MAXIMUM CITY

MAXIMUM CITY

THE BIOGRAPHY OF NEW YORK

MICHAEL PYE

SINCLAIR-STEVENSON

First published in Great Britain by
Sinclair-Stevenson Limited
7/8 Kendrick Mews
London SW7 3HG, England

British Library Cataloguing in Publication Data
A CIP catalogue record for this book is available from the British Library.

ISBN: 1 85619 093 5

Typeset by Rowland Phototypesetting Limited
Bury St Edmunds, Suffolk
Printed and bound in Great Britain by
Clays Limited, St Ives plc

CONTENTS

Praise Allah, Wiggle, wiggle, wiggle –
Praise Allah, Wiggle and dance;
Do that stomp with lots of pomp and sweet romance!
Big Apple! Big Apple!

Lee David and John Redmond,
for the Cotton Club in Harlem
1937

ACKNOWLEDGEMENTS

New York is a city that's tough to survive, let alone write about, and I am hopelessly grateful to all the people who helped me do both. I thank Linda Murray and Peter Yostron in London and Vania Penha-Lopes and Katherine Hughes in New York, whose careful, clever research made the book possible in less than a lifetime. Andrew Shand and Kelly Henry helped in the early stages. Alejandro Correa Ceballos tidied me up and made the bibliography. Noa Kleinman made the index. My father, Reginald Pye, helped on the matter of hunting.

I'm grateful to New York University for the use of the Bobst Library, and the City University of New York for the library at the Graduate Center; and to the Museum of the City of New York, the New York Historical Society and the New York State Library at Albany for their help. The staff of the Municipal Archives in Amsterdam were extraordinarily kind to an unannounced stranger, as was the Prentenkabinet of the Rijksmuseum in Amsterdam. I am grateful to the staff of the British Library in London for their courtesy to me and to my researchers; but most of all, to the New York Public Library, whose Research Branch at 42nd Street is one of the most splendidly democratic institutions I know. Its specialist collections, including the Jewish Division and the Billy Rose Theater Collection at Lincoln Center, were invaluable.

Then there are the hundreds of people who answered my questions, suggested new lines of enquiry and helped me see the city more fully. Some of their names appear in the text and some of them do not want to be named, but I want to acknowledge some special debts: to Margriet de Roever of the Amsterdam City Archives, Pieter C. Emmer of the Werkgroep voor de Geschiedenis van de Europse Expansie at the Rijksuniversiteit of Leiden, Charles Gehring of the New Netherland

Project, David Voorhees and Paul Huey and his colleagues for their help with the seventeenth century material. On the frontiers, I thank Lydia and Ricky Brackett, Hedley Gaujean and Rose D'Haiti for the parties where I found things out, and Bob Allen for his special knowledge of Queens. Yuen Ying Chang, Sherman Eng, Peter Kwong, M.B. Lee and David Leung helped me see Chinatown. Vania Penha-Lopes reported the Brazilian community. Rabbi Yehuda Krinsky helped in the Lubavitcher community. I thank Jennifer Mezzacappa, Donald Olson, Bill Wesbrooks for allowing me to be at auditions, and the Tammiment Library and the Robert Wagner Labor Archive for access to their taped material. Helaine Feldman, Patricia Reed Scott, Jack Goldstein and Patrick Quinn helped me with the theatre. I'm grateful to Sharon Churcher for all her help with the tangled business of Nouvelle Society and the melodramas of the Mob. Peter Derrick generously helped me understand the history of the subway and of zoning. William H. Daly, Carl Weissbrod and Susan Urban fleshed out the story of 42nd Street. For their observations and clues, I thank Nicholas Boyle, Norbert Dittmar, Jill Hamburger, Alain Kihm, Salikoko Mufwene, Swithin Wilmot, Lise Winer, and especially Frederick Cassidy, editor of the Dictionary of American Regional English, for his help with New York's names.

I am very grateful for permission to use material from works in copyright – to Elizabeth dos Passos for a passage from *Manhattan Transfer* by John dos Passos; Hope McKay Virtue for material for *Home to Harlem* by Claud McKay, published by the North-Eastern Universities Press; the University of Missouri Press for *City of Refuge* by Rudolf Fisher; Peters, Fraser and Dunlop for a passage from *Town and City* by Jack Kerouac; Hamish Hamilton Ltd for material for *American Journals* of Albert Camus, translated by Hugh Levick; New Directions Inc. for a quotation from Ralph Manheim's translation of *Journey to the End of the Night* by Louis-Ferdinand Céline; Macmillan Publishing Company, New York, for material from *The Fountainhead* by Ayn Rand, © 1943 by the Bobbs-Merrill Company, renewed 1971; Methuen for permission to quote from verse by Bertolt Brecht; Granville Publishing for material from *The Future in America* by H. G. Wells; Curtis Brown Ltd for lines by W. H. Auden. I quote from *America Day by Day* by Simone de Beauvoir in the translation by Patrick Dudley, by permission of Duckworth. Translation of extracts from Federico Garcia Lorca's Spanish language work *Poeta en Nueva York*, © 1988, 1991 by Herederos de Federico Garcia Lorca, Greg Simon and Steven F. White, published by Faber and Faber, London, and Farrar Straus Giroux, New York. Used with permission. All rights reserved. The epigraph is from *Big Apple* by Lee David and John Redmond, © copyright 1937 by Exclusive Publications Inc, by permission of J. R. Lafleur and Son Ltd, London. I have done my best to trace the owners of copyrights, but if I have failed in any instance, I would be glad to know so that I can make amends in any future edition.

This was a long and bothersome project, and it could not have happened without the sanity and enthusiasm and skill of my agent Anthea Morton Saner at Curtis Brown. I had the extraordinary luck to work with editors – Christopher Sinclair-Stevenson, Penelope Hoare and Peter Strauss – who knew exactly how to support the faltering author and gave me the unfailing sense that they actually wanted to know what I would write, and to be trimmed and polished by Caroline Taggart. Above all, I thank my friends: Linda Melvern and Phil Green for giving me a home in London, and Phil for the cover; Lynda Myles, for all her support; Michael Klein for all his encouragement, and not least for the extraordinary Matt Mullican image on the cover; and Ann Barr, Penny Ciancanelli, Bobby Cohen, Nicholas Faith, Dan Fisher, Vania Penha-Lopes, Jessica Kingsley, Joe Moore, Dayle Schwarzler and Jenny Roper. I only wish that Edith and John Roper had lived to read this. And the book is especially for John Holm – who put up with the monomania, the imperial growth of filing cabinets, the sleeplessness, obsessive questions and odd assignations. Put up, that is, with me.

THE ILLUSTRATIONS

The pictures which head each chapter are: with *Warnings To Travellers*, a detail from Salvador Dali's 'Gangsterism and Goofy Visions of New York' (1935) by courtesy of the Menil Collection, Houston; with *The Manitou*, an engraving of New Amsterdam around 1629 from 'Beschryvinghe Van Virginia, Nieuw Nederlandt...' (1651) by Joost Hartgers, by courtesy of the New York Historical Society, New York City; with *Frontiers*, an undated photograph of 'Immigrants Aboard the SS Potsdam, Arriving in New York' from the Alexander Alland Collection, by courtesy of the New York Historical Society, New York City; with *Audition City*, a Vandamm photograph from 1927 of a Ziegfeld rehearsal, from the Raymond Mander and Joe Mitchenson Theatre Collection; with *Minimum City*, a Thomas Nast cartoon of 'Boss' Tweed from Harper's Weekly, by courtesy of the Bettmann Archive, New York and the Hulton Picture Company in London; with *The Skyline is Politics* a photograph taken during the building of the Con Edison diorama of New York City at the World's Fair of 1939, with thanks to Con Edison for rediscovering and giving us this image; with *The Siege of Mrs Astor's Ballroom*, a photograph taken in February 1905 of guests at the James Hazen Hyde ball at Sherry's Hotel, from the Byron Collection of the Museum of the City of New York; and with *Taking Liberties* an Edward Hopper etching, 'Night on the El Train' (1920) from the Philadelphia Museum of Art, Purchased: The Harrison Fund.

1
WARNINGS TO TRAVELLERS

T HE PLANE GLIDES low above Manhattan on a clear black night. The passengers go scuffling for their bags, reaching for lockers, curling under seats. They start last-minute conversations with their neighbours, because now it's too late for them to mean anything. But some people hang at the windows and look down: the children, the newcomers – and me.

For these few minutes, it seems the city can barely contain all the light within it. It breaks all the rules of seeing, like some optical illusion in which you see either black faces or a white vase; but here you have to work out the heavens from the break between lights, and a million bright windows sketch the pin-cushion of towers that contain them. The softer lights, dappled through leaves, are in parks; the old hills and streams were long ago buried and forgotten; the island has grown out into the rivers, and even the Harlem River runs in a dynamited course. What's below is man-made, artifice up to the sky. The tops of the towers are crowns and pagodas, urns and masts and lighthouses and a helmet of chrome and neon on the Chrysler Building. A schoolboy in Zaire looks at his textbooks and knows that everything must be fine between these orderly towers; Chicago, the book says, is the city with the criminals. You find coloured murals of this skyline in Iraqi military bunkers. For much of the world, this view is the universal sign for being in control of your rich, modern destiny.

The plane skims water and bumps down at La Guardia and we struggle into the real city. Expressway traffic slips in place. Ten years in the city does not take away the sense of shock that the magic simply disappears when you come too close. New York on the ground is a babble of borough bosses, of edgy walkers, the cost of rent and the sour lily smell of crack, and wars between the frontier guards of all the small nations in the city. Passing the frame houses, you wonder who works where any more; the factories have gone. The city has given itself to dealers – in bonds, talent, drugs. If it's a streamlined machine, it is full of ratcheting, revving noise, not the sound of easy functioning: alarms, klaxons, the shudder of a long truck on a broken street, the megaphoned voice of a traffic cop who is chasing a red TransAm. There's no money for cops or services, and the doomsayers talk about a new Calcutta, with the mad and the dying all helpless on the streets. But people who know Calcutta say it has more humanity. If you lose sight of the glamour for a moment here, then memories rush back. A thin man is frozen on a Fifth Avenue sidewalk, his leg in the air as though he died dancing. I buy tree lights late on Christmas Eve, from traders up against steel shutters in bodega doorways on 14th Street, and see, far down the street, the cars still circling and the kids still promenading in the meat market; they are out in their skirts trading sex for smokes, rushing their own death. I remember hearing snow geese beating south over a cold, still city, and crying.

Short of Jerusalem, no city conjures up pictures and stories so quickly, and none of them is comfortable. In TV cartoons, Evil comes up out of the East River like a shiny skeleton and asks where It is. 'New York,' It says. 'My kind of town.' European movie-makers are fascinated by the red-rust decay of the ancient steel highways, and the styled out clubs, and the sense of riches, threat and intrigue in the place; it is a living *film noir*. The city's decline is written like tragedy, man's great achievement punished for hubris with floods of water and geysers of steam and packs of kids who go wilding in the street with knives. It doesn't work, the headlines say. Each year, almost 2,000 people are murdered; each year, there are more than 16,000 felonies reported on the subway system. It may be time to quit the city. To live here seems to require a cold vein of indifference, a way not to see; people edit the city as they walk along, careful not to catch the eyes of strangers, going only where they know they will be safe. Commuters push into the morning city past garbage bags that are stacked like the start of trench warfare. They go down to the Seventh Avenue subway, where a brawny man, all muscles until the waist where he is cut off, pushes himself car to car on a home-made wooden cart. The very steel on the bridges is rotten; it is out of time.

Yet somehow New Yorkers make a city each day, out of this ruinous bric à brac. The city is held together by this act of communal will. This is not a town for casual exploring, and even the rules for buying apartments conspire to make ghettos of people the same age, the same profession, the same credit rating; so those of us who live here have to draw on the myth of the city, the simple view from above. This New York is glitter and danger, corrupt, ambitious, ostentatious, the extreme case of the city. It is the point of the place. Sometimes, it is a way of excusing things, as when people say 'Only in New York' to the guy in doublet and tights in the fish shop, or 'This is New York' when something floating in the Hudson becomes a corpse in a neat green body-bag on the shore.

People come here to find the New York they expect, and since they see only shards of the city, they have to fit those pieces into the myth. The streets are charged with all manner of battles – for socialism, trade unions, egotism and the nature of the future – that, on the face of it, do not need a location at all. People hear that New York is libertine, and so they come to misbehave. They hear the city is like an examination in the arts, and they bring their ambitions along. They see its towers in a textbook, and it seems so utterly different that they pay off the people-running coyotes, and cram themselves into the gas tanks of trucks to get here, sure that New York will be where their lives change. It's true that if they come to be social stars, with a curator for the apartment art, they insulate themselves from working stiffs; but they still know about danger on the streets. Danger is in the myth. People who come to work may never see a limo except on wedding days, but they know the goings on of Trumps and Helmsleys, and how New York is the city of excess. Excess, too, is in the myth. If the city had no myth, it would be only the sum total of its deals and crimes, a cramped and airless place.

The cab is at my building now. There's a man standing in the hallway between the open doors and the locked doors, a shadow. I have to calculate, and imagine who he is before going to the door. I do so with all my assumptions about the risk in the city, the calm that usually settles on this street, what I know about where the drug dealers last migrated. There is nothing simple even about coming home. At moments like these, I wonder if the city is finished. And once the question is out, it needs to be answered. I'm thinking at once of keeping the hallway shadow out of the building, and how better to understand the city, to see the glamour and the raucous, startling reality together.

Suppose we took the myth of New York and picked it apart in its various strands and saw how it came to be. And then suppose we stopped editing the city, that we opened all manner of doors into its story – different lives, different times, the wrong turnings. We could set what has happened in this city alongside the legend, and see if the city has become too weak and fractured to nourish its spectacular story; or if it remains the turntable in millions of lives, the risky, astonishing, essential city.

The man in the hallway is gaunt; the dirt on his hands is like resin on old wood. He does not expect anything. If I told him to go, he would go, looking down. He shrugs.

This is not an encyclopedia of New York. It is a biography, the kind written for a star – myth and the raucous reality held together in stereoscopy. Biography is always personal, the story of a relationship. I have been ten years in the city, wondering at it, reporting on it. This could be a way for me to say goodbye. It could also be a love letter to New York City. We shall see.

There's something curious about the very idea of looking into the history of New York. The one constant in the city is frantic change, which means that the words New York also change meaning: they once, unimaginably, meant a pastoral dream. The city's other names have to be re-invented to fit the state of the myth. It was Old New York Town out of irony, and contrast with the new West; Lil' Old Noo Yawk out of false modesty; Gay New York because the neon and the dancing girls were famous; and Fun City, derisively, because of Mayor Lindsay's campaign in the 1960s to make a declining city seem like a fairground. It was Babylon on the Hudson, Baghdad on the Hudson. It was Gotham, like the English village full of fools, because Washington Irving used the name satirically; but the legend of the original Gotham is that the very clever villagers were only pretending to be stupid. It is the Big Apple because the president of the New York Convention and Visitors Bureau re-invented the phrase in 1971; the 'big apple' is horse-racing talk for the New York tracks, or a mobster's phrase for the boss, or theatre talk for the height of ambition, like 'the main stem', or perhaps jazz talk for New York, although the players more usually said only 'the apple'.

Conservationists complain that the city's whole identity is just as precarious, as buildings are broken down and built up. 'The denizens of New York are such utilitarians,' said a guidebook of 1866, 'that they have sacrificed to the shrine of Mammon about every relic of older time.' The artist Joseph Pennell celebrated in 1911 'the Unbelievable City, the city that has been built since I grew up ... built by men I know for people I know ...' but only thirteen years later he made a new sketch called 'An Orgy of Building'. By the mid-1930s, Edith Wharton considered the social city of the turn of the century 'as much a vanished city as Atlantis, or the lowest layer of Schliemann's Troy'. Robert Moses, the awful angel of New York in the 1930s and 1940s, said: 'There are people who like things as they are. I can't hold out any hope to them. They have to keep moving further away ... Let them go to the Rockies!'

A city that is always in transition never has to worry about what it happens to be at the moment; something shinier or bloodier is coming in its place. The city lives off hope. At the same time, it denies its history. Some of the most important New York records are stashed in private homes, or disused men's rooms or dead subway stations; they lie in trunks, without index or calendar, in the archives of the New York Historical Society. The buildings which survive have changed their meaning. A mid-Victorian church is only a relic to someone whose people were long settled in New York; but suppose your family came from some pogrom in the East, and settled here precisely to forget the past, then that church is a reminder of what was happening in the bad times when it was built. I've seen friends on tour buses shiver at the thought. People bring their history to New York, histories of labour and famine and horror and ambition, and add it to the city; the city changes with each group of new arrivals.

So to find the continuities in the city, the things that define New York besides its place on a map, we need to see the city as a bundle of stories which can be tracked down in the files of Amsterdam notaries, the records of English fox hunts, the diaries and letters of travellers, the guide-books and novels and movies and histories that touch on New York. And voices, too, from newly opened archives and old shipping records; wiretaps and court papers, old magazines and the rich memory of older people. In all this glorious variety lies the clue to the nature and even the meaning of New York: because it is a puzzle. The city has been dreamed into being.

Consider the Martin family in Jack Kerouac's *The Town and The City*, who leave their Massachusetts township and come to New York, uprooted by war, without a cent or a friend. Old man Martin knows only too well that the lights of New York are not for the likes of him.

His Brooklyn home is miserable, its view blocked by a giant billboard of a man with a headache. And yet everyone he knew used to talk about New York – about the financiers who started life as just plain errand boys, and how there's always plenty of work. He remembers a black man bleeding in a men's room who is complaining: 'I been all over and I been beat aroun' and I been busted 'n' beaten, hauled ass off to jail for nawthin, I been everywhere, I been all aroun' – but I ain't nevah been to New Yawk!' And the old man stands facing Manhattan, and is filled with wonder: 'It was too much to believe, and so huge, intricate, unfathomable and beautiful in its distant, smoking, window-flashing, canyon-shadowed redness there, and the pink light glowing on its highest crests as bottomless shadows hung draped in mighty abysms; and little things moving in millions as the eye strained to see. . . .'

Somehow, newcomers learned to give New York such a weight of significance, and beauty and horror. They learned from guidebooks, scandal books, well-intentioned books by visitors, the kind that now lie in the far part of library stacks, waiting for attention. They learned, too, from the movies, and the way in which New York had a meaning far beyond a simple location, and shifting from glorious modernity, to soullessness, to lawless ruin and a metaphor for being modern and neurotic. Out of all this was born the very idea of New York. Our first job is stir the dust, and run some movies.

Daniel Denton was a minister's son, a civic booster, alone in London on business in 1670. Friendly promoters asked him to write a brief pamphlet on all that was good in the New York he had left behind. His is the first English language work on New York City, written to bring more settlers to the island. Denton promises a practical Paradise: a city easily defended because of whirlpools to the north and a strong fort to the south; sweet air and 'the Countrey itself sends forth such a fragrant smell, that it may be perceived at Sea before they can make the land.' There were Indians, but somehow the 'Hand of God' dealt with them whenever the English wanted land – either 'Wars one with the other, or by some raging mortal Disease.' The town itself was 'built most of Brick and Stone, and covered with red and black Tile, and . . . gives at a distance a pleasing Aspect to the Spectators'; but the glory of the colony was the fields around. The June strawberries, for example: 'the Fields and Woods are died red: Which the Countrey People perceiving, instantly arm themselves with bottles of Wine, Cream and Sugar, and instead of a Coat of Male, every one takes a Female upon his Horse behind him, and so rushing violently into the fields, never leave until they have disrob'd them of their red colours . . .' Mrs Denton, for one, liked the strawberry fields; when her husband came home, he promptly divorced her for 'Incontinency, and committing Adultery in ye absence of her Husband then about his Occasions in Europe'. Mr Denton left town for eleven years in New Jersey. His wife was not single for long.

The first thing travellers learned about New York was that it came close to Eden – its summers like Barbardos, and its Arctic winters unmentioned. In the easy years of the eighteenth century Peter Kalm, a Swedish doctor, came visiting. He found a city like a garden, with avenues of shade trees – Lombardy poplar, mostly; a poor man could live the year round on the oysters 'of such an exquisite taste, and of so great a size . . . very wholesome.' The seas were almost absurdly kind. 'They could never find any signs of lobsters being in this part of the sea; They were therefore continually brought in great wellboats from New England, where they are plentiful; But it happened that one of these wellboats broke in pieces near Hellgate, about ten English miles from New York, and all the lobsters in it got off. Since that time they have so multiplied in this part of the sea that they are now caught in the greatest abundance. . . .' This plenty, and the splendour of the trees and the bay were thoroughly proper Republican enthusiasms. Cities lay outside the gentleman's dream of America, of a responsible gentry and a quiet tenantry, which was for the moment masquerading as the whole American dream. Washington Irving, eyes and pen sharpened for urban idiocies, wanted to celebrate his New York child-hood, and he made it sound like a pastoral – 'the bay; the rivers and their wild and woody shores . . . absolutely have a witchery over my mind.'

But the city itself was becoming too grand a fact to camouflage. By 1800, the population of New York was only slightly behind great Philadelphia, and the bay was a busy harbour, but the shadow of Irving's green childhood still blocked the view. New York, Samuel Mitchill wrote, 'is not as well known to its own inhabitants as it deserves to be. There is no wonder, therefore, that strangers and travellers have not done justice to it in their printed writings.' Mitchill tried to improve matters with *The Picture of New York*, the first guide-

book to the city. It was not an easy business. The new United States
of America was a serious, not to say glum, place, and the obvious
glories of a city were nothing to boast about. Architecture was a fine
art, and the fine arts were aristocratic and bad. The city's bustle was
all too unruly to the gentlemen who made the Revolution; Jefferson
viewed crowds 'as sores ... [on] the strength of the human body'.
Mitchill's guidebook had to find an answer to all this. He chose to list
and catalogue all the societies, traders, charities and markets; his is a
statistical geography, with the purpose of proving by sheer accumulation that New York had enough to be worthwhile. He stuffs his book
with patriotic matter, with heroes and battles, but he leaves out the
prominent buildings. Instead, he allows himself purple moments on
the subject of the suburban countryside, the unruffled ocean seen from
Rockaway Beach. He is Jefferson's man, eager to promote industry
and show all the useful things about New York, but not able to bring
himself to sing the city itself.

If you travelled to New York in the half-century after the Revolution, you expected a depository of facts more than a living city. A.T.
Goodrich composed a *Picture of New York and Stranger's Guide to the
Commercial Metropolis of the United States* (1828), stuffed with charts
and tables; but Goodrich felt he needed description as well as a directory. The city had become a phenomenon, something unfamiliar. In
Mitchill's time, New York could be imagined like a family. It seemed
easy to overlook the black slaves, and see only people with the same
skin colour, the same language, the same histories, all crammed
together on the tight little family plot at the southern end of Manhattan. But by the time Goodrich wrote, growth and building had become
the most important facts about the city. Goodrich tells visitors about
the man-made views, like the vista of Broadway's buildings from the
Battery, and not simply the waters, hills or bay. He criticises the
uniformity of the city's grid, and the ugly red stone that is making
the grid real. He sees the natural glories of the harbour, the Hudson
River, and the distant hills of Staten Island, but he fills up his picture
with what men do there – merchantmen and steamboats 'crowded
with passengers and noisy with bells, steam and bugles, and smokey
and foamy in their progress'; and the fine houses, the Battery swarming with visitors. The city has become more than its institutions and
setting; it has life. Goodrich feels able to celebrate it because it is a
matter of national pride that New Yorkers have more, eat better, live
better than in foreign capitals, and London in particular. Cities might

not be the American ideal, but American cities had to be better than any other kind. New York was enrolled in the war of pamphlets, travel pieces, memoirs which followed the Revolutionary War and the War of 1812 – first the British in America, then the Americans retaliating on British subjects, then a free-for-all of 'monstrous absurdities' and 'cumbersome tattle of British travellers' against the patriotic enthusiasm of Americans. Charles Dickens, wrote James Gordon Bennett, editor of the *New York Herald*, was the worst of all the Brits – 'the most trashy ... the most contemptible. ... the essence of balderdash'.

American visitors, too, could be alarmed by New York. If the city was really American, then the meaning of the word was in question. It could not, for a start, mean just American-born any more, nor Protestant and English. It did not mean homespun and honest since there were markets where men could speculate and make sudden fortunes; and the speculation fed off the cycles of good times and terrible times that cost other men their livelihoods. A showy new class emerged, often paper speculators, and set their grand mansions along Fifth Avenue, quite eclipsing an older and drabber aristocracy; New York, which had prided itself on being plain, broke out in a rash of gilt, and footmen and balls and over-*frappé'd* champagne. The city had been peaceful, if ragged and boozing at the docks, and now there were strikes, food riots, campaigns against the Irish – twelve major riots between 1834 and 1857. Poverty became a terrible issue, not just a fact. 'We newspaper people,' said Benjamin H. Day, editor of the first scandalous *Sun,* 'thrive best on the calamities of others' and now there were many. The city was becoming a story.

Asa Greene also ran a penny paper, full of police-court sex and local news – from a rise in boarding-house rents to forthcoming attractions at the Bowery theatres. When he produced a guide in 1837, *A Glance At New York*, he tried to bring the city alive, as once his columns in the papers had done. He sees shoddy building; worse, he sees a confirmed bachelor lean on a wall and fall through to the rooms of a confirmed spinster, who falls herself into fits of propriety. He sees a city which always needs to be newest, best and biggest, even 'a pre-eminence in dirt! That was more than we had looked for, more certainly than we desired to claim.' Town water from the pumps is so filthy that, Greene writes, 'if [a person] stand in need of a physic at the same time, the pump will furnish that, also – without money and without price.' This city is something more than a catalogue of institutions; you could live there. But its small-town kindness is quite gone. Greene regrets the coldness to strangers; 'Hospitality, or anything resembling it, is unknown.' He is resigned to the city as 'theatre of the mob' and the counterbalancing excess of dandies. His Broadway is not an engraved view, but a place for the living, too many of them. To cross, Greene warns, 'with any degree of safety, you must button your coat tight about you, see that your shoes are secure at the heels, settle your hat firmly on your head, look up street and down street, at the self-same moment, to see what carts and carriages are upon you, and then run for your life. . . .'

New arrivals could feed all their fears with the home-grown twopenny dreadfuls which often had a second life as books – *New York in Slices* by George Goodrich Foster, for example. 'Gaslight' Foster was a literary gentleman who drank with Herman Melville, and edited the first American edition of Shelley's poems; but who was threatened with jail because of a forged $300 note, worked as a member of an 'Equestrian Company' and a member of the band for a travelling menagerie. He set up satirical comics for New York, but was promptly buried under libel suits. To make a living, he became a 'journeyman journalist' (his own words), writing 'city items' for the *New York Tribune*: fires, receptions, the Italian opera and, of course, the pig question – should they be banned from the streets? There is calculation in Foster's books; whenever he was particularly short of cash, the quota of lewd women rises. But he seems truly infuriated by the hoodwinking of immigrants, the would-be maids who come to beg for work and end up as brothel playthings for the most proper of stuffed-shirt citizens, the rowdy aristos chasing down pleasure in a pageant of excitements that can also seduce the working man, the honest husband. He hates the local grocery store for selling the liquor that ruins families. He deplores the demon of financial ambition. And he gives details, which exercised the shockability of his readers and made the city seem like a perilous maze. For telling too much truth, he was rewarded by a pompous obituary in a Philadelphia paper which declared that he lacked 'a decent regard for the proprieties of civilised society'.

New York was obligatory as well as dangerous, something visitors had to see; it was not simply the most convenient port for a visitor from across the Atlantic. It promoted itself. Three miles out, the bum-boats met Ludwig Gall's ship in 1819 – bearing boys who touted 'mail-coach, steamship and other transportation companies, boarding-houses, shoe manufacturers, tailors, seed companies, money changers and even the agent of a Dutch land company.' In mid-century, when the ship finally docked, the city came swarming aboard; porters from the great hotels of New York touted for the Astor House, the Metropolitan, the Fifth Avenue. Nobody could miss the 'monster Hotels . . . of which there are a great number', 'truly,' said one British visitor in 1854, 'more like towns than hotels'. They had splendid mirrors and sober dinners (on the American plan, wine cost a great deal extra) and hot water on tap and ice always and deep carpets and, above all, the gilt and marble of the barbers' shops, smelling of *pale rum*. The Fifth Avenue Hotel even had an elevator for people as well as baggage, 'a little parlour going up by machinery'. The British were shocked, they said, by the white satin bridal chamber at the St Nicholas, so shaming for a well-brought up young bride ('the cheek of a brazen woman might be lighted up,' Alfred Bunn acknowledged) and such an unhealthy source of interest for bachelors. But they were even more disturbed by the proof, five storeys tall, that you could hire a little grandeur by the day, and live like a prince without a title or any other certificate of worthiness. 'Such carpets and curtains,' wrote the Reverend A.P. Moor in 1853, 'I never saw elsewhere, except perhaps in palaces.' William Baxter, the same year, stayed at the St Nicholas: 'The looking glasses are set in frames worthy of Windsor Castle,' he wrote, 'and embroidery on the mosquito nettings itself might be exhibited to royalty.' And when the Prince of Wales came to the Fifth Avenue Hotel in 1860, the correspondent of the London *Times* thought the hotel 'a larger and a handsomer building than Buckingham Palace'. Its scale and splendour 'astonished every member of the royal party'.

Sometimes, the sheer numbers of guests was upsetting; the hotels bustled relentlessly. But then the city was literally under pressure, its people crammed together. 'The great characteristic of New York is din and excitement,' said *Miller's Guide for 1866*, 'everything is done in a hurry – all is intense anxiety.' There were warnings to travellers, always: 'Probably in no city in the civilised world is life so fearfully insecure,' Isabella Bird wrote in 1854. 'Terrible outrages and murderous assaults are matter of such nightly occurrence as to be thought hardly worthy of notice.' The sheer closeness of poverty and wealth was shocking. 'Fine ladies can look from their high casements upon the squalid dens of their unhappy sisters,' Edward Winslow Martin wrote in *The Secrets of the Great City*, which is subtitled *Virtues, Vices,*

Mysteries, Miseries and Crime. Sin is everywhere; a bishop announces there are as many prostitutes as Methodists in New York City, a remark made more striking by the fact that he was a Methodist Bishop. And there are the bummers, the men who 'hate the discipline of life'; '"In a city like this, where plenty of good food is thrown away every day, it is a shame for any man to go hungry," remarked one of this tribe, "and I won't go with an empty belly; I ask until I have enough."' In New York, you met men who had opted out of every stolid Republican ideal.

In Martin's eyes the city has become a foreign place, where the ordinary naturally turns bloody. So the ferry lines, all twenty-three of them, are at once the handsome, gas-lit galas passing on the night waters, and the wreckable vessels crashing through winter fog and icepack, and sometimes being pushed and dragged for miles out of their courses. Martin tells only one story about commuting to Manhattan. It is early morning, in November 1868, and the sister ship of the ferry *Hamilton* has been delayed, so the *Hamilton* leaves Brooklyn heavy-laden, with more than a thousand passengers. It is flood tide up the East River; the ferry goes downstream of the slip on the Manhattan side, to be carried to dock by the currents. Close by the piers is an eddy that snatches the bow of the *Hamilton* and runs her with great force against another ship, the *Union*, which is waiting there. The *Union* is almost empty, and rides high in the water, and the *Hamilton* is full and rides low. 'The projecting guard of the *Union* therefore entered the front part of the ladies' cabin at about the height of the seats, and also smashed the rails on the outer deck. This particular part of the boat was, of course, the most densely crowded, and the consequences of the shock were frightful. One boy, George Brewer, who was said to have been outside the chain, was caught by the foot and instantly killed, his head and a good part of the body being mashed to a jelly. Several had their feet cut off below the knee. . . .' In the horror show of New York, going to work becomes a massacre. Even the jolly world of Currier and Ives, 'Printmakers to the People', who stocked the walls of every decent middle-class home with portraits of heroes, pictures of pets, horse races, jokes and religiosity, was founded on a series of studies of ghastly New York fires.

Like a stage melodrama, the city lived insistently in the present tense. Anthony Trollope had noticed in the 1860s: 'In other large cities, cities as large in name as New York, there are works of art, fine buildings, ruins, ancient churches, picturesque costumes, and the tombs of celebrated men. But in New York there are none of these things.' Henry James returned in 1906 after twenty-five years in Europe, fastidious, still a little drunk on Rye and its literary life, and sensed a volatility which was much more than the lack of a past. He wrote: '. . . the newness of New York – unlike even that of Boston, I seemed to discern – had this mark of its very own, that it affects one, in every case, as having treated itself as still more provisional, if possible, than any poor dear little interest of antiquity it may have annihilated.'

James did not take a kind view of this provisional city. 'Its mission would appear to be, exactly, to gild the temporary, with its gold, as many inches thick as may be, and then, with a fresh shrug, a shrug of its splendid cynicism for its freshly detected inability to convince, give up its actual work, however exorbitant, as the merest of stop-gaps.' Cynicism lay in the very fabric of the place – 'the serried, bristling city, held in the easy embrace of its great good-natured rivers very much as a battered and accommodating beauty may sometimes be "distinguished" by a gallant less fastidious, with his open arms, than his type would seem to imply.' James could hardly imagine what force still held together on the shore the 'old sordid facts . . . that seemed destined so long ago to fall apart from their very cynicism – the rude cavities, the loose cobbles, the dislodged supports, the unreclaimed pools, of the roadway; the unregulated traffic, as of innumerable desperate drays charging upon each other with tragic long-necked, sharp-ribbed horses . . .'

And yet the city has 'the power of the most extravagant of cities, rejoicing, as with the voice of the morning, in its might, its fortune, its unsurpassable conditions, and imparting to every object and element, to the motion and expression of every floating, hurrying, panting thing, to the throb of ferries and tugs, to the plash of waves and the play of winds and the glint of lights and the shrill of whistles and the quality and authority of breeze-born cries . . . something of its own sharp free accent and, above all, of its sovereign sense of being "backed" and being able to back.' Money and markets give New York its power, which is itself a moral problem. The skyline is 'crowned not only with no history, but with no credible possibility of time for history, and consecrated by no uses save the commercial at any cost.' The new landmarks seemed to crush the old, 'quite as violent children stamp on snails and caterpillars.' The future city is 'some colossal set of clockworks, some steel-souled machine room of brandished arms and hammering fists and opening and closing jaws.' It could no longer simply be described and catalogued as the writers of guide-books had done; 'there is more than enough of this pressure of the present and the immediate to cut out all the close sketcher's work for him.'

H.G. Wells also arrived in 1906, a man still able to imagine Utopia. To him, New York becomes a symbol of the unstoppable, inhuman force of Progress – 'growth under pressure'; which also means that he sensed a loss of control. Progress itself was what hemmed in the humanity of the place. Skyscrapers are not just provisional, but incomplete: 'Each one seems to await some needed terminal, to be, by virtue of its woolly jets of steam, still as it were in process of eruption.' The city has an energy that human beings can no longer control: 'The great thing is the mechanical thing, the unintentional thing which is speeding up all these people, driving them in headlong hurry this way and that, exhorting them by the voice of every car conductor to "step lively", aggregating them into shoving and elbowing masses, making them stand clinging to straps, jerking them up elevator shafts and pouring them on to ferry-boats.' The city has a 'sense of inexhaustible supply, of an ultra-human force behind it all.'

For a writer whose optimism about the machine-made future was fast evaporating, New York was an object lesson. Wells sees the tiredness on a messenger's face; he worries about juvenile vice, and the way the great mansions along Fifth Avenue look like goods on the shelf of a house shop, and the art dealer who tells his client that if he wants a Botticelli in a different size, he'll have to have one custom-made. He suspects that political corruption is the inevitable mirror of a society organised for business. He sees how the metal pens for immigrants, and the metal wicket which is their gateway to America, are like the valves of some machine. See the difference: that the city is now a machine in itself, and the vignettes of life within the city do not necessarily say anything about how the machine works or what it will become. The city itself gives life, as an English satirist suggested: 'There are days, and sometimes whole weeks, when the nervous tension is maintained like the hum of an electric battery attached to the body.'

You could sit in tired, used up Europe and dream of the possibilities of this America, in which New York was part of a wild and free frontier, but with no disagreeable cows, and with bookshops and cafés – Berlin with hope. Bertolt Brecht fell under that spell, as though he was ready to share Walt Whitman's ecstatic embrace of everything in the city, even its crimes and misfortunes as recorded in cheap novels. You can tell how strong the myth was from the pained way he sings his disappointment at the city's vanished glory, much later:

'Who still recalls
the glory of the giant city New York
in the decade after the great war?
What a people! Their boxers the strongest,
their inventors the most practical,
their trains the fastest,
and the most crowded,
And all that seemed destined for a thousand years. . . .'

Of course he also saw in the city's Depression years the perfect evidence that the social system 'showed more shameful weaknesses/ than that of humble folks'; but he still remembered the glory.

The city in print had become such a wonderful, consuming idea that any failure was shocking. The Depression was enough to spoil the grand modernity of New York. The Federal Writers' Project, government-funded by the Works Progress Administration of the New Deal, produced in 1939 its *Guide to New York City* – a huge thing, an encyclopedia which tries not to be angry when it mentions terrible poverty or exultant when it tells how Greenwich Village came to be the ground where strait laces were untied, where a nation was 'coming into its own artistically'. It is wonderfully rich with facts; you have the sense of an army which has walked each street, sorted through each archive, tried to comprehend an entire city despite the 'dynamism' and overnight changes of its subject. The city was susceptible to human reason and control again, not just some impersonal machine. The guide has a distinct point of view, not in its words, nor even in its photographs which are usually a matter of lifeless record, but in its paintings and prints. In this New York, the towers of Manhattan are lovely things, but they rear out of a working harbour, with the steam of tug-boats as grand as the Empire State; or else they are a vague backdrop to the work of the wharfs.

There are exactly three pictures of the bourgeois life – an auction, a ball, the dining room at Sardi's – out of forty-three; there is one conventional sketch of a landmark, St Paul's Chapel. The real New York, the pictures say, is a Bowery mission, boys selling shoe-shines, a shape-up to hire workers. It is clam shacks and stilt houses and a clubhouse for the Colonial Dames of America which is dwarfed by gasholders, a gingerbread house on Staten Island dwarfed by silos; the WPA liked to put history in its place. Often the city is under snow, not just for aesthetic effect; snow makes the Metropolis grey, or makes the walkers at Columbus Circle drag their feet. There are derelicts propping each other up along the East River waterfront, and crowds tamped down by the girders of the Elevated railway at Chatham Square.

There was a huge divide between the grand claims of the city, and the bad times of its citizens. The WPA Guide is only sensible about the Empire State Building, noting the way the flush windows saved on the cost of trimming stone, the way standard machine-made components make the building truly 'modern', the glories of the view; there is nothing here about man's aspirations or the worth of the race to be tallest, greatest, best. The city's hard glitter is missing, as though it was spoiled by too many human beings in the way. To see it clearly, it had to be built on a stage.

At the 1939 World's Fair, the Con Edison pavilion held a huge diorama of New York City, big enough to fool the eyes with its checkerboard of lights, and the photo files on its making have the force of a fable. Giants tuck suburban trees into place, and haul up the Empire State into its proper place: stage centre, like a star at a curtain call, while Brooklyn leans yearningly in from the wings. The places where people live are a sketch of pale paint; the diorama is a stone parade in a half-circle, a cathedral and a church dwarfed by all the skyscraping 'cathedrals of commerce'. The powers of the city are on display. Tiny workers under tiny manholes, the only humans modelled, are dwarfed in the photographs by visiting civic dignitaries.

And there is something curious about this city; it is meant to be admired, but it cannot be reached. The subway trains are set to run in cut-open tunnels, like some schoolroom ant farm, but they do not bring people into Manhattan; the bridges are only sketched, there is no airport and only a single vessel frozen on the East River. For the moment, a Titan sits on a skyscraper, kicking his wing-tips and feathering the steel with paint; another reverently settles a giant urn on top of the Con Edison building. Film-makers come with a tripod, and take heroic film-making poses for the still cameras. And then the last human beings take down the ladders propped on the Woolworth Building, take care not to tread on St Mark's in the Bowery, and leave the city for ever. To be glorious, Manhattan has to be empty, the illusion of life provided by a schedule of electric lights.

Since the show was staged by the electricity company, its view of the city is not too surprising. The surprise is the crowds. There they stand, waiting for the automatic sunset and the city's glitter – felt hats crammed on men's heads, plaid jackets for the women, a couple of sailors in whites and some schoolgirls in straw hats, and grown-ups running interference. The lights dim, and hands slip round the waists of friends. Even New Yorkers, who live with the smell and troubles of it, take pleasure in the spectacle of the city – the myth made into a model. Without this tight point of view, they have no point of view at all on the city as a whole. They choose this lovely monument over anything more human and alarming.

The emptiness of these towers could be bullied into even more meaning. In the Ayn Rand version, they are proof that the sublime human ego could stave off the mob that admires them, but is not worthy of them. In *The Fountainhead,* Rand discovered the architect ('heroes who have given us some of the highest expressions of man's genius'), especially the flat-bellied, orange-haired variety who can wield a pencil or a quarry drill or an oxyacetylene cutter with equal panache. Such a brute man is the hero Howard Roark, obviously a genius because 'he was usually disliked, from the first sight of his face, anywhere he went.' Roark aspires to perfect selfishness; he would rather dynamite homes he has designed than see his vision compromised. Ranged against him are an effete critic, a rival architect without talent but with social grace and Roark's extremely lovely lover, Dominique, an architectural *maven*, who loves him enough to wreck his career on all possible occasions ('Roark, I . . . I'll still want to destroy you.' 'Do you think I would want you if you didn't?') The enemy also includes those who believe in classical motifs on bank buildings, cathedrals where a man feels awe, women whose 'hips begin at their ankles' and government subsidies for public housing; at the book's climax, after some 680 pages, a private developer takes over a public housing project ('Enright budgeted the undertaking to set low rentals with a comfortable margin of profit for himself'); Roark also marries his lover and builds his masterpiece, but that somehow comes as an anti-climax.

The enemy builds towers which apologise for their height, with detail to 'bring the towering structure down to the humble level of the observer'. But Roark, looking back from the train to Connecticut, sees skyscrapers that transcend the ordinary onlooker: 'They were of their own world, and they held up to the sky the statement of what man had conceived and made possible. They were empty molds. But man had come so far; he could go farther. The city on the edge of the sky held a question – and a promise.' The skyscraper is a hero's building, which should be made by unapologetic and heroically selfish men; Roark's masterpiece, his patron promises, will be 'the last achievement of man on earth before mankind destroys itself' and so peculiarly innocent of altruism. This city exists for ever against a purplish, apocalyptic sky, a state of perpetual storm.

But there was no more agreement on what this city signified. W.H. Auden lands among all those heroic skyscrapers, Rand's monuments to the ego, and finds them using 'Their full height to proclaim/The strength of Collective Man.' Isherwood stands with him in driving snow and sees 'the Red Indian island with its appalling towers . . . You could feel it vibrating with the tension of the nervous New World aggressively flaunting its rude steel nudity. . . . We promise nothing. Here you'll be on your own.' Nobody bothers to look at the political culture of the place to see which might be appropriate; people bring their own metaphors. It becomes easier to concentrate on detail; 'You idiot,' Auden snapped at Stephen Spender, who tried to let in light and brought down the curtains, 'in any case, there is no daylight in New York.' Diana Cooper saw 'how marvellously beautiful the city is, and how much more beautiful than ten years ago. Duff is in a perpetual swoon about it, and is as happy and *sans souci* as a colt'; but she also sensed how bleak the city could be for living things. 'This time, I have nothing to do, only Society to pull against and a sleepless broken nervous system.' New York, the same city that the WPA presented, was in the Second World War a place of luxury for those who could no longer feel at home in the blooded, awkward Europe that they left. Its survival, unmarked and grand, made it the last hope, the proper city for the United Nations, the world city because other cities were in rubble.

It was difficult to read, but tantalising; perhaps it had secret lessons to teach. Albert Camus went on radio to think aloud that in America he might just find some new clue to life. He looked out at New York harbour and saw that 'The order, the strength, the economic power are there.' He sees the idea before the city. When he starts exploring, New York seems 'hideous, inhuman'. He comes to feel that ever more strongly in the rain. 'The taxi's rapid and monotone windshield wipers sweep a water which is incessantly reborn – bizarre feeling of remoteness. Impression of being trapped in this city, that I could escape from the monoliths that surround me and run for hours without finding anything but new cement prisons, without the hope of a hill, a real tree, or a bewildered face.' He cannot bring himself, except intellectually, to care about the place any more. He looks at the man who counts cars in the Holland Tunnel and sees the perfect hero for a modern novel. He truffles off after the exotic – the blowsy, paunchy ladies who end their careers at the Bowery Follies, or the Chinese theatre where he has to make up his own plot because he cannot understand the language. His heart is not engaged any more, and he comes very close to patronising this sad, strange place – so different from the 'ordered, expansive' life he loves (and, in New York, finds only in Chinatown). You have to visit New York, of course, but it is nothing as lively as a battleground or a pleasure resort. It's a goddamn obligation, an exam question for intellectuals (which ends: 'Discuss').

It is also fascinating. To take off from Paris to New York is an event, Simone de Beauvoir wrote, because she is heading for a legend 'and between reality and legend there is no road.' She was flying also to a lover, the writer Nelson Algren in Chicago, and her first days in New York were full of that expectation. Her plane is over New York and 'only in childhood had I experienced anything so dazzling, such excitement and such desire. All the treasures of the Thousand and One Nights, of which I dreamt then but of which I never caught a glimpse, were there. All the fair booths that I had never entered, the merry-go-rounds, Magic City, Luna Park, pantomime décors, birthday cakes, crystal chandeliers that are lit at night in drawing rooms full of music – all these came back to me and were offered me.' In her passion for the place, she knows only too well that she will wake up in nothing but a city; but she goes to sleep remembering the light, the domino buildings. She anticipates the city she saw at the cinema. Each apartment house is like a movie memory and 'What worried me was that these studio decors which I had never believed in should be so real.'

Stars exist in an odd space between what they are on screen, and what they otherwise are; the image shapes the person shapes the image. New York became a star city, its image unreeling on screens across the world. See Frank Sinatra, the Hoboken lad, sit in the taxi with his guidebook to New York in *On The Town* (1949). Lesson One: Manhattan is not an ordinary community or a place, but a foreign land. See the sailors take their shore-leave before a real Statue of Liberty, street scenes snatched from real life; and yet the movie ends with the title: 'Made in Hollywood USA'. Lesson Two: the representation of New York is not New York. The movies conjured up a New York to which New York sometimes lived up – modern towers behind a Fred Astaire dance number, steam and neon as raucous as cheers in a burlesque, dangerous streets, glass corridors crowded with corporate runners, all suspended in the special time that belongs to the screen. Broadway Babes are still waiting, in the Naked City, for each other. 'The greater proportion of New York's stenographers and clerks live alone or in couples in single or two-roomed apartments on the West Side. Their world is that of the cinema,' W.J. Turner wrote in 1929. 'They have no other, for New York is itself a "movie"-picture with nothing but squalor and riches, hard lights, and shadows, and the restless excitement of melodrama.'

The city is somewhere ordinary people are driven to be, but it is a moral vacuum; the old Jeffersonian distaste became a screen staple. In King Vidor's *The Crowd* (1927), John Sims is born on the Fourth of July, just like America, and like America he goes to the city. At twenty-one, a caption tells us, he is 'one of the seven million that believe New York depends on them.' He marries, lives in a flat under the elevated railroad ('It's heavenly inside our flat, but outside it is El!')'. He drinks, dreams, loses his child and his life most pathetically crumbles; his long-suffering wife goes back to her family, to be safe from his dreams. Vidor insisted that 'these scenes in New York do not mean that New York is to be the New York in the picture'; this was an Upper Case picture, about The Man, in The Crowd, in The City. But all the publicity emphasised that the film was authentic – shot on the streets of New York City; and it is this real street life, caught by hidden cameras, that oppresses. 'What chance has a poor clerk in this dense swarm?' Vidor asked reporters, from the comfortable certainty that he would never, like Sims, die of being ordinary. 'I am going to try to show the packed cities turning the cold shoulder to his kind.'

In the elevator, a voice barks: 'Say you, face the front!' to anyone out of line. The camera rises through grids of identical windows until it plunges through a gap that seems arbitrarily chosen, and finds there an office with identical men at identical desks, all making identical lines of figures on cards. John Sims is reduced, in a single sequence, to a point on a graph, given meaning only by the endless straight lines that hem him in. The warmer moments – ambling out for hooch in the sticky snow, flirting on the top of the Fifth Avenue double-decker buses – are there for ironic effect. We know the child must die, and when he is run over in the street, the crowd presses round to leer at a tragedy, and then leaves Sims quite alone. 'The crowd laughs with you always,' a caption says, 'but it will cry with you for only a day.'

The movie business started in New York; there is still an odd creosoted gazebo on top of a building at Broadway and 13th Street which was once a film stage that could be turned to follow the sun. When the movies took off for California, they kept a second home in Harlem and on Long Island. But New York was usually built, painted and filmed somewhere else, which means it was always distilling some idea of the city. The great Sam Fuller was a Manhattan crime reporter, but he worked in a Hollywood studio for movies like *Pick Up On South Street* (1952). When Martin Scorsese rhapsodised about his city in *New York, New York* (1977) it was with deliberate, almost painterly stylisation on an MGM stage, and the skyline behind the credit titles was first painted by a West Coast artist for a Raoul Walsh movie. It isn't the city; it's a quote. Actual New York was just too hard to see – too tall, too busy. It was always hard to represent within the usual rules. Joseph Pennell made prints of New York early this century, and he soon discovered that 'to glorify the skyscraper requires giving up modern perspective.' To make it look right, it had to be distorted, even by the apparently literal camera lens. When Alexander Mackendrick came to make *Sweet Smell of Success* (1957), that wonderfully sardonic nightmare which turns a Broadway press agent into Faust, he had to walk the streets with a camera to work out how little the eye really needs to be sure we are in Manhattan, and how to show skyscrapers by storey-editing. Among other things, his art director, Eddie Carrera, noticed that all you see in nightclubs is smoke and ceilings.

Walking in the city can be a little like walking round a movie studio: all kinds of drama stacked and boxed on stages, and what we see on nightly news or in the papers is the edited version. Stop on 42nd Street for a moment, and look across to the boxing gym above a formal wear shop above a deli. Stop on Broadway and see a chorus line sweating on the fourth, above a martial arts academy on the third who parody their killer high-kicks. In apartment buildings, windows look out on to windows; everyone is audience and performer. Immensely rich people live in what are essentially sets; the Steinbergs built a thirty-four room mansion in a few floors of a Park Avenue apartment building, reached by an elevator, not a driveway and a park. Big-boned Jersey kids come over to cruise the streets of Greenwich Village and gun their engines in the early morning; they're genuinely surprised if told real people live behind the façades. The real city and the screen city are hopelessly confused. The standing city set on the Paramount backlot in Hollywood was based on Commerce, Barrow, Grove and Bedford, four Greenwich Village streets that are still sometimes used as a location, but have to be dressed to look as 'authentic' as the set. Even time and place are muddled. 1902 survives where Fifth and Broadway divide, at the base of the Flatiron Building, if you look closely; the ground floor was used as a set for Warren Beatty's *Reds* (1981). The Mid West, open and green, is a ferry ride from Manhattan; *Splendour in the Grass* (1961) was shot on Staten Island.

This confusion helps the New York set at the gates of the Twentieth Century Fox studios in Los Angeles look more purely New York, from the lions of the Public Library to the back street tenements, than anything on the relentlessly changing island. The 'real' New York is nostalgia by the time it is screened. Jules Dassin's *Naked City* (1948) was 'Actually filmed on the teeming streets of NEW YORK!' But however real the back streets and bridges and peddlers – and Dassin fired them if they washed or combed their hair – the movie mostly reminded the critics of those buildings demolished to build the United Nations between the making and the screening of the film. And imagined New York is so powerful that sometimes it gets itself built. There are art directors' buildings in the city; the Hearst Magazine Building on Eighth Avenue, splashed with urns and statues and balustrades, was designed by Joseph Urban, decorator of the Ziegfeld Follies, one-time artistic director of the Metropolitan Opera and art director of twenty-five lost Hearst movies. It was built as though a matte shot would add the extra floors. Look at Fritz Lang's *Metropolis* (1926) and then at the squat towers, shoe-boxes for Brobdingnag, once planned around Times Square; or the block on the Coliseum site, overlooking Central Park, a bombast of concrete with its endless grids tortured into fancy shapes at top and bottom, with arches between the towers and all its life in the sky. Structures catch up with movies fifty years old, which then were judged to be 'weird views of a possible city a thousand years hence'.

Screen Manhattan can never be just a place. Set aside a few Neil Simon comedies on the stress of the real city – *Prisoner of Second Avenue* (1975), the best and therefore most horrific account of the wet heat and knifing noise of a Manhattan summer – and the city is used in tales of style or morality. New York is the endless party of the Gilded Age in *The Belle of New York* (1952) – playboys and lovely women just waiting to stop being serious, cute and deserted horse-drawn railways, Fifth Avenue like a hill village, sanitised Bowery missions and skating in Central Park ('We're posing for a picture/By Currier and Ives . . .'). The top of the arch in Washington Square opens up, and it becomes a stage from which lovers can hoof up the sky. New York is audition city, where the girls cluster in cold water flats waiting for a break; stars are made, as in *42nd Street* (1933). New York is modern; show *King Kong* (1932–33) atop a model of the Empire State Building, and he's nature against man's achievement, challenging the island where man is most in control, the tallest storey of them all. The city is a state of mind, elegant and neurotic. In Woody Allen's *Manhattan* (1979) we're back to the times when a shot of the skyline went with a whole orchestra, when everything black and white had much more silver in it. Nobody is poor, rushed, violent, afraid, homeless, jobless, unable to get a decent table at Elaine's or even black; without irony, Allen says, 'I intend Manhattan to be a metaphor for everything wrong with our culture.' The city is lovely, but like any good analysand, Allen assumes it is founded on decay. Take a rowboat out in Central Park, as he does, and trail your fingers in the water, and they come up slimed.

Landmarks acquire meaning, which sticks. Central Park is the pure breath of the country, a lovely ghost in the heart of an over-sophisticated, over-concreted town. In *Portrait of Jennie* (1948), the ghost of a pure child appears to a troubled artist there. Milos Forman rebuilds the Sixties there in *Hair* (1979). Troubled theatricals manage to fall in love, shadows dancing sweetly, 'Dancin' in the Dark' from *The Band Wagon* (1953). In *Fifth Avenue Girl* (1939), the bloated capitalist finds joy there with an unemployed Ginger Rogers; he has an ominous, over-gilded mansion; she has the sweet green peace of the park. Crossing the Brooklyn Bridge is choosing a new world, or changing life; think of *Sophie's Choice* (1982) or even *Saturday Night*

Fever (1977), where the disco kids assemble usually with a view of the lovely Verrazano Narrows, until the fatal day when they cross to their dream on a more significant bridge. The city as a whole is an assault course for the ambitious – *How to Marry a Millionaire* (1953), *Breakfast at Tiffany's* (1961) – who want to parlay being young and available into a life. So it is also the dangerous alternative to decent, suburban living. There is an RKO Screenliner subject of 1956, *Where Is Jane Doe?*, which sums up all the warnings to girls not to run from the ranch house and the children. It opens on the suicide of a Plain Jane who fell among Manhattan's flesh-peddlers and wanted to be a model. In ten brisk minutes, it shows how ambition will always lead to degradation in the city, a low credit rating and the return of child-hood acne.

The city is literally a jungle, its laws and contrivances as entangling as vines and as full of killers and animals; in *Tarzan's New York Adventure* (1942), the movie with which MGM killed the ape-man series, our hero sees cab drivers as trail finders, shies from the jitterbug war dance on the radio, walks into showers saying dopily, 'Rain, rain feel good!' and reacts to the kidnapping of his son by swinging, in a double-breasted suit, from flagstaff to flagstaff and then off the Brooklyn Bridge. In *Taxi Driver* (1976), the city is a combat zone of cruising lights, a place so blank it can hold the horror of a child prostitute, her pimp, and also the halo round the golden girl from some smart political campaign, all circulating in the fantasticated mind of the taxi driver Travis Bickle. It is the grim setting for comic-book struggles, as in the invented streets of *Batman* (1988) which are obviously modelled on Manhattan seen through frightened eyes. It is the same in the comic books themselves. When Spiderman finally met Superman in comic battle, the only site that would do was Spidey's real New York City, which transcended in bizarreness the invented Metropolis of Clark Kent.

New York is the future, which is sometimes almost nostalgic and sometimes appalling. In *Just Imagine* (1930), New York is the all-singing, all-dancing staging post on the way to Mars, with ship canals cut under a city of 200-floor towers, policemen suspended from dirigibles to direct everyone's private planes and television to discover D-6 in her home as she scampers flirtily out of frame to put on clothes. Fritz Lang bankrupted a studio to build his imagined *Metropolis* (1926), and his direct inspiration was the Manhattan skyline.

Lang first came to New York in 1924. He was held overnight on his liner, waiting to land. 'There I saw, across from the ship,' he remembered, 'streets lit as if in full daylight by neon lights and topping them oversized luminous advertisements – moving, turning, flashing on and off, spiralling . . . something that was completely new and different for a European in those days.' He pondered a city of the future and how people could remain human there; he imagined the gardens of the rich high in the bright sunlight, and the cottages of the workers, buried with the city's machinery in the dark earth. Light is basic to *Metropolis*; it brings to life the metal robot, and turns it into the rabble-rousing Maria; when the workers rebel and smash the dynamos under her leadership, the first horror is light out of control – manufactured lightning, storeys high. Light is privilege in the city, as it is for the penthouse gentry, as it was for the people who lived in the shadow of the elevated trains because the rents were lower. But as the future began to seem less systematic, imaginary New Yorks grew grimmer. In John Carpenter's futuristic *Escape from New York* (1981), Manhattan looks the way some anxious and judgmental outsiders assume it already is. The crime rate has risen so high the entire island might as well be a Federal prison, which it becomes, and the criminally insane rise up like rats from the subways and sewers. But there are too many people in New York to make filming safe at night in burnt out areas; the film was made mostly in St Louis, which was just as trashed as Manhattan, but less dangerous. 'Don't forget that most people don't know the geography of New York,' Carpenter said, significantly, 'so it doesn't really matter.'

The sidewalk hinges up, and I look down into wet, dusty darkness. This is 29th Street at Sixth Avenue, a nondescript Manhattan block with Korean stores and rag-trade workshops; one o'clock in the morning. The roof lights make white mist out of the rain.

This is just a reminder. The mythic New York is a marvel, a shiny and ominous thing. It animates the history of the city, and makes it quite different from other ports, other metropolises, other cultural centres; only one city is an emotional location as well as a place. But it can be blinding. You forget what is there when you open up the street.

Sergeant Steve Klambatsen goes down first. We are six men, in the criss-cross wanderings of two flashlight beams, slipping on the steel ladder that leads to the concrete stairs below. Black soot calcifies on the walls, on the stair rails, which you know only when you come back to the light and find your hands crusted and stinking. Water drips and floods and makes the stairway slick. The air seems very old. Down below, a train passes and makes a brief vacuum; the pitch-black air comes maliciously alive with soot and water and debris. 'Watch out for needles,' Steve shouts.

The stairs branch into corridors, tight and wet and dark; there are dead bolts and light bulbs on the floor. Rodriguez takes the downstairs; there is nobody. Klambatsen goes to the tracks. A great rat passes through the light. Written in chalk on the wall: 'Charlie Across The Tracks and Up.'

So someone is here.

There's brief discussion. We could clamber down and cross to the other side, but if we find anyone, we could never bring them back across the tracks; too risky. Besides, the tracks are alive: not just the 600 volts DC of electricity in the third rail, but also the scatter of switches for sending trains from one track to another, great joints of steel that shift suddenly and without warning. 'My biggest fear,' Steve says. 'They move with such force they can crush your foot. It's like walking through a minefield.' A tired motorman can't suddenly stop a seventy-five foot train if he spots a man on the line, if he even sees you on the blind corners of the system; there can be eight- to ten-foot drops, the gravel pits, between parallel lines; often there's barely room for trains to pass between the walls. Each year, five or six homeless people die down here; it's remarkable there are so few deaths.

It's agreed we climb back and try the entrance across the street. This other sidewalk opens on to light. A flannel shirt, the wreck of a pinstripe suit hang on the wires. There is a trail of sodden paper and plastic, bits of books, a stash of old *Cosmopolitans*, clothes torn and strewn like harvest trash that is turning to rot. The trail leads down and down, from order to shit; but the residents have gone. At the surface, the cops are preoccupied. A man sits alone in a doorway, smoking, giving a thoughtful wave as we drive away. 'That's him, bet you,' Klambatsen says.

Three or four months back, he went down such an entrance at Delancey and Forsyth. 'We encountered all these wires,' he says. 'I knew they didn't belong there. I thought about bombs and booby traps. We clipped through them and we found the gate itself was wired shut. We followed the wires, down five flights of stairs. We could hear people talking, maybe 250 yards into the tunnel. You never know what you're going to find, who you're going to find.' Suddenly, he's concerned that you do not think the homeless are violent; Klambatsen has only been attacked once, by a man with an address who came with an ice-pick from behind a station pillar, and that was when he was still in uniform. 'They may steal from each other,' he says, 'but it's from each other. The women, they do get raped. Once, some passengers set fire to a homeless man who was asleep.'

There is a parallel city down here. At Delancey and Forsyth, the cops found shower curtains strung across the corridor. Klambatsen shouted to ask who was there. 'One guy comes walking out, all friendly, asking Hey how are you? He and his brother lived there; it was like their house. They tapped into the power rooms, and they'd got a TV, a hotplate, a VCR, a refrigerator and electric heater; there are plugs in the walls for drills if anyone's working down there. They had water and pictures on the wall. They said they'd lived there for eight months. I couldn't get over how friendly they were. I asked how the stuff got there, and they'd dragged it along the tracks from the station – round the blind curve on the D train track. They said they could hear when a train was coming, but you can't. You hear, but you can't tell if it's coming north or south or east or west.'

These cops who go down to the tracks are remarkable men; they're still cops, aware their duty is to clear out a public nuisance, but they're also some kind of social worker. They talk kindly at first, and pull rank later. 'I used to think the homeless were bums, just bums,' Steve Klambatsen says. Now he knows they stick together, come to the same places at the same time, eat together, agree to pretend there can be a lights out time on a twenty-four hour system; usually, the groups are around the same age. At 181st Street, they're black and Hispanic men, drinkers, who live at the back of the station; they light fires for warmth in winter; when the cops come, 'they throw bottles and chairs. They feel they're being ejected from their house.' At Forest Avenue, on the border of Brooklyn and Queens, white drunks, male and female, assemble even in winter on the outdoors, upstairs platforms. At Broadway-Lafayette, there's a cut out in the wall some eight feet into the tunnel, and people sleep there, on a ridge of concrete no more than a couple of inches wide; the passing of a fast train drags them by vacuum towards the tracks. At 57th Street on the Sixth Avenue line, there is a cool, high tunnel that leads nowhere, and between the tracks and the rat droppings, there are mattresses, old Coke bottles, a torn-out ad for an AIDS hotline. At Chambers Street, the well-meaning local branch of Roy Rogers fast food used to leave a basket of chicken by each sleeper on the platform, until the cops had to point out how kindness was filling up the station. At Second Avenue on the F line, there used to be eighty or ninety people sleeping; they got to know that the cops came on Tuesdays, and slept there the rest of the week. Now they're cleared away, it turns out there is always a use for blank space; the hookers take their johns where once the homeless slept.

Nowadays, the cops don't try to clear the terminals; they respond to complaints. They know they only move the problem along, but when they come with buses to take people to shelters, and food and juice and attendant social workers, there is the hope that they'll salvage someone, if only for a night. The truth is that on a bad winter night there are men and women beating on the doors of the buses, starved for a roof and a bed; but mostly, the city shelters horrify the people who most need them. They are afraid of crack, of gangs who run the floors like fiefdoms; 'there are rumours you have to pay for a bed, pay the cliques.' Men sleep in shoes that would otherwise be stolen, in fear that their pockets will be razored open. Since the transit police started trying to work with the homeless in 1982, they've made 42,000 contacts, and three out of five agreed to go to shelters. But in 1988 the figure was down to two out of five, and in the first half of 1989 only three out of ten.

It's not uncommon to find men in security guard uniform, low paid and not able to find the deposit and credentials for a place to live, sleeping in boxes on the platforms. Klambatsen found a kid of twenty-one at Coney Island who had lost his home when his grandma died; he was well enough dressed and worked in security, but he had only $500 and he needed $250 more to live somewhere. He had a job, so he could not get welfare; in any case, you need an address to get a welfare cheque even if you need the cheque to find an address. A kid who's long lived off grandma's social security has no credit cards, no credit history. The people who guard us are down in the tunnels, too.

Anywhere else, life can be organised so that its fragility is hidden; in New York, you see the derailments. Klambatsen found a man and wife together who wouldn't go to the shelters; 'We know,' they said, 'you'd have to split us up.' The man had two years at New York University, his wife a year of college. Their apartment went on fire, the man had a bout of pneumonia and their lives broke. The wife somehow maintained herself, the man went from 180 pounds to 95 pounds. 'This guy was very smart. I didn't know why he couldn't get a job, but then he told me – "There's no place else for my wife to be. I can't leave her alone here."'

A dormitory in a tunnel wakes up. A young black girl is curled up against a young white boy, an old bedspread under them with bags for pillows, another spread over them, a sheen of nylon gold; at the end of their bed is incense burning in a pint Coca Cola cup. They might be in a cheap motel, in their minds.

2
THE MANITOU

t' Fort nieúw Amsterdam op de Manhatans

THE DAY WAS still alive to the Mohicans more than a century later. They told how men went fishing where the river widens to the sea, and how they spotted at a great distance 'something remarkably large, swimming or floating on the water, and such as they had not seen before.' Some thought it was a huge fish or animal. Some thought it was a very large house. They muscled their canoes back to the shore, and sent runners so the chiefs could alert the warriors.

The men on land agreed the thing must be a large canoe, or a house, and that it bore 'the Manitou, great or supreme being, himself ... and that he probably was coming to visit them.' The chiefs assembled. The images of the tribe were cleaned; the women began to cook the finest food; they prepared a grand dance to calm the Manitou. 'The conjurors were also set to work, to determine what the meaning of this phenomenon was, and what the result would be. ... Between hope and fear, and in confusion, a dance commenced.'

The house floated up the wide stream under its odd roof of high sticks and grey cloth; rumour ran just as fast against the current. To Indians who hollowed their boats from trees, a ship built up above the waterline was a phenomenon; other such ships had been close to these waters, but they had never struck upstream as far as Delaware and Mohican territory. The chiefs concluded that 'a house of various colours and crowded with living creatures' was coming towards them. 'It now appears certain,' they said, 'that it is the great Manitou bringing them some kind of game, such as they had not before.' They heard shouts from the floating house, and they wanted to run off, but they knew they must not give offence to the animator of their world. Among the spirits on board, they could see one who was entirely red, and his clothes shone with lace: the Manitou himself. They watched him come on shore with cups and bottles.

The Manitou filled a cup and passed it round, but nobody drank until one Indian chided the others for their lack of manners. He took a swig for the good of the nation, and then he took another. He said it was better for one man to die than a whole nation to be destroyed by the anger of the Manitou. But he had no head for the wine and aqua vitae in the bottles, and he soon began to stagger. He fell asleep, and the elders thought that he was dead. But 'he awakes, jumps up and declares that he never felt himself before so happy as after he had drank the cup.'

Henry Hudson is never more vivid than in that moment, when he steps ashore in 1609 with a handful of bottles. No portrait of him survives, he has no certain father or birthplace and all we know of his private life is that his Amsterdam contract provides for 200 guilders for a wife 'in case, which God prevent, he do not come back or arrive hereabouts within a year.' He first appears on the record at a London church in 1607, taking Communion with his crew before sailing north in the hope of crossing the North Pole. He disappears three years later, murdered in a cold sea. On this brilliant day, he was in the service of the Dutch East India Company, captain of a fragile sixty-tonner called *De Halve Maen*, the Half Moon. He was not even in the right place. His orders were to beat through the icepack North of Russia, to round Novaya Zemlya and force an open Arctic sea route from Amsterdam to China; but the voyage did not go well. A note on the back of contemporary maps by Hessel Gerritz says 'Hudson, not having accomplished anything worthy of note in this voyage, was sent out again the following year. . . .'

The Indians, 'between hope and fear and in confusion', knew the new dance had begun.

'Discovery' is a curious business; 'discovering' a land usually means changing it, not simply being the first from your continent to arrive. Giovanni da Verrazano had blundered into what is now New York harbour in April 1524, and only 'a gale of unfavourable wind' had kept him from seeing Manhattan. On maps from the century before Hudson arrived, Hudson's River is a dagger of straight water in the side of America, in Estevan Gomez Land, named for Magellan's Portuguese pilot who followed Verrazano in 1525. By 1600 Dutch traders and privateers knew Newfoundland well, and there was a flourishing, not entirely legal, trade in furs with the French territories. When the ships went down from the northern fisheries to the Caribbean, to fish for gold in other nations' ships, they knew Hudson's River as the Rio de Gamas. But the river is now named for Hudson, because settlers and politics followed him; and a little because he could fit this accidental discovery into a grand theory of the world.

Hudson was kicking his heels in London in the winter of 1608, hoping for spring and the chance of new expeditions. He had built a reputation on two Arctic voyages for the English Muscovy Company. Each time, he had found open polar sea beyond the icepack, and animals grazing where he expected only crows and foxes. He decided the persistent Arctic sun could clear the ice, just as the slowest fire will eventually warm a house; through the open waters, there had to be a North-East passage, to China and the Indies by way of the Russian shore. But to test his ideas, he needed a ship and a crew. He sailed for the English, signed with their rivals the Dutch East India Company in Amsterdam, flirted there with the Catholic French; he would take any flag, any masters.

Hudson arrived in Amsterdam late in 1608, expecting to settle his new contract with the East India Company and be at sea by March; if he sailed later, he risked running into new ice on the return voyage in autumn. But the Company was a great monopoly, consulting and representing each province in the Netherlands, and the final decision to send out ships rested with the Council of Seventeen which met only two or three times a year; they would next meet in Middleburg on 25 March. Hudson had his contract on 8 January, but nothing else. He was paid to sail around the north side of Novaya Zemlya, and continue until he could sail back south to sixty degrees north on the other side of the world; he was 'to obtain as much knowledge of the lands as can be done without any considerable loss of time.' The Company knew that a mercenary, with crew and ship and eight months' provisions, was beyond their control at sea; they ordered him 'to think of discovering no other routes or passages.' Any other route would run into oceans where the Company had no monopoly; it might even challenge Spanish power, and be an act of war. The cautious Hollanders in Amsterdam wanted only a more efficient trading route.

But they let Hudson too much alone in Amsterdam, a city full of knowledge about the oceans, and Hudson drifted. He went to talk with Dominie Plancius, the head of the Amsterdam school of navigation, who was also interested in the navigable polar sea. Their discussions were dangerous. Plancius had 6,000 shares in the East India Company, and he must have known about Hudson's orders, but he drew their talk to quite other oceans. He was not a Hollander, thinking mostly about profit; he was a Southerner, a Calvinist preacher who had seen the Spaniards burn his books publicly at Ypres, and who fled north disguised as a soldier. He carried the anger of Southerners, who resented the shutting and silting of their great port at Antwerp, and always remembered. They had last seen Antwerp as 'a stage of horror', in Hooft's words, 'the corpses of men and horses in mountainous heaps, the streets dyed with their mingled blood.' They kept alive stories that were like slogans: a pregnant woman pitched by Spanish soldiers into a well, men flayed alive for the skins on Spanish drums, a bridegroom killed in the arms of his bride who is then, in her turn, hunted naked and bleeding through the streets like a spoiled deer. They honoured the United Provinces of the Netherlands, but, even more, they detested the Spanish. When Dominie Plancius said, doucely, 'There are other lands which have not yet been discovered and which God may be reserving for the glory and advantage of other Princes, not willing to bestow all upon Spain alone', he was thinking of stealing an empire by way of revenge.

He pressed on Hudson the journals of George Weymouth, an Englishman who had looked for a sea route across America, and a treatise by Iver Boty on the Greenland seas, marked 'for the use of Henrie Hudson'. The Dominie had changed the subject. Hudson had seen in the Whitehall Gallery in London a botched copy of Cabot's Planisphere, which showed a passage across the whole of America on the same parallel as the southern tip of Greenland. Hakluyt had recently published Verrazano's account of his voyage, along the coast of America, in which he says he 'did not doubt that I should penetrate by some passage to the eastern ocean.' Hudson believed Captain John Smith of Virginia, who reckoned there had to be a passage by Newfoundland which would circle Virginia and come to India; and Plancius warned him the far coast of America was unbroken 'upon the relation of a person who had explored the western part of that same country.' Hudson had orders to go by Russia, but he was thinking of America.

By March, when he should have been at sea, he was fidgeting on shore, and unhappy with his crew. He fought with the Company's chief boatswain about the wages of his English sailors, and he walked

out of his contract. 'He shall remain dismissed,' says the copybook of
the Zeeland Chamber of the Company, 'and even if he came to change
his mind with respect to performing the journey, you shall in no wise
engage him.' The Zeelanders drafted a letter to Amsterdam, which
they thought better of sending: 'We are much surprised at Mr Hudson's strange behaviour and consider it inadvisable to let him under-
take the voyage, for if he begins to rebel here under our eyes, what
will he do if he is away from us?' For Hudson was meeting, hugger-
mugger, a man called Isaac le Maire, another Southerner but a French
speaker, whose family was already its own trading company in Portu-
gal, Italy and Spain, and who had large, unofficial ambitions; le Maire
was a director of the East India Company, but he acted in Amsterdam
for the French. Paris had just realised the profit in oceanic trade, and
the huge political advantages, and was ready to outbid anyone for
the best pilots and captains. Le Maire 'did not venture to talk to the
Englishman except in secret', Jeannin, the French Minister at The
Hague wrote to Paris, but he was working on Hudson's patience.
When the Amsterdam Chamber of the Company found out, they
panicked, and reversed their irreversible sacking; inside a month, Hudson was on his way to the Faroes. A royal French draft of 4,000
crowns for his expenses arrived only days too late.

Henry Hudson very nearly sailed in the name of monarchy, autoc-
racy, a conventional and Roman religious life; not to mention the
King's policy and the nation's interest, supposed to be much the same
thing in war and treaties and trade. Instead, he carried Amsterdam on
the *Halve Maen*, as surely as the provisions. And unlike the Godly
experiments of New England, or the royal companies in Canada or
Virginia, the ideas have an oddly familiar shape. They are the faint
ghosts of an America, and a city, still to come.

Even the smells on Amsterdam streets were rich; warehouses that
smelled of fish and grain in the sixteenth century were now perfumed
with East Indian spices. In Hudson's time, the East India Company
kept back five years supply of mace to force up the price; sometimes
the smell of burning spice could be stifling. Through the huge
windows of merchants' houses, jowl by jowl along the orderly canals,
wealth was displayed as the visible sign of God's favour, granted only
to the elect. Houses were scrubbed quite ferociously clean, as if to

prove that the elect could control and perfect their lives amidst the crime and death of the darker streets. There were enough poor new-comers in Amsterdam for the city to need a public assistance pro-gramme, but there were fortunes in the narrow palaces along the canals, and they looked directly on to the lighters plying from the harbour. The elect rested their power proudly on cash and trans-actions, not land and fortifications; this is decades before Cromwell brought down the walls of the great feudal castles in England, and almost two centuries before the French demolished their court. Amsterdam was, as John Wheeler wrote in *A Treatise of Commerce* (1601), one of the 'new upstart towns in Holland'.

There was an official religion, a watery Calvinism, but also hidden churches for other sects and synagogues; as long as a passer-by could see nothing, the city let heresy be. Some of the English pilgrims who came to America had taken sanctuary in the United Provinces first, along with sailors from Denmark and Germany and Sweden who wanted work in the great trading city and the French-speaking Wal-loons driven north by the Spanish. Lutherans were on the board of the great trading companies even though they were, in theory, her-etics; Jews were influential shareholders while they were still not allowed to set foot in England. When a ship from Amsterdam went discovering, it sailed with hired hands, not settlers who wanted to make new lives abroad. There was no great religious imperative. In Joost van den Vondel's words, 'We Amsterdammers travel wherever profit drives us.' The city's unofficial motto was a proverb: Diversity creates tolerance.

The life of the place was trade. Between 1589 and 1611, the customs revenue doubled there, and the population went from roughly 30,000 in 1585 to 105,200 in 1622. When the French wanted to break the Dutch monopoly on whale oil, they still had to buy the flesh in Amsterdam. The English depended on Dutch traders for sailcloth and cordage, even when at war with their government. Amsterdam bought so many Russian furs in 1640 that the annual Archangel fair was almost bare. The only currency in which you could pay Russian customs duties was Dutch and the English East India Company imported gold ducatoons from Holland for India. Amsterdam had, as Violet Barbour wrote, 'a veritable empire of trade and credit . . . held by a city in her own right, unsustained by the forces of a modern, unified state.'

Venice had once been much the same, and just as Venice was helped

by innovations like double-entry bookkeeping, so Amsterdam's tri-
umphs rested on ideas that were startling at the time. In the middle
of the sixteenth century, the city was Europe's grain basket, as basic
a commodity as you like, but the Amsterdammers devised ways to
trade futures in grain. Elsewhere the idea of selling what you did not
actually own looked like fraud. The city's share markets worked;
shares in the Amsterdam Chamber of the East India Company were
worth a fifth more than shares in other provincial chambers because
in Amsterdam there were always buyers. When Isaac le Maire wanted
to break the East India Company, he did not go to war; he tried a
bear operation against its shares and lost a million and a half guilders.
No European country outside the Netherlands had the habit of speculation that bred the mad, catastrophic passion for tulips, so strong
that men would ruin themselves for a share of a single bulb. And
circumstances drove Amsterdammers to this speculation and clever
paper trading. There was little land to buy in the wet flatlands around
the city, and money had nowhere to go but risk – sometimes making
new land from under lakes, sometimes loans, shares, ships and voyages. In the paintings of Hudson's time, the city is a walled island of
crammed streets set in a neat and featureless green, both water and
land; it seems peculiarly a product of man's will, much more than
cities that hang on hills, or spread around natural harbours.

It had already begun to shed its medieval skin. Hudson signed his
contract just before Printer's Monday, the craftsman's holiday that
falls just after Epiphany. Four years before, Adriaan van Nieulandt
painted the last of the great Printer's Mondays. Lepers came on sleighs
to beg, rattles in hand, in short wide coats with white bands round
their hats; they made a procession of grimace and jerk. They passed
gin-sellers touting their wares in pewter cups, rat-catchers flying their
prey like a flag to show their skill, quacks selling cures for the gall,
city heralds in coats of red and black stripes, and agents for the lottery
for the madhouse, who helped the sales of tickets along by displaying
slightly draped studies of the mad. But look again at Van Nieulandt's
streets. These people are dealing with each other, literally dealing,
and not signifying some immutable social order. Behind the flurry,
there are racks of grey canvas sails and the great scales of the fine
weigh-house, the city's first true Renaissance building, under its
golden weather-vane of Fortune and the sea-god Neptune. There is
no king, nothing abstract and sacramental about power; everything is
for use. Already the city has the smugness that would grow through

the century into paintings of Neptune signing on with the Admiralty of Amsterdam, or a rather sulky Maid of Amsterdam accepting the tribute of mere nations.

Six weeks out of Amsterdam, the sea was crammed shut with ice, and the *Halve Maen* could not pass. The way north, according to the ship's logbook, had already been 'much trouble, with fogs sometimes and more dangerous of ice'. The Dutch sailors who had been in the East Indies trade had sailed full of resentment and they fought with the English crew in the tight confines of the ship; now they said they could not bear the bitter cold. When Hudson tried to run into the Kara Sea, through the straits south of the island Novaya Zemlya, the Dutch first mate and the crew refused to go on.

Hudson had been stopped at the same latitude the year before by a press of ice; he was ready with alternatives to offer to the crew, anything except turning back to Amsterdam and wasting the expedition. They could sail towards America, either around Greenland to Davis Straits in the north, or in the latitude of forty degrees, to what is now the New Jersey shore. Emmanuel van Meteren, who had the story from Hudson, writes that the crew chose the more southerly route, and that Hudson was 'mostly incited to this by letters and maps which a certain Captain Smith had sent him from Virginia.' This decision was made to seem suspicious; a note on maps by Hessel Gerritz says Hudson 'seems purposely to have missed the right road to the western passage, unwilling to benefit Holland ... by such a discovery.'

In the best of weather, the Atlantic crossing took between six and eight weeks, trapped in a box of wood. The sea changed colours like omens, white green to grey. Charts were uncertain; Hudson spent time searching for something called Busse Island, which is actually a shifting icebank. On 15 June, the *Halve Maen* lost its foremast overboard. Other vessels slipped by on their own silent business, which might or might not be legal, and did not stop to hail or help a stricken ship; many were privateers. Everything depended on the crew, and they were what the Dutch called *het grauw*, the rabble or riffraff, with no morals and men's muscles, considered no better than vagrants or the workless. When the *Halve Maen* reached Newfoundland, and Indians came aboard in friendship, the logbook records that the crew 'manned our boat and scute with twelve men and muskets, and two stone pieces or murderers, and drave the savages from their houses, and took the spoyle of them as they would have done of us.'

Hudson turned south, through 'a hurling current, or tyde with over-fals which cast our ship round' and the great heat of July. The fragile shallop, or dinghy, ran against the ship's stern and split, and had to be cast off. On 21 August, 'a great sea brake into our fore-corse and split it ... this night our cat ranne crying from one side of the ship to the other, looking over-boord, which made us to wonder.' On 2 September, 'we saw a great fire, but could not sea the land ... then the sunne arose and wee steered away north againe and saw the land ... all like broken islands ... untill we came to a great lake of water, as wee could judge it to bee, being drowned land....'

They had come to Sandy Hook, at the mouth of Hudson's River, and to haven after their ferocious voyage; 'This is a very good land to fall with, and a pleasant land to see....' The next day, they stood off the south coast of Staten Island and 'saw many salmons and mullets and rayes, very great.' On Coney Island, they caught ten mullet 'of a foote and a halfe long apeece and a ray as great as foure men could hale into the ship ... This day the people of the countrey came aboord of us, seeming very glad of our comming' and bringing green tobacco to trade for knives and beads. 'They have yellow copper. They desire cloathes and are very civill.' But Robert Juet, the Lime-house man who kept the log, insisted the Indians were not to be trusted. Two days later, sailors crossed from Staten Island to Bergen Neck and were dazzled by 'lands.... pleasant with grasse and flowers and goodly trees as ever they had seene, and very sweet smells came from them.' On the way back, their dinghy was surprised by a little fleet of warriors in canoes. Night was down, and rain drowned the lamp; an Englishman called John Colman was killed by an arrow through the throat and two others were injured. The tide was too powerful for their anchor, and the survivors could not find the ship; they 'labored too and fro upon their oares', helpless until dawn.

The ship could not be ignored; the Indians had to act or react. Some brought presents of corn bread or hide, and some set out to kill, in their hundreds. The Europeans could hardly decide if they were naive or terrifying. Hudson visited a house of oak bark, piled with corn, grapes, pumpkins; 'when they saw that I would not remain,' he wrote, 'they supposed that I was afraid of their bows, and taking the arrows, they broke them in pieces and threw them into the fire.' But sometimes the arrows were used, and Van Meteren records that the crew 'behaved badly towards the people of the country, taking their property by force; out of which there arose quarrels among them.' In the Mohican tradition, the elders remembered how their grandfathers had known, even then, that the Europeans 'would soon want all their country'.

On his own ship, the Manitou was just a captain far from home, his authority fragile. He was afraid of his own crew, who 'had sometimes savagely threatened him.' The Dutch mate wanted to winter in New-foundland and then to explore to the north; 'nobody ... spoke of returning home to Holland, which circumstance made the captain still more suspicious.' Many of the crew were sick. Their provisions would soon be exhausted. Hudson could smell mutiny. He suggested they make for an Irish port, but the sailors forced him into English waters at Dartmouth. Foul weather prevented the news of his voyage reaching Amsterdam for two months. By the time the East India Company knew the fate of their ship, the English were at war, and they ordered Hudson to stay put until he could sail again under English colours.

He thought he could go again to the river the next year, but his course took him further north. On the way, Robert Juet, the log-keeper, turned the crew against him. Hudson was bundled into a longboat along with the 'poor, sick and lame men' and abandoned among the ice castles of an Arctic bay. He disappears into the cold and the fog.

After Henry Hudson, a few traders came slipping up from the Carib-bean, lured by the prospect of buying fine furs and, most of all, the beaver for a European gentleman's obligatory hat. On Hudson's river, they could do business without the bother of French or English excise. One man, at least, went ashore to stay from the European ships; Juan Rodriguez left the *Jonge Tobias* with the captain's help, and eighty hatchets, some knives, a musket and a sword. He was a mulatto from the island of Santo Domingo, which today is Haiti and the Dominican Republic; like other people of colour later, he became a go-between for the Indian trappers and the Dutch traders. But the Dutch fancied themselves as traders, not settlers. They carried with them the idea of a settled city, with monuments to survive for centuries, and prop-erty to buy and sell, but they did not plant it. They did not break the Indian nations' belief that land was an element like air, belonging to a man only while he worked it, and cities were moveable communities. They did not even formally claim their new territory; they knew the English had already grabbed and quartered most of the east coast of America, on the basis of an early, distant pass by the Cabots. They were transients in an uncomfortable land.

In Amsterdam, the captain Adriaen Block liked to bad mouth the prospects; he would tell people on the quays of the Rokin that the new trade 'did not amount to much and was poor work.' It was certainly expensive to finance; Block sailed to America on the money of exiles and Lutherans, with most of his profit committed to his backers even before he left port. But he saw something there; he tried to claim a monopoly of the trade, and said he would defend his rights with guns. He ran considerable risks. In 1613 Block brought the *Tyger* and the *Nachtegael* to America, followed by one other ship he did not command. Just as the ice was beginning to fix the waters of Hudson's river, the *Tyger* caught mysterious fire and burned down to the water-line. Her crew were afraid to wait out the winter; they mutinied, snatched the *Nachtegael* while the captain and crew were ashore building a new vessel and set sail for the more familiar comforts of the West Indies. Block was left to wait on the river for the next captains, his rivals. When they came, he had to concede shares in the fur trade to buy passage for his stranded men.

It seems so obvious now that the river was rich and fertile and available; but it was part of that great zone from Trinidad to Maine in which Spanish power was centred, and taking land there was immediately an issue of war. The idea of 'colonisation by free Dutch citizens' had been mooted by Willem Usselincx, and he was a Southerner exiled in Amsterdam, with a Southerner's living grievances. He had been a trader's apprentice and seen Brazilian sugar coming ashore in Oporto, Spanish treasure fleets ballasted with gold in Seville; he proposed a joint stock company in 1600 that would send out settlers, rather than establishing isolated trading posts. His motives were in important part religious; one purpose of the company was 'the furtherance of the saving Gospel of our Lord Jesus Christ and the bringing of many thousands of men to the light of truth and to eternal salvation.' But such grand proposals for the Americas were blocked in 1616 by the Grand Pensionary van Oldenbarnevelt – a Hollander, a pragmatist who was engineering a truce with the Spanish enemy. A truce would keep the United Provinces out of America; it would stop the kind of challenge to Spain that the Southern exiles wanted. It was not until Van Oldenbarnevelt was rushed to the gallows three years later, accused of treason and accepting Spanish money, that even the idea of a grand West Indies Company could be revived.

It would not be the missionary, colonising enterprise that Usselincx had designed. It was a privateering business, meant mostly to chivvy and raid on the Guinea coast and in the Caribbean; the charter provided for two sets of books, 'one relating to trade and one relating to war, each separate', and after the Treaty of Munster in 1648, when the United Provinces had a settled peace with Spain, there would be serious question whether the Company should continue, since much of its profit came from piracy on Spanish ships. Of course, there were high hopes for the new colony in Brazil, which could take in slaves from Guinea and send out the sugar to which Europe was becoming expensively addicted, but almost nobody wanted to go; the Company almost ruined itself in 1638 buying settlers by giving up its monopoly of sugar. The Hollanders already had the East India trade, and they were happy to leave all the problems of the Americas to the Southerners.

North America meant fur, and only fur; there could be no quick profit, voyage by voyage, in farming. When the Company was chartered in 1621 it took two more years to raise all its capital, and the city of Amsterdam subscribed only three-quarters of what they had found for the East India Company almost twenty years before. 'If the colonies should not tend to the benefit of the subscribers in general,' as Pieter de la Court wrote in 1662, 'we cannot expect the companies should promote them.' So the Company was slow in staking out claims to land. Late in the summer of 1623 the *Mackereel* sailed for the Guinea coast and, on her return, anchored off Manhattan Island on 12 December, the Company's first presence in North America. 'That was indeed somewhat late,' Wassenaer wrote, 'but it wasted time in the savage islands, to catch a fish [a Spanish ship] and did not catch it, so ran the luck.'

Next spring, the *Mackereel* was still in the river when the *Nieu Nederlandt* arrived with settlers. There were thirty families, French-speaking Southerners who promised to stay for at least six years; we do not know their faces, but they took their oaths in Amsterdam before a doctor who appears in Rembrandt's *Anatomy Lesson*. Once landed, they scattered like dust on a mirror, from the Delaware to the Connecticut River, and from Director's Island in New York harbour to a point just south of modern Albany; on their own they were meant to occupy New Netherland and prove Dutch title to the land.

Most of them are unknowable. The story of New Amsterdam was sold for wastepaper in 1825 when the Dutch West India Company disposed of its records; it drowned with the papers that went down with Director Kieft in the Bristol Channel, or burned, when many papers of the Dutch period, in process of translation, scorched beyond recognition in the New York State Public Library at the start of this century. 'The story of these beginnings is more confused and obscurer than that of any of the other colonies,' Filippo Mazzei complained at the time of the American Revolution, in his *Researches on the United States*. But we know that six more ships left for New Netherland in 1625, carrying settlers, livestock and provisions. The fleet was spread by storms; the *Mackereel* was taken by pirates off Dunkirk; the *Oranjeboom* was forced by heavy seas to put into Plymouth, seized by customs who threatened to take her seeds, plants and tools, and released very suddenly when the English realised some of the crew and passengers were sick with typhus. Only three ships reached America. They were supposed to strengthen the southern colony, but also to bring the scattered settlers together somewhere they could be defended on Hudson's river. The engineer Cryn Fredericksz had instructions to stake out a fort; the Company's second choice of site was 'the hook of the Manattes, north of Noten Island' (which is now Governor's Island). There were already cattle pastured on Manhattan, and settlers to guard them.

They dug pits for the first houses, lined them with posts and tree bark, put planks and thatch across the top and lived there, insulated from the bitter winter. They went hungry; within a year, the settlers needed food shipped from the motherland. They were Company men. Their cattle were shipped by the Company and distributed by lot; the Company did not allow anyone 'to construct anything special that another has not'; the Company could make what treaties it liked with local nations, order its sailors to do labourers' work or its carpenters to act as soldiers. The Company had to give permission for anyone to leave New Netherland; when the minister Everardus Bogardus, a wild-tempered man, needed to go home to answer charges brought against him, the colony's director 'deemed it necessary to keep the minister here in order that the Church of God may daily grow in strength.'

To be a settler was to take a job abroad; you might not expect to change your life for ever, except by growing richer; there was no

American to want to be. In those early years, the master bricklayer Luycas Jansz Sprangh took a two-year contract in 1633 to help remake the fort on Manhattan; he came to pay off debts to his brother-in-law. Jacob Swenthorst of Hamburg was an illiterate twenty-five-year-old who shipped out with any skipper who would pay him; when he needed 300 guilders to keep his illegitimate daughter in the orphanage, he signed up as a Manhattan farmworker for three years. America was one choice among many. Pieter Pietersz Bijlevelt wanted gold, came to New Netherland to find it, and was disappointed; after eight years, he took wife and family back to Amsterdam, put them on public charity and shipped out for the East Indies to try again. His wife was left to sue for the value of livestock and grain she had left behind on Manhattan.

There was no group of middle-class people as eager to flee Holland as the Puritans had been to flee England; and families of the industrious poor, who signed indentures to work and populate the English colonies, could easily survive in Amsterdam. The volunteers for New Netherland were drifters, or refugees from the endless horrors of the Thirty Years War; many were young and single, many were sailors who could not find any other berth. Some shipped home after only a few years, according to the minister Jonas Michaelius, because they 'were not serviceable to the Company.' The directors ordered the director of New Netherland 'to pay especial attention to idlers, leaving them to suffer want if they are unwilling to do their duty.' For some said openly they had not come to work, according to Michaelius, because 'as far as working is concerned they might as well have stayed at home.'

Within a year, there was a fort – a pile of sod and red cedar, standing among thirty log houses and a stone horsemill whose loft could be used for Sunday worship. The fort never did hold off an army successfully, but it stood for authority; it was the first target for rebels and invaders, and whoever held it would rename it, a claim on all of New Netherland. For now, it suggested there was a government in the village of New Amsterdam, which was not quite true. Isaac de Rassière arrived to be the colony's secretary and found that the colony's first director Wilhelm Verhulst had simply done away with the forms of law, punished what offended him quite arbitrarily and 'the people here have become quite lawless, owing to the bad government hitherto prevailing.' His juniors were problematic, too. To the north, a freelancing Company man had managed to take sides in an Indian

war and provoke a massacre. On Manhattan, when De Rassière threatened the assistant commissary Fongersz with a fine and confiscation
for shipping skins without the West India Company's say-so, Fongersz snapped back: 'I do not consider you a big enough man for that.'
Like other settlers, Fongersz seemed to need an inexhaustible supply
of drink; 'I have seldom seen him sober . . . I have mentioned the fact
several times to [Peter] Minuit who does not understand where he
gets the liquor.'

This Minuit was the obvious choice to succeed Verhulst, and
quickly. He came first to New Netherland to explore the upper reaches
of Hudson's river and was entrusted with sundry inquiries and reports.
It was he who suggested that the Dutch should buy Manhattan.
Amsterdam recorded the deal in November 1626: 'Our people . . .
have bought the island Manhattes from the wild men for the value of
sixty guilders. It is over 11,000 morgens [about 22,000 acres] in extent.
They sowed all their grain in the middle of May and harvested it in
the middle of August.' The price was the worth of thirty beaverskins,
Isaac de Rassière's salary for six months (but not the legendary
twenty-four dollars, which is based on a nineteenth-century exchange
rate, twenty-five times too low). Minuit dealt only with the Carnarsee
Indians, because the Dutch did not yet know the local nations well
enough to realise that some of the 'wild men' on the island had
cropped heads with a kind of mane at the centre. These Weckquaes-
geek people had land around Harlem and Washington Heights, and
they had not been paid for it; the Dutch, as far as they were concerned,
had title only to SoHo.

The Carnarsee sold something that did not exist in their eyes, since
they recognised a man's title only to ground he was presently working; but they knew how serious the deal was to the Dutch. The
newcomers were proper people; they had houses on the island, but
they would not plant until they paid for the land. Minuit's deal gave
the colony title to itself, a voluntary contract beyond simple conquest.
It became a joke, and a talisman. It was memorialised in the hall of
the New York Title Guarantee and Trust Company with white men
landing in America from a rowboat and dealing with Indian women
in European clothes and braves in moccasins and gaiters; it sanctified
not only the white man on Manhattan but every transfer of title
thereafter. In Lamb's *History of the City of New York*, the Dutch bear
books, guns and a crucifix, to show that Minuit did a worthy deal –
learning, order, religion, as well as goods worth sixty guilders. The

Edwardians were more cynical in their cartoons. They show the pear-shaped, pipe-smoking Dutch plodding their new property; across the water the Indians have staged a roaring (and fancy dress, rather Edwardian) party on the proceeds.

At the time, the deal was a detail in the management of a marginal enterprise. New Netherland was a tentative affair, as far as Mother Amsterdam was concerned. When the West India Company threw twenty-three ships against the Portuguese in Brazil, only to be picked off at sea and then repulsed at São Salvador, the Company panicked and abandoned New Netherland to the Amsterdam Chamber. When Amsterdam heard in November 1628 how Pieter Heyn had taken a treasure fleet off Havana, laden with hides and dyewood, sugar, silver and gold, the Company's stock soared; but now there was a source of profit, New Netherland seemed too big, too empty and too bothersome. The pattern continued. There exist no grand paintings of New Amsterdam to match Frans Post's propaganda for the Dutch colony in Brazil – which needed help, as rumours of heat and sickness and failure came back to the Netherlands; Post made his foregrounds into a linear zoo of interesting animals and his backgrounds into distant blue vistas of hills and order, perhaps with settlers visiting a fine cathedral set on a sugar plantation; he very nearly painted profits. There are not even the celebrations of the riverfronts which were made in Surinam when it became Dutch, let alone the intricate pictures of encampments in the Indies: their tents, their colonnades, their high-stepping camels in a mad chorus line. Very occasionally, the Company did publish a pamphlet – in 1661, to attract whatever English dissidents might have been distressed by the restoration of King Charles; 'Six weeks sayle from Holland,' they promised, 'under the best clymate in the whole world ... seed may be thrown into the ground, except six weeks, and the yere long ... heere groweth tobacco very good. ... furs of all sorts, very reasonable ... excellent veneson, elkes very great and large ... excellent fat and wholesome fish ...' It is a desperate pitch. The propaganda for Dutch settlements in America was more usually meant to remind Amsterdam of their existence.

Jonas Michaelius wrote from Manhattan in 1628 that he was constrained to lead 'a hard and sober existence, like poor people', which shocked a man who had left behind the wealth of Amsterdam. 'Food is scanty and poor,' he complained; milk and butter, Dutch staples, were scarce and 'those endeavouring to secure them are jealous of one another.' Manhattan was 'the key and principal stronghold of the country, and needs to be settled first, as is already done; but it is somewhat less fertile than the other spots and causes more trouble on account of the multitudes of roots of shrubs and trees.' For all the new houses rising to replace the 'hovels and holes', Michaelius still felt enveloped by the uncultivated, unplanned wilderness all around him, so different from the man-made fields at home. It was, above all, too empty to be safe.

In Amsterdam, the West India Company was divided – between those who wanted a factory system, with a few traders and no expensive colonists, and those who thought private money might plant New Netherland with settlers. They first sought investors who aspired to be the dukes of the new world – 'patroons', who were granted the power to tax and punish their subjects and call on Patria for defence; in return they had to settle sixty people in America within three years, or thirty on Manhattan, where the need for labour and defence was more urgent. The scheme was hashed out for a year, and somehow Manhattan was excluded. The 'patroons' would have to look to more distant, and less defensible territory.

The jewel merchant Killian van Rensselaer volunteered. He told the Company his schemes were better than 'the many poor beggars whom it now gets'; he dreamed of growing enough grain to trade for sugar from Brazil. But to defend his privilege, he had to use his fists. When he met the leader of the factory faction in public, he 'went at de Vogelaer in such a way on the crowded Dam that he will not soon forget it.' The fur trade was the Company's monopoly, and since it was the only source of immediate income, the Company was not inclined to share. Livestock was scarce; Van Rensselaer had to maintain a breeding farm on Manhattan and was stopped from moving his own beasts upstream by a later director of the colony on the grounds that Manhattan was 'already vacant and stripped of animals and not fit for cultivation'. It was hard to find colonists; most of Van Rensselaer's were men, single and young, and without a trade, many of them country labourers working to pay back the board and lodging he had bought them in Amsterdam while they were waiting for a ship; he may even have conscripted some.

The emptiness was dangerous. Down towards Delaware, the Company fancied it had bought the best whaling tract on the whole south west shore of the bay; until the day they returned to find the fort half burned, the skeletons of men scattered in the fields, the cattle slaughtered and frozen in appalling postures. To the North, the French were wooing the Mohicans. The English pressed into the Connecticut Valley to take the fur trade, throwing out Dutch trappers and mocking their bronchitic language. When New Amsterdam was rebuilt in 1633, the Company's army of carpenters, bricklayers and stone masons had to be drafted for war when the foundations were barely laid. The English were settling on Long Island, and causing trouble in New Amsterdam, and they mattered enough for the colony's director to hire an ensign to write letters in English. The sheer lack of people drove the Company to make concessions – to give away its economic monopolies, the point of its existence, while keeping the job of directing and managing the colony. The Company gave land to any-one who would farm, instead of holding it all. They kept only one absolute monopoly: shipping across the ocean. But even these changes were not enough. The Company was forced to open the precious fur trade to all Dutch citizens, and to allow private ships to ply to New Amsterdam. Individual merchants could trade much as they wanted, unless the few officers of the Company caught them; and the officers were a dubious lot. Pieter Minuit deserted with secret maps to help Usselincx create New Sweden, a rival colony in the same territory between English lands; the next director was Wouter van Twiller, a drunken clerk from Amsterdam, appointed to new glory because he was the son of the sister of the patroon Killian van Rensselaer; and Willem Kieft, who was appointed in 1637, had no administrative experience, nor much apparent skill as a merchant since he had been bankrupted the year before in La Rochelle. The very idea of a trading monopoly was in trouble, only years after it had been financed and chartered.

But New Netherland was not perfectly empty, except to European eyes; the Indian nations lived and farmed and hunted there. They were rivals for land, and irritants because it took force to subject them to the Company's various schemes. They had grievances which the Dutch did not intend to address. They were heathen surrounding nervous islands of European life, their friendship and hatred unpredict-able. There began the long and bloody sequence of wars which the Dutch States General denounced in 1650 as 'unnatural, barbarous, unnecessary, unjust and disgraceful'.

The first cause was hogs. Dutch hogs and cattle wandered the

woods without herdsmen, which was possible because the Dutch
fenced their crops carefully. But the Indians had no fences, and the
free-ranging beasts trod down their crops; when complaints failed,
they killed the animals, even the horses which were scarce and valuable. These attacks were alarming; they were considered grounds
enough for indentured servants out on Staten Island to break their
contracts and move to the greater safety of Manhattan. After the hogs,
came the governors, with their undiluted view of things. Governor
Kieft took it for granted the Indians should help him pay the cost of
soldiers, sailors and fortifications, in return for protection against their
enemies. When he set out to collect from the summer settlements
where the Algonquin gathered their fruit and dried their winter fish,
his skipper saw the stacks of pelts and seized them all. The chief
attacked the skipper, slashing him across the face with a hunting knife;
Indian warriors tried to storm the ship. Soon afterwards, the hogs on
a Staten Island farm were destroyed. Kieft suspected this was part of
some Indian revenge, but the Indians suspected the Company's rabble
of a soldiery. To this uncertainty, add the power of rumour and
anxiety. There followed a punitive raid on the island, the burning of
villages and the killing of some Indians. Kieft fancied he had made a
kind of peace.

But then a young Indian came to buy duffel cloth from Claes
Rademaker, the wheelmaker who lived to the north of the village of
New Amsterdam. The older man was looking through a chest for
cloth when the Indian struck him on the neck with an axe. He said it
was revenge; his uncle had been robbed and killed by the Dutch while
Fort Amsterdam was being built. A drunk Indian shot a Dutchman
who was thatching a roof, and ran two days' journey away before the
Indians came to offer compensation to the dead man's widow; 'they
laid the blame upon our people because we sold the young Indians
brandy or wine, making them crazy.' The Indians also told David de
Vries, who had a patroonship on Staten Island, that they could not
turn in the killer because he was the son of a chief. Kieft went with
these stories to his council, and only one man thought war could not
be successful, and another that it might be best to wait for a ship from
the fatherland. The others said it was best 'to have patience and to
lull the Indians to sleep' or 'to kill the Indians so as to fill them with
fear' or else 'to begin war and to exterminate the savages if possible.'

De Vries had a house upstream, and the Indians came there asking
protection from a new war; but de Vries could not help them because

their enemies at Fort Orange were the Dutchmen's friends. He had only five men in the house, and the boat was iced up in the kill (which means an inlet); he had to take a canoe through the shifting pack ice down to Fort Amsterdam, to ask for help. At Kieft's table, he heard the director say 'he had a mind to wipe the mouths of the Indians.' De Vries saw the soldiers already assembled in the hall. 'Stop this work,' he told Kieft. 'You wish to break the mouths of the Indians, but you will also murder our own nation, for there are none of the farmers who are aware of it. My own dwelling, my people, cattle, corn and tobacco will be lost.'

But Kieft was not a settler or a farmer; he was the Company's man, supposed to impose Company authority with a garrison and arms. 'I went and sat in the kitchen,' de Vries wrote, 'when, about midnight, I heard a great shrieking and I ran to the ramparts of the fort and looked over to Pavonia. Saw nothing but firing, and heard the shrieks of the Indians murdered in their sleep.' An Indian couple came innocently to the fort for protection because they were sure some other Indian nation had attacked them at Pavonia. De Vries helped them secretly away. The soldiers returned with bright, bloody stories – of how children were torn from their mothers' breasts and hacked to pieces, how sucklings were bound to small boards and pierced and killed. The next morning, Indians who had fled came back for bread and to warm themselves against the February cold, and they were murdered. 'Some came by our lands in the country with their hands, some with their legs cut off, and some holding their entrails in their arms ... and these poor simple creatures, as also many of our own people, did not know any better than that they had been attacked by a party of other Indians.'

The lie could not hold. When the Indians realised they had been attacked by the Dutch, they killed all the men they could surprise in the farmlands, and 'burned all the houses, farms, barns, grain, haystacks and destroyed everything they could get hold of.' If they spared the house of de Vries, it was only because he was considered a 'good chief'.

He was the only man besides Jacob Olfersz who would go with the Indians when they called to the fort from Long Island, bearing a small and rough white flag. The Dutchmen met the spokesman for the sixteen chiefs of Long Island, who had in his hand a bundle of sticks; he laid down one for each point. He said the Indians had given the settlers 'their daughters to sleep with, by whom they had begotten children, and there ran many an Indian who was begotten by a Swanneka' or Dutchman. De Vries could count the sticks and he cut short what promised to be a long indictment. He persuaded the chiefs to Fort Amsterdam for presents of peace, over the objections of those who asked 'if they were so foolish as to go to the fort where there was such a villain' as Kieft; they crammed twenty into a canoe and 'the edge was not a hand's breadth above the water.' All the formal conditions for peace were now in place, except one: that Kieft give presents enough to make his change of heart seem trustworthy. Instead, the Governor offered a laughable 200 fathoms of zeewan, the shells that served as currency, for the head of the Indian who killed Claes Rademaker. Kieft would not play the Indian script, and the Indians were insulted by European obstinacy – two cultures, clashing against each other until there was fire.

The war did nothing for the settlers' nerves in their tiny town. The afternoon of 21 March, 1643, someone called Maryn Adriaensen a 'murderer' because he signed the petition for revenge on the Indians; he fell to brooding. He took a sword, a cocked and loaded pistol, and went down to the house of Governor Kieft; his wife asked friends in the tavern to run after him and stop him. He came to Kieft's bedroom and held the Governor at gunpoint, demanding to know what devilish lies he was telling. It happened that the learned Johannes la Montaigne was there, and he threw himself at Adriaensen and 'caught the pan with such quickness that the cock snapped on his finger.' For his threats, the local court gave Adriaensen only three months banishment; it was Kieft who insisted he be sent home to Holland, in chains.

And in autumn, it was the Indians who fell on Pavonia, killed the soldiers who were stationed there, allowed Jacob Stoffelsz to run for the fort but kidnapped his child. De Vries was the only man the Indians were ready to hear, but when he brought two men to the fort to plan the boy's release, 'everyone wanted to kill them and I had enough to do to save them.' He won the boy's freedom, but he also decided that the glories of patroonship were over. He sailed for Virginia to find a well-mounted ship to take him back to Holland, 'because my farms, where I had begun my colonies, were lying in ashes, and the Indians were discontented and desired to go to war again or have satisfaction.'

The record is bloody, and full of shadows. We know about the wars, but not who drove them on. Kieft seems like a stolid, unimaginitive man, who caused massacres by imposing his simple view of things on a very different culture. But Kieft was also unusually interested in the Indians; he told Roger Williams in 1643 that he was pleased 'to draw their line from Iceland, because the name Sachmacken, the name for an Indian prince about the Dutch, is the name for a Prince in Iceland.' His English military commander, Captain John Underhill, on the other hand, was a brutish drunk, who came to New Netherland with a name for abusing the Indians. We know his manners and temper did not improve in New Netherland; court records tell of him trying to crash a party at the city tavern, slashing at the walls so that mugs and glasses fell from the shelves and the doors were pock-marked, being held back for a while by the landlord leaning against the door and the landlady wielding a leaded bludgeon and finally breaking in to threaten to strike with his sword at random. Perhaps it was Underhill who staged the raids and insisted on revenge. Kieft's side of the story was drowned along with him, when the *Princess Amelia* went down in the Bristol Channel on 27 September 1647; it was quite usual for colonial governors to travel with all their records, to be ready to give an accounting or mount a defence when they got home. The irony for Kieft is that his accusers, including the murderous Adriaensen, travelled on the same small ship. They, and their bill of indictment, survived.

In an uneasy world, you cling to ease. You buy and ship it. You prove your Christian virtues by remaking Amsterdam on a blank island. There were canals at home, and so there was a Herengracht that ran where Broad Street now lies, and changed its name to Prinsengracht where it crossed Beaver Street on its way north. The tides drained it for half the day, and left it a ditch of stinking mud; in winter, it froze shut; but it was what a city had to have. There was a windmill on Governor's Island in 1626, and one a few yards west of the fort. Down by the water stood the city tavern, a handsome building, gabled and built of stone with open ground behind it; when it became City Hall, the court secretaries kept the right to sow grain there. New houses were solid and tall, with fine gables and cellars and side aisles for storage, with passageways to make distinct rooms; they were city houses, with more than the countryside division between stables and human quarters. There was a church of quarry stone, begun by English masons in 1641, with shingles of oak that turned slate-blue in the wind and rain. David de Vries had pushed Governor Kieft to give a hundred guilders for the building, and the Governor, who drank carefully at a wedding where everyone else drank wildly, asked the guests for contributions to match his own. 'All of them with light heads subscribed largely, competing with one another; and although some well repented it when they recovered their senses, they were nevertheless compelled to pay.'

These were the elements of a city, clustered at the south end of Manhattan and surrounded by water and wilderness. The town boundary was still a wooden fence, held together with rope and pegs. It divided town and farm, but it was not the town's real defence. That lay in the goods and the mindset of Christian folk in savage lands, telling themselves they were civilised among the heathen. The settlers hung their pictures and treasured their perfumed soap and pearl-handled looking glasses, and bought dozens of fashionable parrots and cockatoos from the Caribbean. On dresser shelves stood fine decorated glass, even fragile Venetian glass, and majolica and faience dishes, often with the blue-white Chinese birds and characters and mandarins that the Dutch so fancied. Outside, they made gardens where the goats and hogs allowed. Brilliant new flowers came from Europe: fine tulips, crown imperials, white lilies and anemones, violets, marigolds and roses. As early as 1643, when Jonas Bronck died on the farm for which the Bronx is named, his estate was thoroughly comfortable: Bibles and psalters, books especially for his children, atlases, charts and the Cosmographia of Petrus Apianus, eleven pictures for the wall and silver-chased tankards to drink from. We know of no local painter working on canvas in the Dutch period, but perhaps the point was to hang what hung on walls in Amsterdam, to remember and be justified.

It should have been a lush life. Even the sandy soil on Manhattan was suitable for rye and buckwheat, De Rassiere thought. There were striped bass in the rivers, and pigeons whose great flocks blocked out the light when they migrated. There were vines and nuts, and the Indians offered new discoveries: squash and maize and pumpkins. Venison was a staple of the settlers' diet at least until the 1660s; venison, in much of Europe, was reserved for the high and mighty, so the settlers were being reduced to luxury. But if ships were late or there were rumours of war, food ran short. Yachts had to travel to New England to barter furs for dried fish. Propaganda for the colony mentioned summers like Barbados, but not the sudden, Arctic winds of winter. The truth had a way of travelling home quickly. In 1639 there were perhaps 400 settlers in New Amsterdam; and in 1655, only 1,170, just under a third of all those living officially in New Netherland. There were never more than half the number of settlers who went to Massachusetts although always far more than Pennsylvania even in the 1660s. These counts are uncertain, and likely to be too low, but the community was tiny.

A quarrel made a terrible din, and often ended in court. Someone called the miller a cuckoo, there's a dubious song about an English minister and his daughter, an angry wife pays a fine for accusing a man of gambling away her husband's money. Everardus Bogardus, the minister, infuriated Director Van Twiller, who took to stalking him with a drawn knife. Bogardus said the director was 'an incarnate villain, a child of the Devil, whose buck goats are better than he' and promised sermons that would 'clamp him so tight . . . his breastbone would crack.' When Director Kieft arrived, with his fancy talk of being as powerful in America as the Prince of Orange in the fatherland, Bogardus drank no less and showed no more charity. Kieft put in chains a man who had tried to murder him, and Bogardus 'fulminated terribly for about fourteen days.' Kieft could no longer go to church for fear of sermons in which Bogardus ranted that 'men aim at nothing but to rob one another of his property, to dismiss, banish and transport.' He would stare at Kieft and bellow, 'In Africa many animals interbreed because of the heat and in this manner many monsters are generated, but in this temperate climate I do not know where such monsters of men come from.' As Kieft complained, '[even] the children could understand.' He took to firing cannon or drumming the military roll-call during the sermon. His men harassed communicants on their way from the church.

The slips along the East River were home port to privateers who went 'fishing' in the West Indies and brought back trophies whose cargoes sometimes stayed in New Amsterdam; the port was a staging post for the Dutch beating back from Curaçao to Amsterdam, or the English trading between New England and Virginia, from whom, Kieft complained in 1642, he 'suffered great annoyance.' Most of all, it was a smugglers' town where furs disappeared to Europe without the Company brand or the Company duty, and even the director stood accused of trying to send home a box of pearls on his own account. Enforcing the rules was thankless, and sometimes murderous. A fiscal's deputy went on board a ship to inspect the cargo, and was asked to go below for a drink of brandy; someone threw a blanket over his head and beat him with a crowbar so that the blood flowed. He climbed groggily down the side of the vessel, and someone dropped an iron cannon ball on his head. Soldiers went to arrest the suspect, a gunner's mate, and the entire crew rounded on them; the Company took no action, for fear the ship might lose time.

Sailors were ordered to stay on board their ships at night, to avoid brawls and thefts and particularly knife fights; but despite the nine o'clock curfew, the colony sometimes seemed awash in drink and its consequences. There was good beer, drunk warm, brewed with hops from the woods; and aqua vitae; and rosa solis, a brandy sweetened with sugar and spices; and wine from the Company store. There was the occasional fine bottle, like the one which led the director Van Twiller to start a drinking rout. He finished the good wine; he sluiced down the cheap brandy. He let off a cannonshot and set alight the thatched roof of the storehouse while the drinkers all sat dumbly watching.

The men could drink in private houses, or in the Company house leased to Philip Gerritsen in 1643 as a tavern. It was filled with the smell of tobacco, smoked in clay pipes; the same pipes were sometimes ground to make a simple flute, a Netherlands fad which crossed the Atlantic. A man could play ninepins and mark the score with chalk on a board, or get up the courage for a game of golf which, on the streets or the ice, was a common enough pastime to be banned when Petrus Stuyvesant declared a penitential day in March 1648. The court records show a handful of men who woke up sore-headed, and claimed they had been too drunk to remember buying any damned plantation.

The fort, meanwhile, was a tumbledown square; 'people could go in and out . . . on all sides'; its inner yard was spoiled with the ashes and filth the soldiers threw there and there was a hopeful regulation that 'no-one is to make water within the fort.' The cannon were off their gun carriages when Kieft arrived in 1639. Boatswains and carpenters were accused of neglecting the Company's ships: 'Skippers must sail them year in, year out without being able to keep anything dry in the cabin,' Kieft complained. Company officers, for all their grand statements, had to worry about food for the soldiers and the cash to pay them; the firing squad became a necessary ally. Soldiers refused to do their work, even for extra pay, in June 1639, and the chief mutineer was shot. In 1646 the problem was 'scarcity of money for the support of the Company's servants ... several persons owe the Company considerable sums.' In February 1647, the soldier Hans Reyger pulled a knife on his superior and wrestled with him, and his mate Dirck Zieken struck the captain of the guard; both men took up their guns and threatened to shoot people on the street; they were 'arquebused'.

The garrison found comfort where it could; Nicholaes Coorn, a sergeant, 'has at divers times had Indian women and Negresses sleep entire nights with him in his bed, in the presence of all the soldiers.' Hans Steen, a corporal, discreetly forbade his men to make a fire while he lay on the bed with an Indian woman. The town's prostitutes went in fear of being banished, which meant they had to work the tavern rooms by suggestion rather than flaunting their possibilities on the street; many women went to court to make sure they were not called 'whore' with impunity.

But there was always Gretjen Reyniers, a rambunctious woman who came from an Amsterdam tavern on board the *Soutbergh* and was hardly ashore before she caused scandal. She stood on the quay and the crew kept pelting her with words – 'Whore! Whore! You'd do it for two pounds of butter!'; so she hoiked up her skirts and told them to kiss her arse. On the slip, later, she 'pulled the shirts of some sailors out of their breeches and in her house measured the male member of three sailors on a broomstick.' Brought to bed of a child, she asked the midwife, casually, if the baby looked like her husband – or like a man by the name of Hudden. She was married to Anthony Jansen, a huge, dark man who was known as the Turk because he was born on the Barbary Coast to a Muslim woman and a pirate. Together, they kept the courts busy, forever claiming debts or welshing on them, uttering or suing for slander; in 1638 and 1639, one case in six involved the couple. Finally, they were banished to Long Island, but not before Gretchen went screeching into the fort: 'I have long enough been the whore of the nobility! Now I want to be the rabble's whore!' And their banishment was not the punishment it seems. The Turk bought land, their daughters married into respectable families, and within five years, they were back in a house on Bridge Street in Manhattan, trading and lending money.

New Amsterdam was a stumbling block to missionaries; the minister Johannes Megapolensis complained that the Mohawks laughed when the Christians prayed. 'I tell them that I am admonishing the Christians that they must not steal, nor commit lewdness nor get drunk nor commit murder ... Then they say I do well to teach the Christians, but immediately add: "Why do so many Christians do these things?"' Kieft himself, in the course of admonishing a sheriff noted for being drunk in the evening and sluggish in the morning, wrote that 'complaints are heard daily of thefts, robberies, shooting of hogs and goats and other depradations, and the same are increasing every day, yes, from all appearances will shortly lead to public plundering and highway robbery, so that it is even to be feared that people will murder one another. . . .' There was talk in Amsterdam that the Company itself was a lost cause; it was about to be driven from Brazil, and peace with Spain was imminent. In America, the Company's men had watched as the private merchants of Amsterdam picked away the choicest prospects.

Something had to be done. From the islands, by way of a long convalescence in Holland, came a martinet strutting on a silver-tipped peg-leg, a military man who liked the world to be orderly and conventional, a politician savvy enough to ask all the directors of the Company's Amsterdam chamber to stand collective godfather to his first-born child: the first Governor of New York fit for a civic statue, Petrus Stuyvesant.

The day Stuyvesant landed, it took all the gunpowder in the fort of New Amsterdam to welcome him. He arrived 'peacock-like, with great state and pomposity', according to his critic Van der Donck. 'The word Myn Heer Generael and such like titles were never known here before.' He was a man who knew that, when real power is strictly limited, it needs to shout.

Stuyvesant was a lettered man, able to cite a string of learned authorities for a legal opinion, but his beliefs were simple: he owed them to his father, a village minister, and he did not stay long enough at the University of Franeker to learn doubt. He had sailed to Brazil as a supercargo, the officer who runs the business side of a ship while the captain sails. He rose to be Governor of Curaçao, the bare Caribbean island with its wind-twisted trees. In 1644 he lost his leg while leading his starving forces against the Spanish on the island of St Martin. He stayed at his post, stump bleeding, until another officer relieved him; he did not give up command until it was obvious the

Caribbean humidity would not allow his wound to heal. When he went back to Holland, he was still only in his late thirties, but tradition sees him as a man worn down; his temper was famously short, perhaps because of pain. But he had to learn patience. The West India Company named him as Director General of New Netherland and the Dutch Caribbean islands, but the States General took their time approving him; he could not sail for America until Christmas Day 1646.

His garrison mind was deeply offended by what he found. The Frenchman Michel Piquet had threatened to shoot the last director, Kieft, and now he added that 'if the Honourable Peter Stuyvesant did not behave himself better than the former director, he too would have to pay the penalty.' Piquet was banished, but he came back to threaten Stuyvesant as he rode to his farm in September 1647. There were local grandees, Cornelis Melyn and Jochim Pietersz, who accused Kieft of assorted crimes; Stuyvesant thought that was treason, and confined them to their homes. Melyn dared to suggest the director ruled only the Company's paid servants and Stuyvesant threw the books at him – *Exodus, Ecclesiastes, Romans*. The settlers, used to their independent courses, found themselves 'vassals and subjects', unable to point a finger at the Company's man because of a Biblical text: 'Curse not the king, not even in thy thoughts.'

But Melyn was not discouraged. Two years after his house arrest, we find him putting it about that Stuyvesant was asking for soldiers, 600 or 700 of them, to resist the English, and that the States General had refused, saying 'it was not wise to go to war with one's neighbours over a foot of land.' Melyn said he was 'greatly surprised that the English had not forcibly dragged Director Stuyvesant out of the fort and hanged him on the highest tree.' He added: 'I have brought Mr Kieft to his grave; I shall no doubt bring Stuyvesant to his, also.'

The city was no parade ground. There were houses out of line; some men took lots and never built on them, and others built higgledy-piggledy across the lot lines. The streets were lined with pig-pens and privies, the wooden chimneys were clogged and threatened the town with fire. Everything needed to be set in order. Each hog must be ringed through the nose, to stop the rooting of the roads. Each fence must be high enough to block the goats, and save the gardens. 'He was busy almost every day,' Van der Donck reported, 'issuing proclamations of various sorts, most of which were never observed and have long since died, the wine excise excepted, for that was a source of profit.' He tried to tame the smugglers by making private yachts moor where they could be seen, close to the City Tavern if they were small. He saw too many travellers trading in the town, especially the Scots, and he ordered that only four-year residents of New Amsterdam, or those who 'promise to reside, or at least to keep fire and light in their own house, here in this country' should keep shops; in place of the waterfront jumble of trestles and booths, he started a regular Monday market. He tried to stop the sale of drink and weapons to the Indians, but the Dutch sailors simply dumped the guns, shot and powder overboard in tight barrels, and recovered it when the various officials had made their inspections. He made new laws to punish those who drank and brawled on the Sabbath. But there was disorder that he could not manage, the sheer diversity in the human matter of the colony. 'On the island of Manhate and in its environs,' wrote the Jesuit Isaac Jogues, 'there may well be four or five hundred men of different sects and nations; the Director General told me that there were men of eighteen different languages.' Stuyvesant was not good at seeing the difference between variety and insubordination.

He changed the meaning of a black skin for ever. On the Guinea coast or in the Caribbean, a black was a slave, a field hand and the property of white masters. In New Amsterdam, the Company promised to supply 'blacks' to prospective colonists in 1629, 1634 and 1640, but few could pay cash or tobacco, as the Company wanted; even in 1661, the Company had to accept payment for slaves in beaverskins, or provisions like beef, pork, wheat or dried peas. Stuyvesant found that most slaves belonged to the Company, and while they might be rented out to do a job for a farmer, they did not belong to an individual; and, besides, all settlers were also supposed to be the Company's men. Soldiers and slaves certainly fell into roughly the same category; the Company built one hospital for both. Kieft asked in 1641 that 'many Negroes from among the strongest and fleetest' be armed with hatchets and half-pikes to raid the Indian camps on the lower banks of the Hudson. Marriage banns were read in the Reformed Church for black couples – thirteen of them between 1639 and 1652, and one white man marrying a black woman. By 1640, there were freed slaves who owned property and who could bring lawsuits: Anthony the Portuguese sued Anthony Jansen for the damage a dog did to a pig, and Pedro Negretto, a day labourer and farmhand, sued Jan Celes for back pay. A black man's word could be taken in court against a white man.

Now this does not mean that black skin was valued like white skin. The worst penalty the local courts could impose, short of flogging or hanging, was to be 'condemned to work with the Negroes'. In the indictment of Michiel Cristoffersen, the killing of a pregnant goat comes before the unlawful wounding of two black men 'one in such a way that he is in danger of death, and the other that he will remain maimed for life.' There were black women working as house servants, but there were laws against adultery with blacks, Indians or heathens – the irredeemable outsiders. Jan Evertsen Bout of Pavonia faced the court for shouting at the fiscal: 'Do you mean to catch me with the black wench? What would you do? I sleep with the black wench and have trod her!' Company slaves were freed, long after they had been promised manumission, but they had to buy their rights annually with a fat hog valued at twenty guilders, and thirty schepels' weight of either maize, wheat, peas or beans. Their children 'at present born or yet to be born, shall remain bound and obligated to serve the honourable West India Company as slaves.'

But until Stuyvesant, black skin was ambiguous. A black man might be almost free, or he might be out splitting rails and burning lime and harvesting the Company's grain. The Company needed all the skilled men it could find, and wanted the blacks taught carpentry, blacksmithing and bricklaying; but Stuyvesant insisted 'there were no able negroes fit to learn a trade'. The Company also meant to integrate its northern wastes with its other lands in the Americas, which meant implicating New Amsterdam even more deeply in slavery. New Netherland was to be peopled quickly, and used for grain that could be shipped 'even to Brazil, in their own vessels . . . and to trade it off there and to carry slaves back in return.' When Brazil was lost in 1654, the Company still had its Guinea outposts, but nowhere to send the slaves. New Amsterdam was the obvious port, a market to satisfy demand from the English colonies to the south.

On a sweltering late summer day, 15 September 1655, the full law of the slave trade arrived on board the *Witte Paert*, the first ship to trade slaves directly to New Amsterdam. The ship carried 300 Africans in that peculiar stench of shit and sweat and salt and sickness that went with the Guinea trade. Stuyvesant imported printed forms for the name of the ship's captain and the port where slaves had been collected on the West African coast, and imposed a ten per cent tax on sales down the coast to the English colonies. It was only a matter of business. Nobody asked what free blacks thought as the *Witte Paert* sailed in.

Stuyvesant's country faith, and his military sense of religious convention, made him hot against Jews or Lutherans or, most of all, Quakers. He was alarmed when Jews came to trade in 1654; when Joseph Barsimson paid thirty-six guilders for his passage from Holland; when others fled the fall of Dutch Brazil the same year and landed at New Amsterdam. At least in Dutch territory a Jew, if not a citizen, could get on discreetly with work and worship. The refugees from Brazil had been granted time enough to settle their affairs but there is tradition that, on the way north, their ship was captured by Spaniards on the high seas, and their treasure taken. 'And God caused a saviour to arise unto them,' David Franco Mendes wrote in the next century, 'the captain of a French ship arrayed for battle, and he rescued them from out of the hands of the outlaws who had done violence to them and oppressed them, and he conducted them until they reached the end of the inhabited earth called New Holland. . . .' Certainly, they landed poor; the clergy, unsympathetic in the first place, suspected they would be a burden in the coming winter.

Stuyvesant saw something worse: a precedent. The Jews had uncanonical holidays, and a Saturday Sabbath; 'To give liberty to the Jews,' the Company noted as his opinion in October 1655, 'will be very detrimental there, because the Christians there will not be able at the same time to do business. Giving them liberty, we cannot refuse the Lutherans and the Papists.' He told the Company he was alarmed by the Jews' 'customary usury and deceitful trading with the Christians.' He insisted they were repugnant to the colony's officials, as later he exempted Jews from military service because of the 'disinclination and unwillingness of these trainbands to be fellow soldiers with the aforesaid nation and to be on guard with them in the same guard-house.' His opinions were not very widely shared. The butcher Asser Levy did keep guard under the Dutch, without complaint; the rules for licensing butchers were changed for him in 1659 so he need not slaughter or even handle pigs. In 1658, Jacob Barsimson was not ruled in default when he missed a court appearance 'as he was summoned on his Sabbath.' When Gryte Maas let fly at Joseph d'Acosta, a Jew, when he went to collect a debt, the court made her apologise for abusing him and his people.

Stuyvesant first proposed to require the Jews 'in a friendly way' to

depart; then he gave orders. He could not know, yet, that the Portuguese Jews of Amsterdam had petitioned the Company on behalf of
their brothers. 'There are many of the nation who have lost their
possessions at Pernambuco,' they said, 'and have arrived from there
in great poverty.' They had been faithful in Brazil 'risking for that
purpose their possessions and their blood'. New Netherland needed
to be filled with people who could trade and pay taxes. More, the Jews
had been guaranteed some rights by the peace with Spain, and they
took it particularly hard that the West India Company's own director
stood in their way since 'many of their nation have lost immense and
great capital in its shares and obligations.' The Company's directors
took the point. They pronounced that Jews, like Christians who were
not part of the Dutch Reformed Church, could live and trade in New
Amsterdam. They could not, however, be mechanics; their religion
must be confined to their own homes, like any sectarians and, to that
end, 'they must without doubt endeavour to build their houses close
together in a convenient place.' They were not supposed to keep open
store, but they did. They were free to own property, but transactions
did not always work; when Salvador Dandradj tried to buy a house
for 1,860 guilders, he was not allowed to pay or to take possession.

Stuyvesant was as fierce against Lutherans, until he was reminded
that the West India Company had three Lutheran directors. He was
especially alarmed by the Quakers. Early in August 1657, a ship
appeared off New Amsterdam 'having no flag flying from the topmast,
nor from any other place on the ship'. When the master came ashore,
he stood before Stuyvesant without removing his hat, 'as if a goat'.
Off the ship came two strong young women, who 'began to quake
and go into a frenzy and cry out loudly in the middle of the street,
that men should repent, for the day of judgement was at hand.' It was
Calvinist dogma to think such warnings nonsense, because the elect
were already saved, and pensionable Company men were clearly of
the elect. 'Our people, not knowing what was the matter, ran to and
fro, while one cried "Fire" and another something else. The Fiscal,
with an accompanying officer, seized them both by the head and
led them to prison.' Their ship, meanwhile, had sailed away, still
anonymous and silent, to Rhode Island, as Megapolensis supposed,
because 'all the cranks of New England retire thither'.

Later that month, the Quaker Robert Hodgson began to preach on
Long Island, where there were English towns. Something in the

Quaker obstinacy, unfazed by rank or arms, peculiarly irritated Stuyvesant. Hodgson was bound to a cart and dragged to Manhattan, and put into a cellar 'full of vermin and so odious for wet and dirt as he never saw before.' His trial was conducted in Dutch, which he did not understand. When he refused to start his sentence of hard labour, he was beaten to the ground by a slave with a length of four-inch rope, dipped in pitch. This continued for two days. He was told his punishment would be worse if he spoke. He spoke. He was hung from an iron ceiling and whipped until near death, left quite alone for two days and whipped again. Stuyvesant might never have been called to account, except that an Englishwoman came to bathe Hodgson's wounds, and persuaded Stuyvesant's sister Anna to plead for his release. Again, the Company intervened. 'We heartily desire that these and other sectarians remained away from there,' they said, 'yet as they do not, we doubt very much whether we can proceed against them vigorously without diminishing the population and stopping immigration, which must be favoured at so tender a stage of the country's existence.'

This is a pragmatic kind of tolerance, not wholly admirable; but in New Amsterdam, as in its mother city, it allowed lives to outsiders despite the brute convictions of men like Stuyvesant. The Company, a tattered and unprofitable business now, was forced by circumstances to play down religious issues, in a century where faith and political loyalty overlapped so often. They required preachers who were of 'a peaceable and moderate temperament', not 'infected with scruples about unnecessary forms, which cause more division than edification'. They tolerated English heretics; Lady Deborah Moody had her own town on Long Island, and she was the notorious English Anabaptist who held that 'infant baptism was no ordinance of God's'. There was one brief attempt to prosecute her for heresy in New Amsterdam in 1643, but after that, she was free to live discreetly. Indeed, by 1661, the Company were enticing English dissenters to New Netherland, with the promise that 'they shall have full liberty to live in the fear of the Lord'. New England might believe each colony was bound to God in a covenant that made it unnecessary to compromise, or even to co-operate, but New Netherland had to make a secular compromise.

Its settlers did not have a common history or a common grievance like New Englanders. Many of them were refugees from war, who knew they could never return home. The territory was only loosely run by the West India Company, and even its local representatives could usually be ignored. The people of New Amsterdam did not turn back to Europe to resolve their problems, as New Englanders often did. Something was changing profoundly in New Netherland. The settlers' common identity was born there. They were already, in their interests and their attitudes, beginning to define what an 'American' might be.

Much of this was profoundly Dutch, especially for children and for women. Children grew up in great kindness, just as in the Netherlands travellers 'were certainly surprised and disconcerted by the softness with which children were treated,' as Simon Schama writes. New England Puritans sent their children away at puberty to be adolescent elsewhere; but when Margaret Hardenbroeck's children went to school in Holland, she spent part of each year with them. Most families in New Netherland clung together unless economic necessity forced a child out of the home, or apprenticeship would deliver a desirable trade. In the early years, apprenticeship sometimes looks like a form of adoption – in 1644, Marritje Hans went to serve the tavern-keeper Philip Gerritsen, who was to provide 'board, lodging and the necessary clothes and also have her taught sewing, in such a manner as a father should or might do with his child.'

Under English law, a woman was her husband's creature, relegated to the same status as a feeble-minded man. In New Amsterdam, a married woman could keep her own surname, own her own property, and protect it against her new husband in pre-nuptial agreements. She did not need her husband's signature to engage in trade, to sue or to be sued. She could choose if she wanted to subject herself to her man and, even if she did, she could always change her mind later. Property was divided equally between children, with no bias towards the eldest son; so Maria van Cortlandt had the management of her father's inn and brewery, 'the disposal of the beer and helping to find customers for it'. Jeremias van Rensselaer was told to consult her about property prices and married her, when she was only seventeen, for her business head and her fine political contacts ('about her figure and face,' he wrote, ungallantly, 'I have not much to write.')

Margaret Hardenbroeck, born to a family of Atlantic traders, came to New Amsterdam as her cousin's agent, married, and found herself with the job of sorting out her dead husband's muddled affairs; it's true she had difficulty collecting debts, but then she had a talent for not paying them. Hauled into court, she would always say an answer was soon expected from Amsterdam, perhaps by the next ship, and when it failed to arrive, she would ask most politely what was the question. She was a 'free merchant of New Amsterdam', trading up the Hudson, north to Hudson's Bay and south to the Indies, after she married again with the very rich Frederick Philipse.

Even the crime figures tell the same story. Under the Dutch, less than one hundredth of one per cent of all the crime prosecuted in the colony was committed by women. Under the British, from 1691 to the Revolution, one crime in six was committed by a woman. A woman has to live, after all.

Divorce was rare, but possible within the civil law; when the English took over, such matters passed to church courts. The law only rarely bothered with sexual morality, but it afflicted both men and women. While Cotton Mather was raging terribly against witches, there was no Dutch law against witchcraft; the only trial in New Netherland took place in 1665, after the first English take-over, when Robert Hall and his wife Mary were indicted at Setauket. The jury found 'some suspicions, by the evidence, of what the woman is charged with, but nothing considerable of value to take away her life.'

Such attitudes must not be stripped out of their time. New Amsterdam was secular, and hard to subject to a single, all-regulating authority, and its laws derived from the Dutch-Roman tradition. It was very different from the other colonies in America. But it was not modern. In peacetime, New Amsterdam's merchants could have their own ways to do business, their own lives to lead; but when the English sailed their men of war across the Atlantic, New Amsterdam was a Dutch colony again.

It was one of the great songs of the century, sung again and again: the song of the war for the seas. The English wanted to be masters where the Dutch sailed. Their Navigation Acts tried to insist that trade to English colonies must sail in English bottoms. The consequence was war – in India, in Indonesia, in the West Indies, even in New Amsterdam. The English were terrified the Dutch would do again what they were said to have done in Amboina, in the Moluccas – a Sunday massacre of settlers in their meeting house, the killing and burning of everything. In 1653, pamphlets said the blow might come from New Amsterdam. Nightmares shipped out faster than news. In the first Anglo-Dutch War, the Lord Protector Cromwell sent four warships after New Netherland in February 1654; the foul weather, as important as any treaty, stopped their course, and they reached New England only in June. They revictualled, they prepared to embark some 500 militia from Massachusetts and some 900 foot soldiers; but the day before the fleet was to sail for New Amsterdam, there was delayed news of the truce between the nations. A few days later, and New Amsterdam would have been English.

The trouble with New Netherland was that it did not occupy all of its territory, or even all of its coastline; only a third of its people lived in New Amsterdam, but that single city was its focus. The settlers were French-speaking, German-speaking, Portuguese-speaking; the port was cramped by privateers and traders on their way between English colonies; Long Island was carpeted with English villages. Stuyvesant went to smoke out the Swedes from the Delaware River only to find that the English had set up the Delaware Company of New Haven. The English complained that the Dutch were arming the Indians of the Connecticut Valley, and Stuyvesant agreed to suppress a trade he did not believe was going on. The New England Commission passed resolutions saying that no foreign prince should trade with the Indians between the Delaware and Cape Cod, and New Amsterdam went into panic. And the Company, in the comfort of Holland, kept telling Stuyvesant to avoid war at all costs.

It sometimes seemed these issues could be resolved in America. In 1650, the New England Commissioners met Stuyvesant at Hartford and, when they had settled the protocol of describing which colony they were talking in, they managed to re-arrange the map; they removed from the Dutch two-thirds of Long Island, the Connecticut Valley and all the east bank of the Hudson, except for a corridor ten miles wide. But more often the news of war, carried fitfully by the traders' ships, was what turned the colonies' heads. Battle in the Dover Straits, reported in New Amsterdam after two months, caused panic; the English again accused the Dutch of being 'in bloody colours' with the Indians; delegates came from New England like detectives to look for evidence in the city. They included Captain John Leverett, who would later command the English militia against New Amsterdam. He took the opportunity to inspect the town's defences and decide how best to attack. When there was such mutual suspicion, the Englishness of Long Island suggested a fifth column. Kieft's brutal commander, John Underhill, returned to raise the flag of the London Parliament at Hempstead and Flushing. And now the Company told

Stuyvesant it was time for action. He must control the traitors 'that we may not nourish serpents in our bosom, who finally might devour our hearts. . . .'

Stuyvesant could have been forgiven the thought that serpents were eating well in New Amsterdam. The town's first poet, the trader Jacob Steendam, published in 1659 the *Complaint of New Amsterdam to Her Mother* even before he wrote the *Praise of New Amsterdam*; he had the colony complain 'I, of Amsterdam, was born/Early of her breasts forlorn . . . From my youth up left alone/Naught save hardship have I known . . .'

The city had its first council in 1653, grudgingly conceded after endless remonstrances to Amsterdam; the English townships of New Netherland had long had their own local governments, and charters written in Holland. Now Stuyvesant's advisors insisted that Manhattan needed a wall, 'to draw in time of need all inhabitants behind it and defend as much as possible their persons and goods against attacks. For the present, it is impossible to protect by stockades the villages, where the people live at great distances from each other and thus carry out the good intentions and orders of our Masters.'

The work went slowly. Stuyvesant had to keep all ships in harbour and all citizens at home for two weeks in May to speed construction. When it was finished, a wood palisade backed by an earth rampart ran on the line of modern Wall Street – the physical and metaphorical line, since the work was done on credit. The Company in Amsterdam was all in favour of the colony paying for its own defence, but it was far away and it also wanted Stuyvesant to avoid trouble with the fancy new City Council. To settle accounts for defending the city, the old soldier had to give away the income from the excise on beer and wine.

In the first Anglo-Dutch war, New Amsterdam was spared by days. In the grumblings before the second, it was clear the English wanted the colony. Samuel Maverick of Massachusetts argued that three frigates and several hundred soldiers could take New Netherland and, more ominously, that the war would be worth it because the fur trade could pay all the costs. Stuyvesant heard about commissioners in New England who might well have come to prosecute that war, but he was promised in a letter from Amsterdam that they were there only 'to install Bishops there the same as in Old England'. It would take commissioners to impose Papistical bishops on the luxuriant heretics of Long Island. And so Stuyvesant went about the colony's business, not hesitating to go upriver to Fort Orange.

He was away in May 1664, when the Duke of York's fleet set sail from Portsmouth, to enforce the royal patent granted in March for the territory of New Netherland. He had still not returned when, in August, the sails of four English warships were sighted off the New Netherland coast. They were the stragglers of a fleet that had been scattered by Atlantic storms, sailing one by one into Long Island Sound – ominous as single birds before a storm. Stuyvesant returned to the city as quickly as he could, arrived on 25 August and tried to prepare defences. But he had only some 250 men to throw against the thousand waiting offshore, and they were a rabble of an army. He demanded every third man from the Dutch townships on Long Island, but they refused to leave their wives, children and homes. Upriver, the people needed all their powder and shot to cope with the Indians. He discovered what he must long have suspected: that the colony could not be defended.

Stuyvesant went down grandly to a tavern on the strand of New Amsterdam, to talk with Governor John Winthrop Junior of Connecticut. He read over the terms of surrender once, and tore the paper into pieces; he refused to show it to the city fathers. At once there was a crowd around him, the 'vassals and subjects' he had once demanded to rule. They shouted that 'to resist so many was nothing less than to gape before an oven'. Stuyvesant told them they should fight for honour, country, colony, but the words fell in the air and he knew the game was done. He bent down and pieced together the English paper. Ninety-three of the leading citizens, including his own son Balthazar, petitioned him to accept its terms.

It took six days for all New Netherland to fall, and it was mostly a peaceful surrender. Some Dutch troops, angry and ashamed that they had not fired a shot, set sail for home at once. The next year, Balthazar Stuyvesant was away on Curaçao, pining for what he remembered as the liveliness of the small town he had left. To his friend Nicholas Bayard, he wrote: 'I would ... recommend that your honour take care of the girls on the Manhatans. Your honour can greet them all for me with a kiss, and sometimes to remember them with a hug. I have also heard that some are already becoming English. . . .'

*

It took longer, of course. The seizing of colonies sounds such a crisp event: nationality changes, and so do culture, language, laws, religion and trade. But Manhattan was not some slave island where one group of overseers could be taken off, and another installed. New Netherland had 9,000 souls, too scattered to intimidate and too varied to be forced into conformity. They stayed. They kept their laws of inheritance, their magistrates, liberty of conscience, the right to leave New York and freedom from being drafted for war 'against any nation whatsoever'. English soldiers needed billets, but officers were told to avoid 'publick controversy', ignoring all 'private storeys of ye Dutch being disaffected to ye English, for generally wee can not expect they love us'.

Besides, the colony now belonged to the Duke of York, brother to King Charles II. His proprietary was fine on the pages of an atlas – from the Delaware River to the Connecticut, from the St Croix to the Kennebec. It looked an important shield against empty lands that might be claimed by foreign powers, the last panel in the English dominance of the coast. But to the Duke, it was cost. The Duke's new lands held the only royal garrison in North America, and the London Treasury never managed to find more than half the soldiers' pay and never on time; the Duke needed taxes just to pay the balance. He kept a household like a mirror of the royal court, with its own keeper of the privy seal and attorney general and groom of the presence, and by 1667, his style had created so huge a debt that a Commission of Revenue was established to manage his affairs. These sensible men did not bother to impose James' Catholicism on Protestant New York, or his absolutism on the Dutch.

The Duke's hold was tenuous. There were oaths of loyalty, and the citizens of New York had their weapons taken away, but in 1673, when Governor Lovelace was away in Connecticut, a Dutch naval squadron breezed up from victories against Virginia, and stood off Sandy Hook to take on water. Dutch Long Islanders swarmed on board to tell the commanders that Fort James was leaderless. The fleet drifted into the Hudson and, after a siege of only four hours, the Dutchmen in the town decided to capitulate to themselves on the grounds that there were no Englishmen to defend them. New York changed name again, to New Orange.

The New England states each held that its covenant with God left no room for alliances with its neighbours. Massachusetts did not care about Connecticut's worries, farmers were not bothered by merchants' troubles; nor did Puritan settlers easily rally to the cause of a Catholic duke. Only in London was New Orange considered a serious abomination. The King's Council for Trade and Plantations reckoned that, if the Dutch could hold on, the New Englanders 'being more intent upon the advancement of their owne private trade, than the publique Interest of your Majesties crowne and Government may ... enter into commerce with them, whereby it is to be feared, they will at present divert a great part of the Trade of England into these Countries, and lay a foundation for such a Union hereafter between them and Holland as will be very prejudiciall to all your Majesties Plantations, if not terrible to England ittselfe.' Again, New Netherland forced a European power to see that its colonies were not simply an extension of itself. There could be a distinctly American interest.

His Majesty could not persuade an obdurate Parliament to pay for seven ships and 600 troops to sort out the problem of New Orange. Through autumn and winter and spring, there was a war of bluster. Even when Massachusetts property was attacked, the colonies' deputies insisted no soldier 'shal be Imployed for reduceing of New York'. In New Orange, Governor Colve threw up new defences, and banned all talk and trade with the English, and waited. Foul weather kept New England ships in port well into April, when traders brought the news from Europe: that probably, as people had it, the Dutch and the English had made peace. Now nobody needed to take action. The Treaty of Westminster laid down that all captured territory 'shall be restored to the former lord and proprietor' and New Orange dissolved into New York again. But it was two years before the Dutch stopped brawling against the English in the streets, shouting, 'Slay the English Dogs!'

The new royal governors arrived, with strict orders and no resources, just like Stuyvesant before them. Royal authority was always limited by what the governors did to survive. They acted like New York merchants, to force all Albany's fur handlers to pass their cargoes through the port of New York and pay taxes there, to give city merchants a monopoly on exporting grain just as New York became the granary of the British Caribbean. Sir Edmund Andros kept a sloop for the coastal trade, a retail store, and perhaps a covert business with Amsterdam, all while serving as Governor. When the Duke of York went on the run in Scotland, a confessed Catholic in a Protestant country and a dodgy heir to the throne, Sir Edmund was recalled, and the Duke's power to levy taxes was suddenly suspended. The city took its chance. For years it had been denied the elected assembly which other English colonies took for granted. Now the Duke's Commissioners realised that only the city could raise the cash that the Duke sorely needed, and they were happy to concede an assembly. The issue did not trouble them much. When the city's draft Charter of Liberties reached London, the Commissioners set it aside while they went over the proprietary's accounts.

The Dutch still defined the city; but they had long been diluted by the sheer variety of men and trades in New York. There were issues of nationality and language to settle and, hidden within them, the issues that had once divided the city's sponsors in Amsterdam: whether New York was a secular or a religious enterprise, whether it could be the colony of any one nation and whether it could ever be controlled from Europe. For this a man was both hanged and beheaded by his relatives; and came back, in a fashion, from the dead.

Jacob Leisler was a gentleman, although you might not guess it from what the English said of him. He was a merchant selling fur and tobacco to the Rhine. He married the daughter of Govert Lockermans, quite famously the richest woman in New York. He came of good Calvinist stock; his grandfather had been an influential minister, his father was Dutch Reformed minister at Frankfurt and his brothers were bankers in Basle. Leisler affected wig and cane on the streets, was commonly addressed as 'Sieur' or 'Monsieur' and had his own coat of arms. He could quote Calvin, which was true of most religious enthusiasts, but he could also quote Cervantes.

Catholic King James went into exile, and William and Mary, who were formerly Dutch but properly Protestant, were invited to the throne of England. Leisler did not think he was being a rebel. He simply insisted that New York should declare for the new King and Queen. By spring of 1689, every other English colony had proclaimed the new rulers. There were draft letters in Whitehall telling all colonial officials to stay in post, except, of course, for Papists; but the letter for Andros, Governor of New York because he was governor of the Dominion that was supposed to control all New England, was written on 12 January and never sent. Whitehall was lobbied assiduously to abolish the Dominion and put back the boundaries between the colonies. New York's government consisted of one fraught lieutenant governor, Francis Nicholson, in his late twenties and his first important post. He tried to suppress all news from London. Perhaps he remembered the end of Monmouth's rebellion four years earlier, and how many hanged for jumping to the conclusion that King James was overthrown. Nicholson was dithering for his life.

In peacetime, a little interregnum might have passed, as long as the courts still ruled and the ships sailed. But the French were on the northern frontier, wooing the Indians whose loyalty was uncertain; they wanted the fur trade and the open lands to the west. New York was alarmed. Worse still, Louis XIV of France was famous among Protestants for daring to revoke the Edict of Nantes, withdrawing tolerance from good Protestant merchants and opening the way to their massacre. Jacob Leisler had helped Huguenot refugees settle at New Rochelle, just north of Manhattan, and he had joined their church because he could no longer slip along comfortably with the compromises of the Dutch Reformed. His own family had been forced from France two generations back for fear of persecution. He came to see New York not as a secular place, but as a place whose religion was going wrong.

A Catholic king had been run out of his kingdom; Virginia was in arms in the Protestant cause, and so was Massachusetts. But in New York, Leisler saw a conspiracy to pretend that nothing had happened. A Catholic ex-governor was still in obvious residence. The collector of customs in New York Harbour, always the most powerful man in New York, was a Catholic. Indeed, for a while Leisler himself was implicated. In spring 1689, he was still the spokesman for the lieutenant governor. In May, his signature appeared on an order suppressing rebellious persons. But on 31 May, his own militia begged him to take over the fort. At first he refused, but on 2 June he walked to the fort and stood aside as forty-nine members of the militia went inside, to claim the government for William and Mary. A Committee of Safety took over the running of New York from Nicholson and, in short order, Jacob Leisler took over the committee.

He tried to clear away the laws made under the Duke of York. He wrote to Massachusetts asking about constitutions, saying it might be a good idea if New York had one like theirs, and asking what was in it. He tried to raise forces against the French, but got little support. Massacre obsessed him, the notion that all those in the Dutch church might be killed, that he knew of 'horrible devices', including 'a plot to massacre [us] on New Year's Day'. He arrested important citizens and confined them in 'nasty places'. He seized mail and read it. He talked murder even if he did not do it, and his talk had resonances in New York that it would not have had elsewhere: people remembered the notorious, murderous Orange mobs who had made the Dutch West India Company possible in the first place, by killing Van Olden-barnevelt in Amsterdam seventy years before. He had grand names among his following – Stuyvesant, De Peyster, Delanoy, as grand as New York allowed – but his enemies saw only anarchs and thugs. Leisler's son-in-law Milbourne had a brother who was a famous Fifth Monarchy dissenter. Leisler had dared make a bricklayer into a mar-shall, a carpenter into a sheriff, and his ambassador to London was Ensign Joost Stoll, who sold booze by the shot and was 'famous for nothing, unless his not being worth a groat'.

But Leisler only wanted to make government right. He was for prin-ciple and religion in a city where the issues had become wholly secular; that made him the enemy of those gentlemen who had comfortable links with the governors that the Duke had sent, whose position and profit depended on those favours. His actions divided families Dutch and Eng-lish, merchants and artisans, even the devout of the Dutch Reformed Church. He went down to the Customs House to challenge the Com-missioners by what authority they sat to collect duty; they asked back, 'What power have you to examine us?' He put authority in question without quite meaning to. When he justified himself, he only made the question more pressing. 'By what law, warrant or Commission did the Prince of Orange go into England and act as he hath done?' he asked. 'And how do you think King William can take that amiss in us who have only followed his example?'

One June day in 1690, the mob caught up with Leisler at Peter Delanoy's house on the corner of Dock Street. They wanted the prisoners out of the fort at once, and they refused to pay the new threepenny tax until the men were released. Leisler agreed, but only if the prisoners would swear they accepted his authority as lieutenant governor. He made authority negotiable, no longer a matter of kings and powers. Soldiers arrived and Leisler put himself at their head. They caught Jeremy Tothill and beat him with swords and the butts of guns, and cut him with a halberd. Tothill and Teunis de Key, with two pistols and a carbine, held off the soldiers while the rioters got away – an Englishman and a Dutchman, allied in a tiny riot. '[Leisler] immediately had the alarm beaten and a cannon fired to call the farmers to arms,' John Tuder wrote, days later. 'The soldiers, with naked swords in their hands, ran like madmen through the streets. . . .'

In London, the ship's captain detailed to bring the new Governor to New York did not want to lose promotion by doing American work; for an absurd time, there was no legal governor. When Governor Sloughter finally landed, Leisler stood on ceremony long enough to be accused of treason. In the pamphlets, he was no longer the equal of his accusers. He was some low-born, foreign, enthusiastic creature. He went to the scaffold talking of 'this confused City and Province', but in reality the city was sorting out its notions rather quickly. He was pushed there by his relative Nicholas Bayard, who insisted that 'if some example be not made of such criminals. . . . their Majesties' government can never be safe in these Collonyes.' But Bayard did not quite mean 'government'. New York lacked grand constitutional arrangements. He meant that source of patronage and authority round which an élite could cluster like calves at the tit; so that there were suddenly dukes of the new English world, while the Dutch found themselves scrabbling to pay the steeply rising price of even a share of farmland. These new men were alarmed by Leisler's learning, lineage and principle. They treated him like a traitor and a killer, and a little as though he was possessed of devils; they hanged him, and then they beheaded him, to be sure.

The new English aristos took their power from lands in the New World. Under Governor Fletcher, the 800 square miles of the Evans tract upstream went for £500 and £1 a year quitrent. Robert Livingston paid less than $600 for the 160,000 acres of Livingston Manor. He could be a city grandee because the English law cut away the old independence of his wife, and sent her, by custom, to the country home. Alida Schuyler Livingston managed his estates, because she could no longer legally trade in her own name. Frederick Philipse, of Philipse Manor, married Margaret Hardenbroeck in part for her business contacts and her ships; under the English, her assets were his and she ceased to be the 'free merchant of New Amsterdam' she once was. But she ran the skin trade from Albany, and left her husband in 1691 with 150,000 acres, and twenty-one miles of the east bank of the Hudson. Colonel William Smith depended on his wife Martha, who sent out slaves to the beaches of Fire Island to harpoon the whales that came too close to shore; Mrs Smith managed her own 'try-works' to render the blubber. Between the grants of land, and assuming every cent of their wives' income, the gentlemen of New York could be very grand indeed.

They had rivals, though. In New York's first elected Assembly in 1691, there were Leislerians and anti-Leislerians, and although each faction could easily slip a skin and reappear among the opposition, what matters is the existence of specifically New York factions. Leisler was found guilty by a jury of Englishmen; his persecutor Nicholas Bayard was convicted of mutiny by a jury of Dutchmen when he sought soldiers' signatures on a petition against Governor Bellomont. The local interests were deadly serious. Power such as the Dutch Company claimed, or the English king, was mostly theory. And New York lacked a constitution to contain this politics of interests. Instead, it was already famous as a city more corrupt than Philadelphia: the minimal city, ruled no more than necessary, sometimes less.

Election days were burlesque. Under Leisler, Robert Walters harangued the election clerk, 'I vote for my son Walters, my son Jacob votes for his brother Walters, and my son Walters votes for himself. That's three, put them down!' In 1695, the grandees suspected the voters of wrong opinions and talked the magistrates into a stratagem: they would grant freeman status, and the vote, to every sailor in port the night before the election. They also arranged for navy men to hang around the polling places, so nervous voters might think there were press gangs on the prowl. In 1701, there were more votes cast in the city's east, west and south wards than there were male taxpayers on the tax list; everyone, it seems, minors, women, visitors or people without property, was so keen to vote that they would not let the law stand in their way. Grandees had to ride through the town, soliciting votes from those they could barely bring themselves to notice; already power and politics had begun to drift apart. Political clubs put up 'tickets' – lists of four right-thinking men, to make the choice at the ballot easier.

After Leisler, there was a New York identity. The authority he brought into question never did quite reassert itself; the most successful eighteenth-century governors of New York were famous for delicate skills in political management, not strategy or dreams. Those who owned the city could not necessarily rule the city, not unless they were prepared to corrupt the voters. Leisler, who meant to defend his religious principles, only demonstrated that this particular city could be nothing but secular.

When Leislerians had power, in 1698, they went to Potters Field and they brought Leisler's body out of the burying pit. They carried him back to the city with honour and buried him again, before an admiring crowd. They rewrote history, as New York often had to do.

A whole century was left to be peopled by imagination, as Arcadia or bumpkinland. Even its most famous historian, Diedrich Knickerbocker, was imaginary.

Washington Irving invented Knickerbocker in 1809 – an old gentleman whose name is Dutch enough to suggest early aristocracy, who was cousin-german of the congressman, friend of the city librarian (or so Irving says). Knickerbocker spent his days trying to find manifest destiny in a muddled stash of papers, in a room on Mulberry Street he never paid for. He left behind only the manuscript of a 'most excellent and faithful HISTORY OF NEW-YORK'. In it, he shows how the Creation of the Universe led to the founding of New Amsterdam, how a single skirmish there led to both the American and French Revolutions, and why the eyes of the gods were never off the place. It is wonderful provincial bombast, and persistent for that reason – all the vainglorious soul of a truly small town.

Knickerbocker's history rests on a handful of authentic documents, but mostly on Irving's wit. He was honest enough about its authenticity. Knickerbocker tells how the sun reflected off the ghastly nose of Anthony the Trumpeter, and cut the river with a hissing hot reflection which killed the first sturgeon ever to be eaten by Christians. If readers doubt him, he says, 'they are welcome not to believe a word in this whole history – for nothing which it contains is more true'. But we want to believe; we know so little, and Irving breathes life into a small town of big-bottomed aldermen, lost in the by-ways of empire, never quite matching up to history. When his New Amsterdam falls to the English, the outraged Dutch can only 'unanimously determine never to ask any of their conquerors to dinner'.

From Knickerbocker, we think we know the governors of New York – pacific Van Twiller, testy Kieft, soldierly Stuyvesant, ruling a town which is orderly through sheer inactivity. The burghers of this cartoon town look drowsily out through a cloud of tobacco smoke. Their silence, Knickerbocker insists, is a sign of deep reflection. Governor Wouter van Twiller seems 'either elevated above, or tranquilly settled below, the cares and perplexities of this world'. Governor Kieft tries to ban smoking because it seems to lead to politics, but in revenge 'a vast multitude armed with pipes and tobacco boxes, and an immense supply of ammunition, sat themselves down before the governor's house, and fell to smoking with tremendous violence'. Put such men on a field of battle, under the great Petrus Stuyvesant, and see men of Manhattan, under the beaver flag that shows 'the amphibious origin of the Netherlanders'; 'the sturdy chivalry of the Hudson. .... all fortified with a mighty dinner, and to use the words of a great Dutch poet, "Brimful of wrath and cabbage"'.

The picture seems sharp, but it is authentic to the 1800s, not the 1600s. If you compare Knickerbocker's burghers with Irving's other inventions – in the satirical *Salmagundi* papers, which first appeared in 1807 – his purpose is clear. In the *History*, Wilhelmus Kieft, Governor of New Amsterdam, devises a 'new and cheap mode of fighting by proclamation' – truly stiff letters take the place of gunboats and infantry. In *Salmagundi*, if insurrection threatens, the great Thomas Jefferson 'utters a *speech*! – nay, more, for here he shows his "energies" – he most intrepidly dispatches a courier on horseback ... with a most formidable army of *proclamations* packed up in his saddle-bags.' The New York militia of the 1800s was a pretty farce. In the pages of *Salmagundi*, the rulers of the United States decree that war is very useless and expensive, but that soldiers may be highly ornamental; 'It was ordered that the tailors of the different cities throughout the empire should, forthwith, go to work, and cut out and manufacture soldiers as fast as their shears and needles would permit.' So Knickerbocker's Petrus Stuyvesant also inherits a militia commanded by 'tailors and man-milliners, who, though on ordinary occasions they might have been the meekest, most pippin-hearted little men in the world, were very devils at parades'. Their men are so hardy they can 'march through sun and rain, from one end of the town to the other, without flinching'.

Each governor has a moral, each policy has a kick. Governor Kieft anticipates the poorhouse that would not be built for another seventy years when he announces that the poor should be put in prison 'there to remain until they should reform and grow rich'. The trumpeter Antony van Corlear climbs the ramparts of New Amsterdam to sound such bad tidings 'as to throw half the old women in the city into hysterics; all which tended greatly to increase his popularity; there being nothing for which the public are more grateful that being frequently treated to a panic; a secret well known to modern editors'.

And Irving's settled doubts about city politicians come from observing his own times. New Amsterdam confronts the English massed at the mouth of their harbour: the citizens decide 'First, that the city required to be put in a state of defence; and Second, that, as the danger was imminent, there should be no time lost; which points being settled, they fell to making long speeches....'

Irving does not imagine the sheer strangeness of a very distant, overlooked community who had to improvise their lives – sometimes so far away they could conceive of having their own, American interests, sometimes tugged closely by the tides of European politics and war. From the beginning, the city had to learn how to survive its own diversity. This true New Amsterdam persisted. The look of the place was distinctly Dutch – a garden of a town, with fine trees, unusually clean with woodwork scoured white with rough brushes and laws which required the citizens to sweep before their houses; the buildings were checkerboard brick, the narrow gables turned out to the street and tipped a little forward so that goods could be winched up to the fifth or the sixth floor. As in Amsterdam, each house bore its history – the date of its building, 'contrived of iron cramps to hold in ye timber to the walls'.

Although the English brought different and Italianate styles, the town still seemed Dutch to Thomas Pownall when he arrived to be the governor's secretary in 1753, and in the early 1770s, the Frenchman Jean de Crevecoeur found 'Dutch neatness', but 'combined with English taste and architecture'. Dutchness persisted for a while in trade, in how to celebrate the New Year, and in the language spoken by the New Jersey farmers bringing fruits to New York markets; the diversity of New Amsterdam was remarked on again in nineteenth-century New York. The colony survives even in the natural order of things. After three hundred years, the genes of domestic cats in New York are still closer to the cats of Amsterdam than to any part of New England – often piebald, often short-haired, rarely orange and never with extra toes.

3
FRONTIERS

IT WAS THE wrong Bergen Street, a natural enough mistake, and I had a potted clematis in either hand. I expected to come up from the subway platforms on to low, narrow streets, full of Saturday shoppers. The Korean greengrocers know who lives where, and on Bergen Street they show a muddle of white potatoes, Caribbean beans, piles of the glossy red apples that satisfy only the eye and packets of pasta; they are not full of edo and callaloo and plantains as they are on Utica Avenue in black Bedford-Stuyvesant, nor asparagus, baby's breath and big green apples as they are on bright, white Sixth Avenue. The signs are Spanish, Italian, English. A brief walk, and I would be at the house of friends. I would work in a back garden which looks out on a settled little Italy, like the backs of tenements in some south Italian town: the vines of melons planted on bare ground, bleached washing plumped out by the wind, the musky, purple Concorde grapes trailing up from their frames and pergolas into thickets of old holly.

But it was the wrong Bergen Street: or, to be exact, the wrong subway line and so the wrong Bergen Street Station. The street above was blank on a Saturday morning. The police rose like a monument in a corner. The rowhouses were neat and shingled, but they died out quickly. Nobody else was walking and the day was hot and the plants were dead weights in my hands. Two Buicks kissed fender to fender, their windows smashed and the seats ripped. The usual steady procession of buildings along a street broke up; houses had been pulled out, leaving rectangles of rubble and yarrow; some were burned out, blackened and boarded up. There was a faint smell of soot. Clusters of kids, sitting high on the stoops, looked down on the solitary white man toiling along. But I was obstinately sure that somehow this road would lead to the right part of Bergen Street, and unable to ask sensible directions because all I knew was that I needed Bergen Street, and this was Bergen Street. It was such a small mistake. I had opened the wrong door, and I was in the wrong country.

You could see New York as all kinds of countries moored up against Manhattan like ships in a dock: different nations, different attitudes, different beers and different law. They are settled for a while, but they do not settle into America, only into a microcosm of the place from which they came. On this unfamiliar Bergen Street, the corner groups of tall black players could be the church team or discussing murder; they might speak Spanish, English, Haitian Creole; they might have some great historical grievance against the fact of white skin or they might be kind to someone lost and tired. I could have stumbled into territory run by drug lords. But the sun was too high to worry. In the concrete shack of the Flying Fish restaurant on a corner, with raucous talk and laughter, some Jamaicans set me on my right way. They were puzzled at the idea that anyone would stray in the city. New Yorkers always have to know their place.

The city is an atlas that has been shuffled. If you grow up in Queens, you know Bombay is in the middle of Colombia, alongside Manila, down the road from Ireland and on the way to Argentina, Ecuador and Italy. It is only ten miles to all those nations from the 59th Street Bridge. Past the bleak, shuttered factories which make electric plugs by the waterside, a little Ireland opens up: *Irish News*, Irish goods, images of the saints in shop windows, cabbage and soda bread on the cafeteria menus. The politics, too, are Irish and national-ist; a friend got drunk in the wrong English accent and found himself at the end of nine gun barrels on a roadside.

The signs turn to Spanish along Roosevelt Avenue, under the lattice of the elevated railroad tracks: the shops are smears of gaudy red and yellow light with a long tarmac shadow in between and the trains pass by like a stage storm, grazing with white light the faces of dark, oblivious girls. '*COMIDA LATINA*' is translated as 'American food', because everything in this America is Latin. The hybrid of '*COMIDA LATINA Y CHINA*' was first eaten here, a product of the long years the Chinese had to wait out in Cuba before their quota numbers for America came through. But only outsiders think this is a 'Hispanic' quarter, and that solidarity can be built on language. Here, they call the Puerto Ricans *animales*. This music shop sells records only from Ecuador; this steak-house is specifically a Colombian steak-house, selling the home-grown beef and bacon; this butcher's sign says he is

Ecuadorean; this pizza house offers only Argentine pizza, with more beef.

Along Roosevelt, the signs are in the square Korean characters for a while. Then the signs offer transport and freight to the Philippines, special deals on Macdonalds' burgers for your family at home. There is Victor's Restaurant where the nations intersect, and a table of thin Japanese sit with two huge Irish matrons, whose arms are big and wasted like washerwomen in retirement. Then made-up mannequins make a line, far apart, in shop windows, each wearing a pale sari. The gypsy fortune-tellers cross back and forth between the nations; Doña Linda down the road becomes the lady Swami when she does business opposite the sari-shops. The banks change as you travel: Banco de Bogotá is a few blocks from the Hong Kong Bank. There is Thai food here, and in a few blocks *este Bud*, the signs say, is *para Usted*. An old dance hall turned into a Christian tabernacle, and in a few years to a Buddhist temple and then to a Hindu temple. Memory doesn't work here.

The nations have alliances as well as wars. Step into the basement of a Greek Orthodox church, where a huge woven shepherd hangs on the far wall. There are tables and synthesisers and white balloons that cling to the ceiling. In a back room, friends in their best suits chop melon. A Korean couple will marry here today. The bride is patiently sitting outside the far door, and the groom, a sparse man, is walking in a daze. She was a clerk and she worked in a night-club. He arrived in 1983 with nothing at all. 'He has a hard life story, she has a hard life story,' their best friend says. 'They understand each other.'

Now he says he wants to be in the dress business, and his friend Park Youn Young will take him for a few months into his own shops where he sells short, gaudy numbers to Hispanics, just to see if he has sense. Park thinks already that vegetables might be a better business, since it requires less English. It has to be something where the goods are quite cheap, the turnover high and the shop rent feasible. When the decision is made, friends get together and collect the money – $15,000 should find a lease and stock. 'Three thousand from him,' Park says, gesturing round the room 'two thousand from him. And he pays back to the one who needs it most. Sometimes it fails, but eighty-five per cent, they are successful.' It seems like every corner has its Korean shop because the nations that have a tradition of keeping their capital moving, and inside the nation, do best. This fact is often resented, especially by blacks who think the Koreans must have some secret source of funds.

There is no priest for the marriage, but 'someone whose words we will listen to,' Park says. 'Who can give advice.' The mothers come forward to light candles. There are breathless fanfares from the synthesisers. The bride and groom exchange promises, and there is a sermon in which the Korean is broken suddenly by 'Marriages are made in Heaven'. And then the party can begin. A trestle is laden with jellyfish and beef, with bacon and chicken and tart pickles and noodles. There is Scotch and ice on the tables. 'We can drink,' Park says. 'We like to drink.'

One by one, the men take the microphone and sing, their voices amplified and adjusted and smoothed down with the whisky. Park tells how the groom's friends had grown tired of hearing, over and over, how much he wanted to marry his bride. She is already in her thirties, which is late for a Korean woman to marry. The friends said, 'Just marry her.' One brought the bales of flowers, and one the drink, another the food. The groom has a long, dazed face and he is shaking everyone's hand; his eyes are bunched with tears. With his bride, he steps out on to the floor, as careful as children who know they are being watched, and they begin a slow, slow waltz.

Some of the nations are secrets, almost invisible on the streets. On Ditmars Avenue in Queens, the signs are in Greek, and there are flags set out in red and green for an Italian *festa*. In between are hidden colonies. A couple go to the counter in a Greek bakery, with its honeyed breads, and the woman answers them in Portuguese. '*Obrigada*,' she says. Maria Cristina and Paulo look at each other. 'You're Italian?' Paulo asks. The woman shakes her head. 'Hispanic?' 'No,' the woman says, 'Brazilian.' Paulo does not want to say that he disbelieves her because she has such a foreign accent, but the woman catches the pause. 'I'm Greek,' she says, 'but I lived in Brazil for ten years.' So Maria Cristina and Paulo can say that they, too, are Brazilians.

There are no ordinary stories among the newcomers, but they have things in common. Maria Cristina studied dance with Alvin Ailey and got bored when she went back to Brazil: 'it was a mess with the new currency and there were no jobs.' Her husband Paulo had no job. They came back to New York, but not to change their lives, since they still consider themselves Brazilian. Brazilians see Brazilians on the street – the ones who don't walk the tight-assed Northern walk, the men in long shorts and the sneakers with no socks. 'You look at the shirt and the shoes,' Paulo says, 'and you can tell right away.' There is no formal community here in Queens, apart from a single Baptist church, and a trinket shop which sells the exact twins of the fists to ward off evil eye, the pyramids for good fortune that are common in Rio. But there is a network of friends who know things, who find apartments for friends, who are each other's company and security. This doctor, this dentist, is known to cut his prices for a fellow countryman.

Friends send back the story on how to enter America. You can no longer slip off a ship at dockside; you have to face down the immigration officer at the airport. You always say you have only come on a visit. You carry enough money, but not too much, unless you can dress to match your bankroll; from a poor country, too much cash makes the officials think of crime and drugs. Customs kept asking Maria Cristina what kind of a dancer she was. They stopped Paulo for having only summer clothes in a biting February, gave him a pink card and questioned him for an hour. 'It's harder for him,' Maria Cristina says. 'He looks like an educated person. He has an American face. It's much easier for him to get a job.' And you know who to pay off back in Rio. For a fee – $150, $200 – the Federales will help you cover your tracks. Brazilians stamp passports each time a citizen leaves or enters the country, so extra stamps imply that you have made other journeys in the time you were really in America. 'They stamp another entry to match the day your US visa ran out,' Maria Cristina says, 'and another departure to make it seem you've been somewhere else.'

Once in the city, it's easy to find a bed to live in but tougher to find a whole apartment and make a separate life. Maria Cristina and Paulo have small, bright rooms on a neat street of brick houses, with all the right electronics and a few chairs and couches found by friends. They had no difficulty finding work. 'But without a visa, without being able to speak English, without money, you know what's going to happen,' Maria Cristina says. 'They ask if you can speak English and as long as you can manage to say "Yes", that's it. They promise they will get you a visa and a green card.' She works in a finance company that does business with Brazil, and she still does not have the green card that would allow her permanent residence. She asks her boss for a raise and he tells her it is too expensive to pay for the visa and the lawyer. 'You earn very little money,' she says, 'and you stay there for ever and ever, and yet they make you believe that they're the ones doing you a favour.' The green card trap affects all the newcomers who aspire to middle-class jobs; but then, Maria Cristina is lucky. Among the Brazilians of Queens, the women mostly clean house or else they're go-go dancers; the dancers asked her to work with them when she first arrived.

The men pick up what work they can. There are cab companies owned by Brazilians that use Brazilian drivers, and there is restaurant work, or selling books on Steinway Avenue on a Saturday, the only form of street peddling protected by the First Amendment guarantee of free speech. Nationalities end up with specialities in the construction trade; the Brazilian skill is putting up the plasterboard at the end of a job, but it's cheap work which goes too fast. 'You arrive and you end up learning it,' Paulo says. 'But I want to be away from these people. There are a lot of class Z people in that business.' The pay is uncertain, but you can't break away from a possible source of future work. 'Paulo's boss is a crook,' Maria Cristina says. 'He said he would put Paulo in the union but that was just *papo furado*, just talk.' Once you're in the union, you can work on Manhattan jobs. Paulo says, 'He's very mixed up. He does pay me, but only bit by bit. In the past at least he had work for me, and he paid me bit by bit.'

Sundays play like Sundays at home. Friends come by, especially if they are renting only a bed in an apartment, or living awkwardly in the middle of someone else's marriage. The day becomes a party. 'We start to remember the good things from home, and here it's a bitch but we have to stay here for a while,' Maria Cristina says. She talks to Jorge, who comes over because he's not married, and he's spending too much time in bars and he doesn't have a girlfriend. 'He talks to a girl, but he gets frustrated because she doesn't understand what he's saying. Everybody holds on to the Brazilian thing. I think people miss what they have there – family, friends – and that's why it gets blocked and they don't learn English. They're only here because they have to be, and so they don't learn.

'People come here with the illusion that they'll build their lives back in Brazil. You're over here because you want to make a life back there. It can't be. It gets hard. That's when people go crazy, many people. You're here to make a better life, but at least you were happy back in Brazil, so maybe that was the better life. If we go back, we start from zero. We know that.'

This is not the stuff of the immigrant myth, in which heroic fore-fathers are drawn to the dream of America; but then, immigrant experi-ence almost never was. The immigrant dream was either to escape horror or to make money, and in either case to reproduce an old life as carefully as possible, with the slight possibility of shifting into the truly foreign land of the middle class.

The frontiers are often uneasy. Often you cross a street and the nation changes. Sometimes the frontier is only time of day. Nicaraguan friends come from New Jersey and from Brooklyn to a party on a neat, painted street in Bedford-Stuyvesant; outside, the children are skipping Double Dutch and playing tag on the sidewalk. The music is from the Caribbean coast, a kind of merengùe. When the streets grow dark, the children come inside, and the grown-ups talk and move a little to the music. By eleven, everyone has arrived. The doors are locked and barred. Everyone will stay all night because, outside on the closest corner, the crack dealers have replaced the kids. 'Almost every night,' Mr Cayasso says, 'we hear a shot. Bang, bang.' They stay because their own quiet street will not exist again until it is light.

Out in Corona, which is distant Queens, there is a dark stretch where the sidewalks are broken and some of the trees have been allowed to die and the streetlights are far apart, which is Dominican territory; where the first kitchens cooked up crack cocaine and the drug trade traps the people after sunset. You can tell the houses that have been raided for drugs; they have plywood windows. But then the road runs under the Long Island Railroad tracks. On the other side of the tracks, at Corona Avenue and 108th Street, the sky opens out over an Italian piazza. It's not that there are stars only here, but that only here do you dare look up at them. On the corner, a long boy in white pants does push-ups on the half door of the lemon ice parlour for the girl who is watching. Kids mill at the pizza place. A pair of young men sit, serious as cops, outside the Corona Café. People come from other boroughs to eat at the PS restaurant on the square, which is elegantly netted with tiny white lights. The piazza has a park, where a courting couple talk softly in a dead-end of white flowers, and in the park there are two extraordinary things. This is, after all, New York City, where the streets are only intermittently safe, but there is a refrigerator in the park full of drinks for the old men playing baci-ball, and in summer there is a colour television so they do not have to miss the other significant games while they play. Nothing is locked, nothing is stolen. The place is protected by gentlemen who value loyalty, and their enforcers. You can walk peacefully, pleasurably on a warm summer evening and see the azaleas that litter the ground with red.

On occasions, the men at the Corona Café put down their cappuccino and call a hire car. They carry long, thin bundles wrapped in newspaper. They travel only four blocks, under the railroad tracks to the open land behind a public school, a deep, dark tarmac blank between high wire fences. They unwrap baseball bats and brag through the Caribbean men who hang out there, who part for them. They lift their bats, and two players take the bloody consequences. Nobody sees anything. The stronger army enforces law on the other's territory; the weaker comes down to the railroad bridge, hears the white boys shouting 'Nigger, get out!' and turns away. They know enough to avoid murder.

In Bensonhurst, in Brooklyn, newcomers from Sicily cluster in a few streets. It's tough for them to make more than $16,000 a year, the jobs are vanishing and the old rule that family would always look after its own is beginning to seem threadbare. Particular blacks and Hispanics may be an Italian's friends, but blacks and Hispanics in general are rivals in a survival game. Each street is a remake of some very distant village, and to move even two streets away is the same as going abroad. Life is not just in Italian, but in each particular Sicilian dialect. It is a tiny, insecure world that defends itself with machismo and guns and baseball bats, ways for the boys to preserve a rickety manhood. When Gina Feliciano got to like Keith Mondello too much, and he was not interested, she said she'd date black and Puerto Rican guys instead. The neighbours were shocked. She said she'd bring in the black guys to fight the Italians. The Italians were waiting, of course; the young men have all the time in the world to let the rumours work on them. Into this nervousness walked four black friends, including Yusuf Hawkins – a boy of sixteen, good-natured, who graduated from junior high school with honours and was going on to a High School of Transit Technology. He came by subway at nine in the evening to see a used car and, for half a block, he had no idea he was being followed. At Bay Ridge and 20th Avenue, there were thirty white kids surrounding the four blacks: thirty soldiers in a war for survival, so they thought, against four kids who were thinking of buying a used car, so they thought. One white said, 'Let's club the fucking nigger.' Another said, 'No, let's not club. Let's shoot one.' Yusuf Hawkins could not have imagined this army out to get him, or known what drove them. He was backing up in terror when two .32 calibre bullets took him down.

Even after his death, each side knew only what it knew before. Bishop Mugavero of the Brooklyn Catholic Diocese spoke approvingly of the 'deep and basic family values' of the 'solid community' of Bensonhurst, apparently not seeing that the notion of family loyalty had been twisted around into defending the community with a gun. Black protesters marched through Bensonhurst, apparently not realising that the notion that anyone can walk anywhere in America is only theoretical, and that controlling these few streets is all the new Sicilians of Bensonhurst can do to control their lives. The next stage was for Italians and the friends of Yusuf Hawkins each to claim the support of a larger racial group. 'I've never been racial in my life,' said a blonde girl, flecked with bits of cheap gold, 'but white people should stick together for ourselves.' Black activists saw in this death a story of racism, indifferent cops and even Mafiosi; because everyone knows that where there are Sicilians, there must be Mafiosi, right? And in the middle of it all, the people on the Bensonhurst streets genuinely did not understand the fuss. 'It's a sin and a crime when a child gets shot,' one bookkeeper said. 'But many white children are also killed in Bensonhurst. When our own race gets killed, there is no big deal about it. What are we? Chopped meat?'

But anything that happens on a frontier is political; it defines the people on either side. This variety is not quite respectable. America tried to deal with variety after the Second World War, building suburban tracts that were homogeneous by race, age, class, income and credit rating – communities carefully separate where differences never butt up against each other. New York is a shocking reminder of difference. In the city you could not be sure what was American and what was not, because so many different things were American. There was no 'melting pot'. But that idea is the fanciful vision of a dramatist called Israel Zangwill, who never did live in America. His play *The Melting Pot* was put before President Theodore Roosevelt in 1908 with wild success. Zangwill talks of all Manhattan as God's crucible, where some great Alchemist is melting and fusing 'Celt and Latin, Slav and Teuton, Greek and Syrian – black and yellow,' as David, a Russian-born Jew, proclaims. 'Jew and gentile,' adds his wife Vera, a Russian-born Christian. The play is their love story, but it has the energy of a sermon. The curtain falls as the band strikes up 'My Country, 'Tis of Thee'; America is celebrated as the place where races merge, not necessarily in body, but certainly in politics and interests.

Theodore Roosevelt approved hugely of this. He did not much like the scruffy, dark-skinned newcomers to America, with their habit of staying Italian-American, or Jewish-American or Russian-American. He wanted them to drop the hyphens and to assimilate, which meant, of course, surrendering their inferior identities and aspiring, however desperately, to his. Teddy Roosevelt did not expect to change. Israel Zangwill, on the other hand, talked of all these fused races breeding 'the coming superman', the American who had yet to be born and who would be 'politically homogeneous'. Neither dream was workable. Until this superman's culture existed, there was nowhere for all the melded Americans to live except in their own particular culture, the one they brought from home; often their jobs, homes, friends and marriages depended on it. Being a melded American required shifting out into the middle class and disappearing behind another set of frontiers into unfamiliar territory.

In New York, you are never far from all the differences inside America. Difference, of course, has its history.

Being truly different was being black in the minds of most white New Yorkers in the 1700s. To be black was to be mischievous, hard to understand, truthless, beastly, ungrateful for being 'better fed and clothed, and put to less labour, than the poor of most Christian countries'; 'silly, unthinking creatures', but also cunning, some other kind of human. This was an otherness in which some whites had to be instructed. New Yorkers were often hauled to court for 'entertaining Negroes in their houses contrary to law'. The Mayor and Aldermen were attacked for failing to prevent 'Negroes from playing publickly in the streets on Sundays'. But other whites, especially the slave masters, were constantly trying to shore up the boundaries between their own free state and their human property.

In New York City and County there were perhaps 945 black slaves around 1700, and 5,362 whites, but outnumbering was not enough. The masters were alarmed by Elias Neau, who tried to bring Christian teaching to the slaves. He was a Huguenot who had once been made a galley slave for his religion, an obstinately enlightened man, seen by an Anglican priest 'creeping into Garrets, Cellars and other nauseous places, to exhort and pray by the poor slaves when they are sick.' He was a walking reproach to the brutality of slave masters, and a practical problem since the slavemasters feared they might have to free any slaves that Neau converted. They came to see sinister meaning in the fact that Neau's school met at night, although Neau wrote: 'I am moreover obliged to keep my school by candlelight; because in the day time [the slaves] are employed in working. . . .' And when, in 1712, the slavemasters' fears all came charging down the streets in what seemed like a full-blown insurrection of slaves, Neau's constant contact with black people and his concern for them became a scandal. 'This barbarous Conspiracy of the Negroes which was first thought to be general opened the mouths of many against Negroes being made Christians,' wrote John Sharpe, the garrison chaplain. 'Mr Neau durst hardly appear; his School was blaimed as ye main Occation of it, and a Petition had like to have been presented if the Governor had not Stood to his Cause.'

On the night of 6 April 1712, two dozen slaves met at midnight in an orchard in the East Ward. The slave masters blamed Neau, but almost all the rebel slaves belonged to masters who opposed Neau and his teaching. Some said they bound themselves to secrecy by sucking the blood from each other's hands, that a free black who knew magic gave them a powder to rub on their clothes that would make them invulnerable; but such stories were told to emphasise that blacks were alien and fanatical. They certainly had pistols, daggers, swords, guns, clubs, staves and axes. They waited until the moon was setting at two o'clock and set fire to an outhouse. Nothing alarmed the town like fire; everything was wood, and water was scarce. A fire was a perfect ambush. The citizens came rushing to it and the slaves were waiting to shoot and stab. A great gun was fired at the Fort to bring the town to arms, and the rebels backed off into the woods, or took refuge with friends in the town. They knew there was no escape. On the way, at least six killed themselves, and one also shot his wife. The *Boston Weekly News-Letter* reported later that 'Three have been Executed according to Law, one burnt, a second broke upon the wheel and a third hung up alive.' The slaves were punished as though for treason, and the town was in a state of panic.

New laws were passed to control them like aliens. A slave must carry a lantern with a lighted candle at night, and only his master could provide it. No more than three slaves could meet together without their masters' consent. A slave could have a gun only in his master's presence or with his master's consent. No Negro, Indian or Mulatto could own houses, tenements or hereditaments. And this law, and the even more stringent ones which followed it, concerned race just as much as the state of slavery. Hosey and John, slaves who won clemency after the 1712 rebellion, insisted that they had been free subjects of the King of Spain, but Governor Hunter could not free them without better proof than their own sworn testimony. They had landed at New York as prisoners of a privateer and they had been sold as slaves on the grounds that they looked swarthy. Lighter-skinned prisoners were assumed to be freemen, and kept as prisoners of war.

In a hard time, in a hard country, men looked for some action they could take when nature and politics seemed outside their control. The winter of 1740–41 was brutal. Snow drifted six feet deep inside the city, and the Hudson was clogged with ice; grain prices soared and by February, the money collected to feed the city poor had all gone. The New York *Journal* reported imminent war with Spain and danger from the French and the suspect loyalties of the Iroquois. The town was hungry and frightened. A white woman heard a slave say, 'Fire, Fire, Scorch, Scorch, a little, damn it, by and by' and the next day there were four fires in the town. When the slave Cuffee was seen running from the scene of a fire, there was a shout that 'the negroes are rising'. There was talk that the slaves who had stolen Geneva gin five years ago, and been whipped for it, now proudly and illegally assembled as 'the Geneva club'.

Everyone knew that disgruntled slaves had used fire to get revenge. Sawney was a troublemaker of nineteen, heard at the neighbourhood pump God-damning all white people, and saying he would set them all on fire if he had the power. He tried to burn down his master's house three times, and once threw 'fire over alderman Bancker's fence into his yard', and had to be sent back to Albany. And there was room for grievance. The slave Quack's wife was the Governor's cook, living in Fort George; when he tried to visit her, he was clubbed by a sentry and pitched back into the street.

The night of 28 February, someone robbed the merchant James Hogg and his linens fell into the hands of John Hughson, who kept an unrespectable tavern where slaves could come together in their tens or their twenties for 'penny drams'. The constables questioned Hughson's young serving girl, Mary Burton, who was serving out her indentures in the tavern. Two weeks later, Fort George went up in flames. It seems a plumber had been using live coals to repair the metal of a gutter. A week later, a chimney caught fire and burned off a roof. A week after that, a careless smoker tipped out his pipe in a hayloft and burned down a storehouse. There were eight fires in six days.

The constables went back to Mary Burton, this time intent on making a link between the robbery and the fires, because they were already sure that the fires must have their own story. Perhaps they were thinking of how able-bodied citizens ran to a fire, and saved what they could out of the flames; a nice way to thieve was simply not to return the salvaged property. But little Mary Burton gave them much more. She said she 'would acquaint them with what she knew relating to the goods stolen from Mr Hogg's, but would say nothing about the fires'. The magistrates took this to mean that Mary knew the hidden story. They offered her a hundred pounds, they frightened her with talk of damnation and she told them an epic. She said there was a plot by the slaves to burn the town and kill all the white inhabitants, except for the inn-keeper John Hughson who would then be crowned King of New York.

Her story was peppered with oddities – fires that she said were set at night but did not break out until noon, a revolution which spread itself out lazily over almost a month. But at last there was something to correct in hard times, a whole rebellious nation inside the city. A tart called Peggy Kerry was hauled in, named as a conspirator by Mary Burton because she did a little business with slaves as well as white men; there were more black men than women in New York and more white women than men, and the town needed a lesson in what happened when a woman crossed the race line. Slaves were arrested, and their confessions published even though none of them confessed until death was imminent; two of them were bound at the stake, with the faggots already burning, when they began to talk.

These alarums produced a problem. It was convenient that blacks were thought dangerous, but not that they were supposed to be capable on their own of grand conspiracy. The justices thought even the scum of the town would not make common cause with blacks without some extra, perverting factor. New York required evidence of white devilry, and thought immediately of the foreign Catholic Church.

A Latin teacher called John Ury was accused of being a Catholic priest in disguise. He was sentenced to death as the mastermind of the Great Negro Plot. Ury was notorious for his refusal to drink the king's health which made people think he might be Catholic. People found it easy to think that Catholics were agents of Spain. Now that Catholics were involved, the rowdy Irish soldiers could be accused; they had always been outsiders living in the town, and they had the accents of Popery. Jerry Corker was supposed to have said he had a mind to burn the fort, and he had been helping the plumber who carelessly left live coals in the gutter of the fort. Private Edward Murphy said, according to his accusers, 'Damn me, if I won't lend a hand to the fires as soon as anybody.' The trials became much like the Salem witch trials – anybody could be accused as long as only the usual suspects were involved. But they stopped abruptly when Mary Burton began talking against people 'in ruffles', the gentry of the town. Sense returned. Most of the accused slaves simply went back to their masters. There was no attempt to tighten the laws on slave conduct, or to take greater trouble to see them enforced; it was as though the town realised there had been only a few fires, a few robberies and a generous amount of false confession.

The truth of the matter did not count for much. Almost half the black men in New York were in jail at the height of the panic, and that was held to prove that they could not be trusted. Slaveowners brought in black women for domestic work and pushed out black men, which neatly solved the problem of having black men without partners in the town. After three years, it seemed the Great Plot was 'almost forgotten', as the town's Recorder Daniel Horsmanden complained. But Horsmanden saw the whole story of conspiracy as a lesson in the divide between black and white; he published a great haystack of a compilation about the trials and the plot. His intent was 'that those who have property in slaves might have a lasting memento concerning the nature of them'.

Once the otherness of black men was established, they were the object and subject of riot. Riot was, in the years after the Revolution, a quite ordinary way for the citizens to discipline some group of suspects or troublemakers. In some white minds, the separate black institutions were a claim to parity that had to be resisted with fists and stones. After the Revolution, ruffians tried to break up the black theatre, tearing the curtains, stripping the actors, bringing down the lights and beating the proprietor. In 1807, trustees of the African Church complained that unruly boys were breaking up their services. Black cookhouses and oyster stands were harassed, and blacks knocked down and beaten in the streets.

The frontier affected everyday life. A black woman could stand on a public omnibus, but not sit. A black man could travel on the exposed decks of a Hudson River steamer, but not in the cabin. By law, a black man could not vote if he had less than $250 in property, and if he had more, he was excluded by custom. Black orphans were refused by homes until the Colored Orphan Asylum was founded in 1836; they had to live in jails, or find their own Fagin who would run them as beggars or chimney sweeps. There were black balconies in theatres, black pews in churches, black seats in courtrooms. Those who wanted to abolish slavery, the 'abos', were first accused of being 'amalgamists' and wanting to mix the races. The strongest opposition came from whites who feared black labour as their competition; the newcomer Irish, who were much more worried about the settled whites, were not yet involved. Integrated meetings were disrupted. Churches were invaded and wrecked on the slightest rumour of a mixed marriage. The mobs made their point with melodramatic signs. One night in 1834, they turned their attention from the 'abos' to black preachers, and from the preachers to blacks in general. They conceived their own Passover, a bitter parody of *Exodus*: white families were told to put lights in their windows so their homes could be passed over when the wreckers came to call.

But there was a sense of solidarity growing inside the blows, a kind of black nationalism. In 1801, there were twenty 'French Negroes' clustered on Eagle Street before the house of Jeanne Mathusine Droibillan Volunbrun, and 200 other blacks joined them. The black nation of Haiti was being born out of the French possession of Saint Dominque. This armed committee had formed on the New York streets to free Haitian slaves. In 1819, the slave catcher John Hall tried to take an escaped slave to a Hudson River dock, but ran into a black crowd. In 1826, blacks waited outside the courthouse where a runaway slave family from Virginia faced a forced return to the plantation. One woman was 'swaggering about the Park with a stick in her hands, crying out – where are the Virginians?' The slave handlers were stoned and bloodied, and the riot went after a white man in Ann Street nearby, shouting, 'Kill him, kill him!'

In colonial New York, blacks were invisible and unimportant; almost everyone who mattered was white, right and English or else long-settled Dutch. The whites were not various enough for variety to be an issue. Peter Kalm records that Germans who tried to settle around

1709 were harassed, their land stolen and their men roughly punished when they dared to fight back; beaten off to Pennsylvania, they warned friends and relations to avoid New York. The Irish were rare arrivals until the Revolution. But when there was a United States of America, the story changed. Immigrants crowded in from Europe – more than five and a half million between 1815 and 1860. Many of them were the wrong nationality, and most lost social standing by crossing the Atlantic and had to start again in the otherwise cosy middle-class family of New York.

Ludwig Gall came to escape the chaos of the Napoleonic Wars, and soon knew he was from another place and the wrong tribe. He was charged twice the local price for food; an American told the bartender, 'You know he's a foreigner' and the price of a bottle of beer went from a quarter to three quarters. He was rooked of half his dollar deposit on six bottles (he may have been growing careless, on seven quarts of beer a day). 'You *never* hear an American complain about cheating and overpricing,' he wrote. 'He simply grabs the first chance to recover his losses in the same way he suffered them.' In the saloons he met clerks and officers from Europe who could not find work that suited them and were reduced to giving French lessons for a few hours a day; only one of his acquaintances was making useful money – $20 to $25 a week – and he was a clerk who had realised that nobody needed his skills, invested in a razor and set up as a barber. But even the barber harboured thoughts of going to home to Europe, as soon as he had the money. It was all too foreign in New York. Gall was offered tea, black or green, at the evening meal. He was given a rounded knife and a two-tined fork to eat peas. In the Tontine Coffeehouse, which served as the city's Exchange, every gentleman kept his hat on, in defiance of European manners.

Once the war of 1812 was settled, and the port of Liverpool was open again, the Irish began their long pilgrimage to America. They came as day labourers, weavers, cartmen, put away in special neighbourhoods; when an Irishman tried to move into Harlem Common in 1825, a mob stoned his doors and windows and tore off most of his roof. Their jobs had to be defended. Irish cartmen attacked Connecticut rivals who dared to use larger carts. In 1826, the unfortunate Isaac Anderson was driven off a carting job at a construction project at Dandy Point; he was working too fast, and the Irish carters accused him of being an Orangeman. The Shamrock Society reported in 1817 that there were already 12,000 Irishmen in New York, a sizeable fraction of the foreign-born, even though its advice was not to stay in the great cities, 'because as much will be spent during a long winter as can be made through a toilsome summer, so that a man may be kept a moneyless drudge for life.' They commended the freedom of the Irish in New York: 'Here they are never accused of sedition, or rebellion, or conspiracy against the Government. They are never disarmed by a military force; and no magistrate trembles when they provide themselves with ammunition.' But they did not tell how the Irish had to fight for those things at the heart of their lives.

Parades on St Patrick's Day in the 1790s were a line of straw effigies called 'Paddies' that mocked St Patrick. In 1799, the Irish fought back when a 'Paddie' procession made its way along Harmon Street and one man died. On St Patrick's Day in 1802 some Irishmen collected around sundown on East George Street and beat passers-by with clubs and stones, shouting: 'Huzza for Dublin, we'll show the Americans freedom!' In 1803, the Common Council outlawed the 'Paddie' processions. It was as though New York at last had to face the fact that it was more than a Protestant, English colony.

But the conflict did not stop. On Christmas Eve 1806, 'highbinder' thugs assembled before a Catholic watch night service, and guards had to be set to protect the worshippers. On Christmas Day, the Irish heard rumours that the highbinders were coming back to tear down their church, and also their houses. The watch tried to calm them but the Irish had no reason to trust the English accent of the authorities; highbinders and native-born Americans fought against the Irish, who fought against the watch.

In the 1820s there were riots between Orangemen and Catholics, a bloody European conflict which continued relentlessly in New York. The Irish were always aware of the hostility of the Protestant and the English. In March 1828, an Irishman died of tetanus in a boarding house, and the local doctor began a routine autopsy; but an Irishman broke in on the operation and would not believe that the cuts were for the 'purpose of surgical inspection'. Instead, he spread the story that 'a Protestant physician was cutting up a Catholic for the mere gratification of sectarian animosity, or of vampyre taste'. A mob assembled, and was persistent enough to drive the doctor out of the city.

Settled Americans were alarmed by the new voices, the new muscle; the flood of newcomers between 1840 and 1860 was the heaviest ever in proportion to the settled population. Wages were down, jobs become scarce and the newcomers took the blame for the peaks and crashes of the economy. Hatters made twelve dollars a week in 1835, and only eight a decade later. Tailors said the price of a coat had been cut in half between 1842 and 1847. Cabinet makers in 1846 made eight dollars a week, but they remembered making fifteen a decade before. Employers, they complained, went on the ships even before the immigrants had landed and offered jobs at twenty dollars a year and board. Craftsmen were used to a little security, and now they could not see a way to put aside money for sickness or old age.

The issues went beyond money. American politics was supposed to include everyone in a grand American identity, but that identity was Anglo-Saxon and established. Newcomers, the Irish especially, were excluded; Thomas Mooney, an Irish emigrant agent, warned them that 'every demand for a fellowship with respectable society, grounded upon the law of the land, will be rejected with contempt'. The city began to think that the best immigrants passed swiftly through: 'The worst part of the refuse class which is thus thrown upon our shores, here clan together and remain in the city, nor can they be persuaded to leave it,' the New York Association for Improving the Condition of the Poor claimed in 1851.

The machinery of personal charity broke down in a bigger city, but the poor still reckoned that the rich owed them a duty. In February 1837, when bread, meat, rent and fuel were all rising in price, a mob went down to Eli Hart's flour store and dumped his stocks; some women gathered flour in their aprons, but most of the men felt they were inflicting a punishment on Hart for failing in his duty to be charitable. 'No plunder, no plunder,' some tall, athletic fellow was shouting, 'destroy as much as you please!' When the Gibbons' house was wrecked in the riots of 1863, very little was stolen; even the grand piano was set on fire, broken up and carried away in fragments. The Gibbons brothers were punished for an excess of possessions as well as their abolitionist views.

The newcomers could not be tidied away. There was never enough housing for them. 'Six poor women with their children were discovered Tuesday night by some police officers, sleeping in an alleyway, in Avenue B between 10th and 11th Streets,' the *Daily Tribune* reported in 1850. 'When interrogated they said they had been compelled to spend their nights where ever they could obtain any shelter.' Some built shacks, but others simply drifted through the streets, worried and baffled and hungry. Cholera, typhus and tuberculosis went with poverty and overcrowding. There were no more apprentices in workshops, because there were so many skilled adults to be hired cheap. The children spilled on to the streets, and if poverty was a moral failing, they were the visible signs of sin. George Matsel, the first New York chief of police, found their numbers 'almost incredible'. They were ragged, knowing, 'idle and vicious children of both sexes', carriers of disease and the germ of crime, an alarming contrast to the neat innocence of decent childhood. And they were everywhere. On the street corners they sold the hot corn that New Yorkers loved, and the baked pears and tea cakes and hot sweet potatoes. They sold newspapers, blacked shoes, held horses. One small boy made his living catching butterflies and selling them to the owners of canaries.

Street gangs, and the fire companies which were much like gangs, did battle to keep control of who drank at their taverns, who did business in their community, and who lived next door. Newcomers were considered 'emigrants', with the country of origin all important, rather than 'immigrants' who could be defined by their choice of America. They ran their working lives through tight groups of friends and relatives, people like them, all the same faith and nationality; they found jobs together, set wages together, set the pace of work together. That was particularly true of those who could organise their own work – longshoremen on the docks, cartmen, workers in lumberyards or quarries, the men who dug ditches or paved streets or shifted coal. On the docks, the Walsh Brothers ran their stevedoring business through 'an endless retinue of cousins,' who served as 'workmen and spies'; business was family business. The work might be seasonal and erratic; most longshoremen needed sidelines working boats or making bricks or running delivery teams. But it was desirable work, to be kept in the family. It also happened to be open to both blacks and whites and, since it required living close by the docks, blacks and whites had to live side by side.

The Longshoremen's United Benevolent Association, an Irish group that was always in the St Patrick's Day parades, tried to claim the work for 'white men'. Their sense of 'white' was flexible; fifty years later it meant Irish or German, so that Poles and Italians could be kept out and officials spoke of so many gangs of white men, and so many of Italians. But in 1855, 'white' meant only 'Irish', so that Germans could be kept out, and the pressing issue was black longshoremen, hired after a dock strike. The Irish Longshoremen's Society came down on the piers and terrified the blacks into quitting. One black was hit in the head by an Irishman; he turned and fired a pistol, and suddenly there were 200 Irishmen around him, and he was lucky to escape with his life.

In April 1863, the longshoremen struck for a standard wage, and some of them were replaced by blacks. This time, racial violence spread from the piers into the tenements. Longshoremen beat up blacks and the cops who tried to protect them from lynching. On 1 January, President Lincoln had freed the slaves by proclamation and they seemed like an imminent threat to the jobs and the lives of the dockside workers. 'Contrabands', the slaves who escaped to the Union lines, could be imported to take jobs in ironworks as well as on the docks. The Catholic Archbishop John Hughes said slavery was best left alone, and those who wanted to abolish it were signs of 'lawless liberalism', 'Deists, Atheists, Pantheists, anything but Christians'. He complained that factories with Irish workers had shut down to force their workers to enlist. He was sure there was an anti-Catholic conspiracy. The Civil War divided Catholic and Protestant, Irish and English, and anyone nervous about their living from the blacks of New York.

In March 1863, with the north in military trouble, Congress ordered a draft. Unmarried men between twenty and forty-five, married men up to thirty-five could be chosen by lottery for war. Only citizens were called, which meant that only white men could be drafted. Whites could buy their way out, for $300, and the price became an issue; labourers, Maria Lydig Daly wrote, 'say they are sold for $300 whilst they pay $1,000 for negroes.' Lincoln's Republican government was held responsible for some future invasion of black workers, and for the risks that white soldiers would have to run. On 13 July there began a terrifying series of riots in the city, a panicky class of white labourers striking out against not just the draft but the government, the rich, the cops and most particularly the blacks. Irish women used crowbars to tear up the rail tracks on Fourth Avenue. Shops were shuttered, work sites abandoned. Any home that might shelter a policeman was burned down. If the mob caught a policemen, he was stripped and beaten about the face and head until he could no longer be recognised; they de-faced authority. Along Lexington Avenue, rioters ripped through rich homes, wrecking and occasionally stealing 'pictures with gilt frames, elegant pier glasses' which were the huge mirrors set between windows.

Around three in the afternoon, the mob attacked a nine-year-old black boy at the corner of Broadway and Chambers Street. By nightfall, they were out laying into black men and boys in the tenements. The fine brick mansion of the Colored Orphan Asylum on Fifth Avenue was in flames, and the mob uprooted the trees and fences that surrounded it, destroying any trace of a black presence. The city was terrified that it was in the throes of some Confederate plot. Bridges across the Harlem River were burning, the telegraph lines had been cut, the Weehawken and Fulton ferries were under attack, the track of the Hudson River Railroad was ripped up. But after one day's show of resistance to the draft, which had quite general support, the riot changed. It became almost entirely Irish, and its enemy was the black community of New York.

William Jones was caught, hanged and then burned, so his blackness was reduced to ashes. Tenements that held black families were set on fire, and their furniture put on bonfires in the street. Anyone who kept a boarding house where black men lodged was taken out, stripped and told to get out of the neighbourhood or face the rope. A sailor called William Williams walked ashore and asked directions of some Irish longshoremen; he was beaten and, when he was on the ground, the gang took turns to knife or beat or kick or stone his fallen body. Daniel Greenlief saw the incident and said, 'After the occurrence there were several cheers given and something said ... about vengeance on every nigger in New York.'

Murder had turned into an obscene ritual, to whiten the city. There was a crippled coachman called Abraham Franklin hiding in his rooms along with his sister. He was hauled out, dragged through the streets, and hanged from a lamp-post. The military arrived and cut him down, but when they moved on, the corpse was again strung up. When it was finally cut down a boy, Patrick Butler, came out of the crowd and dragged the body through the streets by its genitals. The crowd cheered. It was as though all the menace of blackness was being exorcised by the boy.

The violence spread against Germans and Jews who owned stores. The mob thought store-owners must be Republicans, supporters of emancipation and the draft, and they threw stones before investigating any individual's loyalty. A few Chinese peddlers were beaten up because they were suspected of knowing white women. The neighbourhood was being cleansed of strangers, rivals, politicians who were not in the Irish interest, cops who tried to control the drink trade, anyone who did not belong in the tight net of families. This agenda was clear and brutal. It was resisted in Greenwich Village by black families who found weapons and made themselves a temporary army, but this was piecemeal resistance to imminent threats. Many more black people fled the city for the countryside of Brooklyn, or the New Jersey hills, and they had difficulty reclaiming their jobs when the riot was over. Some grand families made a show of employing black servants in place of the Irish, but that was nothing compared with the new humiliation of blacks being thrown bodily off any kind of public transport by the white drivers and passengers.

And the clearest sign that the rioters had won was in the papers. In 1867 *The World*, whose Democrat sermons helped inflame the riot, ran a huge survey of 'Negroes in Gotham'. The *World* could not quite resist a little obvious colour in its report – it introduced Snake-Eyed Mary, an enchantress living all alone on Staten Island at a place known as Babylon and alarming all the 'lowest class of New York negroes'; but it set out to prove that there were black bankers and fashionables and lady-like tea-drinkings, that blacks were not the ones who needed help. Instead, their enemies had to be bought off because their lawlessness terrified respectable New York. The mob were 'strange wretched abandoned creatures that flocked out from their dens and lairs,' to Mattie Griffith, with terrifying ways: she saw 'a colored man hanging on a tree, and some men and women setting him on fire as he dangled from the branches.' With these images in mind, it seemed so much more sensible to let the immigrants' friends at Tammany Hall take New York, on condition that this brutish self-interest was never seen again.

Something else was settled in the draft riots. New York was now obviously a city of nations. Newcomers no longer seemed to bother to adapt to American ways, as Ludwig Gall had found so difficult. They organised their own theatres, amusements, military organisations and national organisations, churches, trades unions and newspapers, 'almost as impervious to American sentiments and influences as are the inhabitants of Dublin or Hamburg,' as the New York Association for the Improvement of the Conditions of the Poor complained in its 1868 annual report. Anything about the Italians, say, could be explained by what everyone thought they knew about Italy. So an overcrowded slum was nothing to Italians, not after Genoa, and defective drains were something that princes had to endure in

Venice, according to *Harpers' Magazine,* which later reported that Italians were 'generally peaceable, but, perhaps because of the lawlessness that has prevailed in Italy until recently, nearly all of them carry arms habitually'.

The assumptions were almost always far worse than reality. The NYAICP thought the Italians on Jersey Street looked like 'a pestilential breeding, law-breaking colony' but closer acquaintance confirmed only the first of those impressions; 'no more peaceable, thrifty, orderly neighbours could be found than these Italians'. Russian Jews who were crowded into tenements were regarded as filthy people, unless social workers noticed that their homes were brighter and cleaner than the halls or stairways of the rotted buildings in which they lived. Of course, the real world of the newcomers was hidden; what most people saw was villains or models, coming in by their millions across the frontier in New York harbour.

Rocco Corresca was bought from the orphanage, aged eight, to beg in the streets of Naples. He overheard his grandfatherly protector discussing the cost of making him into a proper cripple, the kind that makes people shudder. He decided to run away. He heard about 'a far off country where everybody was rich ... Italians went there and made plenty of money, so that they could return to Italy and live in pleasure ever after.' There was even a man who pulled out a fistful of gold and said he had made it in America in only a few days.

The same man found Rocco work in the engine room of a steamship, carrying the coals; only later did he realise that he should have been paid in wages as well as passage. 'We were so long on the water,' he said, 'that we began to think we should never get to America, or that, perhaps, there was not any such place.' He was met at Ellis Island by a man called Bartolo who claimed to be his uncle, who set him to work picking rags and bones for almost no money; 'Bartolo told us all that we must work for him and that if we did not, the police would come and put us in prison.'

After a year, Rocco broke away from his *padrone* and paid a man in Newark five dollars to get him work. Even Northern Italians had the habit of going long distances for work – in French factories, German mines, Swiss tunnels and anywhere there was construction work – and following *padroni* who found the jobs and set the wages. America was simply the extreme case.

Sadie Frowne came from Poland, her passage paid by New York relatives who took up a subscription. 'We came by steerage on a steamship in a very dark place that smelt dreadfully. There were hundreds of other people packed in with us, men, women and children, and almost all of them were sick. It took us twelve days to cross the sea and we thought we should die, but at last the voyage was over, and we came up and saw the beautiful bay and the big woman with spikes on her head and the lamp that is lighted at night in her hand.' Two million Jews from Eastern Europe landed at New York between 1880 and 1914, unable to stay among the pogroms and the hatred where they were, and unsure what they would find somewhere else.

This coming to America was an epic story, touched up and glorified by later generations, but really a matter of hunger and humiliation. R.H. Sherard went steerage to New York in 1902 from the French port of Le Havre. On the train to the docks, he saw 'elation ... on all these faces, under the dim flicker of the oil lamp, and joy was making all these people exuberant and vociferous.' They had a sense of escape to a land where 'Oh, Giuseppe, to think of it! People eat meat every sacred day that the Madonna gives.'

But at the docks, past five in the morning, each petty official was a tyrant to a trainload of people who were only in transit, settled nowhere. On board, no crew member would answer questions, not even the cabin boys. No knives were issued to the emigrants 'for, being poor, we were naturally men of criminal and sanguinary instincts.' They had to snatch for food and bribe the stewards for a glass of fresh water. Leaving the ship, each one was made to sign a paper as a condition of going ashore: a statement that they had no complaints about food or bedding, and were issued their lawful rations of wine and water. The migrants were being taught their place, which is quite different from the place they leave behind: they were probationers for a new life.

There is worse. 'At all times ... a vague fear harassed even the most contented. The question that each one constantly asked of himself was: "Will they let me in?" Many had heard of the American Emigration laws for the first time on the boat.' When buying his ticket, Sherard was asked if he had thirty dollars – which he thought was essential for admission to the United States – but not warned that he could be turned back for medical problems. At the end of the voyage, all steerage class had to parade on the wet, cold deck before the ship's doctor for 'inspection', three hours 'with the spindrift driving over us, crushing, steaming, swearing and foul. There were men and women in the mass who were sick and many fought, and all blasphemed.' Sailors off duty slipped through the crowd, clutching the breasts of the women. And the talk became alarmist on the approach to the city, as it always had. Robert Louis Stevenson was 'amused, and then somewhat staggered by the cautious and the grisly tales that went the round. You would have thought we were to land upon a cannibal island. You must speak to nobody in the streets, as they would not leave you til you were rooked and beaten. You must enter an hotel with military precautions; for the least you had to apprehend was to awake next morning without money or baggage, or necessary raiment, a lone forked radish in a bed; and if the worst befell, you would instantly and mysteriously disappear from the ranks of mankind.'

In the harbour, the newcomers stepped down on to the old, smoky barges, slow, crowded and without seats, that plied across to the immigration station – at the circular fort of Castle Garden on the Battery until 1892, on Ellis Island in a ramshackle wooden hall until 1897 and then, while the Island was rebuilt in iron and brick, briefly at the Battery Barge Office, where the small-time plunderers concentrated and cut off a likely prospect like a dog cuts out a sheep, and followed newcomers on to the elevated trains, sometimes promising a boarding house, sometimes menacing and robbing.

Finally, in December 1900, there was a frontier on Ellis Island: a permanent federal immigration station. The exhausted newcomers toiled up stairs, their baggage all unwieldy and their children clinging to them, and struggled down again for each stage of the inspection. First, there was a rudimentary medical check. Even in the 1920s, the British Ambassador reported that 'the line of male immigrants approached the first medical officer with their trousers open'. Then, the newcomers pushed forward to the inspector at the metal wicket. On a busy day, it took perhaps two minutes to decide someone's life.

In the confusion of the Island, and the deep tiredness after so many days in steerage and so many hours on the deck of a slow barge, the newcomers met the graft of the city. 'Roughness, cursing, intimidation and a mild form of blackmail prevailed to such a degree as to be common,' Edward Steiner wrote. 'The restaurant was a den of thieves, in which the immigrant was robbed by the proprietor, whose employees stole from him and from the immigrant too.' Change a twenty-mark gold piece, and you could expect to lose three quarters of your money. Inspectors jostled alongside the flashier newcomers, suggesting that a little money would make it easier to land. One girl from Bohemia stood in tears, because an inspector had promised to pass her quickly if only she would meet him at a certain hotel. 'Do I look like that?' she asked Steiner. Some immigration inspectors signed blank cards which allowed the interpreters or the labourers to detain anyone. The chief inspector marked 'Hold' against the name of anyone who showed to have money on the steamship's manifest; these gentry came directly and only to him before they could land.

R.H. Sherard knew he could go home when he had cleared immigration, that nothing was at stake; but still he felt like some dangerous beast, forever hemmed in by bars. He said he was carrying only eight dollars. He was taken to the detention centre on Ellis Island. When William Williams took charge of the Island in 1902, he found the detention quarters filthy; they were known as pens, bolted and barred. The beds were caged bunks, two feet of space between them, the room airless and often one hundred degrees in summer. The only common language was a bludgeon. The most vicious of the wardens was a Portuguese who was himself awaiting deportation. The dining room was littered with grease and bones and bits of food; at times there were no knives, forks or spoons. There were occasional, gratuitous lectures on how to be a good citizen. There was time to wonder why all these other people were being held – which were suspected of being contract labourers, or likely to become a public charge, and which were known polygamists, or wanted criminals, or runaway husbands shopped by a wife back in Austria, and which had been paid to leave some country that was over eager to be rid of its paupers. Some, especially women and children, were 'temporary detainees', held for five days so their friends or family could claim them, and then either deported or handed over to the missionary societies. 'As to the Jewish ménage,' Sherard wrote of a couple who had landed with him, 'the old man showed me his card and that of his wife. Both were marked "Senility". I had not the heart to tell him, that the cause of their detention was perhaps the only one which cannot be overcome.'

The newcomers had very various expectations. Jews from Russia wanted to be clear of the pogroms. Italian farmers wanted money to buy land of their own back home. Some families went back and forth, undecided where they should settle, or what America was meant to mean to them. The immigrant dream of America was new. Once, America had been the pastoral of its own imagination. People came for land. Few dared grumble publicly at what they found, although one bilious Welshman, signing himself Hiraethlon (which means homesick) complained in the New York paper *Cymro America, or the American Cambrian* of the friend who had persuaded him to emigrate. 'I gathered from his letter,' he wrote, 'that here "wine turns the millwheels, and one gets five pounds for sleeping in the morning", that money grows on trees, and that the fat birds fly about already plucked and roasted, crying "Eat us!"' He found, instead, bed-bugs as high as skunks; watered milk; poor, rough, boggy and sandy land; a chronic shortage of money; and liberty – 'the liberty to walk barefoot if you don't own shoes'.

But that was before the Civil War. By the turn of the century, newcomers arrived for the money to be made building cities or starting businesses. One barber had been shaving and cutting for months in someone else's shop when the proprietor chose to retire, and offered the business for a few dollars; the barber accepted. Later, it would be said that if you made it in New York you could make it anywhere; the city was tough. But the barber liked to say: 'If you can't make it in New York, you can't make it anywhere.' The city was volatile, and that meant opportunity.

Settled Americans knew that something new was coming from Europe: the masses, their politics and the notion of their culture. Between 1800 and 1914, Europe's population rose from 180 to 460 million; the pressure to leave was overwhelming, especially where the harvests were scrimpiest, the growth of industry least likely and the people least able by reason of religion, class or ethnic group to manipulate any of the levers of power. In Europe, this glut of human-ity produced a violent reaction. Flaubert became suddenly aware of the crush of people not like him, and snapped that 'one could not elevate the masses even if one tried'. Nietzsche proclaimed that 'a declaration of war on the masses by higher men is needed'. The masses were half alive, clever people said; there were too many of them to be known. They crowded out art and God and life.

And yet these masses had their place, their destination: New York – a sudden invasion not just by millions of human beings, but also by a most disruptive idea for an America which set itself up to be middle-class. Once the flood began, the city could never even pretend to be just a monument or a settled place; it became endless events, lives changing, accents shifting, language being grafted with exotic new words and notions so that even the means of describing the city change as the people and buildings of the city change.

Leon Trotsky took an eighteen-dollar apartment on 164th Street, and marvelled at the gas cooker, the phone, the automatic service elevator and (most marvellous of all) a chute for the garbage. He went too deeply into work with American socialists to learn much about the city; as the family was packing to leave, his son, recovering from diphtheria, used his first outdoor walk to try to solve the vexed question of whether there really was a First Street, and had to be sent back by the cops. But Trotsky was sure that here was 'the foundry in which the fate of man is to be forged'. 'The fullest expression of our modern age,' he said, 'city of prose and fantasy, of capitalist automatism, its streets a triumph of cubism, its moral philosophy is that of the dollar. ... As I look enviously at New York – I who still think of myself as a European – I ask myself: "Will Europe be able to stand it? Will it not sink into nothing but a cemetery? And will the economic and cultural centres of gravity not shift to America?"'

He saw, as usual, the general principles, and he was dazzled by the great city. He did not see how the city was divided into nations, and some of those nations had devised their own, enclosed world – from a City Hall to a criminal style. Inside each of those nations, the story is always shaded differently.

The bakery window has sweet fat men with red sugar lips and fishes that are washed with pink. To one side, is the entrance of the Lee Family building on Mott Street, the Main Street of the Manhattan Chinatown. On the fourth floor, Man Bun Lee works behind the steel door of the family credit union. The walls flutter with orange strips that show the New Year contributions from each member, and from friends. A new shop might give money 'out of friendship to the Lees'.

Chinatown works through associations like this one: for people from the same family, or the same place. Once, they found newcomers somewhere to live, fed them free (except for a nickel for the man who washed the dishes). The old ties were strong enough to enable people to find work, and to make almost sure it would be underpaid. Other nations worked the same way. Italian barbers used to work with men from the same village, and took the lowest wages in the city as a result. It was tough to organise Jewish workers against their boss if they shared a hometown or a synagogue. Abraham Cahan used to keep on his fellow townspeople even in slack seasons, but 'this, I confess, was not without advantage to my business interests,' he wrote, 'for it afforded me a low average of wages and safeguarded against labour troubles.'

The Chinese associations could also find money for new businesses, in a trusting fashion: thirty people would chip in ten dollars a month and, when anyone needed capital, he could put in a bid for it. The highest interest won. 'We still have this operation,' Lee says. 'You just rely on honesty. There's no law to get back the loan.' Fifteen years ago, one of the associations lost its entire building when a member took away $400,000 and the courts could not insist that he paid back. In 1977, the Lee Association alone had $2 million in assets, as well as two buildings then worth another $3 million.

M.B. Lee almost died that year.

'It was Sunday night, 11 July, around 10 p.m. I went back to the restaurant and my wife called me to remind me to take back something for home. I said it was too early – why don't you come out to the restaurant and stay a while? I sat in the front table.' A young man came in and asked to talk to Lee for a minute, which was usual enough; Lee is an elder of the community. But the times were not usual at all. Nicky Louie, leader of the Ghost Shadows gang, was under arrest. Lee had denounced him, demanding stiff bail. Lee had set up a committee to resist the extortion of gangs like the Ghost Shadows – the 'red package' paid for permission to open on a gang street, the 'gifts' and 'loans' so casually demanded, and the constant threat of violence to anyone who refused. One young man in the rag trade turned down gang protection, was dragged to a basement where he ate a lighted cigarette and his fingers were smashed with guns.

Lee stood up from his front table and walked out into the street with this drifter who didn't give his name. 'I walked out with him and he starts to pull his knife and stabs me three times before I realised I was stabbed,' Lee says. 'I used my left hand to defend, that's where I got the cut. I still have the scars.' Lee was in hospital for three weeks. The Mayor of New York called, and President Carter sent his best wishes. The drifter, Allen Pang, went to jail for attempted murder. The police tried to charge Nicky Louie with assault, but could find no witnesses. 'We had formed a business committee not to pay off the extortionists, and it made this young kid mad,' Lee says. 'Because the young kids got their money from the gambling joints, and if you clean them up, the kids can't get nothing.'

Everyone knew the gangs had tried to murder Lee. It was, the paperbacks shouted, The Year of the Dragon. The notion of a youth gang was well understood anywhere in New York. 'Some people think I irritated the youth gangs but not so,' Lee says. He is most matter of fact, looking down through the line of old jade plants and the dusty windows to the rush of Mott Street below. 'I think it's the job done by some of the Lee Family Association. I suspect the man who stole the money from the association that lost its building; that person had business with the head of the Ghost Shadows.' He shrugs. 'They wanted to get rid of me, to control the whole thing. Five million, remember.'

Gangs and tongs dissolve. We glimpse a battle for institutions that outsiders do not even know, on which lives and futures depend. We open the door to Chinatown as the Chinese see it.

The Chinese were a sideshow first in New York. The 'new Circus' at the corner of Broadway and Anthony Street, June 1808, starred 'THE YOUNG CHINESE' who promised 'a variety of comic attitudes and vaultings, over his Horse in full speed'. In 1834, there was a Chinese Lady at the American Museum, 'as usual', a tiny bundle who sat among drapes and urns, sipping tea 'in native costume'. The great showman Phineas T. Barnum bought the American Museum and the Chinese Museum in 1850, and 'imported a genuine Chinese lady and her attendants to preside over his temple of curiosities. This celestial houri, who rejoices in the euphonic name of Pwan-Yekoo, is now prepared to exhibit her charming self, her curious retinue, and her fairy feet (only two and a half inches long) to an admiring and novelty-loving public.' She was the supreme curiosity, between the eight foot giant and the famous Siamese twins.

A few Chinese came to live outside the coops. Sailors jumped ship in 1847 from the three-masted junk the *Ke Ying*; they settled on the Lower East Side among the other Chinese in rooming houses on James Street, and often took Irish wives and lovers. Chinese men sold Caribbean rock candy and cigars on street corners in the 1860s; perhaps they were sugar-cane workers from Cuba who had drifted north. Lou Hoy Sing left his ship in 1862, married an Irish girl, lived on Cherry Street and one of his sons became a New York policeman.

Quimbo Appo made his money in the tea trade, a man of great charm but a mean drunk. He cut his first wife's throat, and converted in the 'Tombs' jail to what cynics called 'Tombs Christianity'. He was pardoned and sentenced again for killing a Pole. When he was released after five years, he married an Irish woman called Cork Mag, a warm creature who could not bear to see the hunger of her neighbours. She fed them with Quimbo Appo's money, but without his approval. They fought mightily. Once, she threw him bodily on to a hot stove. He drove a knife clear into her body. Finally he was sentenced to seven years for killing a neighbour, and after three years in jail, he was declared hopelessly insane. He sat silent and staring in his cell, a man quite unsettled in America: another exhibit of a Chinaman.

There were only 137 Chinese men in the whole North Atlantic region in 1870. It was a time when black labourers were grudgingly accepted, their votes courted and their names known to neighbours, but the Chinese still remained yellow shadows, whose vague menace could be exploited by politicians. Their muscle had cut the transcontinental railways; now they were out of work and biddable. There was talk that coolie labour could replace black slaves. A Massachusetts shoe firm tried to bring in Chinese workers to break the unions. New York, with fewer than a hundred Chinese, staged 'a great anti-Chinese demonstration of the working classes'; Mayor Oakey Hall denounced them as inferiors, who brought paganism, incest and sodomy to America (since none was allowed to bring a family, incest at least must be a mistake). Nativists found in the Chinaman a perfect target – 'gross, sensual, grovelling, a liar, a trickster and a cheat,' said the third volume of the *Anthropological Review*.

For a laid-off Chinese labourer in the 1870s the choice was the active hatred of Western towns or life in the cage of the Eastern cities, despised, but clustered together for protection. You expected nothing from official New York, but at least it was possible to find work in city laundries or restaurants. A man could make his whole life in a laundry, curling up on the ironing tables to sleep at night, cooking up rice and greens in the back room. In February 1883, Chinatown had its first newspaper, the short-lived *Chinese American*. Its launch issue told of a fireball falling to Earth, a Burmese elephant which died in Beijing; the front page was spiced with tales of illicit love in

Chinatown; but the advertisements all spoke of a more practical world, of washing blue and cheap laundry machines.

This New York life was only temporary, the price paid for a real life back in China. Everyone dreamed of being buried there; the worst punishment possible was to refuse a man's body passage home. After three years in a white graveyard, the bones are grubbed up and sent back in containers to Hong Kong, where they lie in a temple, neatly labelled and addressed, in case someone from the hometown can come to collect them. America admitted only a few working Chinese males, so it was in China that a man had his marriage, and perhaps made children in the few months before he had to return alone to America. Families migrate again in each generation. The grandfather of the banker Sherman Eng was born in America a hundred years ago and went back to China to get married. Eng's father immigrated to America in 1968 on quite another odyssey, from China and then from Brazil. Eng himself came to America from Hong Kong.

The grandfather and father of M.B. Lee, who once was unofficial Mayor of Chinatown, both lived in America, but Lee was raised in China and sent with his father's dollars to a high school run by the American Mission. He was offered a chance to come to America as someone else's son, because there were doctors in Hong Kong ready to fake the blood tests for a fee, but his real father wanted him to stay in China to learn enough Chinese. 'A kid comes to this country at fourteen, then twenty years later, he's a hundred per cent American, except his face and colour. You forget your own culture,' Lee says. 'You go back to get married, but you can't bring your wife to here. Maybe your wife gets pregnant in those three months and you have a boy or a girl. In three years' time you make enough money to go to China again and then for the rest of your life you may never see your wife again. Educated Chinese said they would never marry their daughters to an overseas Chinese. You make her a living widow.'

In this transitory world, even the merchants' families lived frugally, crammed up in four box rooms with the wash tub for a bath. In the 1930s, you might have bumped into Charlie Louie on the streets. He was a laundryman who wore the same black suit he owned the day he landed, had his hair cut once every three months for twenty-five cents. He lived each week off a ten-cent bag of sugar buns for breakfast, and rice and dried fish or preserved vegetable for lunch and dinner; but as he shuffled to and from his laundry, he knew the real man that he was in China. There, he had married a young woman, built a new house, bought a few acres of rice field and a wife for his cousin. He was a man of substance. And life in America was so insubstantial that, while you could always borrow the money at five per cent a month to buy a wife, it was simpler to visit the 'common women' who had come to Mott and Pell to make their living. They were easy enough to find; there were fifty boys, a few of them Chinese, acting as 'common women's dogs', hanging around to tell strangers where to find a lay, or waiting for their woman to shout down when she wanted beer or opium.

These streets seemed to ache with desire. The men lived six or eight to a room, sometimes in labyrinths of dingy corridors and rickety stairs, sometimes in cell-like spaces dug down as many as six levels below the street; they were lonely and crowded all at once. By the Depression years, there were girls who worked 'delivered goods' and went very early in the morning to the laundries; a Brooklyn man found such a woman naked on his cot and she refused to go unless he 'loved' her. He bought her off with thirty dollars. A taxi dancer sent out five hundred invitations to her Chinese 'sweethearts' for a party they were far too busy to attend. She kept the gifts. A laundry-man of fifty went nightly to the dime-a-dance palaces, where you could only talk to the women on the other side of a partition; the company of one woman was said to have cost him three laundries.

Gambling helped pass the time. The headquarters of the fan-tan syndicate were under the Joss House on Mott Street. The house gave credit, and the games were not skewed to the banker, as in Western casinos; the house took seven per cent of the winnings. There were lotteries up and down the street; the domino game of pai-gow, where you throw to make a perfect four; tze-far, in which you choose which one of thirty-six characters in a bag will best answer a most opaque riddle posted on the wall, and you win by pure luck.

The first gaming houses had men at the door to shout that the game was open, come and play, but the cops learned to recognise what 'Moi Han La!' meant. Watchmen were posted at the door to keep out whites. Professional arrestees earned two dollars each time they went quietly in a raid. There were also legendary victims. Chan Tai had been a great swell with a house in the smart suburbs and butlers, six cars with white chauffeurs, nurses for his grandchildren; but he gambled past his luck. Chinatown knew he was ruined when they saw his daughter-in-law buying ten cents worth of rice in an Italian store. It meant the Chinese had all cut off credit.

At 10 Pell Street, a dark back alley stopped at a barricaded door; if you were known, the door opened on to a wood yard, and you could climb the doubtful stairs, along a porch to a second locked door. Beyond, there was red and lacquer and smoke that lay across the stale air in layers; there were bunks with wood blocks for pillows, with maybe twenty men and women 'hitting the pipe', drawing on the sweet, spluttering drug from elaborate pipes (the best were made of lemon wood, to complement the opium smell of burning orange peel). There were waiters buying a holiday from loneliness, Irish women feeding a hunger for the drug and only occasionally a voyeur come to play with danger; serious white smokers had their own mid-town houses which, like the one on West 46th Street at Seventh Avenue, rigorously barred the Chinese. There were twenty or so places in Chinatown where you could buy opium, and a regular trade in preparing the drug from the raw gum.

In Chinatown, you could heal the emptiness of life. The streets were alive with red and gilt, with dragons and banners; it was home for the eyes. You could buy spices, clothes, use the merchants as banks, or find the future in the Joss House on Mott Street. The Joss of Chinatown is Duke Quan, a Chinese Hercules or Samson. Each supplicant stood before him and shook a prayerbox, and took advice by which numbered stick fell out – whether to buy a concubine or a laundry, which numbers to play in the street lotteries. At the better restaurants, clustered on Mott and Pell Streets, you could take Air Bladder of Eels or Sturgeon's Head, Beche de Mer or Pig's Paunches, washed down with palm root wine or white rose wine; each restaurant had a hen coop at the back with live birds, and a recess off the dining room with a cot for those who had eaten too well. Seven farms on Long Island grew winter melon and bak choy for Chinatown. In basements, the barbers cut hair and shaved without soap and practised the special craft of making up the bulk of a slow-growing pigtail with silk; each had a battery of ear tongs, ear scraper, ear picker and ear brush to complete the job.

The Chinese were separate, and therefore nameless, an agglomeration of bodies who were not quite men. Deputy Police Commissioner Carleton Simon once seriously proposed to end the street gang wars by deporting every single Chinese. The first day Louis Wing joined the board of the New York Laundry Code in the 1930s, an American lawyer asked casually if it would be all right to call him 'Charlie Chinaman'. The old bachelors had no children to push their way into the city's life; you still see them eating glumly in the rice shops and sometimes, on the street, they stand quite still in the middle of all the confusion, staring.

White visitors came to see their life of work and poverty and managed to feel a frisson of horror. They imagined a kind of criminal fairground just a cab ride away. Doyers Street, with its dog-leg shape, became known as 'the Bloody Angle'; in all America it was said to be the street where the most men had been killed. The cops shut off the arcade that ran from Doyers Street to Mott Street, so killers could not escape. Each unfamiliar place was made sinister in the imagination. The Chinese Opera House was lodged in the basement of a rooming house on Doyers Street; some 500 men could perch on the rough, wood benches, their hats on and their cigarettes lit, chatting and eating and drifting in and out. The shows unfolded for six weeks, or even six months, as slow to change as life. When the Chin family heard the current show was anti-Chin, they turned out the gaslights, broke chairs and used the legs as clubs, and battled until the cops arrived. But in the 1930s, the cops used to clear the whole theatre in mid-performance, afraid, they said, that the smoke and gongs and the shifting crowd were perfect cover for murder. Tour barkers promised trap doors, poisoned corpses, hide-outs like palaces and lethal knife-men. In the 1930s the Greyhound Bus Company maintained an 'opium den' for the tourists to see. The Joss House was open to everyone except the Chinese.

All the city knew this gaudy story: the tong wars, the civil strife of Chinatown. A 'tong' is only a society for mutual aid, from the Chinese word for 'town hall'. The Hip Sing Tong worked for sailors and labourers, and the On Leong for the merchants. But mutual aid means protection, and each major tong had its enforcers – the predecessors of the Flying Dragons for the Hip Sing Tong and the Ghost Shadows for the On Leong. Times were rough, and the best defence was other people's fears. When the tongs fell out, there began a melodrama of a war. The challenge, the *chun hung*, went up on bulletin boards, gorgeously inscribed; it traduced the birth of the enemy tong, mentioned various low animals, and ended by setting a time and a place for the final extermination of such scum. The plain red flag of the 'highbinders', the hatchetmen and gun men of the tong, was raised at tong headquarters. The quiet of expectation settled for a while. At a Bowery 'department store' guns were sold, or taken out of pawn – a lending library of Colt six-shooters, holster guns and the double action pistols that were prized above all others. The assassins went out with the guns strapped to the inside of their arms with rubber bands; they wore half a dozen shirts, and beneath that, a suit of mail or else an armour of quilted paper, bullet-proof; all that protection made the gun battles even more deadly, because only a shot to the head had any effect.

Exactly at midnight, the usual hour, the guns blazed out of nowhere. The shooting was never precise; Hip Sing's prime assassin, Mock Duck, fought with a revolver blazing in each hand and his eyes closed. The war was abruptly over when the cops arrived, and the bodies were tugged out of sight.

This was a show, whose point was to control gambling. At the turn of the century, some basement fan-tan rooms paid off the Hip Sing Tong, the organisation of sailors and labourers; but most of the action belonged to the merchants' tong, the On Leong. Mock Duck demanded half the On Leong's take and war dragged on for six years. In 1909, the matter of Sweet Flower opened the battlegrounds again. She was sixteen and lovely, bought by a tong official in San Francisco for $3,000; but that arrangement was upset by the authorities, and Sweet Flower, a free woman, married a gardener and came to live at 17 Mott Street in New York. Her first owner demanded his money back; he was a Hip Sing man. Her new husband refused; he was an On Leong man. On a smothering August day in 1909, someone broke into the apartment on Mott Street, cut Sweet Flower to death and severed her delicate fingers. On Leong demanded reparations – a roasted pig, a Chinese flag and 10,000 packages of firecrackers. The *chun hung* was written. This time, the war lasted a year; fifty tong members died. A year later, three bands of On Leong raiders laid siege to the Hip Sing headquarters and at least five people died in the erratic gunfire, including a conductor from the Erie Lackawanna railway who had been looking for souvenirs.

Ordinary law did not apply. After the bloodshed of the first tong war, the New York Court of General Sessions actually partitioned Chinatown like some grand imperial arbitrator – with Mott Street handed to On Leong, and Pell Street to Hip Sing; so that it was an American judge, Warren W. Foster, who set the territories which still apply to tong members. In the second tong war, Chinese diplomats intervened; the shaky peace was made by a committee of forty distinguished Chinese persons, appointed by the Chinese minister in Washington. In 1930, Beijing sent the first secretary of the Washington mission as a peacemaker; but the tongs would not listen, because serious money was involved – one minor tong was taking $500 a day from gambling in New York City. A foreign ambassador intervened quite matter of factly in the politics of two Manhattan streets, as though they belonged in reality to China. The police tried to prosecute senior On Leong officials for murder when a Hip Sing man was killed, although the magistrate ruled there was not 'a scintilla of suspicion of murder against these men'. The rules of war applied: a general should suffer for a wrong done to his enemy.

This Chinatown was still a place with the manners of men on their own; it was brusque, jostling, watchful. Nobody wanted to inform because the bail system would let the criminal back on the streets in a day, and he knew just where to find you. Besides, you looked after your own; to turn in a family member to the cops would mean losing face. This world needed a government.

The stairs of the China Society are broad and institutional. Grandmothers clamber up them, heads pulled down into their shoulders like tortoises. One is in stillborn tears because she can't understand where her food stamps have gone. One needs the English Secretary to translate letters from her grandchildren and tell the family news; she may not read Chinese too well, either. There are men who have no birth certificates, and know a letter from their family association or the Society will satisfy the social security clerks. There's a man who thinks the English Secretary is bound to know the name of a silk printing importer. Schoolkids say the gang youths are beating them up outside their school and the Fifth Precinct won't do anything; the English Secretary calls to make sure the cops understand the complaint. And the English Secretary, a Chinatown reporter and manager of his cousin's apartment building, does all this for $900 a month. Every two years, the job goes to a man from Toisan, the Canton district which sent out the traders and sailors who used to be the Chinatown majority. Two years later, the job goes to someone from somewhere else. It's easy to see why it gets tougher to find a Toisan person.

The China Society registered in 1884 with the Peking Imperial Government. It was six more years before it registered with the government of New York State as the 'Chinese Charitable and Benevolent Association', which is not quite the same thing. Its purpose was to bring together the organisations which were already established in Chinatown – the family societies, the societies for people from a particular place; the tongs, including the Kuomintang, whose flag used to fly above the CCBA on Mott Street and the two rival powers – the Hip Sing tong and the On Leong. The CCBA was to Mott Street what City Hall was to New York, and it was sometimes just as unclear whether it existed to serve or gouge the people. In the '20s, one President of CCBA set up house with a sweet, expensive flapper – as father and daughter, he insisted – and Society funds went missing. Another had cards printed which announced that he was the Chinese consul, much to Beijing's surprise.

A President-elect, on being told his election was 'irregular' was required to refund the bribes his rival had paid out to buy votes; because it was worth putting out $500 for even the job of office boy, which paid only fifty dollars a month. The China Society taxed Chinatown. It recorded every site where a Chinese person had a store, and, should another Chinese want to open for business there, took a fee 'for basic property right'. The Society's registers were meant to stop the Chinese competing too closely. There was a port tax of three dollars a head for any Chinese person leaving America, levied until the 1950s, and the office boy was meant to hang about the stores to see if there were rumours that anyone was leaving; 'whoever leaves New York City for China without paying the port duty,' said the rule book, 'is to be stopped at any port or railway station and fined $30'. Most transactions seemed more binding if registered with the Society, which naturally required an insurance premium or a fee. As for the charity and benevolence that had been registered with New York State, that was sometimes neglected. During the Depression, some Chinese starved to death in New York City. One man died slowly in a room directly across Mott Street from the CCBA.

Crossing the ocean changed everyone's standing. Among the laundrymen in the 1930s were men who had college degrees, who had been army officers, reporters, teachers; there was one semi-professional politician and the man who had invented the moisture blower for laundries – the same Louis Wing who was appointed to the city's laundry board. These men resented the power of the family groups and the Chinatown swells who thought of laundrymen as a 'pack of pigs'. When the city government demanded a $1,000 security bond from them in the 1930s, the laundrymen needed protection. They wanted to stop the cartoons that the white laundries displayed, which showed Chinese washermen spitting on shirts. But the CCBA did not appreciate rivals; its secretary called in twenty gunmen from the tongs to stop the speeches at the Chinese Hand Laundry Alliance. The tongs immediately understood it as a kind of treason to the powers of Chinatown.

For this is a conservative place. Over on Pell Street, Benny Ong, Uncle Seven, is a grand gentleman who makes an honoured daily progress from the office of the Hip Sing tong on Pell Street to his usual dim sum table, whose children's children's birthday parties are honoured by gifts from wise people who often give significant numbers of dollars, $660 for example. He is used to dealing with the senior cops he knew when they were still patrolmen. He remembers when detectives came into the gambling halls and looked around and announced there were no white people, which had to be some kind of violation. 'I'm going to fine you a case of Scotch,' the cop would say, and Uncle Seven sent his driver to buy a present of ten cases, to be safe.

Much has been forgotten about Uncle Seven. In the 1930s he was a foot soldier in the tong wars and served time for murder. In the 1970s, he learned farming for a while on a prison farm after incautiously bribing an honest immigration officer for early warning of raids on his gaming halls.

There is also good Peter Woo, deep in his golden age, a tubby man with stooped shoulders, whose jet black hair creeps back on his polished skull; he owns Tai Pei Liquors at 53 Mott Street, and in its basement he started the Chinatown Democratic Club because he was most interested in American politics. He would tell anyone that he campaigned for JFK. If he was known for anything, it was as an old horse-player, always in the Off Track Betting office. His school mates were startled when Federal agents raided houses in Queens and found 820 pounds of heroin there. This time, Chinatown spoke of shame. Mr Woo was one of them: an old-timer from Toisan. He sold seafood and ran a restaurant before he went into the drink business; he was a proper merchant. And now he was charged with behaving like the new people, the ones who came after the immigration laws changed in 1965, and Asians at last were no longer treated as the group who would somehow ineradicably stain America.

Chinese from all over Asia now arrive with money, set up businesses like gift shops and restaurants just to keep their money safe or to wash it clean. They have converted Mott Street to a tourist mall. In 1981, four of the six established grocery stores on Mott Street quite suddenly shut down, to be replaced by a drugstore, an ice-cream parlour, a glossier fish and vegetable market, and a fabric shop. Old-timers complain that the newcomers pay anything for buildings, and demand anything for rent. You want the right to sell your vegetables off sidewalk crates outside a fish store? $1,200 a month. You want to sell umbrellas on the sidewalk on Mott? $1,500 a month. Park Avenue is no more expensive. Zoning laws long ago froze the heart of Chinatown so that a half-million building sells here for four million. Man Bun Lee says: 'People used to think you come downtown to rob a Chinese-American, you always get something because they carry cash'; the best estimate is that Chinatown has maybe two billion dollars in the bank. Some of it is savings; mortgage officers say that $70,000 is not an unusual worth for a doorman at an unfancy building. The place is still frugal. But much of that money, the Chinatown elders say, comes from gentlemen who are covering their involvement in drug activity. Chinese criminals now control three quarters of the heroin trade in New York City. Each known dealer has a link to a Chinatown shop, like Peter Woo, or a restaurant, like Johnny Eng of the Ghost Shadows, known also as Machinegun Johnny.

The order that the CCBA once represented is now broken open. Chinatown has many dialects, and the people come from all over China, by way of Taiwan or Singapore or Hong Kong or the boats out of Hanoi or Amsterdam; the ones from Fukien go to Harlem as strong-arm protection for the fast-food places run by the ones from Malaysia, a division of labour according to place of origin. Some arrive with fortunes and skills, sometimes to stay, sometimes on a visa to run a branch of the business in New York which acts as an insurance policy if anything goes wrong at home. Some are looking for some-where, anywhere to settle; there is a Chinatown travel agency which sells mostly tickets to Belize, the erstwhile British colony in Central America. Some arrive because, by luck or forward planning, they already have family here which gives them priority on the immigration lists when the time comes to escape Hong Kong or mainland China. Or they come illegally, packed three or four into the trunk of a car that is crossing the Canadian border; the ticket costs $25,000. Anyone who actually had that kind of cash could go to a lawyer and an embassy, and have his case argued, not risk suffocation on the long run south; but the $25,000 is a notional fee, which has to be paid off in labour. 'They can work in a dishwasher job for the rest of their lives to pay off that debt,' according to James Goldman, a special agent of the Immigration Service. At least one of the 'arrangers' who plan the smuggling journeys and stock the safe houses along the way is the owner of a Mott Street restaurant.

Otherwise, 'what is now in vogue,' Goldman says, 'they go into the gangs.' Newcomers from Fukien tried to take over from Canal to Grand Streets, in the heart of Little Italy, and enough were busted to splinter their force; but they have successors like the Green Dragons of Queens. Nowadays, the headquarters of the Dong An – 'Eastern Peace', otherwise the Flying Dragons gang – is a full block to the north of Umberto's Clam House, famous for the settling of disputes among other, Italian families, and close to the social headquarters in Manhattan of the *capo di capi* himself, John Gotti. The Big Circle gang has its origins with dissident Red Guards in the People's Republic. The old business of extortion – 'dipping in the fragrant oil' – continues, and has spread out as Chinatown spreads out, but it is no longer the main business; Chinatown has changed, and is no longer so passive about those who would tax it outside the law. The gaming halls have phone bills for calls to London, Amsterdam, Hong Kong, Singapore, Dallas, the Philippines, California and even Londonderry in Northern Ireland; Amsterdam is the turntable for the Triad narcotics business, and Londonderry suggests gun-running. The game has grown. But in between the criminals and the alarms, people make lives; just as the Irish did, despite the Westies, and the Italians did, despite the Black Hand, and the Jews did despite Arnold Rothstein and the liquor bandits.

Old men dive down into basement barbers, mah jong tables on the side; younger ones prefer to lie six in a line on padded chairs, belly down, while women in blue skirts and white blouses walk their backs, balancing by bars across the ceiling. Fan-tan is too slow for the rush of the place; you go down into bare rooms to play a seven-card game like poker, highest card wins. A Chinatown waiter can play on credit on his own streets, and he has no time to travel, so there are always games; but the gangs that used to run casinos now want to run buses to Atlantic City. The real change is that the Chinatown newcomers were allowed to bring their families to America, and they can't afford to lose like the old-timers. Come the Fourth of July or Chinese New Year, men and boys go in the next door to the good sea-food restaurant on Mott, or the red-brick building on the corner of Mulberry and Bayard, both warehouses for illegal fireworks; then they stalk the sidewalks shouting out their deals. You hand over cash; you get a shopping bag, in full view. By evening, the sidewalks are red with waste confetti from the firecrackers.

Ken is back in Chinatown this summer, a rangy, big-shouldered nineteen year old, on the classic mission of an immigrant's son: to join the middle class. He is American born, *juk sing*, 'the bamboo closed at both ends' – tangled up with Chinese culture, but apart from it. He wonders what he would tell his children about China and Chinatown. 'I think,' he says, 'I would leave this to their mother.'

He grew up three blocks from Canal Street, in what used to be Little Italy, where the banners still brag 'Welcome to Historic Little Italy' but where the shopfronts have Chinese signs. Chinese kids look at the live turtle in a fish shop and say 'Mama Mia!' The family started in a fifth floor walk-up under the roof, too hot in summer and too cold in winter. They learnt from Italian neighbours how to go on rent strike; 'Chinese are quiet. But the Italians – don't ever get them mad. . . .' In time, they moved down to the first floor, to an old dentist's office with the living room still divided by a blind. 'The chair was still there when we moved in,' Ken says. 'My mother saw it.'

'The only reason we'd go out of Chinatown was to see a movie or go bowling or something like that,' he says. 'It's a place where I feel more at home. I can keep in touch with things that are going on. I was in a restaurant and word got around they had two people who had AIDS and one had died. It wasn't in the newspapers or anything. Things spread fast, especially the bad things.' When he went away to junior high school, on 21st Street, the whole idea was that he should 'get away and mix with Americans'. He was irritated most by the teachers' assumptions that 'you have to be good at math and science, because you're Chinese. The truth is, the newcomers seem good because they arrive from Hong Kong and they're put in a lower level. They just know the stuff already. It's a snap for them.'

In this world, the gangs are never too far away. The 'youth gangs' were once rather middle-aged, newcomers organised by the established tongs to protect their gambling halls and discourage others. But the tongs lost control and now the action is random. The new kids had been promised a golden mountain on Mott Street, and they found only minimal wages and a dormitory bed. 'Today, the young people got smart,' M.B. Lee says. 'They will do whatever they like to do.'

Vietnamese kids came here, knowing nothing except guns from the war in Cambodia, arriving as bona fide refugees; they work Canal Street under the name Born To Kill. BTK spend their time, like kids, among the sweets in a bakery on Lafayette, but they will shoot on the streets. In a Canal Street massage parlour they announced a stick-up and shot dead a fiftyish businessman, Jack Luy, who dared to ask why they were robbing the place. 'They have spiked hair, they look fourteen or fifteen,' Ken says. 'They look so short. You look at them and it's like a joke. And then they open their coat, and they're flashing a gun.'

The real danger from the gangs is seduction, not death. Recruiters sometimes use their fists on kids, but usually they're cruising by with available girls in flashy cars. They show a kid how to eat well and send back the bill signed 'Ghost Shadows', or how to grab cash by asking for it in multiples of 36, which every merchant knows is the significant number of the Triad criminal empires. Once involved, you can hardly escape. Informers die 'by myriads of swords'. One was found cut hundreds of times with a razor blade, and left to die on a meat hook. Another had a bullet in each eye, one in each ear and one near the mouth, because he had seen, heard and said too much. Ken is grateful that the gangs passed him by. 'Once they find out that you don't speak Chinese,' he says, 'usually they'll leave you alone.'

Ken studies business; he will break out of the routine of Chinatown. At ten in the mornings, you see the men line up to board the 'buffalo cars', mini-buses which leave Chatham Square to take waiters and cooks to restaurants that may be two, even seven hours away from the city. Once there, the men sleep in dormitories to save money, work the day round, and see their families maybe once a week, some-times only once a month. They never visit on weekends, because those are the busy restaurant days; they come home Tuesdays, when their wives must be at work. To get a job, you pay twenty dollars to register with an agency, sixty dollars if they find you work; the monthly pay, out in the Hamptons, might be $1,200 a month. It would be better yet to work in Chinatown, but that's for the settled men, not the newcomers, a dream for when you're over forty. Chinatown pay is not as good, despite the succulent tips front of house; waiters admit they sometimes hate the fish stall of white, bland faces expecting to be fed, because they are so incurably, impenetrably alien.

Then at seven in the evening, each evening, the women with their used up eyes surge through the streets. You can hardly find space on the subway platforms at the Chinatown stations; the third-floor garment factories let out the shift through iron doors, the sidewalks are crammed with the curbside vegetable sellers (tonight: cauliflowers in a skin-tight shine of celluloid, in grey-white mounds). These garment jobs are essential; the husband brings home cash, but the wife brings home health insurance for the family. Bosses like to say piecework is truly Oriental. It's convenient, since 'it's easy for my mother to come out and go back,' Ken says. 'She could pick us up from school.' But the women work for companies who often change their names, on a piecework scale that shifts like a foreign exchange; you can never be quite sure what you should be paid. Outer Queens is cheaper than the Dominican Republic. Old ladies will sew alongside you for only eighty dollars a week, out of pride in working; and also because they are determined not to register for any kind of government help which might spoil the visa chances of family members still coming to America. The machines stop, and the old ladies chatter and hiss about the newcomers. Half Chinatown's population of some 100,000 arrived in the past five years. At the bench on 41st Street, in a litter of swatches of cloth, the Chinese women understand this new migration in terms of whether they will eat, where they will get to live, a continent away.

Parents cling to their kids in Chinatown, because they hope the children will live their lives for them, since they will never have time. 'My mother would always say I could go out, even though I knew she was at home worrying. She wouldn't approve if I went out with a girl who's not Chinese. She wouldn't forbid it, but I don't think my parents would approve.' His parents tell him sometimes that they came out of horror at the Communist system, and sometimes that they did it all for him. You can see by the advertisements in the Chinese papers that the parents are big customers for computers to help their kids and VCRs to entertain them; the economy that wraps all the sparse furniture in clear plastic will always break down when it comes to the children, because if it does not work for them, then there was no point at all in the drudging and the tenements. And the children change. Ken and his parents hardly share a language any more. His father carries a pad to note down any word he does not understand. Ken speaks a little Chinese, but he cannot read or write it; 'I feel bad about it sometimes,' he says.

The older people want to help. A student sees his father in the garden, wearing pyjamas as in the old country; he is embarrassed. He asks his father to do as they do in America. The next day, he looks out and there, between the melon vines, is his father in pyjamas; but now the knees are shredded, as Americans shred the knees of their blue jeans.

The father looks up for approval.

Black slaves built the wagon road to Harlem, when the village was first settled in 1658. But Harlem was not black until a real estate boom collapsed in 1902 and frightened landlords began renting the older buildings, rougher tenements. Harlem had been charming blondes singing lieder to the zither, or so the sentimental memoirists remembered. But blacks always came in when whites had been distressed by new railroads, rough newcomers or the cost of mortgages; 'only after a house' had a 'bad name', according to Pastor R.F. Hurley, would the owners allow it to be rented to 'coloured tenants'. A murder at 31 West 133rd in 1905 pushed out the white tenantry, but opened two blocks to African-Americans. In Greenwich Village, they felt under pressure from newcomers; there was no love between blacks and Italians, or 'chattering foreigners' in general. There were race riots in the Tenderloin and on San Juan Hill. The building of Penn Station pushed blacks out of the '30s in Manhattan. Harlem was their refuge.

Any white group – Jews, for example – was divided up by class and origin and income, so that Guggenheims did not expect to live on the Lower East Side; but blacks were blacks before anything else. One man wanted an apartment on Central Park West in 1901, and the white residents formed a West Side Improvement Association to keep him out. The same attitude trapped blacks in the city itself; the next generations could not expect to escape to the suburbs. The *New York Times* in 1903 was reporting the troubles of respectable black families in neighbourhoods where there were 'desperadoes, gamblers and moral lepers'. Rents were higher for black tenants – by ten to thirty per cent – and families took in more boarders to survive. The overcrowding bred a 'peculiar susceptibility' to tuberculosis. In all this calamity, blacks were dispersed through the city. In Harlem, they could make their stand.

Into this black city came two streams of migration. One was driven north by the boll weevil, by flood and drought and the various natural disasters of 1915 and 1916 that made the already precarious life of a sharecropper in the South quite untenable. In the 1920s black life became city life, not rural struggles. 'Harlem became the symbol of liberty and the Promised Land to Negroes everywhere,' wrote the Reverend Dr Adam Clayton Powell Senior. Puerto Ricans also came; by 1930, there were some 45,000 concentrated in East Harlem, and the barrio was forming. Other West Indians came, the 'Jews of the race', denounced as clannish, pushy, crafty, shouted down in the streets as 'King Mon', 'cockney', 'ring-tail'. A Harlem song says that 'When a monkey-chaser dies/ Don't need no undertaker/ Just throw him in de Harlem River/ He'll float back to Jamaica.' They came up easily to New York under the quotas for their 'mother countries', which were almost never filled. It was a rite of passage for Bahamian men to come up to Harlem, to hear the music and drink the wine and sleep out in Central Park.

But West Indian kids went in awe of their parents, West Indian men did nothing in the house, and West Indians were considered strait-laced, prim and all too sexually proper; they were outsiders. Those from French islands had Bastille Day dances, from British islands held coronation balls, from Danish islands kept the picture of the King of Denmark in their homes. Former British subjects sometimes went to the British Consul if they faced trouble in America. The Pullman Company, which employed only black conductors, would not employ West Indians 'because of their refusal to accept insults from passengers quietly'. Those who had come up from the South in their own country, and those who had come from the islands, were separate kinds. Radio shows discussed 'Intra-Race Relations in Harlem'.

Rudolph Fisher has his Southern innocent think in *City of Refuge*: 'In Harlem black was white. You had rights that could not be denied you; you had privileges, protected by law. And you had money. Everybody in Harlem had money.' The innocent sees a black traffic cop bawling out a white driver, and he understands at once: 'Black might be white, but it couldn't be that white.'

Marcus Mosiah Garvey came up from Jamaica, 'a little sawed-off, hammered-down black man' who preached pride in an African heritage and a future in Africa. He dreamed of the black man's government, his king and kingdom, his President, his country, and his ambassador, his army, his navy, his men of big affairs. By the end of 1918 he could sweep five thousand listeners at a time into his dream, in halls like the Palace Casino.

But Garveyites were outlaws to the respectable black bourgeoisie, to the reformers who wanted caution, and Garvey himself was under constant watch by the ever-white J. Edgar Hoover. He founded the Black Star Line, a ramshackle shipping company with a single, exhausted ship, whose colours – red, black and green – were later adopted as the colours of the 'Negro nation'. And he began to weave into his fascistical dreams the real divisions within the Harlem nation. He talked about skin colour, the way power seemed drawn to those with lighter black skins; he called a black rival a 'white man' and was sued successfully for libel. He was a West Indian, ridiculed by the established American blacks, who in turn attacked the likes of W.E.B. Dubois, the scholar and reformer, as that 'cross-breed, Dutch-French-Negro editor' who deserved a 'good horsewhipping'. He said he thought the Ku Klux Klan more honest than the National Association for the Advancement of Coloured People. He thought it reasonable that, until his perfect state could be established, blacks should work for a little less than white men, to keep the goodwill of employers. He constructed an identity which depended on blacks facing frontiers that they could never cross.

Garvey's revolution was all flags and bombast, no answer to a city where businesses, E. Franklin Frazier wrote, divided into two kinds: 'Those that employ Negroes in menial positions and those that employ no Negroes at all.' The moderate, polite reformers also had dubious tactics. They announced a Renaissance in Harlem which would justify blacks to the white world. It would be made by the 'talented Tenth' of all black Americans and a reasonable claim on attention; 'civil rights by copyright,' as David Levering Lewis writes. Almost all of them, except perhaps Langston Hughes, wanted high Negro Art and the singing of spirituals, but looked down on the blues and on jazz. They liked Fletcher Henderson's Rainbow Orchestra because 'the funkiness and raucousness of jazz dissipated' under his direction, and whites knew how to listen. Jazz, on the other hand, was born out of a meeting of players and listeners; it was audacious, sensational and even salacious, not a proper version of black life. Claude McKay in *Home to Harlem* tells how the bands sounded out the end of the work day and a release from the crowded rooms, the menial work of Harlem. 'The first notes fell out like a general clapping for merrymaking and chased the dancers running, sliding, shuffling, trotting to the floor. Little girls energetically chewing Spearmint and showing all their teeth dashed out on the floor and started shivering amorously, itching for their partners to come. Some lads were quickly on their feet, grinning gaily and improvising new steps with snapping of fingers while their girls were sucking up the last of their creme de menthe. The floor was large and smooth enough for anything.'

Zora Neale Hurston complained that the 'Niggerati', the grand, downtown ambassadors of the black mind, wanted to found a Negro Theatre when the real black theatre already existed – not where respectable whites could find it ('A creature with a white head and Negro feet struts the metropolitan boards') but out in the cabarets and jooks, the unorderly places whose name speaks of stabbing and screwing. 'Butter Beans and Susie, Bo-Jangles and Snake Hips are the only performers of the real Negro school it has ever been my pleasure to behold in New York.'

You could tell the power of such dance and such music because it alarmed respectable people; but it also alarmed the 'Talented Tenth'. They wanted a white-face Harlem, and they did not connect with the extraordinary life down in the streets. They did not quite see that the music, the night-time abandon of Harlem was what pulled outsiders uptown, chasing gin in the 'buffet flats' and 'barrel houses', or cocaine, or simply a hell-tickling horn, or a hot night with a fine woman or, of course, a fine man. 'It is a house of assignation . . . this black city,' Eric Walrond wrote in the black journal *The Messenger*. And something was missing in this capital of black America: the machinery by which blacks could make their own future, even if whites decided not to approve the Renaissance. New York was the only major American city which did not have one single black-owned bank.

The Depression came and Harlem's glory faded. If you were poor and in the South, you still had few other places to go, but in Harlem the median family income had dropped by almost half between 1929 and 1932. The flood of newcomers did not stop, newcomers who had no hope of work, who had been sidelined by the schools in the South and could not now catch up. White immigrants used to have a sense of loyalty to the place from which they came, and the people from it; they had networks which found jobs and money and homes. Blacks were running from the impossibility of a sharecropper's life, and sometimes from the southern cities in which they had taken brief refuge before coming north. When they hit New York, they were nothing except black. Jews could see how to rise within the needle trades that they dominated, Italians in the construction business, but blacks were reading the newspaper job advertisements and scrabbling for anything on offer from anyone. A black fruitseller says the price went up as he walked into the wholesale fruit market. A guitarist in a Harlem band had once tried to work at a defence plant, but the personnel office told him 'no Negro can be a shipping clerk' and he was told to apply for a porter's job. A marine engineer from the Caribbean ended up working as a handyman. 'No, no, if you were a black man, you couldn't get a job as an engineer in this place here,' he says. 'You want them to kill you? That was a white-man job. Do you think that you could go near an electrician's shop? Do you think that you could go near a bricklayer's job? They kill you.'

You wonder why there was herb juice to cure your consumption, powders to keep the wife home at night, potent powders, blessed handkerchiefs, 'cockroach rum' and signs which read: 'Jesus Is The Doctor. Services on Sunday.' Nothing more rational worked, or could be afforded. The best hope was miracles, or the pride that comes from stepping away from Satan. 'The devil runs every theatre,' a black pastor preached. 'He collects a tax on the souls of men and robs them of their seats in Heaven.' Eternal rest was the next good thing that could happen. Even W.E.B. Dubois himself, who so wanted to prove the black genius to the white world, was writing in 1934 that 'it will be necessary to our own survival and a step toward the ultimate breaking down of barriers, to increase by voluntary action our separation from our fellow men.' If nothing else worked, perhaps frontiers might.

Bishop Amiru Al-Minin Sufi Abdul Hamid, a huge and bearded man, broke out of his Universal Holy Temple of Tranquility to march against any white business that dared to discriminate by race in Harlem. Jewish merchants were alarmed, because this was the 1930s and they said that Hamid had praised Hitler. The merchants sponsored inter-racial banquets at which the decorous of Harlem denounced Hamid's tactics, including his willingness to shake down merchants of his own race for contributions to his Negro Industrial and Clerical Alliance. George Baker, alias Father Divine, mentioned to his congregations that he was God; a judge who dared sentence him as a public nuisance died suddenly ('I hated to do it,' the Father said), a rival and glorious preacher George Wilson Becton left this world, and Father Divine's career was certain. He took his 'debaucherated' flock and he promised to retake, reincarnate, reproduce, reiterate and rematerialise their intelligence, skills and ability. 'I reincarnate them,' he declared. As religious doctrine goes, it was not especially opaque. He bought Marcus Garvey's *Negro World* and filled it with news of his fifteen kingdoms, all the way from California to Harlem. Women flocked to him, surrendered all, and financed a fleet of Cadillacs and a mansion and a chain of hostels and cafeterias where a black person could live and eat for almost nothing, a kind of Harlem Heaven. The Sufi and the Father came together before a gigantic rally at Rockland Palace to shout against discrimination in housing and hiring. And in face of the powers of Harlem, of God and the Bishop, nothing changed at all.

In almost half of Harlem families, nobody was working. But in only nine per cent of them was anyone able to find a Federal relief job. Harlem General Hospital had 273 beds for 200,000 people. Two black mothers and two black babies died for every one white mother and white baby. Out of this time came the organisation known as the Nation of Islam, calling for the total separation of black and white America, and the notion of Haile Selassie as a hero, and a rage which was prepared to use steel and fire inside Harlem against the white merchants and white property, against foreigners in a promised land. When the rage came first in 1935, on a slight provocation, it took down two million dollars' worth of property; and it came again and again. Some people chafed bloodily inside their frontier.

One side of Eastern Parkway in Brooklyn, there are bright painted bars and vivid shops and signs in Spanish, and the kids on the streets have flounces and blue jeans, and there is the sometimes blare of a car that is stuck about with speakers and louder than a concert; the faces are black and tan. Cross the highway, and the world seems for a moment to fade. The signs are plain. There are silver menorahs in the shop windows, and pictures of the Lubavitcher Rebbe – the spiritual leader, the worldly focus of this nation of Hasidim, the most pious and sometimes the most joyful of Jews. He has a fine white beard and awful, understanding eyes, but they are turned aside. There's a joke about the Rebbe's followers in this part of Brooklyn: 'How many Lubavitchers does it take to change a light bulb?' 'Two. One to change the bulb, the other to write the Rebbe about it.'

Some frontiers are chosen. The Hasidim carry theirs with them.

Pale, white, serious faces look far away from strangers, as though denying them. If you live locally, as many blacks and Puerto Ricans do, it's hard not to take offence at your own persistent invisibility. The world ends for the Hasidim where the last Hasid lives on a street; the windows are shuttered and blinded, not to see out unnecessarily and not to be seen. The women wear wigs of dead auburn nylon, not meant at all to look like hair which might arouse the men, and they are covered scrupulously. Husbands and wives do not touch in public. In the narrow grocery stores, customers twist to avoid contact. The men have beards and ringlets, wide hats crammed on their heads, and coats and kaftans that are long and black. There is a whole hierarchy of the devout, from the double-breasted dark suit that is buttoned from right to left, by way of the beards and side-locks, the *kapote* overcoat, the *shtreimel* sable hat, the *bekecher* which is the long silk coat with pockets in the back, up to the Rebbe himself who wears slipper-like *shich* and white knee socks called *zocken*. A man is judged by his holiness, and his standing is spelled out wherever he goes; as it once was in the tiny town of Lubavitch in Byelorussia.

The late Lubavitcher Rebbe came to America in 1940, fleeing the prospect of annihilation in Eastern Europe, and bringing his 'court' of followers; just as the Bobover Hasidim came, and the Satmarers who now live in Williamsburg, down by the Brooklyn Bridge. The Lubavitchers settled very soon in Crown Heights, and they have stayed ever since – even when other Orthodox Jews were complaining of the 'incompatible' newcomers, black and Hispanic, all around them, and feeling pushed out of their old neighbourhoods and resenting the way the newcomers seemed to be rewarded as a minority while the holy Jews, a tinier minority, could not pull in the city and Federal grants. The Lubavitchers stayed because the Rebbe told them to. Perhaps he had been moved on much too often in his life; his father was imprisoned and then exiled by the NKVD in Kazakhstan. But he certainly said there was no reason to run from useless fears, and no reason to destroy a community and risk its dissipation in some suburb and he said that in Jewish law other communities had to help the Lubavitchers stay in their chosen, stable place. Middle-aged and older people could hardly find the money to change their lives. It seemed as though the rest of Brooklyn was seized by white panic, but this particular nation, now 25,000 strong, stayed put.

This day, the men flock like starlings to the hearse which will carry away a cousin of the Rebbe for burial in Israel. Each carries the big-lettered Hebrew texts on whose pages the characters seem carved. There is a rumour that the Rebbe himself may appear at a doorway, and the flock darts away quickly for a sight of him; but he is not there, and they come back raggedly to the cream-coloured apartment house that is now their synagogue. They put the body into the hearse with a kind of yearning. From a window above, Rabbi Yehuda Krinsky watches. 'A young lady in her thirties died. A child of seven. An old man of eighty-six killed by an automobile accident, going to a function,' the rabbi says. 'I was myself astonished at this happening in a week, a week and a half. Perhaps we should be more charitable, improve our ways. Did we do something bad? Did we hurt somebody?' There will be discussion on what the deaths may mean, and what this community should do, because nothing is without significance.

The colourlessness of their world, its run-down look and the sunless faces is an outsider's illusion; to the Hasidim, everything has a soul, and there is a bit of the light of God in the leaf of a tree. They live with peculiar and mystic wonders; their children still read the stories about the Golem, the clay superhero of the ghetto, a story that even conservative Jews find quaint. But they also maintain Jewish law, they say, and live as a Jew should live. Their table is something like an altar. A Hasid seeks to 'sanctify his life and sanctify the world around him, whatever that surrounding may be,' the rabbi says.

The streets are calm, as though they are defended. It has not always been this way. Go back to 1970, and you find blacks and Jews squabbling over the Crown Heights poverty programmes. A Jewish anti-poverty worker is assaulted, the Crown Heights Jewish Community Council is bombed. On Yom Kippur, the Lubavitchers heard how fifty Puerto Rican men and boys had broken up the most holy services of the year at a tiny, unmarked single-storey synagogue in Boro Park which looked for all the world like some small factory. Hasidim patrols went after Hispanic men, and Hispanic men tipped garbage cans at Hasidim.

The different Hasidic courts had their own rivalries, and sometimes fist-fights over them, and also their own strategies. In 1973, the Satmarers were demanding Yiddish street signs and Yiddish civil service exams, which seemed to them the first logical stage in their claim of equality; but to outsiders, it seemed odd and arrogant. The city was being asked to support their taste for separation. An old Jewish plumber was stabbed in the chest and belly as he went home after Sabbath services in Boro Park, and suddenly hundreds of Hasidim invaded the local police station, screaming, punching, swinging clubs and hurling rocks, gutting the filing cabinets and scattering the papers of a whole bureaucracy, pink, blue, yellow and red, over the floor in a blind anger at the goyim for allowing Irving Sussman to die. Now Hasidim complain that incidents on their streets, when their security patrols have clashed with blacks for example, are over-reported and made too significant; but in this case, they invested a miserable city crime with their own huge significance. The Hasidim had attacked the cops, one said, because as Holocaust survivors they naturally thought they were facing storm-troopers. Irving Sussman, it turned out, was stabbed by a bunch of Hispanics who had spent the night robbing Hispanics, blacks, Italians before they came to a Hasid.

A world view so utterly different from the secular city, from secular or even Reform Jews, could seem profoundly skewed; but it was ordinary enough in the confrontational politics of the 1960s. Blacks and Puerto Ricans and the newcomers in Brooklyn ran up against the stubbornness of the Hasidim, and each side attributed powers and menaces to the other. In Crown Heights, the long-established blacks resented the new Jews in their midst; the old ones, they considered, had been friends. A black contractor was killed by cops, and the community went to protest outside Lubavitcher headquarters, as though somehow the Hasidim were responsible for what the police did. Hasidic patrols began to stop and question blacks on the streets; seven blacks went to the assistant minister of a church on Atlantic Avenue to complain they had been beaten because they would not let the patrols check their identity.

There were disputes over city money used for housing, when blacks claimed that a Lubavitch landlord had simply taken away the most basic services because he wanted to let only to his fellow Hasidim. Even though there was little or no competition for work, there was competition for city and Federal money, and for housing, and for streets which worked to the manners of one group or the other. The bigots of the Jewish Defence League resented the way, as they saw it, the city was being handed over to blacks and Hispanics. The middle-class and professional blacks of Crown Heights resented the way the Hasidim took no interest in them, the way the physical community had acquired internal frontiers which were unofficially policed. They somehow did not notice that there were sometimes blacks in the patrols.

But the Hasidim stayed, and the blacks stayed, edgily together. Anywhere the Hasidim congregate, there's pressure on property prices because they want to live within a few streets of each other, and the rest of the community may feel as though they were being displaced; it can never be an entirely easy relationship. For the Hasidim live in a world which only partly coincides with the secular world; they would be monks and nuns if Judaism approved of removal from the mundane. There are few New York sights more striking than the black-coated, bearded Hasidim walking the diamond block on 47th Street, their heavy cases full of glitter, their negotiations on the street, their messengers who carry off Jiffy bags of jewels to the nearest post office and are almost never intercepted. Their clothes are the clothes of the Poles and Russians who were once their overlords, a compromise between looking ordinary in eighteenth-century Europe and needing to keep the head covered in God's sight. They dress in order to know always who they are, and to be protected against sin by the knowledge; it sometimes disconcerts other Jews that once the men with beards were pious rabbis, and now they may drive trucks. Their manners are quite separate; it's hard for anyone who is not a Hasid or at least an Orthodox Jew to do serious business in diamonds because trust goes with the whole identity. They separate the sexes, when the law requires them to be equal. Their marriages are often arranged; 'to see that people are compatible. Some people are materialistic,' the rabbi says. It matters that a bride has no relations married to gentiles, and no heretics in the family. Rabbi Chaim Stauber, who runs a mental health clinic among the Satmar Hasidim of Williamsburg, has told of parents who go out walking late at night with their retarded children so that nobody will see. Mental sickness is close to sin, and it throws doubt on whether the child's sisters can marry.

They have hardly anything to do with gentiles because their life is too absorbed in the Law and their faith, in a society which still talks politely about assimilation. There are a few Lubavitcher doctors and dentists, one woman who is an attorney and one in public relations, and a Hasid who teaches at Columbia University 'with a black beard down to here,' Rabbi Krinsky says; the Lubavitcher Rebbe himself was at the University of Berlin and the Sorbonne, and has a degree in engineering. But that only gives him special knowledge when he advises against college for most Hasidim, on the grounds that colleges teach heresy and mix the sexes. Besides, the Hasidim do not need degrees. Mostly, they work as 'operators', which is a rag trade term, or in the diamond business; work is not the point of life, as long as a man has enough for charity. Or else they serve as a kind of conscience to the Jewish community of New York, which not every Jew appreciates.

The law of kosher is precise; there is room for worry about each detail. To avoid the sin of gossip, a good Lubavitcher wife will ring the Maimonides hotline while cooking to hear the teachings of the day. The hardware stores have water pots between the stacks of boxes, to serve as a ritual bath for any new forks or plates or pans that might not have been made within the Law. The Hasidim's exactness holds up much of their economy; they are trusted by other Jews. For who else knows if the egg noodles are made from eggs without blood, or the sugar and salt are unspoiled by substances which are *hometz* – grain exposed to water for more than eighteen minutes – or if the person who says so is reliable? The truly observant have *hashash*, exquisite anxieties, that flour may contain moths, which requires a special sifter. They must be concerned that linen and wool do not mix, which requires a special laboratory. They would rather buy the round matzoh from D. & T. Shmura Bakery in Crown Heights, an unmarked storefront which produces unleavened bread from wheat cut in Hasidic fields, ground in a Hasidic mill, mixed for not a second more than eighteen minutes and baked at 1,000 degrees for only thirty seconds. They need the Frig-O-Matic Sabbath Zeiger, which turns the refrigerator motor on and off automatically so that no human accidentally turns on the power by opening the door. All these things are expensive. Between the demands of the Law, and the size of Hasidic families – five or six children is common and the community will help support them all – poverty begins in Crown Heights below twice the annual income of some other communities.

The Lubavitchers are not the extreme of the Hasidim. The Satmar-ers in Williamsburg close themselves off; the Lubavitchers reach out to other Jews, teaching and showing the Law. On Broadway just before Sabbath, the Mitzvah Tank goes by (a *mitzvah* is a blessing), in a roar of music and megaphoned reminders to be home by sundown. Lubavitch families bring strangers to Sabbath, to show the power of the Jewish rituals. Satmar rabbis put up posters which warn: 'Satan has put on different clothes to confuse the people with a new machine which calls itself video.' Lubavitch uses satellite link-ups, continent to continent, to show the lighting of the Hannukah menorah. 'Our children speak Yiddish first,' a man from Satmar says. 'Not until five do they learn English. Our children do not communicate with the outside world. They see no TV, read no newspapers. Yiddish is the Mama Loshen, the mother tongue, and that is all they need in our community.' The Lubavitchers talk to outsiders, patient as Rabbi Krinsky in his office overlooking the dark-coated men who are still milling there, and lining the synagogue stairs. The Satmarers are silent, except when the scandal is too loud to be suppressed. Their community is notoriously divided, over just how much of a blasphemy the state of Israel may be, over whether to support the late Rebbe's widow or his successor; gates have been torn from synagogues, cars burned and men stabbed in that dispute. There is even a Satmar version of a supermarket tabloid, edited by Chaim Shaulson. A computer technician, same height, same Hasidic dress, walked out of Shaulson's office and was stabbed, pulled into a car and beaten and thrown back to the street shouting, 'I'm not Shaulson.' It seems Shaulson had written about where charity funds really go, and discussed the dissent within Satmar. He has also been indicted for taking cash from the Grand Rebbe's secretary – $50,000 for stopping the flow of disagreeable stories.

Such stories shout out of these closed communities, making them for a moment seem ordinary, just like the rest of the texture of the city; but lives cannot be reduced to occasional scandal, not on any side of the city's frontiers. The men who cluster at the Eastern Parkway synagogue are there for remarkable reasons, as followers of the Rebbe who has, in Rabbi Krinsky's words, 'done so much to soothe the ache and pain of a wounded people'. They do not think of assmiliating; a Jew who has assimilated is a painful sight to the rabbi. They celebrate their particular ways in a city full of such particular communities, not all of them as easily marked out. Some of the energy of the city, its full life, is the contrast and sometimes the clash of these nations. Much of its politics is about keeping the frontiers calm.

In their own nation, the Lubavitcher end the annual cycle of reading the Torah. The men in their best sable hats and their fine silken kaftans dance out in the street and circle the synagogue, faces alive with wine and vodka and something much more. One thing the frontiers protect, most surprisingly, is joy.

4
AUDITION CITY

SOMETHING CHANGED THE day Colette unwrapped. Her apartment on Pearl Street was swags and drapes, all of it; it was a pink, billowing, romantic world stuck about with figures and devices: her art, and also where she lived. Colette is a performance artist, a small woman from Tunis who presents herself as a porcelain doll, boxed and photographed and always wrapped in ribbon and chiffon. But she unwrapped in the middle of the eighties, and sold the wrappings; she ended the performance, and went to Germany. All that was left of a heroic work, where the art and the life were the same thing, was memory. And it was Colette who, for a performance at a downtown club called Area, hung a banner with the motto of the age: 'FUCK ART,' it said. 'LET'S DANCE.'

Everyone did: preppies, druggies, straight, gay, nouveaux, ancients, gargoyles who edited fashion magazines and movie executives and frockmakers and waiters. They came downtown to visit a different life, something possible only in a city like New York where voyeurs are taken for granted; they fed on the energy, the fantasy of the kids. Everyone was an 'artist', which is a style of life, even if they did not make art; 'artists' are daring, energetic, full of life and defiance, shamans and revolutionaries, or so the myth says. There was also sex. The usual social barriers were irrelevant in some meat-market sex club or some arty dance palace, which also meant they were never threatened. You could go visit the anarchs in their Bohemia. The point of the place was to go too far, which is a tradition. The difference was that a Victorian Bohemia was shocking for unwed mothers, men who did not have careers; in the 1970s, it took cross-dressing, hog-tranquilliser and fist-fucking. But there was also an element of play, bad children breaking rules. Outlaw parties began. There was the party on a hulk of a boat that came in, black and lightless, to a pier by the meat market; some of us stayed in a speedboat behind, having seen the same ship sink a year before. Annie Flanders' birthday party on the Williamsburg Bridge was almost a success, until the cops saw it on the eleven o'clock news.

All this was famous, part of the story of New York. Crowds lined up before the doors of clubs to be judged and, if approved, admitted. Midwestern teenagers wondered if they would pass the door at Studio 54, and see for themselves the man in the moon with a coke spoon over the dance floor. Rudolf, a Berliner who ran Danceteria and, later, a club called Mars in the meat market, stands outside to cast the evening, worrying on cold nights that red noses made it difficult to judge who is fabulous enough; 'I wouldn't have the heart,' said one of his old associates. 'That's why you hire sadists called doormen.' A club called M.K. offered a window from which insiders could look down on the waiting mob; but no mob came. At Underground, a Union Square club, bouncers pushed a man out after a fist fight with a man in a red leather jacket. 'Hey, do you want to get me shot?' he said. Minutes later, he was still trying to scramble back when the man in red pulled out a 9mm semi-automatic pistol and started firing into the knot of people waiting to get into the club; but the doormen were implacable, their judgement final.

It was shocking when Colette unwrapped. She was leaving a city where so many Bohemias leave traces, where there was an art community and a social role for the artist and even the artist-doll; where the myth of an artist's life intersects with money and a market. Of course, she left just as downtown began to fade. Sex was no longer play, after AIDS. Money felt the need for walls and protection. Drugs roughed up the city streets, and made dangerous even the simple job of towing the cars parked illegally at a disco. The crowds at club doors needed police escorts. But New York was still the obligatory city for actors, artists, writers, a city big enough to sustain both a market in talent and a myth of seriousness. When you lie in bed dreaming of being a star, you know which plane to catch.

Even the city's manners are like auditions: a competition. Nice, middle-class couples, all dressed up in credit, go before co-op boards to argue why they should be allowed to buy an apartment. The brushed and bright accountants and brokers and lawyers and bankers all storm purposefully in a cloud of health and fear, never once letting up on selling themselves to the world. A new therapist practises the right smile, the right manner, for the first private client to come through the all too expensive door. Very young girls from Tennessee are learning to smile for *Vogue*. At certain restaurants you audition for the dining room, and the ones who are not called all line the bar, believing the maitre d' when he says, 'Just five minutes.' Kids in black, faces peaked, carry portfolios trailing to the ground. An art world posse at a miniature golf course, 21st Street, tees off through gorillas and gazebos, with one of their number being scrutinised. Cleaning ladies, whose names are glued to lamp-posts, wait for the call-back. At Bergdorf Goodman on a Tuesday, the buyers will look at anything designers bring in; everyone in the trade knows Calvin Klein started that way. In the Belasco Room, upstairs at Sardi's, actors on a line of little red and gilt chairs read a play before the author, his friends, and, they hope, the Money; but nobody knows what the Money looks like. A woman enters with huge henna'd hair; we hope. At the gym, the farm boy auditions well enough to be some lady's private trainer, and a bit more; he has a weekly treat, he says, shining with pride. 'Shit,' he says. 'She sends me to the chiropractor.'

On corners in Bedford-Stuyvesant, men wait in the early morning for work: the Haitians, the Nicaraguans complain, get chosen first. You stand there, anonymous muscle, hoping that this day there will be a labouring job, and that the foreman will choose you; you can only wait. In the 1930s, on Stone and Pitkin Avenues in Brownsville, there were four different corners where the men waited, one for carpenters, one for bricklayers and so forth; they were known as the *beerzha*, which is Yiddish for slave market. Sundays, the men went out early and were there until the afternoon, just keeping in touch with the bosses. Anne Filardo says: 'My mother used to say that my father's funeral would be postponed because the cortège would have to go by the *beerzha*.'

On Burnside in the Bronx, the black women used to stand waiting for house-cleaning jobs, and the white women would drive by. 'What they would look for,' Geraldine Miller says, 'is the ones with the most scarred knees, the ones who had crawled around on their knees the most.'

Longshoremen waited at seven before the aluminium doors of the union halls and pushed through for the shape-up, some with tooth-picks behind the ear to show they would pay the boss to work, sometimes so many that the stevedores had no way to choose. 'He took a handful of cheques,' Sam Madell remembers, 'and he threw them out among the crowd. The longshoremen were pushing each other around and fighting with each other to pick up a cheque.' Get sunburned on a holiday, and the boss would turn you down as inefficient; play softball and the boss said he'd paid for that energy. From 1966, the men with work were called by telephone, and only those without work had to go to the shape-up. Now, the system is computerised and the shape-up is gone. 'But if you're sitting at home waiting for a phone call, you don't know who gets hired,' Wesley Shipman says. 'They're turning this job into a factory job, and it never was that,' Peter Bell says. 'Guys hate it.'

Audition City.

The Music Building stands on a sticky, broken block of Eighth Avenue, looking like another pile of offices and sweat-shops with a deli down below. You pass a black-painted chimney of a corridor, and rise in a matte black elevator that goes too quickly, so the fifth floor chords are still chiming when you reach the tenth. MALE ROCK VOCALIST WANTS WORK RANGE CLEAN POWER PROFESSIONAL ONLY, a sticker says. On each floor, the rooms are twenty feet by twenty, with doors like strong-rooms; inside, the speakers are huge black blocks jumbled between padded walls and nuts, rugs, sawdust, nests and rushes of wire and a cage on wheels. Gyda says, 'Gross, you could put a human in there.' Gyda is auditioning today: Gyda Gash. Gyda is a real Norwegian name, and Gash, she says, 'is made up'. She's in long Spandex shorts, a purple top over a tight Gothic belly, suspenders marked with skulls and bones, a tattoo, and a peaked cap marked SNAKEBITE crammed on to hair which starts powder blonde and goes abruptly red. She's been playing and writing with an ex-boyfriend 'but for the past month nothing's been happening. I get depressed if I don't play. I used to be like the Cycle Sluts – sing back-up, in sessions – but I always wanted to play. I need to play.'

The room's airless, but if you throw up the grey windows, the whole fifth floor comes in like friends. The microphones smell of beer. On week-ends, and Friday night, Jennifer Mezzacappa and Lisa Greco have the room to practise; they're going to be Shebite, or Cool Whip, but the name's not yet settled. They need a bass. 'Someone,' Gyda says, 'put a bass guitar in my hand.' They start singing that old, raucous Nancy Sinatra number about boots, and all the walking they are going to do; Gyda roars it. Lisa says to Jennifer: 'She's hip, she's loose.' Jennifer says to Lisa: 'I like her.' Gyda moves on to the next audition.

'I'm jealous. I don't mind saying it.' Jennifer has a boyfriend who plays in a group with its own rehearsal space, good equipment, and a line of gigs. She has three brothers, all musicians; she got an electric guitar at twenty-four when her youngest brother got his. She's feisty, small, pretty, in levis, pink high-tops, a haltertop until 'my guitar is sticking to my skin. Gross.' She carries school notebooks with her own notation for music and lyrics; she writes punkish songs, for bellowing, 'anti-men,' she says. Lisa was a dancer and choreographer until she had eye trouble, and now she can't quite bring herself to go look for the better waitressing job she knows she needs. Jennifer used to be a secretary at *Business Week*, and now she is office manager at a firm that makes expensive drapes. 'I am,' she says, 'moving into sales.' But they have this other wild, autonomous life.

They've been this route before, Lisa on drums, Jennifer playing lead guitar in a group with two other women called Charity Ball. Their picture is in the deli downstairs, a dark-haired foursome who aren't quite elegant, yet. But their singer bawled for six months and had no voice left; she would not take voice lessons and she had some sudden physical disability which meant she could not play guitar. The bassist turned up for a football crowd in construction boots, torn jeans and a T-shirt, under a week's grime; she believed in political statements. Neither one turned up for a Cat Club gig which Jennifer had begged from the manager, calling and smiling daily. Charity Ball was dead.

They liked playing Long Island dive bars, local and friendly, four sets a night. 'At the fourth set, I was cooking. I was doing things I hadn't even thought of doing. But you have to do cover tunes, you can't do your own tunes. It's more prestigious in New York,' Jennifer says. 'You want to play CBs because everybody – Blondie, Talking Heads – was discovered at CBs.' The reality is waiting two years for a gig somewhere like the Bottom Line, off Washington Square, then having the manager call one evening to ask if you have a 'following' for Tuesday at midnight. Lisa says, 'Clubs have to pay the rent, they want you when you have a following. But your friends are artists and musicians and they can't go every time you play. They can't pay the cover and the drinks. But you bring in a hundred and fifty friends, the clubs want you.' One bad night, the set rolled on for two hours more than it should, and they came back to the Music Building to find it locked. They sat out on the sidewalk, drum kit and guitars around them, with their roadie, a fifty-year-old in a frock called Laverne, or Auntie Roadie. They waited and waited, with all the shadows.

They wait now for Astrid. She's Spanish, a 'perfect musician', but she changes things and re-arranges things and she can't stand when Jennifer's chords are not precise and clean. 'She's not raunchy,' Jennifer says. 'I mean, I'm not into raunch, but. . . .'

She turns, hot and smiling. She says: 'We're going to be stars, you know.'

You come to New York to be a writer, a painter, a performer; it's a question of identity, not just work. You come for the community of people who think the same way, for the publicity, the support systems and the possibilities. You can learn here. You can be judged here by your peers; you earn respect. There are far more comfortable cities to struggle in, but only this one lives at the exact intersection of an idea and a market. If you suffer along the way, that is also part of the myth. Each star's story proves the point, and if anyone should seem to fail, they need the myth even more because it proves they still have possibilities.

They tell each other Dustin Hoffman was once the coat-check boy at the Longacre Theatre, then a stringer of Hawaiian leis, the man who held patients down for electro-shock therapy, one of the hundred actors who refiled all of *Time* Magazine's clippings, and a toy salesman at Macy's, where he tried to sell Gene Hackman's two-year-old son as a walking, talking doll. Hoffman hated his birth and life in Los Angeles, and dreamed of New York from the start. 'I used to go see *Dead End Kids* every Saturday,' he says, 'and wish I could be a member of that gang getting out of the East River.' New York came to mean seriousness and soul to him, the high art of the Theatre as opposed to the quick glitz of Los Angeles and the movies.

Everyone knows Robert de Niro hung out on Hester and Kenmare, a quiet boy so Marty Scorsese remembers. He became a jobbing actor, and studied with Stella Adler, one of the acting teachers whose reputation brings newcomers to the city, and helps define its seriousness. Everyone knows, too, that Tom Cruise was a waiter in New York until he auditioned for Zeffirelli and was pronounced *bellissimo*;

after which, he had a career. The city is where you start, and prove yourself.

It's not just a man's myth. Bette Midler picked up $350 working as a film extra and ran away from her Hawaii home. She hit Los Angeles briefly, and ran away again to the sleazy Broadway Central Hotel ('I developed a lot of wind, running from all manner of strange people'). She made the chorus, and then the juvenile lead in *Fiddler on the Roof*, but she was a go-go dancer in a Broadway bar when the call came to play in a New York institution: the Continental Baths, a few floors of sexual abandon for gay men in the basement of an Upper West Side hotel, with musical interludes. At the baths, the more members of Midler's audience wore clothes, the more she was a star.

It takes time to concentrate so much hope and work in a place. In the small town of colonial New York, an ocean away from what it still considered civilisation, the theatre only washed ashore. Richard Hunter wanted a licence to produce plays around 1700; nobody knows if he succeeded. In 1703 Anthony Aston, a strolling player, crept into New York 'full of Lice, Shame, Poverty, Nakedness and Hunger' and gave some performances. There were amateur theatricals: in 1732, Mr Heady the peruke-maker presented *The Recruiting Officer* in a ware-house belonging to Rip van Dam. The first professional company in America, led by Walter Murray and Thomas Kean, came up from Philadelphia to give shows in a makeshift theatre on Nassau Street. But the community of theatre – egos, limelights, star attractions – arrived on the *Charming Sally* in 1752 with William Hallam, from the famous Hallam Company of London. His troupe worked Wil-liamsburg for nine months and came north to New York the next year. They opened Sir Richard Steele's *The Conscious Lovers* on 17 September 1753 at the New Theatre on Nassau Street.

You could turn up at showtime or else 'gentlemen and ladies that choose tickets,' the playbills said, 'may have them at the new printing office in Beaver Street'; a ticket guaranteed a seat but not any particular seat, so the servants were sent an hour ahead to keep the best places. Playgoers expected to pay less if they arrived later, down to half-price at the end of the third act, but Hallam's management could not afford these London habits; they announced on 20 December that 'nothing under the full price would be taken during the whole performance'. 'No person whatever,' the posters said, 'to be admitted behind the scenes.' In summer of 1767, the company opened the first permanent theatre in America, an unmarked shed with double doors on John Street. 'It was principally of wood,' William Dunlap, the actor-manager, remembered, 'an unsightly object, painted red.' The company was divided into salaried actors and the far grander 'sharers' who took home a cut of the box office; the new house would 'yield to the sharers $800 when full, at the usual prices.'

Theatre was royalist, loyalist and frivolous, a sign of attachment to London ways, as well as an affront to more Puritan communities. By the time of the Revolutionary War, the John Street Theatre had become the Theatre Royal. Soon after the British took New York in 1777, the British military occupied the theatre; it was their diversion while they held the city. Officers took the female parts until ladies of the town could take their place; after which the officers kept all the star parts, hiring civilians only for walk-ons.

Even as the war was ending, the British stayed on stage – seventeen productions in 1782 as they awaited defeat and evacuation, a quite surprising zest for show business. The military had to hunt the plays they knew from London. They advertised successfully for copies of *The School for Scandal* but could not find *Maid of Kent*, nor the score of any of the operas they wanted. After the defeat of Cornwallis, British soldiers poured into New York, nearly doubling the population; the box office was busier than ever, for fewer performances. But they lost their impresario, Dr Hammond Beaumont, and American players came back to claim the city. John Henry, a leading player from Hallam's Company, delivered *A Lecture on Heads* and *A Monody, called the Shadows of Shakespeare*; the 'Celebrated Isaac Levy' did conjuring and palming; there was the show of 'A Curious Fish, almost in the shape of a Woman'. These visitors were flexible men. Dennis Ryan's company arrived in 1783 after its success among the patriots of Baltimore, but sang *God Save The King* between the acts. And the military were confined to benefits and playing 'Some of the Characters' in Ryan's *Macbeth* and *Tamerlane*. They last appeared on stage a month before the British were finally shipped out of New York.

Their enthusiasm for the stage was awkward. Republicans had already dismembered one playhouse on Beekman Street, according to William Dunlap; the theatre was for Tories. When Hallam's company came back to New York in 1785, there was furious debate about whether they should be allowed to play at all. Dr Logan thought theatre was fit only for monarchies. Mr Smiley thought amusements led people to forget their political duties. Mr Finley thought the stage spoiled taste by representing unreal characters. Mr Whitehill thought no regulation could prevent the vice and immorality of a theatre. Republican arguments, and good plain democratic talk, added weight to old Puritan objections to the stage. The Quakers tried to run the players out of Philadelphia; in Boston, actors had been arrested on stage for acting; Congress banned plays throughout the Revolutionary War. Actors always carried 'characters', testimonials to their moral standing, from town to town, so as to avoid trouble. Plays were often presented in disguise as 'lectures', 'moral dialogues', 'pantomimical finales'. New York was friendly to players by comparison, as friendly as the South, but the city did not actually trust actors. David Douglass built a new theatre on Cruger's Wharf, but he had no permission to perform. He said he would open instead a Histrionic Academy and everyone assumed the grand title was a subterfuge.

Hallam crept back very carefully to Manhattan. He tried lectures in August 1785, with prologues and pantomimes, and waited until October to risk a play. For all the debate, he was not prevented. He set the style for all New York's theatres for half a century: an actor-manager who believed in two principles – 'Keep down the expenses' and 'Divide and Govern'. He quickly lost his lead comedian, Thomas Wignell, who set up a Philadelphia company and started a fierce theatrical rivalry with New York. He lost John Hodgkinson, who opened the Park Theatre in 1798 with William Dunlap, because of Mrs Hallam's habits. Hodgkinson was driven to publish a pamphlet about the lady's drinking – about the night the hairdresser complained she was 'so senseless she could not sit in her chair', about her 'strain of Invective and Abuse' when Hodgkinson tried to keep her from reeling on to the stage, and her next day apologies, and her husband's promise that 'I'm sure she will never forgive herself, or drink any Thing but Water as long as she lives.' Mrs H. was the first of a long line: the flamboyant and monstrous American theatrical drunks.

This theatre was a theatre of stars, joined at each town on their travels by a 'stock' company of local players; that was true of Manhattan theatres as well as the sticks. The volatile, boozy Kean and the grand Macready and the downright alcoholic George Frederick Cooke all sailed in from London, but there were also Rachel and Fechter from Paris, Janauschek from Prague, Modjeska from Warsaw, Ristori Salvini from the Italian circuit. A European success helped the New York box office: Thomas Abthorpe Cooper arrived from Edinburgh and played Macbeth for very little, went back to London where his Othello was a triumph, and came back to command $750 a night and the job of co-manager of the Park Theatre on Park Row. Since the stars were likely to land in friendly New York, not Puritan Boston or Quaker Philadelphia, they logically booked their tours there; New York became a theatrical hub, with the most theatres of any Eastern city. But this was only convenience, and actors could still thrive in the provincial life. Nor did New York guarantee taste. It was the 1880s before Clara Morris could escape the hoots and hisses of audiences in Cleveland and Cincinnati for success in New York, and then go back home as a star – 'lifted high into popularity,' as she wrote, 'by the whim of the first city in the land.'

Edwin Forrest was the first true American star. He went to London to make his obligatory success, but he was hissed and booed. He blamed the claque of his unyielding rival Charles Macready. But in New York, he was a hero. He was a different kind of actor, a roaring boy out of the Bowery. James Murdoch remembered he was 'often charged with rudeness and violence in his impersonations and even ridiculed for muscularity of manner'; he had a basso voice, made rasping by his passion for cigars. He played inspiring, high-flown parts, like *Spartacus the Gladiator* with his broad chest bare, his waist cinched with warlike brass and his massive calves on show like monuments.

He gave his *Macbeth* at the Broadway Theatre on 7 May 1849, the same night that Charles Macready himself was due to open at the Opera House, the grandest of the New York theatres. Now British actors were not always popular in New York. In 1834, the British had been hauled off the Bowery Theatre stage by an angry crowd and replaced by authentic Americana – a minstrel show. Macready was the gentleman's favourite, but the streets were with Forrest. Seeing the danger, Macready's management arranged yet a third Macbeth, to be played by the Bowery favourite Thomas S. Hamblin at the Bowery Theatre itself. The Scottish play was never so popular. But if Macready hoped that Forrest's fans would be busy elsewhere, he knew he was wrong when the curtain rose. Forrest's men reared up throughout the theatre. They bellowed, 'Down with the English hog!' They hurled chairs and lemons and rotten eggs. Macready's exit was sudden, careful and unrehearsed.

Philip Hone wrote in his diary that 'this cannot end here; the respectable part of our citizens will never consent to be put down by

a mob raised to serve the purposes of such a fellow as Forrest'.
A committee of merchants petitioned Mayor Woodhull to protect
Macready's later performances. On 10 May, there were 300 police and
200 state militia and even two brass cannon covering the Opera
House, keeping the whole culture of the New York rich from the
rough hands of Forrest's supporters and the Bowery gangs. The mob,
too, knew what they were about. Hand-bills urged them to 'express
your opinion this night at the English ARISTOCRATIC Opera
House'. There were 20,000 outside the Opera House, including ring-
leaders thrown out of the theatre, and they howled at the soldiers:
'Tear it down! Burn the damn den of the aristocracy!'

The mob found cobblestones piled up nearby, where a sewer
was being dug. The troops crouched under a hail of stones. Inside
the theatre, Macready would not leave out a word of the play.
Outside, Colonel Duryee threatened to withdraw unless he could
fire into the mob. The sheriff gave his permission, because the
alternative was to surrender the streets. Duryee's men first fired
over the heads of the mob, but the warning shots only made the
men furious. The troops next shot point-blank into the crowd. It
was the first time such a thing happened in America, the state
firing on its citizens; it was done in defence of Society. Thirty-four
people died, their bodies left casually on Astor Place like the
remains of some bloody picnic.

The stars had the power to raise passions. They almost eclipsed
the other people on the stage – the 'teapots', who stood with a hand
on one hip to speak. Each had a 'line of business', the type of role
assigned for a lifetime; like some orchestra with its first and second
violins, big companies hired a first and second soubrette, a first and
second walking gentleman, and the soubrette would still be fluttering
and flirting in her sixties. Teapots had their settled ways of falling,
fainting or stabbing themselves. They moved as precisely as the scenery, and as illogically; as late as 1870 Clara Morris was quite shocked
at a director who actually thought up reasons for actors to change
places on stage. Edgar Allen Poe, reviewing a comedy in 1845, noticed
the 'rectangular crossings and criss-crossings of the *dramatis personae*
on stage; the coming forward to the footlights when anything of
interest is to be told'. Anna Cora Mowatt, whose play he was
reviewing, remembered rehearsals lit 'by a single branch of gas, shooting up to the height of several feet in the centre of the footlights. It
sent forth a dim, blue spectral light'. She mainly noticed that, the day

before the first night, the cast still needed to carry their scripts in their hands.

What was seen on stage was manifestly faked. 'One may be charmed,' wrote Samuel Haynes Jenks, editor of the *Nantucket Enquirer* in 1825, 'by the exhibition of spectacles nowhere else discernible among the phenomena of this world ... whole streets and blocks of tenements are shoved forth ... upon the same boards, with most magical effect, without the dislocation of a single brick, or the shattering of a pane of glass – and vast forests, or stupendous mountains are unrolled from above; their bases resting conveniently upon the aforesaid wooden ground, and their summits sublimely enveloped in the canvas obscurity of the clouds beyond.' There was resounding thunder, and hail like quarts of dried peas in a tin, painted cylinders and striped dowlas, for the pleasure of the spectators, 'lots of reputation to performers, food for critics, opportunities for puffs, and a free ticket to Major Noah!' It was usual to heckle actors on the front stage, rag them and even stone them; the audience was all too intimate.

But the apron stage began to disappear, and the whole show moved behind the proscenium arch, as separate now as a picture. Hefty, realistic sets for Shakespeare came into New York first, brought in steamers by stars who would use the new railroads to take them on tour. Theatres became capable of mocking reality. The Madison Square Theatre had a double stage so that two sets were ready all the time to be swung by counterweights into place. Spectacle replaced intimacy. At Niblo's Gardens in 1866, ladies went in heavy veils so nobody would know they had seen that shocking show *The Black Crook,* a ballet with a melodrama grafted awkwardly on, and full of 'all that gold and silver, and gems, and lights, and women's beauty can contribute to fascinate the eye,' according to the *Tribune.* But the most remarkable part of the show, to many in the audience was a kind of stage never seen before in America – 'every board slides on grooves and can be taken up, pushed down or slid out at will. The entire stage may be taken away; traps can be introduced at any part at any time, and the great depth of the cellar below renders the sinking of entire scenes a matter of simple machinery.'

Anything, it seemed, could be counterfeited on stage; actors were part of marvels, not just some tap-room entertainment. There were explosions, collisions, collapsing viaducts, a whole new genre of railroad melodrama; Augustin Daly in 1867 strapped his hero to the railroad line as a locomotive rushed closer, in *Under The Gaslight.* The gold rush of 1848, the fight against the Indians, came on stage; and so did the poverty of the cities. Dion Boucicault used the panics of both 1837 and 1857 in his *The Poor of New York*. This new subject matter was hugely successful, and it changed the logic of the theatre. Instead of shipping just a star, who worked on the fixed set of the local theatre, these shows had to be transported at great expense with every effect intact. Companies went with them, because stock companies could hardly cope with the technicalities. And now actors owed some loyalty to the individual show. Daly, and A. M. Palmer who ran the Union Square Theatre, abolished the 'line of business' and cast their companies as they saw fit.

Instead of playhouses which took in stars, there were shows out on tour – starting in New York, where a show or a player made a reputation, mostly booked in New York, because Chicago shows paid less, and depending on New York as the only fixed point in a touring life. When vaudeville expanded, it, too, was booked from New York; the offices where an act learned its fate were in the Palace Theatre, the house where every act longed to play. Actors could once spend lifetimes in some small town, and feel quite grand enough, but now they had to be in New York or on the road. And the foundation of this change was a change in the law. Until the 1870s, anyone could get away with stealing the text of a play. Of the many productions of Gilbert and Sullivan's *H.M.S. Pinafore* hardly any paid royalties. But Dion Boucicault lobbied successfully to give a dramatist the sole right to 'act, perform or represent' his show. The writer had the power that actor-managers once had. A play was not just the basis for a hundred different, unofficial performances each night, but a legal entity, a show, which could be cloned only with New York's consent.

A show could now be as complex as those David Belasco productions which later became operas – *Madam Butterfly*, *Girl of the Golden West* – but which were born as 42nd Street extravaganzas. The scenery moved behind the actors. The audience saw sunrises and sunsets. The stage was divided into three areas, and the action cross-cut between them: Indians, settlers and cavalry for example. There were 'living photographs' on the stage. In *Girl of the Golden West* it took thirty-two men, 'a mechanical orchestra' to present the snow in its sprays and drifts, the cabin shivering in the wind, the 'click, click, click' of freezing snow driving against the walls and windows. This 'reality' could compete even with early films, and since those needed the full blaze of sunlight, it had even more dramatic range; Belasco lit beautifully, and minimally, to make an asset out of chiaroscuro.

The aesthetic change produced an industry. New York in 1873 had half the population of Paris, but spent three-quarters as much on entertainment; a city of newcomers, single people in small, cold rooms, went out for pleasure. And the industry produced a whole society. Union Square was the heart of the theatre district in the 1880s – where the dramatic agencies booked the touring shows, the costumers, wigmakers, printshops and theatre bookshops clustered along with the offices of Samuel French, the *Dramatic News* and the *Sporting and Dramatic Times*. Many actors lived within a few blocks. It was a social place; actors did the rounds of the agents each day, checking to see what might be available, registering with each agent the details of their wardrobe, specialties, speed of learning and physical characteristics. They were notorious for loud shop talk, so everyone knew they were players, and for the 'saffron hair, painted eyes and eyebrows' of the women, the silk sashes, straw hats with ribbons and the 'russet shoes' of the men. On their Rialto they were front and centre; Augustin Daly had to insist that his companies dressed and talked more modestly.

Because of the theatre, the Square saw chorusgirls, husbanding their one fashionable dress for interviews, or else trying to raise the money to buy it, although the supply of 'mashers' and 'stage-door Johnnies' was more reliable on tour. There were the 'supernumeraries', the extras supplied by brokers – human props, often not told what the play was about, who reacted accordingly. One line of grenadiers, cued to shoot off their muskets, produced a total silence. Each man had unloaded for fear of an explosion, thinking the others would cover him. There were the first schools for actors – the Delsartian techniques of harmonic gymnastics – and charitable groups: the Elks, the stuffy and business-like social club in every American small town, began with a group of actors meeting at the Star Hotel in New York. And everyone wanted to know what happened in this world – of naughty girls, since the magazines almost always called their half-dressed models 'actresses', and the stars. Everyone knew that Sarah Bernhardt had been a huge social success in London; but the grindingly proper matrons of New York decided to snub a mere actress and only men came to her reception at the Century. In 1880, the *New York Sun* ran an extraordinary series of interviews and reports about an actor who was feuding with his plumber over a bill.

The idea of an actor's job was re-invented on Union Square. Acting was no longer just a matter of taking cues, remembering as many lines as possible and keeping out of the way of the star, although those things mattered. Actors created, not just repeated, the show. This individual performance was something open to anyone on stage, not just the star. It is a kind of paradox: because of the huge machines of those commercial spectacles, acting had become an individual art. Actors began to talk of the 'profession'. The American Society of Actors lobbied for a law which would have set a minimum standard of excellence for any actor appearing in New York State. But actors could still be stranded on the road by a dubious manager, and their annual income put them only in the middling middle class – somewhere between clerks and postal workers. They longed for the comfort, the toilets, the heating of a New York theatre when they were out on the road. They longed for a living wage when they were in New York. By the 1900s, some took to hanging around the new movie studios by Union Square in the morning, hoping for jobs; if there was nothing, they could still see the agents in the afternoon. Some of the women went on the streets. Anyone in the show business could see that there was a formidable syndicate of theatre owners and booking agents that an impresario like David Belasco could fight only with difficulty. Against the syndicate, against the Shuberts who had arrived to battle the syndicate and bought so many theatres they became one in their own right, the actors organised.

It was the summer of 1919. The Actors' Equity Association, six years old, called a strike. Equity ordered the cast of the new musical *Chu Chin Chow* out of rehearsals; only four obeyed. A week later, 1,400 of the union's 2,700 members crowded into the Astor ballroom and decided on a full-scale action. The managers understood the threat. They tried to make sure that Equity members could not work in vaudeville, movies or burlesque. They sued the union – Florenz Ziegfeld tried for an injunction and the Shuberts sued 200 union members for half a million dollars for breach of contract. But twelve shows shut down overnight. Frank Bacon, a stock company veteran of twenty years, finally had his first star role on Broadway in a show called *Lightnin'*; but he chose to come out. W.C. Fields and Ethel and Lionel Barrymore were the hosts of benefit performances. Eddie Cantor refused at first, but, as he said, the likes of Ziegfeld only paid his wages and 'the people who associate with me call me "scab".' Billposters would not put up the posters for a non-union show. Teamsters would not handle a manager's baggage. And it was a strike like no other; it lit up like a carnival. Players on the picket lines gave impromptu shows. There was a parade from Columbus Circle to Madison Square, a glory of chorus girls, and stagehands, and stars, a suitable celebration of the new 'profession'.

The elevator's crammed at 890 Broadway, the last surviving rehearsal space in the city for a musical. There are dancers who love each other and want to beat each other and know that what's waiting upstairs is the very last job of the summer. There are careful smiles. 'Too many doughnuts,' says someone who's archly inspecting a dancer's belly. 'My taps have no more rubber on them,' a girl says. They spill out into a corridor that's all bodies, propped up against doors and walls and then one by one, they walk into the long and mirrored rehearsal room. The gofer hands over their eight by ten and their resumé. They look at the line behind the wood table: director, choreographer, music director, producer, secretary. In the corner of the room a woman in a black dress is doing the splits.

Each says, 'Hi!'

First, they sing. There are lost voices, sliding voices, CinemaScope voices that project the middle of each vowel but cut off the top and the bottom. A black man sings *Honeysuckle Rose* like a seducer, a white woman sings it out like a brass foundry. An Italian boy says, 'It's very early. I'm not sure it's there yet.' Another says, 'I had to do "Bridge Over Troubled Water" yesterday and it blew out a bit ...' One tries to be social before he's sent off: 'I saw it at the run-through and she had her fingers caught in her pearls and she was – like – choking herself. ...' They're trying to be slick and they can't hide that they need this job. Either they go play in this musical in an upstate park, or they work out the summer as waiters.

'They've all done this before,' the director says. 'It's worse with the young ones, there's tears and they're angry and they want to know why. You can't ever say – you weren't good enough. You say – you didn't fit. But they know.' The clutter of bodies in the hallway is down now to the last thirty-five. Each resumé goes in a pile: chorus, first alternate, LD (for last ditch). The room's cleared and the choreographer takes over. Four by four, they tap, tap, tap, the others watching and echoing them in the moved equivalent of a whisper. At the end of each number, the taps rattle still like the last of the rain. Together, they shake the building. 'Step soo-ten-oo, fan kick . . .' the choreographer says. 'One Buffalo, two Buffaloes, slap . . .' as in 'shuffle off to Buffalo.' 'The steps aren't very hard,' he says, 'but I'm interested in the interplay.' The whole troupe giggles, making a schooldays' joke. 'Interplay,' someone says, and they're laughing out loud.

Everyone is kind; it's the process which is harsh. There's a dancer, a little older, whose sodden hair is swept back to make the shine look deliberate, whose sweat seems to seep from the spine; he's having trouble with his taps. He has a screwdriver in his pocket to fix everything. There's a blonde hanging back, in powder pink, her hand under her sweats to fan her breasts. She has a cold look. At 3.30 she says she needs to collect her daughter. 'Thanks for understanding,' she says. 'Thanks for hearing me. I'm off to pick up my baby girl.' As she leaves, there's a whisper that she was a star, that 'she was never known for her singing.'

'She was cold, non-communicative and all the rest of it, but she came,' someone at the table says. 'That has to say something.'

'Yeah,' says someone else. 'She's broke.'

'Most of what you get is rejection,' says Patrick Quinn, first vice president of Actors' Equity. 'When people hang on sometimes, you wonder about the stupidity, or the tenacity. We survive with lots of therapy, a supportive group of our peers. But you're never allowed joy in this business. If you get a great contract, a great part, you're not allowed to shout about it.' You come to New York for the theatre, but a showcase job in an off-off-Broadway hall can earn you just carfare. 'There's no such thing as a pure Equity member. You have to be in SAG for film and TV, AFTRA for radio or live TV or taped TV. I have to say no to theatre jobs because that's not where the money is. And if our members go to Minneapolis, they make enough money to live in Minneapolis – but not to be in New York and Minneapolis at the same time. They have to choose.'

And yet New York still rules Equity, even though only 17,000 of its 39,000 members live in the tri-state area, and the volume of TV and movie work in Los Angeles is more lucrative and steady. 'It used to be,' Quinn says, 'that an actor from New York was properly trained.' Most commercials are still cast in New York, maybe seventy per cent, and most soap operas, maybe sixty per cent, which are good money and a good start for actors. The soaps make stars, and they put talent in a showcase, but the producers rule: you make your deal before the audition, just in case they really want you, and the shows have an inexorable cycle. Each thirteen weeks, any actor may fall under a car, suffer amnesia, contract an incurable and sudden disease or simply be forgotten. But if you also have a Broadway show, you're excused Wednesdays and not made to shoot after seven in the evening. You have a chance.

'There are lots of people who prey on actors here,' Quinn says. There are classes for everything, some given by casting directors; some sign up to get known. 'I've seen contemporaries of mine give musical theatre workshops,' Quinn says, 'and I know they can't chew gum and move at the same time. Maybe they have every cast album of every show, but that's all.' Everyone knows there are always some 20,000 others in town, just waiting to get an Equity card, and yet the business is contracting. 890 Broadway is the last surviving rehearsal space which can handle production numbers. Broadway Arts and Showcase became the Carnegie Apartments. The King on 43rd Street is a frock factory. The rent for the Minskoff rooms has tripled. 'They're talking about rehearsing in Hoboken,' says Quinn. 'Can you imagine running from rehearsal to a commercial audition in Manhattan?' Dinner theatres prefer concerts to shows. The Guber-Gross management used to take out ten shows a summer on tour from New York, but now they can cast out of towners, and save by using non-union talent. The TV commercials business slumps with the economy, or with the TV ratings – during a writers' strike that made prime-time TV less attractive, fewer actors worked on commercials. It's a volatile, treacherous business.

'But the saddest thing,' Quinn says, 'is people leaving the family. . . .'

The young John Steinbeck, out in Stanford, California, wanted to be a writer, and he knew what he must do. He shipped out on a freighter bound for New York City. He laboured through the days and hoped at night to meet writers, to be among his own kind. But he never did find the right doors and in time he went back to California. Still, he had no doubt that he could define himself as a writer, that American writers had a trade, that writers lived in New York, that you went to New York to become one; the city was somehow the heart of the writing dodge. Of the four things John Steinbeck knew, each has a history bound up with the harbour, the trades, the market and the meaning of New York.

In small-town New York, in the eighteenth century, Hugh Gaine advertised in the *Gazette*: Bibles, prayerbooks, Church and Meeting psalm books, a *History of the Five Indian Nations*, an *Account of the Earthquake at Lima*, Ovid and Virgil in Latin, mariners' compasses, writing paper, 'also choice good bonnet-papers' (which lined a lady's bonnet to keep it clean). He sold functional things, among which were books. He offered books that a gentleman would have known from the classroom, the Ovid and the Virgil, and books for praising God, a single work of local history and a topical book. There was precious little fiction for him to sell, and even when fiction began to appear in quantity, it was British fiction. There were no American publishers until the 1860s who were not also printers or booksellers. And nobody could define himself simply as 'a writer' because no New Yorker could make a living from his pen until at least the 1820s. The obstacle was 'the game'.

The New York book trade lived off British books until the 1890s, and lived fatly because it did not need to respect copyright. Anyone who could get hold of a book could copy, print and sell it. London was not complaining, because London was stealing American work just as enthusiastically. 'The game', as the publishers called it, was being first. A new novel by Walter Scott, a new instalment of Byron's *Don Juan*, was pirated with breakneck speed because a slow pirate ran the risk of being pirated in his turn. Publishers bribed clerks and printers in England to see advance sheets; they shipped the sheets into New York, and raced to print. The Careys of Philadelphia bought sheets of a new Scott novel from Edinburgh fourteen days before it was published, and still reckoned they would beat the New York pirates by only three or four days. The Careys' copy of Bulwer's *Rienzi* arrived off the same New York packet as the one destined for the rival Harper Brothers in New York. The Careys sent it to twelve printers, had sheets at the binders by nine the next morning and books on the New York stagecoach that afternoon; they had to hire every passenger seat, and still the books were in the bookshops only a day before the Harpers' edition.

All this was supposed to be democratic, bringing books to as many as possible; the publishers said copyright was an unnecessary charge on the poor reader. As printers, they had gone from colony to colony before the Revolution helping to invent the idea of a common American culture, and now they claimed they were publishers only for the common good. But 'the game' changed them. In the first years of the nineteenth century, half the fiction published in America came from smaller towns and not from Boston, Philadelphia or New York; but 'the game' was all about best-sellers, printing and distributing them fast, and that could be done efficiently only in or near a major seaport. The draft of the New York harbour, the numbers and speed of the ships that brought the books there, gave New York the edge. It helped that the New York audience was larger and richer and more eclectic than Boston's.

'The game' dealt only in established goods, which meant British books; there was no provision for an American best-seller. Even when hack work began to be profitable, life was hard. Fitz-James O'Brien, otherwise known as Fist-Gammon O'Bouncer, was a brawler of a man who staved off hunger by writing long, commercial poems and died a terrible death for a talking man – of lockjaw, in the Civil War. At a low point in the 1850s, he picketed the offices of Harper Brothers with a sign:

ONE OF HARPER'S AUTHORS
I AM STARVING.

For a start, books were far cheaper in America, and the profits less; remarkably few publishers were able to survive the 1820s, even though they took their material and its fame ready made. For his romances, James Fennimore Cooper bought the paper, hired the printer and took the whole risk; early editions of Cooper are famously corrupt because chapters were printed and the type broken up while Cooper was still writing. Publishers were printers looking for work, like the Harpers, or booksellers who needed stock to exchange with other booksellers to fill their shelves, like Appleton, whose dry goods store filled up with books until he became a publisher for lack of space to be anything else. New material did not appeal to such men; they liked sure things, and school books, medical books, Bibles. In the great cholera epidemic of 1832, Appleton made money with *A Refuge In Time of Plague and Pestilence*.

Until Washington finally accepted international copyright in 1891, seventy per cent of the books published in America were by foreigners; when the copyright laws changed, and foreign material was no longer almost free, seventy per cent were written by Americans. But in the meantime, 'the game' made martyrs on both sides of the Atlantic – Walter Scott, dying in debt despite his vast success in America, and Edgar Allen Poe, ruined and dying while Europe praised him to the skies.

The trade does look a little familiar. Harpers hired the first publisher's reader in 1830 to deal with the manuscripts arriving daily. 'Literary advisors' acted as editors, while the printers and booksellers did the accounts. Book publicity was assiduous. Edgar Allen Poe complained that Harpers had sent him nine letters about a single book in 1835. His review began: '– Well! – here we have it! This is *the* book . . . "attributed to" Mr Blank, and "said to be from the pen" of Mr Asterisk: the book which has been "about to appear" – "in press" – "in progress" – "in preparation" – and "forthcoming": the book "graphic" in anticipation – "talented" *a priori* – and God knows what *in prospectu* . . .'

But the whole machinery of the trade was strange and arbitrary; it could have been designed to confuse booksellers and keep money out of the hands of authors. In New York and Philadelphia, finished books were advertised in a fine quarto catalogue and sold off at auction twice a year – the Trade Sales. Book dealers bid on the entire print run of a book, with prices that hung on chance and appetite, and sometimes prices so low that a book was simply withdrawn to wait for a better day. Publishers scrapped to have the first sales and often disposed of books at bargain prices under the table. Some auctioneers could stay interested, title by title; John Keese was their master. 'If a book had any special points about it – smutty or otherwise – he knew where to find them,' I.S. Lyon wrote. But Merwin of Bangs, Merwin, the Park Row salerooms, was unpredictable: 'Occasionally he would allow his dander to get up a little, then he would knock down a valuable book for little or nothing before his buyers were half done bidding on it.'

Out of the proceeds the author need not expect a royalty. George Palmer Putnam, a refugee from carpet-selling, did offer Elizabeth Barrett ten per cent of the profits of a volume of her poems, and Thomas Carlyle a proper royalty on his *Cromwell*. But until the First World War, some authors had to pay respectable publishers to see their work in print. Authors complained at the lack of advertising, and that there were no books in the store. Publishers could botch and titivate the text as they wanted. When publishers did not cheat, they were ungenerous; Henry Holt in the 1880s declared a royalty over ten per cent immoral, and refused to give any author a written contract.

Authors often had friends or relatives who negotiated for them in times when travel was arduous; after the 1880s, they more and more had agents. Publishers naturally found this, too, immoral. Walter Hines Page frostily described in 1905 the publishers 'who keep "literary drummers", men who go to see popular writers and solicit books. The authors of very popular books themselves also – some of them at least – put themselves up at auction, going from publisher to publisher or threatening to go. . . .'

Literary life began in the literary societies – the Uranians, and the Debating Society and the Belles Lettres which followed in the 1790s. Their members were gentlemen lawyers who liked books, and their futures were uncertain in the harsh political debates which followed the Revolution. Hocquet Caritat, the most fashionable bookseller on Manhattan in the 1790s, tried to establish a salon with rare books and the chance of conversation, but he forgot that readers wanted only serious, practical stuff. They did not want to meet the men who wrote books. Those gentry gathered in the backroom of Wiley's bookshop on Reade Street, known as The Den; James Fennimore Cooper was often there. They shared a rather careful kind of jollity over dinner at 'The Bread and Cheese Club'. In time, this taste for the company of other men who wrote books would help define a 'writer', but too late for M. Caritat. His vision of New Yorkers as sociable and literate as Parisians ended in bankruptcy. It was magazines and newspapers which eventually made it possible to make a scanty life by writing. Meantime, 'writers' stood in need of a myth to give themselves dignity. The life of Edgar Allen Poe helped greatly: the heroic drinking, the flashing eyes that fascinated women, the feuds, the hoaxes and the obligatory death in either a gutter, a garret or some saloon. Being a writer, or an artist, was not at all respectable; even Edith Wharton, from a fine old colonial family, was regarded by the social classes as an outsider. Uncertain income was a fact of life; William North drank prussic acid in 1854 because he could no longer stand the poverty of a journalist. Writers told each other it was heroic to live outside the rules, since they could not afford to keep them. They became, in their own word, 'Bohemians'.

Their world had a centre: the table in an alcove under the sidewalk at 653 Broadway, in Pfaff's saloon, where hacks and poets ate the crisp fried fish, drank good champagne and respectable Burgundy from the barrel, sighed at the kind, full breasts of the Saxon waitresses, 'while,' in the words of Walt Whitman who liked to sit a little to the side, 'on the walk immediately overhead pass the/ myriad feet of Broadway.' Whitman was a watcher, not a boozer; he could be shocked by the regulars. He was horrified when Ada Clare, Queen of Bohemia, advised her lover to go back to the country, seduce the girl who had been sending him such passionate letters and then come back to report what he had learned. But then Whitman was an editor, astute enough to cut his own loves out of his poems.

'Bohemia' could be a phase, or it could be a lifetime. 'Ada Clare' had come to New York from Charleston, South Carolina, in company with her grandfather. Her name was her pen name, chosen when she published her first slim volume of poems at nineteen; at the time, she wanted to be famous as a 'Love Philosopher'. She was more famous for her love child, and for boldly signing hotel registers as 'Miss Clare and Son'. She declared: 'The Bohemian is not, like the creature of society, a victim of rules and customs.' But her income depended on her Charleston properties and after the Civil War she had nothing. She took her notoriety and worked in the theatre. A black and white terrier bit her sharply on the nose, and she expired of rabies, on stage, during a performance of the melodrama *East Lynne*.

Her 'King of Bohemia', Henry Clapp Junior, fared little better. He edited the *New York Saturday Press*, a raucous and funny paper and the ancestor of every counterculture rag; he even allowed the *Press* to denounce Bohemians as 'a peculiar mixture of the seedy, bloated, whiskey-sucking, kid-gloved, airish and pretentious'. He insisted that 'the real Bohemia includes all the best writers in this metropolis'. But Clapp died a pauper, in the asylum on Blackwell's Island (which is now Roosevelt Island, in the East River). 'There has rarely been a more pathetic picture,' wrote the *Daily Graphic*, 'than this poor old man presented, reduced to rags, consumed by a horrible thirst, and utterly without hope for this world or the next.'

Those who only passed through Bohemia took a mildly cynical view of such tragedies. Towards the end of the century, the glut of national magazines gave writers a more regular income, and bound them more closely to New York. Edmund C. Steadman, known as 'Pan', had passed through Pfaffs on his way to making a Wall Street fortune. 'If there had been a *Century*, a *Cosmopolitan*, and a score of other paying magazines,' he said, 'I suppose that Clapp, Arnold, O'Brien and the rest would have been as "conservative" as our modern authors, and would have dined above-stairs, and not under the pavement.'

Already there was reputation in the writing game, sometimes too much of it; Charles Dickens complained that people lined up to see him wash his face when he toured America in 1842. In the jolly optimism of the 1850s, the publishers thought they could raise the tone of the trade. They organised a joint book auction in New York City that eclipsed Philadelphia and Boston for good; it helped that railways and canals now linked Manhattan to most American readers. To give this coup some glory, they proposed a 'Complimentary Fruit and Flower Festival to Authors'. They invited all the literary figures they could remember, some of whom came. They filled the useless emptiness of the Crystal Palace with bunting and cornucopias, a fiery gas sign that read HONOR TO GENIUS and a perilous gaswork statue of History whose brow lit up with tiny flaring lights. Only fifty women dined as authors, but nine tenths of the spectators were women; everyone noticed. The city looked on with some interest. And the authors listened hungrily, willing to tolerate a twenty-minute Episcopal blessing and seventeen official toasts, ready to tackle symbolic still lifes of cold meats meant to represent Graces Supporting a Basket of Flowers or Serpents Destroying a Bird's Nest, all to have something, at last, from publishers.

It was rare for the trade to honour writers. But there were high-toned ladies holding *soirées* and *conversazioni* for them, imitating what they fancied was the French salon and being much mocked for it; Ann Sophia Stevens has a country bumpkin in *High Life in New York* decide that 'swarry' and 'conversation-anny' must be medical talk for 'hysterical fits'. The mode went with a general enthusiasm for things French, fuelled by the teachers left over from the Paris Revolution and the Napoleonic Wars; even popular papers put Paris nightlife alongside the latest winners from the New York horse races. But it had much more to do with being urbane, unvulgar and arrived. Your social climber in a satirical novel – as in Donald Mitchell's *The Lorgnette* – schemed to be invited to some grand lady's soirée; 'To be sure, they sneer at her, but it's sheer envy; besides one sees the lions, and as they say, a great many first-rate people.' A 'writer' could be a 'lion' almost before he could make a living.

The literary climber needed to know Ann Lynch, later the wife of Professor Vincenzo Botta, whose salon flourished for a half-century – surviving the 'wizard spell' of Edgar Allen Poe, and the boorish silence of Horace Greely, and including the likes of Emerson and Melville. It blossomed again after the Civil War, and helped set the tone for serious-minded snobbery: a careful shabbiness, the floors covered only in Chinese matting rugs, the supper undemanding with sugary cakes, the drinks either coffee or some nicely imprecise 'old Italian wine'; an appetite for the foreign which inclined to France and culture but which was meant to help define what was American; a concern for personality, rather than work, and a romantic taste for extreme and even rather disruptive personality. The true literary life was not found in the study, with pen and paper; it was a drama, made to be watched.

Here was Oscar Wilde, 'often seen in public carrying a lily, or a sunflower, in his hand'. He sits down in the autumn of 1882 to a dinner party of eighteen 'fashionable girls'. Anna, Comtesse de Bremont, admires 'his splendid youth and manly bearing' and somehow understands 'his feminine soul, a suffering prisoner in the wrong brain-house'. He sits between an amateur actress and the daughter of a millionaire, almost outshining them in his black velvet coat and knee breeches, his black silk stockings and low shoes with glittering buckles. And what makes this dinner, which in another town would be simply amusing or grotesque, into a New York dinner is the element of publicity. The Comtesse fancied herself at 'a medieval banquet presided over by a disguised mummer', for Mr Wilde is playing the author, an important part of his stock in trade. The ladies, in their turn, are defending Mr Wilde by inviting him to dinner. They feel that Wilde alone, by his publicised example, brought interior decor to replace the horsehair sofas and coarse stoneware of early America, that he brought civilisation with his sunflower; but the Press has been barbed. So they make sure reporters know he capped the dinner by saying, 'America reminds me of one of Edgar Allen Poe's exquisite poems – because it is full of belles.' They cry: 'Behold the tribute of the belles.' And they rain roses down on their hero, in time for the morning papers.

The more New York papers were sold around the country, the more New York doings were reported, the more would-be writers came to understand that they needed the city: it offered work and notoriety and the company of people like themselves, and the prospect that lovely women would invite them to dinner. New York provided a set of rules for being a proper writer – 'it was correct to wear long hair,' Julian Street said, 'be dunned by one's landlady, owe bills at little restaurants and generally jeer at the conventions and the dull folk who heeded them.'

A writer had to be lucky to have money to care about; in a serious-minded, practical country, full of people advancing steadily in material ways, that made him a rebel without the need to do anything more. John Reed came to Greenwich Village as a middle-class revolutionary, rather removed from the real socialist firebrands of the Jewish Lower East Side; he came to do 'a little amateur starving', as Julian Street said, but also to make himself visible, a celebrity who would be commissioned by the uptown magazines. The Village was full of those artists and prophets that Edmund Wilson praised for leaving behind 'the shame of not making money. . . .' Artists, you notice: a craft that would quite soon aspire to rule Bohemia.

Artists understood the act that is not what it seems to be, while writers were literal-minded. Ellis O. Jones, an associate editor of *Life*, called a revolution in Central Park. A gratifying number of ambulances and soldiers with machine guns turned up, but almost nobody else; Jones blamed the fiasco on rain. But Gertrude Drick understood the rules of art far better. Her revolution was staged on the top of the Washington Square Arch in 1917 – with three artists, including Marcel Duchamp amd John Sloane and three theatricals. They pushed open the door in the west pier of the arch, and scrambled up the stairs in the brick interior; they brought wine, hot-water bags to sit on, balloons, Chinese lanterns, food and candles. Drick called them to attention and read a proclamation, which was mostly the word 'Whereas'; she declared Greenwich Village independent of America, for ever. The conspirators fired off toy guns, which could hardly be heard from the street below. They settled down to a wickedly pleasurable picnic in the cold January air. The proclamation was meaningless, the event unseen, but it claimed a huge significance. It was a political act which left no trace except balloons.

The artists, clearly, were on to something.

In eighteenth-century America, an artist only travelled: Baltimore, Charleston, Norfolk, New Orleans, Philadelphia, Newport and New York, making paintings of the gentry and then moving on. If he settled in a single town, he taught amateurs; M. Quesnay taught French, dancing and drawing at the New York City Academy. And then the amateurs took precedence over his own work. The American Academy opened with casts of famous statues for the students, and never allowed mere painters to forget the expense to which gentlemen had gone on their behalf. So gentlemen amateurs were 'invited' to hang their pictures, but only 'the most distinguished artists' were 'permitted' to do so. The professionals were dismissed as a snarl of men, semi-literate, quarrelsome, and often barely competent draughtsmen.

If artists knew anyone, it was writers – Samuel Morse, in the days before he became famous for his code, was a painter who knew Fennimore Cooper; Thomas Cole, the landscapist, knew William Bryant. Writers might produce commissions of some kind; they wrote books that needed frontispieces, and their articles and stories needed woodcuts. Francis Alexander, the painter, had come to New York in the first place because an itinerant book peddler showed him illustrated books and the best seemed to come from Manhattan. But the New York market was tough. 'Not one landscape painter in New York has received from a gentleman of New York a single commission for the last two years,' Thomas Cole complained in 1829. Samuel Morse thought of moving to New York. 'There is no rival that I should fear; a few more years may produce one.' When the National Academy talked of art and the cities of America they did not expect New York to dominate; they talked fancifully of the great works that would surely come when American cities competed, as Florence, Rome and Venice had done. But the Academies never did make an art world. They were full of the old paintings, the dusty busts that New York painters loved to copy; like the museums that followed them, they were signs of what wealthy men could give, not the core of anyone's life.

In the eighteenth century 'specimen' paintings sometimes appeared on the walls of shops and taverns, and even in artists' studios. The first true art show in New York, covered by the first New York art critic, opened in 1802 at the Columbian Gallery, an offshoot of the City Museum which Tammany founded when it was still a benevolent society, and not yet an engine of political corruption. Prints and paintings were crowded into the gallery, the best of them 'placed so *low* as to render it impossible to have a good view of them *without lying flat on the floor*', according to the anonymous critic of the *Morning Chronicle*. Half were originals, half prints of varying and dubious quality; a surprising number were American subjects, worked by American artists. There were views of Washington, and a madwoman by Pine, 'a flower pot and flowers by *a lady of New York*', a picture called 'The

Chymist' which had been cleaned so ruthlessly that it was only a shadow, some insipid landscapes with moons and ruins, a painting of 'an extraordinary late discovered animal', perhaps a 'My-Attic or Mountain Ram', and a work called *The Genius of Modesty preventing Love unveiling Beauty*, which the critic thought would offend chaste eyes and which he knew allowed the city wags to make raw remarks 'in the presence of fair ones'.

The show was a success, but it offered little comfort for painters. The appetite for great works was less important than the merchant collector's inclination to spend time with young artists, to be patrons and to damn well patronise. The painter John Vanderlyn even addressed Aaron Burr as 'My dear patron'. Philip Hone, worth half a million when he retired at forty-one, bought work by Thomas Cole for patriotic reasons even though he thought the work 'too massy and umbrageous'. Samuel Morse complained that most collectors 'give as their reason their wish to encourage the artist. . . . Who purchases a coat or a table, or a book, to encourage the tailor or the bookseller?' But at least these infuriating new men were willing to back their taste, unlike the closed chapters of Philadelphia and Boston. They even showed off their taste: a rich grocer, Luman Reed, opened a gallery on Greenwich Street to show his collection to the public once a week. And this taste infected the nation, because so many professional men and merchants made their way to the city once a year, to see the new styles and to learn how to be urbane.

Slowly, a community came together. The two main dealers in the 1850s were on lower Broadway, just north of the engravers and the dealers in supplies. The nearby Appleton Building, belonging to the publisher, had room for eleven artists on its upper floors, and it was publishers of books and magazines who gave artists an income; all of the Ashcan School of New York realists at the turn of the century, shocking with their images of street life put down in a swaggering style, had been newspaper illustrators. Side streets off Broadway had clusters of studios. The great gothic pile of the New York University building on Washington Square housed many artists, Winslow Homer among them, as well as a classical school and some scientific societies.

Between Spring and Prince Streets, in the large room over the hall of the Church of Divine Unity, the Dusseldorf Gallery opened in April 1849; its owner and promoter was John Boker, otherwise the New York agent for Mumm champagne. The walls of its high, sky-lit room were panelled with pictures; when one was sold, another was shipped from Dusseldorf. The pictures were allegorical, historical, ambitious – nothing less than a martyrdom or *Germany Awakening in the Year 1848*.

But the single most important canvas was a group study of a bird shoot at the Grafenberg, with guns, a dog, a dwarf, many men in beards who seem to have been clipped from a catalogue of portraits and stuck in place, and a basket on the floor which suggested a picnic, but actually contains trophies. The point of the picture was that these were the artists of Dusseldorf, all out together in a common pursuit, showing professional solidarity. They hung, huge and carefully lit, an emblem of the notion of acting as a guild, instead of squabbling as small-time craftsmen. The New York artists applauded, and they learned.

They held an auction for the widow of a landscape painter and a testimonial for poor John G. Rand, inventor of the collapsible paint tube. They met together, talked together. Ten artists were among the forty-two founders of the Century Association, the club for literate and thoughtful persons. Artists went to live at the Tenth Street Studios, built by Richard Hunt, who briefly held an architecture school there. John Ferguson Weir arrived in 1861 at this community, in a cold room with a high sky-light which made him suddenly very aware that he was 'an isolated stranger in a large city'. He unpacked his things, set up an easel, unwrapped a roll of studies, just for the sake of handling familiar things. He knew that coming to the city was more than an adventure; 'it meant for me the burning of one's bridges connected to the past, something to be pushed to a finish in winning a place in the profession.' He was amused when his neighbour, old Regis Gignoux, the landscape painter, advised him: 'Young man, let me give you the advice of an old painter: make your reputacion first, and then learn how to paint afterward.'

But he knew that an artist had a profession, and he knew in which city he had to be; and both those certainties were quite new.

Teddy Roosevelt arrived with all the gravitas of an ex-President, although he had been out of office for three years, and all the glamour of a radical: he preached a New Nationalism which would curb big business and still build a swaggering, virile America, a new Renaissance. His opinions, being those of a man who was again a candidate for office, came in a spotlight. On 4 March 1913 he walked into the

Armory of the 'Fighting Irish', the 69th New York Regiment, on Lexington Avenue. All the military life of the Armory had been put away. The huge open hall had a dome of yellow streamers, and eight-sided rooms had been improvised and skinned in burlap and hung with sober greenery – from the Massachusetts Tree of Liberty, the designers suggested. Ahead, in a straight line, was hung the history of modern art, with Americans, English, Irish and Germans stashed in rooms to the right, and the famous French put to the left, in a sequence that ended in cubism. But up in the gallery, the band of the 'Fighting Irish' played.

The show, Roosevelt reckoned, showed 'our people' the 'art forces' which were active in Europe, and of course he would not stand against all change. He examined Marcel Duchamp's *Nude Descending a Staircase*, a sharp-angled and unfleshy diagram. It was a shocking idea because nudes stay still to be idealised and nudes are lovely things, odes to the 'Female Form Divine'; a senator came to see if the nude might be obscene. But Roosevelt thought his Navajo rug was better art. He passed a Matisse figure with only four toes on one foot, the Gauguins and Rodins and Kandinskys, and he sniffed at the cubist work; like the coloured pictures in the Sunday papers, he said. He saw lines like a cave painting, and disapproved of the backwardness. He was kind enough, but he raised his manly, self-reliant, adventuresome morality against this new art, the upriver squire playing at frontiersman. As for the seriousness of it all, he said we should treat most of the pictures like mermaids at a P.T. Barnum show.

Other critics were more direct. They worried that foreign art might lead Americans back to a colonial and dependent kind of taste, a regular imitation of Paris. But Mable Dodge, a patron of the show and famous for her fine Fifth Avenue salon, told her friend Gertrude Stein the show was 'the most important event that has ever come off since the Declaration of Independence, and it is of the same nature. . . .' She knew very well the long tyranny of sugary Paris salon art on New York taste. The *New York Times* said cubists and futurists were close to anarchists; and there, Mable Dodge would have been able to agree. She liked the idea that art, elevated to a spiritual pursuit, would somehow subvert the machines of civilisation. She paid a stiff price for those ideas, having later to co-exist with D. H. Lawrence and Frieda in Taos, on principle.

There was talk of Ellis Island art, meaning the art of the new and suspect immigrants. The name of Gertrude Stein, an expatriate and a Jew, was invoked and mocked for its foreignness. This kind of anti-Semitism was complicated; there was also a myth, attractive to American promoters, that landing on a free continent would liberate the genius of those, like the Russian Jews, who had so long been confined by ghettos and pogroms. 'Genius' came to mean, sometimes, this sudden flowering. But even in the 1930s Thomas Craven, wanting to attack the modernist taste of Alfred Steiglitz, chose to condemn him as 'a Hoboken Jew without knowledge of, or interest in, the historical American background'.

Modernism owed no allegiances, or said it did not; it allowed artists to fly outside a specific history, to ignore alarmingly what defined everyone else. But then Mable Dodge did not approve of history, either: 'The majority are content to browse upon past achievements. What is needed is more, more and always more consciousness, both in art and in life.' If you happened, like the newly rich and like many Jews, to find no place for yourself in ready written, all-American history, modernism was an obvious refuge. And modern taste was associated with new money; the Museum of Modern Art would later be new money's answer to the old guard at the Metropolitan (although the Met bought Cézanne's *Colline des Pauvres* at the Armory Show). New money was being a little less radical than it might seem. By the time of the Armory Show, Paris had already approved Van Gogh, Cézanne, Gauguin with great retrospectives; both the taste and the work of the moderns arrived with a stamp of approval, just like the art the robber barons had bought. But if it was as safe as the taste of earlier generations, it carried the kick that it had the power to make those earlier generations furious.

This new taste had its own perfect subject. New York was the home of the masses, and the mass future; its playground, its Versailles, was Coney Island. At the turn of the twentieth century, Coney was still a retreat for gangsters, writers and the rich; then the trolleys and sub-ways brought out the millions to a gaudy fairground, a place to put away your conscience – join the crowd of thousands to see a real live elephant electrocuted! see an incubator baby cling to life! see the bearded lady who will not cry! roll up! roll up!

In Steeplechase Park and Luna Park and Dreamland, the steel wheels and skyroads were a parody of the way New York flaunts its own iron bones – the tangles of roadways on high stilts; massive, articulated bridges; tunnels under the tidal harbour. Driving from the

Bronx into Manhattan, strung on steel vines in a gorge of concrete, is a lot like a slow rollercoaster ride. The machinery of Coney Island became a perfect emblem for some artists who wanted to show the whole city as a machine, and glorify it, or disable it; and since New York itself was becoming a great subject, an icon as sure as any Madonna, the images of Coney Island are a double distillation of the place. They try to show the life, not just the monuments.

These painters were beginning to be a little afraid of the machine. Joseph Stella might paint like a Futurist, but he was not as blindly in love with speed and violence as his Italian colleagues; closer to the reality, he was writing prose poems about New York as a 'monstrous dream, real like a chimera, an Oriental delight, a nightmare from Shakespeare, unheard of riches, frightful poverty....' He painted skyscrapers as knife-like lines that menace the eye, awe-inspiring machines to which mere humans were irrelevant. But in *Battle of Lights, Coney Island* he painted all the dangerous pleasure, the 'carnal frenzy' of the place. He shows the beams and walls and towers of light at Coney, brilliant enough to disorient ships thirty miles out at sea and pre-figuring a Manhattan planted with towers full of light. But he shows them for what they exactly are: only metaphors for the force, the energy of electricity and light. At Coney, Stella moved away from his realistic studies of miners and crowds to a style which could cope with his alarmed sense of awe at the city – a rush of colour to represent the city's real force, which was often hidden by the streets and bodies he could literally see.

There is the same tension between the chic machine and its human consequences among the icon-makers of the Left. They couldn't help revelling in machines and progress, even as they condemned how they were organised and managed. So their Coney Island is, at first, a kind of education in the wonders of machines, a surprisingly still place unlike the frenzy Stella painted; Louis Lozowick, in the review *New Masses*, made Coney Island as flat and clever as a diagram. Because it had machines, it had possibilities. But Art Young, in the 1930s, spat venom at the place. It was now a trick played on the masses, Looney Island, where the merry-go-round spins like a top and throws off its passengers, where a breeze costs 10 cents from the Fan Concession Company.

*

The Ashcan School were left puzzling how to be grand and humane at the same time. The Academy students, imitating old works within an agenda of genre, landscape and portrait, were left to deny very loudly that their agenda had been taken away. After the Armory Show, nothing could be the same, although it would be thirty years before the scale of the change was clear.

The trouble in the meantime was Bohemia, the very myth that brought the aspiring world to New York. Caroline Ware wrote a long and ponderous study of Greenwich Village in the 1920s, and diagnosed 'art, sex, and a disdain for the pursuit of wealth'. This Bohemianism was a romance that writers, artists, actors wove around the troubles they faced in selling their labour, which was a real issue, but it looked very much like troublemaking and impropriety and even danger. The cops came hunting Reds and anarchists, and hauled off girls who smoked in public to be charged as streetwalkers; newspapers told Villagers to grow up, get serious and go home.

Bohemianism could easily be packaged for day trippers from Brooklyn or the Bronx. In one 'hang-out' of the 1920s, a long and narrow room in the basement of a tenement, you sat at bright tables for sandwiches and ginger ale; in these Prohibition years, you carried your own gin. No girl went unapproached. There were a few middle-aged men out for a pick-up, and some older people with an artistic or literary past, but mostly the faces were young and pale, their eyes bruised all around with drink. Prohibition made drink more urgent, people more drunk; since all drink was illicit, there were no more manners for drinking. A young Chinese Communist came in, to find someone who could help him translate and analyse his work. Two young Southern girls, 'who obviously came from substantial homes and a cultivated background', danced together, always drunk. Ware was told that one girl was the joke of the place because she tried very hard to be a proper lesbian, but took a few drinks and danced with men. And something very curious had happened. Writers, artists were not genteel professionals; they did not, on the whole, dine with lawyers or bankers, and they certainly did not go to Mrs Astor's ball. They did something that seemed trivial in a practical society where leisure was a side issue and newspapers did not even have sports pages until the 1890s. But writers had a style of living that everybody thought they knew. By the 1920s, people turned to the label of writer or artist 'as a means of satisfying themselves or of giving themselves status in a society in which art was the one recognised form of divergence', or simply explaining their lack of dull ambition. According to Ware, gay women in particular chose that means of making a way of life that suited them. Indeed a truly successful writer might drift back to selling books and having credit, which was not what a 'writer' wanted at all.

Suppose, though, you were serious about art. For the serious painters of the 1930s, New York was a frenzy of a place, which allowed them both to live poor in a loft and to look out on the vast, boiling subject of the streets – 'unknown, uncozy and not small scale,' as Edwin Denby said. The painter Willem de Kooning liked to show Denby how the neon, the broken light, the spots and fissures made compositions out of the flat fact of a sidewalk. Serious artists came to the city because they had no choice; imagine being born into a heartland vacuum, with a very proper library, perhaps a music circle, but almost no kind of plastic arts beyond the occasional civic statue. They did not expect recognition in the city, only the possibility of doing their work; they were proud of seeming to fail in material terms. The critic Lewis Mumford had laid down that 'there has never been a place in our present industrial system for the artist, except as a flatterer of the rich and idle, or as a mere servant of business enterprise.'

They talked a lot about manual labour, about working wheat until they were bloody to the elbow, about tracking across America as a hobo, about working, like De Kooning, as a house painter; all this showed they were practical, American and male. For the fact that art was deviant made being properly male a terrible burden; it had to be proved, over and over again. Simple abstraction would not do, because it was associated with feminine decorative arts; abstraction had to claim a male and ritual function, a shaman's power, and to be about something. And personally, an artist had to booze and screw like a hero. Think of poor Jackson Pollock who'd get drunk, paw the girls at the Cedar Tavern and ask them all to 'go fuck'. On his worst night, friends took a call girl to the bar and she said, matter of factly, 'Yes.'

When the government counted artists in the 1930s, with a view to a national make-work scheme, it seemed that half America's artists were in New York. They had practical reasons for being in the city. There were schools like the Art Students' League, which were meeting places; the instructors, the fellow students were artists, too. There was the chance of seeing, sometimes, something new: the Brancusis that American customs tried to seize, a Matisse retrospective at the

Valentine Dudensing Gallery. Europeans had come to New York – John Graham, the cavalry officer from Kiev, with his collection of African carving and his news from Paris. David Smith remembers Arshile Gorky working the edge of a painting perhaps a hundred times 'to reach an infinite without changing the rest of the picture, based on Graham's account of the import in Paris of the "edge of paint".'

But in the Depression, the city was cold and hungry. A little money filtered into artists' pockets in the 1920s, but now nobody could afford to buy; by 1933, art prices were down by half from their peak in 1929. Worse, the scrappy jobs that nobody wanted, the ones that kept a painter alive, had vanished, or were now desired by thousands. Charities brought home the would-be Bohemians from Paris – 700 of them in 1931 – but the New York artists had nowhere to go. And the closer they came to real pain, the more ordinary they became; their special loneliness and poverty was drowned out by the millions who shared the same lot. Rod Godfrey, who was about to sell work to the Metropolitan Museum, slept in subway stations. The great Ben Shahn could not find work as a lithographer, could sell no paintings; he stole a few rolls for his children. Isaac Soyer taught ancient Hebrew to keep alive, but who could afford to pay him? The established Marsden Hartley wrote to the Treasury Department: 'I was never rich ... for I was never a best seller but with the passing out of the old style collector there is little sense of security anywhere so I have lived more precariously the last two or three years. ...'

The shock was great. Poverty had no special meaning. It guaranteed nothing. Artists needed cash from the Works Progress Administration to survive; this modern notion of art had its first, uncomfortable relations with government. Artists, who defined themselves as solitary creatures, had to acknowledge some community; that was the condition of their dole. Unformed political ideas, in the heart of a city which seemed to be collapsing in on the poor, were sharpened and defined. The worship of Paris was spoiled by anger at the notion that somehow the dealers who sold the French moderns were, in the words of the artist Max Weber, 'deliberately and maliciously sabotaging and maligning native American art'. The critic Forbes Watson complained that, 'The American artist saw that picture buying in New York was dominated by Paris dealer agents. ... even minor talents, if quoted on the Paris picture bourse, could sell perverse and disingenuous work. ...' There was a ten-dollar prize for a slogan to change things;

the winner, rather hopelessly, was 'I AM FOR AMERICAN ART'. Self-interest dictated nationalism, but the politics of the left forbade it; and besides, the progressives like Arshile Gorky fancied themselves bankrupt aesthetically alongside Paris. The Bohemian ideal had been quite simple; the Depression turned it into a dilemma.

So there was talk, endless talk – factional fights and political spitfires and old Hans Hoffmann's studio school where he preached the 'push and pull' theory, and his students sometimes took years to decode suchlike phrases which they had so carefully noted down and memorised. Hoffmann taught the grammar of painting to classes whose innocence would have startled Europeans; in New York, it was a new thought that a painting was a two-dimensional illusion. Artists who might have been political cartoonists before, now tried to marry theories of politics and art. The Museum of Non-Objective Art opened, with its calla lilies and its piped Bach and the pictures hung close to the floor; it was Solomon Guggenheim's collection brought to the public by his eccentric mistress Baroness Hilla Rebay von Ehrenweisen, whose pictures were always and infuriatingly prominent, along with those of her long-time friend Rudolf Bauer. The museum employed custodians like Jackson Pollock, who learned to love the Kandinskys shown there. The great Surrealist and Cubist shows at the new Museum of Modern Art brought theory with them, nourishing stuff to replace the simple, individual myth of being alone and struggling.

That myth was too commonplace now it made artists share an exact identity with the men in the cardboard houses in Central Park. The blurring of the boundary which kept art special alarmed *Partisan Review* in the 1940s, which was obsessed with beating back 'mass culture', keeping 'art' separate and significant, afraid that the paintings could be as submerged in the mass as the painters had been so recently. But it was uncomfortable to admit that the special quality artists owned was ambition – a taste for significance; the coming New York School of artists, the abstract expressionists, could never quite stand the idea. Think of Pollock's drunken anger at the people who helped him to success, De Kooning's high-handed ways with the dealers and patrons who admired his work. Artists were still in love with the way Bohemia proved that they mattered without anyone having to judge them. They wanted to return, but the Depression took away Bohemia's meaning. It was left to critics like Clement Greenberg to insist, sentimentally, that 'the fate of American art is being decided – by young people, few of them over forty, who live in cold-water flats and exist from hand to mouth.'

It took a cataclysm to end New York's provincialism once and for all: the Nazis moved into Paris. The art market collapsed, the capital of art was in the hands of registered, bloody Philistines, and many of the artists got out – some to New York, the only world city which was cosmopolitan enough for them, and safe. When Marcel Duchamp first made the journey, in 1915, he had come for the easy way an artist could stay aloof from movements or categories because they hardly existed. He rather grandly announced, 'The only works of art that America has given are her plumbing and her bridges.' During the Second World War, Duchamp parked himself in a building on West Fourteenth Street and gave his profession as breathing; it is said that he played chess brilliantly with naked women; he made a little money matching the right picture with the right collector, and nothing more. For a charity show of Surrealist art, he tied a gallery in string, miles of it webbed and tangled.

You notice that there were commissions in New York, in the war years; there was money. There was also a sense of starting from zero. Duchamp thought Americans were less freighted with the past. 'They can skip all that tradition, more or less, and go more quickly to the real.' He no longer patronised American art. Like Camus after the war, or de Beauvoir, he suspected that there might be clues to the future and to life in New York, now that Europe was scarred and smoked and bleeding. But these possibilities were not exactly practical. He thought great artists had to go underground, to be discovered after their death. Art had been too neatly integrated into the market, which meant pay, but also constant production. The city was still the necessary condition of making and selling art, but it was no longer its proper subject.

De Kooning was painting for Container Corporation of America, to sell cardboard boxes. Jackson Pollock made a sketch to sell County Homes at Tarrytown NY. Pepsi-Cola handed out $2,500 a year for an art prize, won in 1946 by Boris Deutsch for a rather silly painting of *What Atomic War Will Do To You*. Corporate America had discovered culture, but as a subdivision of nationalism. America would be top nation, the strongest economic power; there had to be art to go along with this, a cultural identity. Braque, Picasso, Léger were in decline,

America in the ascendant, the critic Clement Greenberg wrote; 'the general social premises which guaranteed their functioning have disappeared in Europe'. Experiment had once been the province of the starving Bohemian; now the gallery owner Samuel Kootz, whose time as a movie huckster gave him a vivid sense of art propaganda, wrote to the *New York Times* that 'now is the time to experiment ... Money can be heard crinkling throughout the land.'

Almost everyone was working by 1944, and their savings were prodigious; they had a whole new range of possibilities. Freedom of expression was one of the values for which America was fighting – modern, progressive; so the artist was duty bound to express himself. If the work was sometimes brutish or crude, that only showed the virility and the power of the new America, and how individualist and risk-taking its artists were. Art had to be 'new', like the new model car or the new soft drink; and then it could be folded neatly into consumerism as another consumer good. Kootz himself staged an art show at Macy's department store, and Macy's rivals, Gimbels, stocked a Rembrandt *Portrait of a Child* for a classic, loss-leading, winter bargain basement price of $9,999. 'Contemporary paintings,' promised *Life* magazine, 'fit into rooms of any period'; and if you wanted to stand out, to claim some status, you bought the paintings that *Harper's Bazaar* shot as backdrops to frocks, lovely and classy things by Mondrian and Léger that sold to the same wives of lawyers and industrialists who bought couture.

One other cataclysm shaped the particular work which this market would consume: the bombing of Hiroshima, the desire to paint fragmentation and apocalypse and angst, and to draw on inner furies because the outer world encompassed impossible horrors. There need be no more dubious nationalism, and no more lefty social realism. Feeling, and myth, neatly took the artist out of taking a stand on reality, and being suspected as Red or radical. The buyers were in place, and the mood, for abstract expressionism – the triumph of the New York School.

Washington, unlikely as it seems, was a front runner for world culture capital during the war, somehow expecting to integrate mavericks and avant gardists and poets and trouble-makers in that most immaculately political city. But artists lived in a myth, and New York City was now built into that myth; Jackson Pollock told *Art and Architecture* in 1944: 'Living is keener, more demanding, more intense and expansive in New York. . . .' American art was largely New York art because New York dealers knew how to make it seem so, and their slogans turned into reality. The Federal Government almost sponsored a grand show called *Advancing American Art* which was meant to tour the world; the Feds smelt Communism and withdrew in alarm. But a Paris show of artists from the Kootz Gallery in New York was indirectly subsidised by the Government as a way to battle the Reds of Europe. The Federal backtrack generated enough middle-class crossness to prove that successful artists were still proper outsiders, but their incomes now were more than twice what the vast majority of American families earned. The keepers of the myth emphasised the threat from senators who hated art and the loyalty mongers; but the United States was officially represented at the Venice *Biennale* in 1950 by De Kooning, Pollock and Gorky, all hot and heavy New York heroes. The fact was that art and success were keeping company. Simone de Beauvoir in the 1940s was told how an artist could no longer be poor and lean on his friends, because a free dinner, a loan of money were scornful charities that broke up friendship. She had the classic New York conversation with a Greenwich Village designer:

'"But if they are great artists they succeed and make money," B. said.

"Supposing they don't succeed?"

"Then they are not great artists."'

Artists could preen, now. The painter Alfred Leslie had been a body-building champion before he turned to art, and the dealer John Bernard Myers wrote that his 'narcissism shifted from the muscle-building Mr Bronx to where the action was: Abstract Expressionism.' Artists had to be sociable, to promote themselves and not simply expect their work to be discovered; Myers was in despair that Robert Goodnough, although pushed and touted and fretted over, still worked as a freelance carpenter and removal man because he simply would not go to his own openings. And the definition of the avant garde grew clubbish and exact as it made money, with the newly important gallery owners serving as arbiters. The painter Byron Browne was rejected by Kootz for being too close to reality, and his paintings dumped to prove the point, sold at Gimbels for fifty per cent off – humiliation by sales ticket. Browne was dead, of a heart attack, within a year. Nobody liked to remind Kootz of his back room, stocked with Picassos in case the American heroes did not sell.

*

Jasper Johns came to New York in the 1940s because it was the perfect 'elsewhere' from the South Carolina where he grew up, an evasion as much as a destination. 'In part, art represented an unknown place – something foreign to me, something not familiar, something distant from my background.' His teachers suggested the city. He stayed only until he was drafted into the army. When he was discharged, he knew Japan, where he had been stationed and South Carolina, where he could not return; he says: 'I would not have known where to go except New York.' When he returned, he fell into the company of artists, as if he was not seeking it. 'I must have learned from them, but I didn't see it at the time,' he says. 'I did realise that "being an artist" was different from "going to be an artist". Work was the central issue for these people.'

The city was the only possible accident, because art is sold as well as made there. But Johns had no access to the market until he met Robert Rauschenberg. 'To me, Bob was a successful artist – he had exhibitions in galleries, he had the background. He entered a period when he had no gallery affiliation – something happened. He was no longer exhibiting publicly. We were very close, sharing our ideas and our criticisms.' They survived together, sometimes making money by designing windows for the department store Bonwit Teller. Rauschenberg taught Johns to quit his regular bookstore job, to live day by day and always to work. Johns even tried to paint a Rauschenberg, an extraordinary thing for a man who thinks work and identity are hard to distinguish; 'It was play,' Johns says, firmly, and then: 'There was a period during which the two of us formed a society and that was sort of that.'

Leo Castelli, then a new dealer, came to see Rauschenberg's work in the Pearl Street lofts; and Rauschenberg insisted Castelli come downstairs to Johns's studio, ostensibly to get ice. 'I had what I call my epiphany,' Castelli says. 'The crucial event of my career and my gallery. Really. There was this extraordinary work, of which I'd had only the barest glimpse – a few days before, in a group show at the Jewish Museum, the famous *Green Target*. I didn't identify it as a target, you know; it was just an extraordinary green painting. It was work with this very subtle emotion that everyone, ignorant or wise, seems to respond to.'

At Johns's first show, in January 1958, the work was a prodigious, scandalous success. The subjects were banal, the scale unheroic, the surfaces sensuous, and soul was not exposed in paint as the Abstract

Expressionists required. But it was a success in an art world that was not yet a matter of headlines, one of the last. The possibility of going down to a gallery and finding significance for sale was beginning to excite the city. Pictures came with theory attached, so that their seriousness was guaranteed. But Johns was not accessible; he paints no obvious feeling and no agenda. He slipped away from New York to a studio at Edisto Beach, aware of a rift with Rauschenberg and also a 'sense that art is like show-business'. He refused to face paparazzi, or dine with all the collectors who wanted to buy his work. He broke the rules obstinately.

But he came back. He did not return for the sociability of the art world, not when Rauschenberg has said he is 'cautious and terrified of extending himself and I don't know how he survives'. He is not in the art world itself, and he does not need to concern himself with the market. 'I never understand money,' Johns says. 'I don't understand why it behaves in the way it does. It makes me think one is not independent of the society in which one operates. That thought is always frightening to me.' He did not come back for the ease of working, and in his rooms of white sofas he is very far from Bohemia. Certainly, he came back for friends, but he is much too private to say so.

'I came back,' he says, after a long pause, 'for the cultural riches of New York.' He is on the edge of a giggle.

5
MINIMUM CITY

'I GOT A crime scene,' the police dispatcher is saying. 'What do they want? Operations was notified. What the hell they got going over there?' It was two o'clock on the morning of 10 January 1986. If they'd told Operations, then something bad was happening with someone famous. The dispatcher ordered radio silence. 'Tell them not to even mention it, whoever goes down there.'

Out near Shea Stadium, the cops went after a Ford LTD and stopped it up against a chain fence. The door came open. They saw blood, a four-inch knife and a big man with his left wrist cut open in a rough Y, maybe a half inch deep, and his wristwatch lying undamaged on the floor. His face was so white it had sweat for veins. The cops recognised Donald Manes, the borough president of Queens, chairman of the Democrats in that county, a 'boss' of New York City; and he was very close to death.

In hospital, his hand stitched together, Manes said two men had been hiding in his car. They had blackjacked him on the neck and the back. He said he'd felt metal on his neck all the time he was driving. As the story was told around town, it grew fantastic – UFOs had landed, or maybe hookers, cross-dressing hookers, with blackjacks, maybe three of them. By now, not everyone believed there had been a crime. Any time two politicians gathered, they wondered how Donny Manes had fallen in such trouble, and why he was so depressed. And then the cops held a press conference, timed for the six o'clock TV news, and the Chief of Detectives Richard Nicastro did something very rare: in public, he questioned the story of someone who had made a complaint. 'In the absence of anything else,' Nicastro said, 'I mean, you don't have to be a genius, there's only three things that could have happened. Either it was an accident, which is kind of far-fetched. It was perpetrated on him, which is remote. The third one is self-inflicted.'

On 21 January, reporters crowded into Manes' hospital room and saw him propped in bed, wrapped in a blue robe. He read out a statement. He never looked up from the paper. 'The wounds I received that night were self-inflicted,' he said. 'There were no assailants and no one but me is to blame. The fact I came to be in a state of mind permitting me to do such a terrible thing to myself is very painful for me to deal with.' He said nothing else. He waved to the reporters with his bandaged hand. All the hidden ways of the city were suddenly exposed: functional, obscene, essential like organs on an operating table.

There is a fountain that once stood by City Hall in Manhattan until Mayor Fiorello la Guardia removed it in the 1930s as an insult to women: a blocky male holding down wicked, fish-tailed women marked 'Vice' and 'Corruption'. It is called 'Civic Virtue'. It now guards the two neat blocks of Queens Boulevard where the politicians hang out, and the lawyers who nurse them and sometimes want to replace them, and the bureaucrats who administer the borough the politicians run. In the bars and the restaurants, they heard the news about Donny Manes with alarm. They knew Manes from the days when he was a young liberal reformer, a fan of Adlai Stevenson. They watched him bend around to the practical give and take of borough politics. He was affable enough, but too gruff to make the public big time. But in his own place, he was pragmatic and therefore powerful, one of the city bosses. 'Some people play great tennis,' Councilman Morton Povman said. 'Don plays great politics.'

Everyone thought they knew him, until he cut himself. That put dissonance into the ordinary view of the city's ordinary business. A boss could feel guilt. There could be deals a man would rather die than face. Donald Manes knew how New York really runs, and he could not live with the knowledge.

His nemesis came from the same machine. Michael Dowd is a gregarious, burly man, a heavy smoker with a touch of diabetes that had a little to do with the drink. He is a lawyer who wanted to be a politician – 'a typical young Irish kid looking to make his way up in the party,' according to Matthew Troy, then leader of the Queens

Democrats. In 1979, he was approached by the founders of a company called Computrace, who needed offices. Computrace helped the city collect its debts, especially unpaid parking tickets. Dowd heard their story and liked the sound of the contracts so much that he bought forty-one per cent of the company. It was only a sideline because his reputation as a criminal lawyer was growing, but it was a useful one; Computrace was a success.

In 1982, Dowd took lunch at a restaurant called Tutto Bene with Sheldon Chevlowe, one of the city marshals who collect overdue fines and carry out evictions. 'I've heard,' Shelly said, 'you're due to get some more big business from the city in July. If you want this new business, you're going to have to take care of some people.' Dowd knew the ways of the Queens machine, but even he was startled. 'We're starting to do good,' he said, 'and now they want a piece of my hide? Why do we have to pay when we're the best?' Shelly said, 'You think that makes a difference?'

Dowd began passing the envelopes to Shelly late in 1982; he paid maybe a total of $30,000 in used notes. He didn't condone it, he says, but he thought it was necessary. He never knew where the money was truly going, although Shelly had told him at that first lunch, 'Believe me, Mike, there's nothing in it for me.' But he found out, when Shelly was laid in the ground the next year. After the funeral, Donald Manes himself came up to Dowd and told him that in future the envelopes should go to a man called Geoffrey Lindenauer, who was deputy director of the Parking Violations Bureau, which employed Computrace. Dowd was startled. 'I've looked out my window and seen Manes going down the street with the President of the United States, arm in arm,' he said. 'He was the most powerful political public figure, certainly in Queens. The Mayor called him his best friend and said he didn't make a move without him.'

There came a time when Dowd would not pay any more, even though he knew the city's contract with Computrace would not be renewed. He went off to play racquetball with the boss, and Manes tried to 'work something out about another way to pay' through his strenuous breathing. But Dowd had had enough. He told his friend Peter Maas, 'I didn't want a foot on my throat for the rest of my life.' He went to talk to the Feds.

It should have been a prosecutor's dream: putting the heat on a borough boss, who would tell all the stories that were to be told. But the Feds met Manes, and realised they could not insist on anything.

The man had fractured. His own lawyer said Manes 'could talk, he could listen, he could understand – but he would just tune out.' He was being visited by nightmares. Twice in those weeks, Michael Callahan came to Manes' home, stayed for a while, slipped discreetly out of the back door and went to a pay-phone, checking to see if he was followed. Callahan identified himself in an 1982 trial as a close associate of Joseph Trocchio, a member of the Genovese crime family.

On the night of 14 March, Marlene Manes called her husband's psychiatrist from the phone in the first floor bedroom, with Manes himself on the kitchen extension. She wanted to find him a hospital bed. His daughter Lauren could see he was fretting, opening and shutting the knife drawer. The doctor put down the phone for a moment to answer his doorbell; when he came back, he could hear screams from the dangling phone. Manes had pulled an Ecko Flint knife from the drawer and driven the nine inches of the blade into his heart. He died almost at once.

In the communal memory, the great New York scams belonged to 'Boss' Tweed in the 1860s, a flashy villain who was unrepentant to his jailhouse death, or to Mayor Jimmy Walker, a wit and a poser exposed in the 1930s, who sailed away from the city for exile in Europe. Donald Manes, the men on Queens Boulevard reckoned, was ordinary: a family man with a mock-Tudor house, and a second home at the shore that he bought cheap and three kids at college at the same time, a middle-class guy on the usual financial rack. Villainy had become ordinary and systemic, like a party ticket. Manes told his buddy Geoffrey Lindenauer that he planned to run for mayor, and then Lindenauer would see how to really make money.

This Lindenauer was a quack, an unsuccessful one who ran the Institute for Emotional Education in a nice building near Gramercy Park. He offered to sort out sex, emotions, self-esteem, all the raw issues, at forty dollars for a half-hour session. He practised psycho-drama. Sometimes, he admitted later, he also fucked the patients; the Institute became notorious for its sex therapy, its 'financial therapy' and something called 'milieu therapy'. He was Dr Lindenauer on the strength of a degree in 'church history' from Philathea, an unaccredited Bible college in London, Ontario. But he impressed Marlene Manes, a psychotherapist herself, who started visiting from time to time. She introduced the Lindenauers to her husband. Marlene and Geoffrey seemed the closest of the four, but the two men were friends; they would go off together fishing, or shopping, or on slimming cures in upstate New York. Lindenauer thought Manes was his best friend.

Perhaps Manes put $25,000 into Lindenauer's clinics in 1973. If he did, it was a poor investment. The clinics closed the next year, for no respectable reason. Two years later, Manes eased Lindenauer into his first city job: assistant commissioner in the New York City Addiction Services Agency. Nobody asked questions because that is what bosses do. When the agency folded and its work went over to New York State, Lindenauer was salvaged, and made administrative manager of the Parking Violations Bureau, which collects parking fines. Stanley Friedman, the boss of the Democrats in the Bronx, made the arrangements at Donald Manes' personal request; you arrange such things through the party. Lindenauer was properly grateful, since rather few owners of failed sex clinics are put in charge of such a cash machine; in New York, only the bureau which collects property taxes has a more impressive cashflow. Lindenauer began to feel guilty about the money Manes had lost in his clinics. 'So why don't you pay me back?' Manes asked.

Lindenauer first sold a ring that belonged to his wife, and handed Manes $2,500. Then Manes suggested he could make more money if only he would make life easier for Datacom, one of the debt-collecting agencies that served the Parking Bureau. Datacom was willing to pay for ease. 'Donald said to me, in this way you can start to repay me.' The first bribe was $500 in cash. Lindenauer took it back to Manes and handed over half. 'Where is the rest?' Manes asked. Lindenauer said he'd thought the two men were partners; but he said immediately that he must have misunderstood. Perhaps it was a test, because in later deals Manes settled for half the money. Lindenauer began slowly to learn the rules. Every man needs his 'rabbi', his protector, and he needed Manes. Manes 'always preferred to deal with lawyers because they have licences to protect' and could not blab like company executives. And Lindenauer discovered that not even lawyers were always to be trusted. 'The bottom line,' he said, entirely without irony, 'is that I never got the right amount.'

The parking bureau had a problem with illegible parking tickets, and the difficulty in spotting scofflaws who simply ignored the tickets they received. A company called Citisource claimed to have a four pound hand-held computer that the New York parking police could use. The deal was peculiarly sweet; instead of a few test machines, the contract called for a city-wide system all at once at a cost of $22.7

million. To get the deal, Citisource hired Stanley Friedman for his influence and sold him 167,500 shares of stock at a penny a share. When Friedman unloaded in December 1985, he got six dollars a share. But this deal somehow slipped the company's mind until the city had cleared the contract, even though it seemed to make Friedman the company's largest shareholder. This may have something to do with what Geoffrey Lindenauer told a Citisource executive: 'If Stanley does not get the stock, your company's deal is dead.' Friedman was eventually convicted of holding the stock for Donald Manes and Geoffrey Lindenauer, something he always denied.

Eight companies, and Citisource, bid for the contract, but the game was rigged. The proposal was rewritten so that computer makers like Motorola had to show they could also do routine keypunching and microfilming while the computers were made ready; Marvin Kaplan, boss of Citisource, happened to have a company which already did just that for the city. Lindenauer handed all the proposals over to Citisource, who wrote their own evaluations – 'Motorola: Buck Rogers kind of stuff. Inadequate,' they said, and 'Citisource: Excellent.' Lindenauer had them typed out as if they were his own. The selection committee taped their meetings and Lindenauer handed the tapes to Citisource so they knew precisely what was being said and could tell him how to answer. Towards the end, some shrewd official asked if Citisource could actually manufacture a working printer. Lindenauer announced that he had been to the plant and seen the machine work. But when Citisource went public on the strength of its contract, papers filed with the Securities and Exchange Commission told a story rather different from the one the city had accepted. The design and making of the machines was to be sub-contracted. There was no 'pre-production' prototype, no 'officers' of the company to supervise everything. There was just a notion and a profit.

To make sure of the deal, Friedman was easing his way into the offices of the deputy mayors to ask why budget officials were taking their time on the contract. Friedman was an illusionist, the kind of politician thrown up by the remains of a once-great Democratic machine; 'He has lived closer to the line of chutzpah than the other county leaders,' one elected official said. He had no great record in getting his own men elected, and his borough was poor and shrinking. He was a Jew repudiated by Jewish voters, whose power rested partly on the remaining Italians and Irish of the Bronx, but mostly on his skill at keeping black and Hispanic leaders at each other's throats.

'You walk in there relaxed,' an observer said of the Bronx delegations meetings up at Albany, 'and you walk out sweating, listening to them attack each other.' More, he was a politician who never bothered with elected public office. He left his one lifetime job, on the city Board of Water Supply, when he became the Bronx Democratic boss. 'I am on no public payrolls – city, state, federal or otherwise,' he declared. But when he entered a room, a brash man dressed with a permanent cigar, power entered.

He played the favour game – when to give them, which to take and how to remember, always. His father, an aide in the parking bureau, used to help him 'fix' parking tickets for friends. Under Mayor Beame, he was the fount of patronage; he even chose which kids got summer jobs on strict party grounds. Mayor Koch liked to complain that Friedman, a registered lobbyist for the taxi fleet owners, had virtual veto power on city laws about the cab trade; but he was one of the few intimates who was invited, every four years, to the private midnight inaugurals of the mayor. His men ran the State Insurance Fund, the city commissions on planning, tax, taxi and limousines and even the civil service. He was chairman of the Bronx Overall Economic Development Corporation, which ran millions in federal, state and city loans to local businesses. He divided up patronage with Donald Manes, boss to boss; in 1986, for example, it was his turn to name the city clerk. For all this political power, power that derived from his position in the Democrat Party, he never needed to listen to all the grand, hot ethical talk that came from City Hall. 'This is the system,' he said. 'It may be deplorable, you may not like it – change the system.'

But it was a hidden system that went about nervously. Manes complained of his financial troubles, and then, when the money was flowing, complained he might have to go bankrupt because he could not account for his income. Lindenauer collected cash by the urinals of Manhattan restaurants. When he delivered to the Queens Borough Hall, he only pointed to his pocket and went to Manes' private bathroom to divide the cash. Graft was oddly like a drug, in its rituals as well as its pull. Lindenauer even told Manes he wanted to quit. 'I was very scared. I told him I was having all these meetings in bathrooms and he wasn't.' Manes insisted it would take another year to set up all the contracts. Lindenauer was trapped in the politics of a dime novel. When he wanted to know how many shares Friedman held for him, he started to say a number. Friedman held up his hand. 'He wrote the number on a piece of paper,' Lindenauer remembered. 'He had a large plain ashtray on his desk. And then he ripped it up and then he burned the paper.' At his trial, Friedman had to explain why he did not report what he took to be a shake-down by Lindenauer and Manes. 'There was no way I was going to blow a whistle on a good friend without talking to him first,' he said.

Friedman at least was robust. Manes and Lindenauer had closed themselves off in a sour, addictive space. According to Friedman, Manes said Lindenauer was losing his mind, off the wall, out of control. Marvin Kaplan, chairman of Citisource, also thought Lindenauer was a problem. 'The Fat Boy's becoming a pig – he's getting greedy,' he once said to Friedman, who agreed. 'Yeah, he's becoming a pig. He's stupid.' Lindenauer took the whole business personally. He needed his associates, and his boss, Lester Shafran, director of the bureau, to be just like him. Again, graft worked oddly like a drug; the addict went recruiting. He encouraged Bernard Sandow, an executive with Systematic Recovery Services Inc., to be a friend to Shafran, but Shafran only said, 'Bernie, the best way to share your success with me is to continue doing a good job.' That was not what Lindenauer wanted to hear. A few months later, Shafran mentioned to Sandow that he wanted a new TV set and a VCR, and Sandow provided. In the years that followed, Sandow gave the bureau chief tickets to Florida and tickets to *Cats*, a gold money-clip, a new kitchen, the videotaping of the bas mitzvah of Shafran's daughter; each time, Sandow reported the gift to Lindenauer and Lindenauer was 'very happy'. In the end, Shafran was taking money in folded newspapers at lunch, or down in the men's room.

Lindenauer could not afford to lose him, and nor could Sandow. In the presence of a government informer, both men had lunch at Hisae's Restaurant in Manhattan to discuss how to persuade Shafran to stay in his job. They talked violence, flattery, women, money, a flight to Chicago to meet powerful people, the promise of becoming an international financier and shifting millions through Switzerland for political grandees, the more remote promise of becoming 'head honcho of all transportation on a national level in Washington', and, when that was done, a truly gold-plated future as a consultant. But their real power over Shafran was different and pernicious. When Sandow went to see him next, Shafran's first question was, 'Are you wired?' Lindenauer had made Shafran suspect the world just as he did.

On 26 December 1985, Manes and Lindenauer knew their deals were being investigated. Three days later, they met in Manes' living room. Manes asked: 'Are you going to run? Are you going to leave town?' Lindenauer said he had no money left; all his $250,000 in bribes was gone. Manes leaned across and said: 'If this had happened to Shelly' – he meant Sheldon Chevlowe, the first intermediary – 'Shelly would go like this.' Manes put his finger to his head and pulled a trigger. Both men shivered. Manes' father had killed himself, and so had Lindenauer's father, a New Jersey lawyer convicted of trying to slip a bribe to a cop. 'Donald, nothing has happened yet,' Lindenauer said. 'God forbid, if something should happen, I wouldn't turn you in.' The next day he went to his friend Dr Jerome Driesen to ask if there was a way to 'commit suicide but not make it appear as if it was suicide.' Driesen's answer was practical: what Lindenauer needed was the cash and the nerve to leave the country.

Manes arranged to meet Lindenauer across the street from Stanley Friedman's law office in Manhattan; but when Manes was crossing the street, a car stopped and asked him where Friedman's office was, and Manes panicked. Everything now happened with the expectation that the FBI was watching. Manes made a new appointment: outside Dr Driesen's office, two hours later. 'He was nervous, he was erratic,' Lindenauer remembered. When Lindenauer said he needed $400,000, Manes said, 'What are you, nuts?' The two men began walking, two big sets of shoulders in the tent of their coats. Manes started to hand over an envelope, and then pulled back, several times. The two men got into Lindenauer's car and Manes finally handed over the envelope, stuffed with $58,000.

They met again only once, at the ceremony where Manes was sworn for a new term as borough president. 'He wanted to know if I was going to go,' Lindenauer said. He had meant to run, but he was still talking with lawyers about safe countries and extradition laws and suchlike when the federal agents arrived.

This is the city Donald Manes knew. Mayors do not interfere with the borough bosses. The mayor, his candidates and the borough presidents sit on a powerful Board of Estimate, approving what the city spends and how the city is built, but none of them stays for the big votes. Those go by proxy. The City Council talks about the city, and nobody listens. But there is an apparatus that governs the city, and everyone knows how to find it, cajole it, grease it.

In Manes' time, typists at a Department of Buildings office kept jars near their desk for contributions, which made the documents flow that much more quickly. Landlords bribed ten dollars a case in Brooklyn to rush eviction cases through the system. Sewer inspectors worked punishing days in bars, taking cash from contractors who did not get paid until their work was approved; slow paperwork was ruin. Throughout the city machinery, a little money helped things happen. If you paid, anything could be overlooked. Stephen Harasti, an electrical inspector for twenty years, walked on to a Queens building site and went to look at the fuse box. 'I don't wanna look too goddamned hard in this place,' he said. The contractor, who was actually an undercover cop said, 'Twenty enough?' Harasti took the cash and said, 'Plenty, plenty.' The system made it simpler for supermarkets to pay off Consumer Affairs inspectors, rather than give good weight or keep to health rules; nine inspectors were indicted in 1980. Restaurant inspectors expected to be paid off for a dishwasher that did not reach the right temperature or a freezer that was too warm; in one clean restaurant, where the owner did not speak English, the inspector was reduced to drawing a raw little caricature of a rat. The owner understood and reached in his pocket.

Money eased negotiations. Alex Liberman, New York's director of lease negotiations, told witnesses to lie about the money they'd given to his synagogue, or directly to him, around the time they wanted the city to lease their trickiest bits of property; $2.6 million was involved. Herbert Ryan, a taxi commissioner, took $1,400 from a city detective who pretended to want the exclusive right to have his unofficial cabs collect passengers on the streets of Queens and Brooklyn; the money was simply part of a proposal. Nova Scotia Fish Products wanted to move its plant from Greenpoint in Brooklyn to a city site in Bushwick; City Councilman Luis A. Olmedo agreed to swing his local community board's support, in return for $12,000 for him and for friends. In court, he said the money was a legitimate public relations fee. As for why he did not walk away from the 'construction executives' who on another occasion offered him thirty per cent of the first public contract he landed for them, he said they were 'big men'. He was 'too afraid'.

The system looked after its own. Councilman Vincent Riccio was indicted for finding his mistress Natalie Kachougian a cushy, no-show job on the Temporary State Commission on Child Welfare and having the city pay her $18,000; his own lawyer said the story was a 'trashy love novel'. State Senator Vander L. Beatty siphoned off some $200,000 from the Bedford-Stuyvesant Urban Development Corporation between 1979 and 1983; he 'placed ghosts on the payroll, and wrote out cheques for the enterprise to political allies, friends, family and personal staff members for services never rendered,' according to the US Attorney. 'He then forged their names or otherwise had close associates endorse and cash the cheques for him.' The Bed-Stuy organisation never did anything much, except take money from New York State; its board, managed by Beatty, never met, had no members, never convened, never voted on anything. Beatty took J. Moise Michel, the corporation's executive director, to lunch when Michel was worried about cheques to a 'Joseph Salmon' and a 'Douglas Edwards'. 'I don't think these people exist,' Michel said. All business-like, Beatty answered: 'What I think is you ought to write up something about what they did.' He thought it best to call them 'consultants'. The city, after all, was spending $2 billion a year on consultants.

Informers lost their good jobs, got flesh wounds, were railed at by the mayor. On occasions, they died. Enrico Mazzeo was pulled out of the boot of a rented car with four bullets in his head. Mazzeo was a sad case – back living with his Mom, without job or money but with a cocaine habit that needed constant feeding. Five years before, he had been director of leases for the bureau which runs the Staten Island Ferry, and the parking lots and concessions around its docks; he had been the working landlord of the newspaper stand called, nicely, 'Terminal Industries'. He ran several businesses out of his ferry office; if you called the numbers in Yellow Pages, a phone rang in his desk drawer. He had somehow managed to spend more than his salary on renting a Long Island mansion. His aspirations were written on his number plate, which read GATSBY.

But most significantly, he shuttled back and forth by city limousine to the law office of Roy Cohn, where he was 'a ubiquitous person', in Cohn's words. He was a minor civil servant, but courted and on occasions defended by Cohn himself, the operator of New York's 'favour bank', where favours become a kind of currency. Cohn helped out city bosses and disco owners and cardinals and mobsters and publishing moguls and clung to such a strict cash economy that the Internal Revenue Service spent decades trying even to estimate his affairs. At Cohn's office, various companies had their headquarters.

The business of some of them was parking lots, a good cash business, and the concessions leased from the ferry bureau. Rick Mazzeo liked to say he went to Cohn's office because it was 'the only way to get the rent on time', but the city's Department of Investigations thought Mazzeo was Cohn's bagman. By understating the number of cars on each lot, Cohn and his associates could skim hundreds of thousands of dollars – $700,000 at one lot alone – and someone had to deliver the spare cash.

When finally this game was up, Cohn yelped and threatened the auditors with writs, which only shows how important the cash had become. Mazzeo left the city's employ and in late 1982, he was sent to jail for charges based on the odd fact that he had found $564,000 to put into his sideline companies while earning $15,000 a year from the city. The Feds kept hinting at other charges they could bring, and Mazzeo hinted he might talk. He tried to bully Roy Cohn, a hopeless task, into setting him right with the city. He told one reporter Stanley Friedman had done all he could to protect Cohn's leases. He lay in his car four days before he was found.

Politicians looked to politicians to protect them. Mayor Koch suggested, after Stanley Friedman had been convicted, that the jury must have been anti-Semitic. When reporters brought up Friedman's activities, Koch shouted: 'Why are you saying these terrible things about him?' The city's investigations department hated to embarrass the mayor. The city seemed to have no official memory when it came to protecting itself. In 1982, four years before the Manes scandal ripened and broke, the comptroller of the Parking Violations Bureau warned Investigations that the bureau was corrupt. Investigations decided that there was only a management problem and its own official memory was that the bureau had somehow been cleared; it took the FBI to bring up the subject effectively.

The political machine took precautions at the polls. State Senator Beatty was also convicted for trying to rig an election. When he lost a Democratic primary, his supporters hid in the ceiling of the men's room until the election board office was deserted, and then swarmed down to change the voter records, slipping in the buff forms which show someone has voted. Brooklyn primaries were quite usually rigged in the 1970s and 1980s. One man voted ten times in 1970; in 1976, his job was to lead groups of bogus voters from polling place to polling place, casting 550 illegal votes. A voter does not need identification to vote, not a driver's licence, not anything; you need more proof of identity to borrow books from a city library. The Elections Board is appointed by the Democrat and Republican county organisations, stuffed with patronage employees whose skills are minimal; sometimes, they failed to give printers the proper samples of election forms, or legible lists, or either on time. The machine can harass independents off the poll, just by showing they miscounted the number of signatures on their election petitions, even by one name, or misnumbered the pages. In 1985, the Justice Department sent observers to only two places – to Mississippi, to make sure black voters were not intimidated, and to New York City to make sure that Spanish-speakers were not sent away from the polls because nobody could translate for them.

Then, the city has been held so long by the Democrats that the party is the government. The county leaders in Manhattan, the Bronx and Queens – like Friedman – virtually appoint civil court judges simply by naming them as Democrat candidates. Patronage assigns jobs because the city lacks the machinery. The strength of the city Democrats makes the opportunities for the local ones. People still go down to the Democrat clubhouses because they help people, help fight some Dracula landlords and move the drug pushers on and find a lawyer or a summer job or a city official who cares if a street light has gone dead. Even with welfare services, and rules for entering the civil service, the clubhouse is useful. Joe Maggio of the McManus Democratic Club on West 48th Street says the club used to hand out turkeys and coal to the poor, and find patronage jobs for everyone, but nowadays the candidates elect themselves with TV advertising. But a woman comes into the storefront office, and the club says it will help her find an apartment; she's gleeful. She'll be back to put out nominating petitions or take round campaign pamphlets. And Joe Maggio congratulates himself. Politics is run by people who give money, he says, so the politicians would vote for cockroaches if the Cockroach Association just had a political action committee. 'At least,' he says, 'the party has the interest of common people at heart.'

The burying places used to stink in summer, a *memento mori* on the air. It was the first clear sign that inside all the bustle and power of New York City, there was only a weak official machine. In the 1800s, doctors thought the stench from vaults and graves held the particles of yellow fever. Builders saw the graveyards as a ragged obstacle to the growth of an orderly city. The Common Council took action and banned all new burials within city bounds. But the churches objected. They said they held the graveyards on city leases which allowed more funerals. The city claimed it had police powers to abate a public nuisance. The issue of the charnel stink went to the courts, which ruled that the city had both a private and a public nature, that it had property and the duties which went with it, but that it could also make rules of public health and city expansion. But this power to control itself was derived from the State of New York. A city had no citizens, no legal standing of its own, and no power to rule itself; it was a creature of the state.

This nice legal point mattered to the lawyers who dominated civic affairs until well into the 1870s, and are still talking. In law, New York City is a very slight thing compared with the rushes of new population on its territory and its dizzy growth. Lawyers were pretty sure in the 1800s that the city could make rules against smoking in livery stables and open fires on the deck of docked ships, because the city could make by-laws 'for the Public good'; but still it seemed wise to ask the State legislature first. The city had to ask permission to move the municipal powder magazine in 1807, urgent as the move was; the city poor were often evacuated under its walls during epidemics and blasting to make new roads was threatening to blow the magazine's walls. Laying out the grid of Manhattan required a petition to the State Assembly; so did a by-law that banned the inspection of meat south of Lispenard's Meadow.

Pigs occupied the streets, 'prowling in grunting ferocity'; they were food for working families, an unofficial cleaning squad, and a bristling, risky nuisance. When the city successfully prosecuted a pig-owner in 1818, not even counsel for the city argued that it had the power to ban the pigs on its own. To make any kind of change, New York's fathers needed compulsion, since the people of the city no longer shared assumptions about what should be done, and their duty to do it. To keep the power to compel, the city fathers had to nurse their political links to Albany. The city was proud, thriving, a new Venice, but it was also a paradox: a highly political place, where all manner of issues had to be resolved urgently, which was officially a place with no political institutions worth the name.

*

Into this gap came the Society of St Tammany, an 'improving society'. For as long as New York was America's capital, Tammany was a 'national' improving society. In 1787, the society held the first of its grand celebrations of the Fourth of July, which in time would be famous for both passion and tedium, with 5,000 people listening to the Declaration of Independence and patriotic speeches in a hall full of smoke and summer sweat, followed by flag-waving and fireworks. Its first leading light was John Pintard, a universal kind of man without whom no New York movement could begin, who was political enough to be involved in the planning for the Erie Canal, learned enough to be a founder of the Literary and Philosophical Society of New York, and simple enough to believe that Tammany's 'democratic principles will serve in some measure to correct the aristocracy of our city'.

Tammany's first chief, called the Grand Sachem in the manner of the Algonquin tribes, and installed at the Society's 'wigwam', was certainly a democratic figure: a furniture dealer, paperhanger and upholsterer. In a republic which still hankered after the rule of a landed gentry, this was a radical notion. It began the tradition in which Tammany claimed to be the 'true home of the working classes' that included 'all sober, respectable mechanics of New York', and organised so well on behalf of the new Democratic Party that in the 1850s it was reckoned a third of the electorate would 'vote for the devil himself if he had Tammany's endorsement'.

This machine grew slowly, at its most powerful when there was a mass franchise and thousands of newly arrived voters. Until then, the city was a muddle of powers. In a wooden city, where arson was a main concern of the watch, the firemen were heroes. They answered to a chief engineer, who answered to the Tammany Common Council, but according to Philip Hone in 1836, they were 'so courted for political objects that they appear to consider themselves above the law'. The Council disapproved of the boys who ran with the firemen, the 'volunteers' who helped to drag the engines and clean the equipment, who lived for the rough exercise and the honour of being alongside the companies. Solid citizens saw them run an engine down the sidewalk for the sake of speed, or move it from the firehouse before the official firemen arrived. Hone suspected they were 'idlers and vagabonds who raise false alarms in order to get out the engines'. But any insult to the 'volunteers' was an insult to the firemen. Magistrates tried to ban the boys from the firehouse, and even seized a fire company's engine when the boys played up at a fire to the point of riot. Tammany and the firemen were at odds.

Without explanation, the Common Council decided on 4 May 1836 to sack James Gulick as chief engineer of the department. The message reached Gulick as he was fighting a fire on Houston Street. When the ordinary firemen heard, they set down their pumps and hoses and Gullick had to talk them back to work. They suspected politics. They petitioned for Gulick's return, but his reinstatement was delayed while Whigs and Democrats wrangled over who should be president of the aldermen; Tammany could not control even the body which could give orders to the firemen. In September, all but five of the city's forty-nine fire companies resigned. Tammany announced it would find 'new and equally efficient men in their places', but it could not. James Gulick stood for public office against a Tammany man, and won handily at an otherwise close election because the firemen had formed a voting bloc of their own. They threw their support to Aaron Clark for mayor, and he also won handily over the Tammany candidate. Even money and patronage worked against Tammany, since firemen were not professionals, and they strongly objected to the Council's idea that assistant engineers should be paid $500 a year. The firemen stayed resolutely amateur for thirty years more, a city service that the city could not control.

Tammany was only beginning to acquire patronage, a system for finding jobs for newcomers and taking their votes in return. It was a socially useful version of the Washington placemen who quite usually owed their jobs to party, but it appalled visitors. On Charles Dickens' trip to America in 1841, he had been horrified by the way even guards in a New York lunatic asylum had to belong to the right party; in *Martin Chuzzlewit* the losing party in a city election 'found it necessary to assert the great principles of Purity of Election and Freedom of Opinion by breaking a few legs and arms, and furthermore pursuing one obnoxious gentleman through the streets with the design of slitting his nose.' Tammany was identified with the new immigrants but until the 1860s, the rolls of patronage show, it was not a peculiarly Irish organisation; only the lowest of its placemen were Irish.

Its radicalism was the cautious kind. In the 1860s, Tammany took up the causes of booze, parochial schools and religious freedom; but it was careful to keep a distance from the working men's meetings that were thought seditious, and the working men that federal troops in 1857 had to hold back from the Customs House and the armoury. Tammany intended to survive, to be the body that even the Fifth Avenue Hotel Association, gentlemen Democrats, needed if they were to be voted into power. But it stood four square for whatever the working classes needed to get them to the polls. It gouged out money to make its political machine work, from tarts or bawdy houses or public works; it offered protection before there was a police force, and then it offered protection against the cops. It imposed a kind of system on all the missing aspects of the city. Tammany could get people employed, working and elected, while reformers could not pass the ballot box and did not have the levers to run the city. Its success horrified its literate, thoughtful enemies. They feared universal suffrage, thought only property owners should vote on public works and wanted the city run like a business by 'men of standing, moral weight and courage' like themselves; they talked as though the legal fiction of the city was real and New York was no political entity at all, only the old private corporation.

Democrats ran the city, Republicans the state. Rural virtue shouted its mouth off in Albany about that terrible, alien place called New York. New Yorkers denounced the upstate Republicans as 'vampires [who] feed by means of corrupt legislation upon our city treasury'. The Democrats pointed out that the city controlled only a quarter of its own spending. It was already famous for dizzying change, but the city itself had the power to change nothing. In the battles over building the Broadway railway in 1857, the Chief Justice of New York State argued that the city might have the power to surface a street or repair it, the traditional matters connected with a street, but that was the limit of its jurisdiction. It could not license some new use of a street. In 1857, Albany decided to exploit this fact after a half-century of reticence, and interfere enthusiastically with the running of the city.

Upstate politicians talked freely of corruption, but then everybody talked of New York corruption. In the late seventeenth century, city elections were public burlesques. In the 1790s, the Federalists were ruthless in doling out the city payroll to their supporters. In 1854, reformers complained of 'cormorants in every department of the government'. On that pretext, police, fire, health and the building of Central Park were all shifted from city offices to state commissions. Albany took back the power that, in law, it had always had. The crisis might have been avoided if Tammany had shown any sign of sharing the spoils, for the state brought no great reformation; in 1861, Simon

Chittenden stood up at a taxpayers' meeting to say that 'free men will not much longer put up with the robbery, the corruption, the infamy which have disgraced city government'.

By the start of the Civil War, the two great divides in New York city politics were already established. There was the tussle between the state and the raw, wild city it happened to contain, which led to passionate campaigns for home rule. There was the long struggle between the newly built political machine, which could make things happen in New York, and reformers who, for the most part, could only try to stop them. It was New York's ill luck that the man who wrote a new charter for New York in 1870, brought powers to the city and invested the mayor with them, had his own agenda. William Marcy Tweed was planning to steal New York.

19 October, 1871. The outer room at the Department of Public Works was full of official men in smart clothes, wearing the diamonds that rogues wear. In his inner office, Boss Tweed sat at his desk with scissors, snipping nervously at any bit of paper he could reach, a big-boned, slouchy man whose silence and thoughtfulness were unusual. For a decade, he knew just what to say; if anyone challenged his influence, he simply asked 'What are you going to do about it?' and grinned because he knew there was nothing to be done. But now a reporter was telling him that the books of the Broadway Bank had been opened and there was proof of his exact transactions. His way of talking changed. 'I don't know anything about it,' he told the reporter. 'What can I do?' he said, knowing there was nothing to be done.

Eighteen months earlier, in 'Tweed Plaza' where Canal Street runs into East Broadway, there were fireworks and gunpowder and banners and balloons and Fink's Washington Band playing loud. The William M. Tweed Club marched onto the square, under a banner with a woven portrait of the 'Boss' and assorted mottos, including 'Let justice strike the blow when ingrates dare the field'. His Tammany followers were shouting in favour of Senator Tweed and his brave struggle to bring home rule to New York City. 'I congratulate you,' the Boss said in a letter to the crowd, 'upon the restoration of municipal rights. I trust our victory will, by wise use of its fruits, result in raising our party above the plane of selfish aggrandizement.'

Remember this scene. Boss Tweed was a manipulator and a thief on a wonderful scale, but he was much more; he magnified the politics of New York City until it worked. He understood faction, and ethnic faction in particular; his constituency was Catholic, partly German but mostly Irish. He turned the Democrats of Tammany Hall into a rough machine which could bribe, bully and cheat its way to continued power. Treasury bills did what party discipline would later do. He brought back powers to the city and especially to its mayor. He rode a building boom to power, glorying in the expansion of the city, and taking his 'rake' on it. He understood the new, ebullient nationalism that followed the Civil War, the process of Americanisation. He also understood, all too well, debt financing and how to water stock.

In a city with minimal government and little concern for new-comers, Tweed was also friend of the immigrant, able to slip new men into city life when the city itself resisted. In the wards, he and the other Tammany leaders would help an Irishman get naturalised or find him a job on the city payroll, or bring down coal and food when the newcomers were hungry or cold. In the State Senate, Tweed sat on the Committee on Charitable and Religious Societies and bent the law to finance the Catholic parochial schools; earlier Democrats had tolerated common-school teachers who proselytised from the Protestant Bible. He got money for Catholic orphanages, hospitals and dispensaries, all ways to soften the cold edges of the city. Still, to worthier citizens, he was an affront: gaudy, brutish, corrupt and somehow alien, although he was a Scotsman like some of the founders of colonial New York. He acknowledged, as they could not, the mean-ing of giving every man the vote; he worked with the 'dangerous classes'. Upstate Republicans were terribly afraid that either New York was run by Tweed's Democrats or else it would again explode and burn as it had done in the draft riots of the Civil War.

The Boss was a walking affront – a bankrupt in a merchant city, who had failed at his father's business of making chairs; who traded on his reputation as 'Big Six', chief and hero of the fire-fighters of Engine Company Number 6, a standing rebuke to New York grandees who no longer did such civic service; an uneducated man who had read law for himself, infiltrating the rich man's knowledge without bothering to take on the duties of a professional. He was the horror of the evangelical, teetotal middle classes – a defender of Popery, who owned a corner grogshop with a retired prize-fighter behind the bar to ladle out booze called 'tangle-leg' and 'kill-me-quick' to loyalists.

He drank on the Sabbath, he wore a diamond which once had belonged to rajahs, he lived in a mansion at Greenwich, Connecticut and a Fifth Avenue palace at 43rd Street where fountains played and the walls were hung with good all-American paintings; for Tweed had an eye. He was one of the people, the successful one. Above all, he had the power to change things, which respectable, lawful gentry so obviously lacked.

He was never mayor, never governor; he was elected to the State Senate only in 1868. '. . . It pays Mr Tweed much better to put other men in responsible positions, and be content himself with pulling the wires that move the puppets,' as the *New York Times* wrote. His power lay in organisation. He was Grand Sachem of Tammany Hall, and through Tammany he controlled every Democrat nomination in the city, and the machine that engineered their votes. He was Chairman of the Court House Committee, which allowed him to skim nine million out of its twelve million dollar budget. With the bright, would-be literary fellow Mayor Hall and Controller 'Slippery Dick' Connolly, he formed a Board of Audit in 1870 which somehow managed to pass $6,095,309 in fraudulent claims against the city out of the $6,312,641 that it examined. He was part-owner of the New York Printing Company, which printed for the city on very generous terms. He controlled the city's Department of Public Works and all it spent. It's not enough to say Boss Tweed was an embezzler on a monstrous scale, or to paint him as the architect of a welfare system before its time. Instead of good intentions, the Boss had something new in New York: a system.

His supporters did not mind if he was a thief, since he stole mostly from the city; men worth under a thousand dollars were not taxed and there were hardly enough taxpayers to make a revolt. Tweed closed the books of the Tax Commissioners in 1870, so that nobody could check who else was paying what. Railroads, given Tweed's famous position on the board of the Erie Railroad, did particularly well; the Dry Dock, East Broadway and Battery road, for example, was down on the books for real estate worth $152,000 and other property worth $100,000, even though its real worth on the stock market was four times as much – $1,176,000. The city's tax rate was a fraud in itself. Tweed's tax bills in the State Assembly allowed a rate of only two per cent, but that was two per cent of the value of every bit of property in the city, whether or not it paid tax, and the nominal capital of every company whether or not it had ever been issued. Since the real tax base was much smaller, real taxpayers paid much more. Tweed also understood debt, which gave him generous pickings and left the taxpayer, apparently, with only interest to pay for the moment. The city's growth had rested on debt from the 1850s, when work on opening new streets first went ahead before all the taxes from local landowners were in the bank. In the railroad capital of America, railroad bonds were an obvious model. During the Civil War, the city acquired a war debt in the name of patriotism and the nation – to pay bounties to the families of volunteers, to buy substitutes for those conscripts who wanted to slip out of the draft and to repair the damage done by the riots and lynchings that the draft provoked. But debt was a device that politicians were not used to judging, not until it began to frighten them. In 1871, the Citizens' Committee reckoned it would take only three more years for New York's debt to equal the assessed value of all the real and personal property in the city.

Elections were Tammany's masterpiece – expensive, at a million dollars a time on the estimate of the *New York Herald*, but ruthless. They were glad of luck, as when a Republican police commissioner took to chasing other Republican factions out of the rooms they had hired for election meetings, but they never relied on it. Immigrants from Ward's Island were brought over to Manhattan, and the corner loafers joined them at headquarters in each election district. The Secretary held a book of names, picked at random out of city directories, and of addresses – most of them hotels or empty houses owned by good, solid Democrats; each man was issued with a name and an address and went off to register to vote, four or five times in each district, before moving on to the next. Somehow the cops never did quite recognise familiar faces, and the election inspectors liked to ask no questions; which was not surprising, since many of the inspectors were Tweed's own men, some of them notorious, some of them plain criminal. One, in the fourth senatorial district, had a sinecure at $100 a month with the Water Police but made his living as a gambler. On election day, he led a gang of eighteen 'repeaters' from precinct to precinct, sometimes grabbing the register to reel off names, always moving too fast for any honest inspector to check. The Deputy Superintendent of the Bureau of Supplies, responsible for checking the bills the city paid, was William Hennessy Cooke; he was famous as the leader of a gang of election day 'repeaters' who were paid fifty cents a vote. In five districts of the Sixth Ward the number of registered voters was actually larger than the number of men living in the ward – native, naturalised and alien all together. Observers from other parties were beaten or warned off or even arrested by the police. And still, as a kind of insurance, Tammany adjusted the registers and sent out the old wooden ballot boxes already filled with votes for Tammany, or had them filled before the polls opened.

All the city's business was off-kilter. A saloon keeper who had not paid off Tammany might find he was suddenly served a last notice to pay water rent, even though he had no faucet in his saloon. Charles Jacobus, a jobbing carpenter, used to wait at his Pearl Street office for messengers from Tweed's department, who ordered up work; the city books showed he had been paid $20,000. 'I have never received a single cent of that $20,000,' he said. As for the $7,050.75 that the city claimed to have paid him for plumbing, 'I never have done a cent's worth of plumbing all my life.' A small city office, supposed to lay water-pipes, managed to spend $10,605 in a single month on envelopes, pens, paper and ink; they bought from Manufacturers' Stationers and W.C. Rogers. The city needed $11,593 worth of mats, spittoons, water coolers, brooms and axes between 18 April and 6 May from Edward Marrenner and, astonishingly, another $15,164 worth in the next three weeks. Somehow Tweed's department spent its two million dollar allocation, and another million on tick, and still the roof of the Hall of Records leaked so badly that the titles to most of New York were at risk; the thousands supposedly spent on carpet for City Hall stairs had covered only two short flights; the city's markets were tumbledown things, where stallholders paid for whatever repairs were done, despite the $76,217 that the city claimed to have spent there; the courtdoors opened to anyone, even though the books said they were equipped with dozens, even hundreds of rotary locks; and the $51,714 spent on furnishing the Department of Public Works itself left the outer rooms of Tweed's headquarters shabby, unpainted, mostly uncarpeted, with the entrance lobby scribbled over in pencil. A remarkable number of bills for all this work came to $999 or $998; bills above $1,000 had to be checked.

Tammany dealt in 'jobs' – contracts that friends could take and profit from. Streets were suddenly improved with 'Belgian pavement', charged to property owners who did not see the point of the improvement. 'All the squares below Fifty-Ninth Street,' complained the *New York Times*, '[are] in a state of chronic chaos, overrun with men, who seem to be amusing themselves with pick-axes, spades and wheel-barrows, with no object but to pass the time away, and no result but "confusion worse confounded". The scene,' the *Times* added frowstily, 'has an aspect delightfully pastoral and primitive.' There was no secret about how Tweed profited from all this; the printed contracts from the Commissioner of Public Works – one of the various sinecures held by 'the multiplied Tweed' – made his 'rake' official. Suppose a contractor was laying sewers or culverts or manhole frames or inverts; on page two of the contact, the city demands that all these be bought from Commissioner Tweed, whose prices are two to three times the usual. The pipes were made in the Long Island foundry of John H. Keyser, where Tweed was a partner. For every foot of sewer laid, Tweed held back twenty cents of the contractors' payment to repair the roadway, even though the contract insisted that the work be done before the contractor was paid. Any time a contractor wanted a certificate of work done, the commissioner got ten dollars; 'a simple blackmailing demand,' said the *New York Times*, 'for $10 whenever this cormorant had to sign his name.'

Anyone who needed to know the next great surge in the city had only to check where Tweed and company were buying land. There was the Broadway widening scam, the great Croton water scam; by his own law, Tweed as Commissioner of Public Works could buy land in Putnam County for the city's water supply, and the official Tweed bought Lake Gilead from his unofficial self for a quarter of a million dollars. A few months earlier, he had paid $25,000 for the land and water rights. When Tweed put down $300,000 for land near Essex Market, everyone knew the market would soon be demolished and a new, much more lucrative one built. He paid $130,000 for a hundred feet of Broadway frontage which just happened to back on to the new extension to Madison Avenue; together, those lots were about to be worth a million. A frame house burned down in Yonkers and Tweed's name was on the deeds; it was the first indication the city had of where its next reservoir was to be built.

The machine was waiting from the moment a man landed on America at Castle Gardens, and came out all bewildered in a strange town. The Commissioners of Emigrants were 'reorganised' in 1870, and stuffed with Tammany Sachems. The only man allowed to sell bread, milk and provisions to the newcomers was a politician's brother. A state senator had the lucrative franchise to move immigrants' luggage. If newcomers stayed in town, the only boarding houses that could tout at the gates had paid off Tammany. If he was heading west, the ticket agents for the railroads paid off Tammany; and if he was 'unassigned', then they were made to go by the Erie Railroad, where Tweed was a director. Even the paupers paid, indirectly; another politician's brother had the contract to ship them across to Ward's Island.

A Thomas Nast cartoon in *Harper's Weekly* shows the Boss squatting over the bones of New York on some dilapidated crag, a sharp and sallow bird with a huge white belly and a few beaky attendants; the caption reads 'Let Us Prey'. Nast also showed him as an obese Roman emperor at the circus, with SPOIL written where it should be SPQR, complaisantly watching the hideous Tammany tiger rip a cloak marked 'law' and a head-dress marked 'ballot' from a few dying ladies. He was seen welcoming immigrants, and the new men were shown as baboons, spoiling church and schools and 'usurping all your rights'. This Nast was an annoyance to Tweed; 'My constituents don't know how to read,' he said, 'but they can't help seeing them damned pictures.' More, the Tweed ring could do little about mockery. Its skill lay in cutting back public information, so that what everyone knew could never quite be proved. The tax rolls were closed, the city pay roll went unpublished for three years and all the citizens heard was Tweed's men demanding cuts and economies, but in a budget that was never published. Annual reports due on 1 January 1871 were withheld until June, and a pair of rich men with interests in the building boom that Tammany unleashed – John Jacob Astor was one – were hustled into city offices to certify that everything was 'all right', even though New York County could not write a cheque to pay its share of state taxes.

Most comment, even so, was kind. Tammany advertised hugely – in five years up to 1871, the city paid out $5,180,995 for official advertisements, in twenty-six daily papers and forty-four weeklies within the city. All that money was a wonderful incentive for newspapers to stay friendly, even more so when Tammany threatened to cut the numbers to nine of each. Tammany was also kind to the desperately underpaid hacks, finding them city jobs or pensions or simple bribes.

Without solid information, even the Ring's implacable enemies – the Republican *New York Times* under George Jones, for example – had to rely on insults. 'Extravagant', 'unprincipled', 'degraded', the

Times said, casually mentioning the Sultan of Turkey; 'corrupt', 'rapacious', 'jackals', 'objects of pity' and 'branded men'. The Tweed gang, Jones imagined, longed to be part of the city's respectable élite, and were perpetually barred. When Tweed gave $50,000 to the poor one Christmas, the paper gleefully quoted a Philadelphia opinion that this was 'a judicious investment of an embarrassing surplus of stolen capital'. But nobody was stirred by all this rhetoric, not until the Ring made a very usual kind of mistake; they disappointed a one-time Sheriff, James O'Brien, who was expecting his own particular cut of a city fraud. When he realised he would get nothing, he found someone prepared to copy from Controller Connolly's secret account books, and he took the proof directly to George Jones.

The *Times* savoured the facts, letting them slip out to the public almost reluctantly: the inflated bills, the fraudulent payments, the lies and the padded payrolls and the 'jobs' and the complaisance of judges. It was the first time an American newspaper had investigated and presented facts that spelled out crime on this scale, an excuse for Jones to make his sales copy a touch more self-important and a true political event. Tweed tried, of course, to bribe Jones. He tried to confiscate the *Times* building because of some technical defect in its title; he owned judges enough to succeed. 'Sands, the secret agent and spy of Tammany,' the *Albany Evening Journal* reported, 'is trying to buy up a few shares of the *Times* so as to get an excuse to annoy that journal by mandamuses, injunctions and kindred appliances.' But from 8 July 1871, and the first printed report, the Ring was on the defensive. Tweed had to say out loud that he did not fear lynching. He also said: 'If this man Jones would have said the things he has said about me twenty-five years ago, he wouldn't be alive now. But you see, when a man has a wife and children he can't do such a thing.' The Boss balled up his fist. 'I would have killed him,' he said.

Every bit of his success now seemed to turn on him. The building boom gave Tammany cash and a following, but now the bricklayers' unions began to agitate for an eight-hour day; Tammany workers wanted their share. Tweed understood debt, how to issue revenue bonds against taxes yet to be collected and 'accumulated debt bonds' on top of that, and bonds for special investors at seven per cent. But the dealers in bonds were becoming suspicious. The city's debt almost doubled between 1866 and 1871, to $82,057,000, and the sinking fund to pay it off was stuffed full of city bonds; the city's savings banks had soaked up almost fifty million dollars in the same dubious paper, and they were trapped into buying more to make sure their interest was paid. When the *Times* printed figures which confirmed the suspicions of the markets, New York suddenly had no more credit, and even Rothschilds' name could not persuade European investors to buy.

The Irish had followed Tweed, even the middle-class Irish who wanted nothing to do with their troublesome, Fenian countrymen. Mayor Oakey Hall was their man, so literate he fancied his speeches could have been written by Thackeray, so stylish he tried to force his designs for costume jewels on Tiffany's and so political he turned out for St Patrick's Day in a green shirt embroidered with shamrocks and emeralds, and eye-glasses on a green cord; he had not a drop of Irish blood, but he was a walking statement that, had he been Irish, he would still have been mayor. Tweed stood for drink against the temperance thugs in the police force, for tavern-owners and sociability, issues which mattered to the newcomer Irish and Germans.

But on 12 July 1871, at just the wrong moment, Tweed's men misjudged the city. The Loyal Order of Orange had paraded in 1870 to celebrate 'William of Glorious Memory', and uptown Catholic labourers had laid into the parade to such effect that five died, and hundreds were wounded. In 1871, the cops forbade the Protestant parade, and the Catholic hierarchy tactlessly applauded. Wall Street was furious; for more than two hours, Protestant businessmen queued to sign a petition. They were angry that the city had surrendered to a Catholic mob, and their minds were full of the newspaper images of the Paris Commune and its violence, and memories of the draft riots of 1863. So the police ban was rescinded by Governor Hoffman, the parade went on and a Catholic labourer, asked if the city would stop violence, insisted the authorities would only 'sit at home and drink punches and smoke cigars comfortably after dinner'. A riot, licensed by Tammany, was announced.

At midday on the 12th, the city's work sites began to empty of labourers. The wharves shut down; unfinished buildings were deserted. Quarrymen and pipe men were reported on their way to where the Orange parade was to assemble. Armed men marched on Eighth Avenue to make sure that every labourer stopped work. The police tried to intercept the marchers on 42nd Street, but enough got through to 29th Street where the Protestants had assembled; they stoned the crowd, and they stoned the troops who were guarding them. Tammany's men were out with their white flags and their fine

speeches and their attempt to make New Yorkers angry at the presence of the troops; but they failed. The soldiers opened fire on the
crowd. At least thirty-seven people died, and sixty-seven were hurt.
And the respectable classes saw the end of their devil's bargain with
Tammany; they had surrendered the city to have it orderly, and now
chaos had returned.

The men out laying the Harlem sewer had not been paid, nor the
men paving South Street nor the men who were laying small pipes;
Tweed's men offered their own personal security for monies that the
city could not pay to labourers, and Tweed himself paid the pipe-
layers and nobody missed the irony. Tweed and his men were
injuncted to behave properly, and insisted in court that they had
always done so, but the hangers-on at City Hall understood what the
injunction meant. The man who supplied carriages was cursing his
luck at asking, just too late, for a warrant for $600. Labourers milled
around, asking uselessly for 'the man who buys the time on the Croton
Works' – someone who gave ready cash for wage claims from the
building of the upstate water system. The mayor asked the Controller
to resign. The *Times* gleefully wrote, 'The Ring No Longer Round'.
There were rumours of Tweed's own resignation. The Boss sometimes said he was sick of politics and public life, but he was nominated
for State Senate by acclamation. He seemed to take strength from the
crowds that massed to see him at 'Tweed Plaza', where Canal Street
and East Broadway meet. 'This is the only true and proper way,' he
bellowed, 'to meet those who traduce and revile me', and the crowd
cheered. It seemed for a moment that his political machine would
survive disgrace.

But on 26 October, the *Times* carried the final proof against Tweed:
not just suggestions of overspending and impropriety and fraud in his
department, but the vouchers from the Broadway Bank which showed
how he had profited directly from the Ring. Between May and September 1870, he had banked $1,037,192 and all of it followed the same
route: a request for payment from the city, the approval of the Board
of Audit which he had created in 1870 as an instrument of home rule
for the city, the issue of a city warrant, payment to some in-between
who promptly wrote a cheque to William M. Tweed. He was banking
public money which was supposed to go to those who had done work
for the city. There was no ambiguity. 'I thought Bill Tweed was smart
enough to cover up his tracks,' one Tammany man muttered, 'but the
morning papers don't show it.' Orders of arrest were issued for

Tweed, and bail set at a million dollars. The day before his arrest, he shifted $975,000 worth of real estate out of his name to his son Richard's, and Richard in turn signed the property over to such companies as the Pottier and Stymus Manufacturing Company, where the 'Boss' and the company were much the same thing.

On the day of Tweed's arrest, a deferential deputy sheriff pushed the warrant at him and asked what he could do to make the Boss comfortable. Admiring friends milled around in a kind of grand levée at the Metropolitan Club. In court, Tweed was committed without bail, but he was not taken to the cells; instead, he waited in the office of the district attorney while Judge Barnard, soon to be impeached himself, prepared a writ for habeas corpus and released the Boss on bail of $5,000. The good middle classes were alarmed at the confidence with which Tweed could manage the law, dismiss the criminal charges and the civil suit against him as 'this thing', and be re-elected to the Senate in a spectacularly fraudulent election. His portrait still hung in the office of the city controller until 1 February, 1872, when it was ceremonially replaced. His frauds lingered; a manufacturer of water meters sued the city for $283,500, the price of 4,050 meters which Tweed planned to buy, store and sell to the city for perhaps a million. But the November elections gave them real consolation: the reformers won, because Tammany's usual bloc vote was split with Democrat reformers. The *Times* put up a massive headline: 'New York Redeemed'.

William Marcy Tweed was convicted of fraud and grand larceny, sentenced to life imprisonment, kept himself out of jail for a while by argument and, when that failed, escaped from Sing Sing and took refuge in Spain where he was recognised from one of Nast's bitter cartoons. He was returned to New York and the Ludlow Street Jail, where he died on 12 April 1878. James Ingersoll, the furniture maker whose name was on so many false warrants, spent some time in prison, but was pardoned for the sake of his evidence. No other member of the Ring was jailed. Oakey Hall was acquitted, and served out his term as mayor. Controller Connolly fled. None of the lawsuits against Tammany came to trial, but the city did recover $894,525 from the estates of two dead men – at a cost, in fees and expenses, of $257,848. And the 'Boss' was laid to rest, without irony, in a perfect white lambskin – advertising his innocence to the last.

*

25 May 1932. It was a mob shot from the movies: five thousand people cheering, hollering, elbowing forward at the steps of the old Tweed Court House. Judge Samuel Seabury came early in a phalanx of purposeful assistants, each with a briefcase, each in a grey suit: a moral army out to bring down Tammany. Some of the crowd hissed. A limousine stopped, and out stepped Mayor Jimmy Walker in neat, pressed blue, his grey fedora reserved for waving. Now the crowd had its favourite. All 5,000 of them swept forward, with hollers of 'You tell 'im Jimmy' and 'Attaboy' and 'Let 'im have it, Jimmy!' His honour played them like a true vaudevillian. He put up his hands to show he was a fighter, he ducked and he weaved, and when the cheers were loud enough, he slipped out of sight.

In the courtroom, the Hofstadter committee of the New York State Assembly, charged with examining the government of New York City, came to a tenuous kind of order. Today, they had summoned the Mayor of New York City to answer questions about his financial affairs. But the hearings were about something more than the casual way Jimmy Walker acquired bonds and money. 'This administration is the greatest opportunity Tammany Hall has ever had,' the *World* wrote in 1926, a year after Walker was first elected mayor. 'For the first time it is in power with the consent and with the good will of the whole city.' Walker promised a new Tammany, cleansed and devoted to the public business, and New Yorkers were waiting. 'Should they decide that there is no new Tammany,' the *World* predicted, 'the gentleman who will be responsible is the Hon. James J. Walker, Mayor of New York.'

This new Tammany ruled Greater New York, which in 1898 added Brooklyn, Queens and Staten Island to Manhattan and the Bronx. The change acknowledged that New York City dominated the region, that the economic power concentrated on Manhattan was the ruler of even the most obstinately independent tract of Brooklyn; but its form was a political compromise, the dream of city reformers adjusted into a Republican scheme to hold power. City and county administrations overlapped and duplicated each other because of careless writing in the charter, and Tammany stuffed each available payroll. The city employed at least ninety Democrat district leaders, not to mention their children, relatives and clients.

Jimmy Walker was Mayor of the whole of New York City, but mostly he was the Mayor of Manhattan, the speakeasy Mayor, proper for a good-time city in love with its streamlined, skyscraping self.

Never mind that New York was a sprawl now, and Manhattan only its old heart; Walker was Tammany, and Tammany was the Manhattan Democratic Party, and the administration set aside the needs of the outer boroughs. Its mayor was often at his desk by three in the afternoon. He was the fashion-plate Beau James, whose shoulders were famously padded on top of a pipecleaner body. The women kissed him and rained roses on him and the men cheered his jokes. The night he was re-elected, he was uptown in a showgirl's arms, and she was in only her costume and a police blanket. The Cardinal had to rebuke him for such public adultery. He gambled for high stakes; he had to flee a Long Island casino as the cops arrived, barely disguised in a kitchen apron. It was for him that the black-glass 'Casino' rose in Central Park, a properly swank retreat where Walker maintained an office with moire walls and a gold-leaf ceiling, and a chorus line to entertain the Tammany faithful upstairs. He reflected the rowdy glamour of the city, the Vanity Fair of it. In bad times, he could always slip away to Europe for a while.

But when the bad times persisted, Walker grew melancholic; his doctors feared a nervous breakdown. The breadlines assembled, and the streets filled with purposeless men. Italians and Eastern European Jews still poured into the city – 300,000 or so between 1920 and 1930 – and blacks came up from the South after the First World War, 170,000 by 1930; they crammed into tenements, and when the Depression came, they suffered terribly. Hunger was an imminent fact. Families in the Cameroons sent $3.77 to help feed 'the starving' in the city. And sharp Mayor Walker was moved by the pain, but he knew no way to act; the city's machinery did not connect with its problems, any more than it could support its glamour. The city's charter, the city said, forebade make-work schemes for the unemployed. The first city relief effort during the Depression was a Tammany fake; women with maids qualified, and some men with four cars, and on Staten Island nine out of ten of the recipients just happened to be registered Democrats. The other systems for helping the unemployed were a maze of confusion, eight different schemes, each with a separate rulebook. Private schemes were too small for the scale of the problems.

Jimmy Walker's city was evaporating before his eyes. For decades, New York had been famously, wilfully modern, forever changing, 'the only city in the world,' as the French historian Bernard Fay wrote in 1929, 'rich enough in money, vitality and men to build itself anew in the last twenty years, the only city sufficiently wealthy to be modern.' But by 1931, Times Square, as Mary Agnes Hamilton discovered, was 'packed with shabby, utterly dumb and apathetic-looking men, who stand there, waiting for the advent of the coffee wagon. . . .' There were breadlines, beggars, a bottleneck of lost lives turned out in shabby clothes – a million and a half unemployed. Great skyscrapers stood unlet, unfinished, blind without windows. The Empire State Building, tallest in the world, gold-medal winner, rented mostly the view from the top to tourists by the day.

The Depression had exposed a crisis which had been masked by the glorious, skyward growth of the imperial city. In fifteen years, New York's population had grown by fifteen per cent, its budget by 250 per cent. Scam by rake by steal, Tammany spent the city. The IND subway system cost maybe $400 million more than outsiders thought possible; anything that couldn't be moved was faced in granite for as long as Tammany men controlled the quarries; schools had to be rebuilt within a year of opening. The city was borrowed to the hilt, so that a third of its tax take went to pay interest and, at the start of 1932, New York had to ask the banks for help to meet its payroll, and was refused until it trimmed its spending. Even this trimming was blocked by Tammany; only schoolteachers, who did not pay the right dues, could be fired in quantity. All this could happen because, in 1927, for example, the value of all the property the city taxed rose by twelve per cent; growth allowed Tammany to steal at will. But in 1932, the tax roll grew by only one per cent, and defaults and mortgage crises made that figure theory. The finest city in America, and its financial capital, had come to the end of its credit. Jimmy Walker was an entertainment, not an administrator, and New York was, as Alva Johnson wrote, 'colossal, astonishing, fascinating. But politically, New York is a failure.'

Samuel Seabury, the moralist, was unwilling to believe that. His spine was the spine of four generations of Episcopal ministers, a mixture of social certainty and moral steel. In his first weeks on the City Court bench, when he was twenty-eight, he ferreted out a courtroom racket by which the Metropolitan Street Railways had the power to choose the jury any time the company faced a legal action. The offending clerks were fired, and Tammany men came to remonstrate with Seabury, who ordered them out of his office. Seabury wrote tracts in favour of city ownership of utilities, because he said the system of private companies with special privileges was a constant source of temptation to the corrupt. He had Tammany's nominal support when he ran for governor in 1916, but they did not deliver on the day, and he did not speak in their favour. When his campaign failed, he was convinced that Tammany had 'knifed him'. He walked out of public life, and settled for collecting his rare books and his extremely substantial legal fees. Fourteen years later, in August 1930 he was looking for first editions in London. He heard the call to purge the city by investigating it. First, he looked at the magistrates courts, as referee for the Appelate Division, and then he examined the machinery of the city itself, as counsel to the assembly committee charged with looking at New York government. He checked every bank book, every file, with dogged, relentless young assistants; Walker said the Judge had taken so many records that he 'left most of the departments anaemic, so they weren't able to carry on'. Out of all this, Seabury built an indictment of a system that was starting to seem almost ordinary.

Consider his file on the Mayor. James Walker had taken $26,535 worth of bonds from a taxi financier, just before the city considered new rules for the taxi business. Ten of those bonds were from the Reliance Bronze and Steel Company, which sold 104 traffic-light posts, made in bronze, to the city. His financial advisor, Russell Sherwood, had gone suddenly to Mexico City and showed no signs of answering the committee's subpoena, which left unexplained a million dollars lying in accounts that the Mayor could touch. A corporation with its own legal team paid the Mayor $15,000 in fees, years after he left the law to take civic office. He took gifts from the newspaper publisher Paul Block, who also owned a company that was bidding to tile the new subway stations. Block's ten-year-old son had been walking on Fifth Avenue one day, it was said, when he began worrying about whether Mr Walker had a car, and a home, and enough to live on, and his kind father conceived the notion of making money for the Mayor.

Walker took to Europe in 1927 a $10,000 letter of credit bought by a promoter of the Equitable Coach Company, after Equitable had won a bus franchise in the Board of Estimate. The Mayor's own performance had made that meeting memorable. He skipped all other items on the agenda and called the roll for the Equitable matter immediately; the hundreds who had come to object did not even realise the vote was over. One rival company's president yelled his objections: 'We will not,' the Mayor said, 'permit you to use the Board of Estimate to shout and get a lot of publicity for yourself.' Another bus president tried to protest, and Walker told him he was through speaking. 'But I haven't started,' he said. 'You don't know it,' the Mayor snapped, 'but you have concluded your address.' The decision had taken fifty seconds. Later, it turned out that the Mayor had relied on the word of a dead man for Equitable's financial standing, that the company had no money and no buses; the wildcat service on the avenues had to continue while Equitable scrabbled to begin to exist. It was, said the Transit Commission, 'a financial cripple'.

All this was circumstantial stuff. Some concerned only the Mayor's brother, a doctor, who kept taking cheques for 'medical services' from William J. Scanlan which just happened each time to be half the commission that Scanlan had just made on sales to the city. Other doctors split their fees with Dr Walker when they dealt with city workers hurt at work. These fees seemed rather generous. One doctor charged twenty-five dollars for a 'sacra illiac support' [sic] when his patient complained only of a cut finger; one sent in a bill for strapping a man's foot, when he thought he had hurt only his left thumb; another charged for four x-rays of a hand in order to treat a bruised toe. The doctor, a stout and phlegmatic man, blinked at the notion that anyone could fuss about such matters. The Mayor liked to say all this was down to Seabury's political jealousy; the Judge could not get elected, while Walker was mayor by acclamation.

Seabury was beet-red in the heat, the sweat running on his face. He did not use the word 'bribe', but he left the thought in the air. The Mayor challenged him to speak out. The Mayor sat, his spectacles swinging in his right hand, all the better to look directly at the Judge; but Seabury had been warned not to look him in the eye. He made little jokes. He was asked if he had met a particular broker and shaken his hand. 'Due to the activity I have been in since 1910, I do shake hands with a great many people I don't know and try to make them believe I do,' he said, 'but please don't tell them about it.' The room adored him; Tammany's crowd cheered. He was told of a secret brokerage account, denied all knowledge of it, but said, 'I hope he proves it is mine. I will try and collect it.' But the real drama was in nothing he said; it was in the evasions, and the manifest bitterness between the two men. They were reformer and politician, moralist and member of the machine, at war here in a small courtroom.

Whatever Seabury found, there was a crowd ready to cheer for Jimmy Walker. In the Prohibition years the letter of the law had separated from how the city actually lived in a way that was obvious to everyone. In New York, sentiment was all 'wet', which is to say that Prohibition was hardly ever taken seriously. A dry and high-minded nation pushed social drinkers, gangsters and bootleggers together with gamblers, politicians and cops on the take. Spy-holes and fake names and passwords, a parody of criminal conspiracy at the speakeasy door, were everyone's game and played with pleasure. 'You go to a locked and chained door,' Stephen Graham wrote. 'Eyes are considering you through peep-holes in the wooden walls. There is such a to-do about letting you in. Someone for the first time must be sponsor. You sign your name in a book and receive a mysterious-looking card with only a number on it. The bartender says to you suggestively as you sign your name, "And you will please *remember* your address."' There were bars with virtual airlocks, and bars where you had to show the print of your palm on the glass doors; after-hours joints in Harlem, where the stoppered gin went back in the pocket if the cops came, and men's bars where the whole establishment would shut if visitors stayed on the stairway and would not go away; there were Italian bars with shuttered green wooden cupboards for private 'meetings' with your girl, and beauty parlours where, through a tiny back window, a hirsute hand pushed out glasses to the women.

All this was a matter of style since, as one bar-tender admitted, 'The police notify us of a coming raid. But it costs us heavy.' In the Bowery, anyone could walk into the saloons on the East side, and take what he wanted of the raw liquour they sold. Between there and police headquarters on Grand Street lay 'Bootleggers' Row.' Seabury discovered in Queens that the operator of an illegal still simply paid a fee to Inspector Thomas W. Mullarkey, who himself had a part interest in a still. Bronx speakeasies hung blue cards behind the bar as proof they belonged to the Liberty League, which also protected them from the cops. When ordinary social life surrendered to criminal chic, any argument for law and order sounded downright frumpish.

Real crime slipped across this fuzzy boundary into new territory. Naturally, the political clubs sold booze without interference. When Police Commissioner McLaughlin led raids on the People's Regular Democratic Club of the Fifteenth Assembly District, the local boss, Peter McGuinness was infuriated. 'I am going to take the matter of these raids to City Hall,' he said, 'and even to 14th Street', which meant Tammany, evidently an authority higher than the city, 'and see whether a police commissioner can do such things and get away with it.' Two weeks later, McLaughlin resigned, and even the oldest friends of McGuinness were impressed. Some political clubs were also gambling houses, protected with sentries and 'ice-box doors' as well as their connections. They were a sanctuary in which criminals and gunmen could rest up.

'It is easy to get a pistol permit in New York,' said Supreme Court Justice Selah Strong. 'All you have to do is see your district leader and have $250 with you.' When armed thugs stole the cash and jewels from guests at a dinner to honour Justice Albert Vitale in the Bronx, the Justice simply went to see friends at the local Democrat club-house, and everything was restored within hours. If the police did invade the clubs, magistrates would always listen to the kind words of the Democrat bosses who appointed them; such influence, as the district boss James Brown said, 'is how we make Democrats'. At the Perry Club, a murder was committed, an eyewitness gave the killer's name to the district attorney and absolutely nothing happened next. Seabury noticed that out of 514 people arrested in raids on political clubs in 1926 and 1927, only two were ever convicted of anything.

The cops learned ethical relativism from their political masters, and applied it vigorously. In Walker's time, the special scandal was the framing of innocent women, quite at random, by the vice squad. Chile Mapocha Acuna, the 'human spitoona', was the key informer. 'He made violent love to me and told me he owned all the soft drinks stands in the Penn Station,' Angelina Coloneas testified. 'He finally gained my confidence and asked me to marry him. He asked me to visit his room and see something he had bought me as a wedding gift. A few minutes later, two policemen rushed in and arrested me on an immorality charge.' She gave the cops, her bondsman and her lawyer $800, and she was discharged. But two months later, the cops broke in, sprinkled some white powder in a pair of slippers and arrested her for possessing narcotics. 'I was discharged when I gave them $400 – every cent that I had. They were disappointed because I couldn't give them another $800.' Coloneas was relatively lucky. The girls, however innocent, came back bruised and sometimes bitten. Some of them worked off their obligation to the cops by starting a new career on the streets.

New Yorkers knew the inner machinery of things and the irrelevance of the public, official front. Seabury had somehow to make them angry at what they knew. Suppose you wanted to build a gas station where it had been forbidden, or to change a family house into a site for shops or an apartment block, then you could either take a chance on the judgement of the Bureau of Standards and Appeals, or else buy the sure thing: the advice of the fire department horse doctor, Dr Doyle, whose connections were almost infallible. Suppose you wanted to do business at the Fulton Street fish market, then it was only an extra business cost to pay your respects and a percentage to Joseph 'Socks' Lanza, the union negotiator for the United Sea Food Workers local. Those who worked union labour paid him a tax, and those who did not had to pay him for keeping the union out. Without paying Lanza, no boat docked, no wholesaler could find a porter to take fish to his market stall, no retailer could carry away what he had bought without the imminent risk of finding it sprayed with kerosene. Nobody parked near the market without paying Lanza, or the wheels mysteriously parted from their wagons, and sometimes the wagons went up in spontaneous fire. Suppose you wanted to teach in a city school, the going rate was $200 until the Depression deepened and more desperate young women tried to raise $1,000 to buy a job. It was hard to make any deal with the city without employing some offshoot of Tammany, or paying the tiger direct; architects charged the Tammany fees to the city, as an expense, and the city paid. The legal firm of Olvany, Eisner and Donnelly were particularly valuable when the city seemed unresponsive. For nine years, North German Lloyd Steamship Company could not find a pier in Manhattan, but their troubles ended when they handed over $50,000 for 'legal services'. The firm's senior partner, George Olvany, was a former Grand Sachem of Tammany Hall. But you did not have to be grand, or even grown up to pay the tiger. School principals chose school doctors and allowed them to charge as much as a dollar for a minute-long examination; parents had to pay, or their children were out of school.

Money stuck inexplicably to the fingers of all kinds of public officials. James McQuade, joint leader of the Greenpoint district, somehow put away $510,000 in six years on an annual salary of $12,000. He said he'd borrowed the rest to feed 'the other thirty-three McQuades', but could not offhand remember from whom. 'I got enough,' he said, 'to do the rest of my life if I die today.' Asked how much that was, he shook his head. 'Nothing. You can't be worth much when you have thirty-four in the family.' Seabury's investigators never did discover the source of McQuade's fortune. Whether for his stonewalling or the needs of all the McQuades, the Brooklyn boss gave him a sharp raise in salary. Sheriff Thomas Farley of New York County couldn't explain $360,000 in his bank, except to say that he took the money from his safe deposit box at home – 'the good box I had', 'a wonderful box'. His tin box stood for all the graft by Tammany's men.

This graft had very public effects. Public lavatories were a sinecure for the widows of Tammany pensioners who curtained off the unsightly stalls to make a cosy room where friends could take tea. The city beaches were guarded by lifeguards who did not all know how to swim; parents warned their children away from the lifeguard huts because that was where the raddled, salt-skinned tarts hung out. The most modern city, all glorious in the sky, had horse-drawn carts in its parks. Citizens who could live with this contradiction did not suppose that city government was full of righteous men, not with a Board of Aldermen, some of whom could add, voting on the city's budget, and a Mayor wedded so closely to Tammany. The new building code was delayed in 1931 because the county bosses were frolicking in Florida, and the Aldermen did not like to vote without their instructions. It was already a matter of bravado to say: Only in New York, and look away.

So Seabury went for Walker, for the flirty, sparkling face of the whole rotted system. He could not help attacking also the awkward fact of democracy. Walker argued that he could not be held accountable for anything in his first term as Mayor because he had been re-elected, and that wiped out all past offences. It was impudent talk, since Tammany's man was elected as much by muscle and graft as by public enthusiasm. 'Hey you, only push down the first line, de Stars, or I'll knock yer block off,' as one thug told an East Side doctor from under the curtain of a polling booth. Teachers asked to administer the literacy test to new voters were assaulted if they failed the boss's men; when one complained, a cop said, 'I saw and heard nothing. How do you expect me to arrest the local district leader?'

But an election was still as close to the people's will as anyone could come. Seabury had to convince the voters that Walker was not what he seemed, and that they could not have known. He had to show Walker as a private kind of crook, the public official who could not explain his assets. When the Mayor left the courthouse at the end of his testimony, he faced the possibility that Governor Roosevelt would remove him from office. But Tammany let it be known that, if Roosevelt acted, they would simply re-nominate Walker and re-elect him. They would answer, in their own way, what Walker insisted were 'aspersions against our fair city'.

That was not how it happened. Governor Franklin Roosevelt summoned Walker upstate, and examined him closely; Walker decided to resign. Tammany now had to face the fact that Roosevelt would be elected president with them or without them, and rather than face humiliation, they grudgingly supported the man who had forced out Beau James. Their revenge was to oppose Roosevelt's chosen successor as governor, and to defeat him, but Tammany never again had the same national clout. People noticed that Walker had more or less admitted that Roosevelt had good reason to distance himself from Tammany and the ex-Mayor, which said nothing for either's reputation. After the Mayor's resignation, the price of New York City bonds rose two points in a day, instead of the usual, minimal fractions of a point.

On the steamship *Conte Grande*, bound for Italy, the Mayor walked his dog, consulted his secretary George Collins, drank water very obviously with every meal and put out a bit of prose to any reporter who passed. 'I may take a short trip in North Africa or Corsica and chase the elusive mufflon from precipice to precipice,' he said, 'or let George Collins do it.' He dreamed of quaint villages and being like any other American tourist; 'One can have too much popularity,' he said. He performed like a rather faded star, the kind that no longer listens to the questions because there is no answer except the performance itself. And in the city, Jimmy Walker's real audience settled down in the movie houses with their popcorn and judged the politicians rowdily as they appeared on the newsreels. Greenwich Village booed Walker loudly one week and was kindly the next. On Broadway, there was a swell of dignified applause for Seabury and faint claps and snickers for Walker. On the Upper West Side they booed Walker outright, and in the Tammany stronghold of Yorkville, they sat stonily silent, waiting for the whole catastrophe to sail away. Only in Brooklyn, at the Valencia and the RKO-Albee, could Beau James still count on the applause he loved.

*

He was small, fast, square, in a black sombrero, a cartoon power dashing and squeaking through the city machine. 'BREATHTAKING ACTIVITY,' said the *World Telegram*, 'REPLACES TAMMANY SOMNOLENCE'. In 1933, Fiorello la Guardia was elected Mayor of New York City. He began a frantic campaign to make a drama out of the dumb, stolid city machinery. He came armed with certainties about his city, 'the greatest and most daring experiment in social and political democracy'. He wanted to wash clean its bureaucracy and its lives; 'If I cannot be the mayor of a clean American city and protect its morals; if I cannot be the head of a decent city government, I don't want to be mayor.' In 1929, Walker and Tammany had defeated him ignominiously, but Seabury's revelations put him back on the ballot – this time as a Fusion candidate, neither Democrat nor Republican. He stood for a responsible city, a technocratic city, a city which had skills instead of placemen and perhaps an impossible city; in himself, half-Jew, half-Italian he was a fusion of more than half New York. And his way of changing things was frenzy.

Where Walker was absent, or indolent, La Guardia was action. 'Running a city resembles running a house,' he liked to say, 'and if the servants are honest ... then the house can be managed well and economically run.' Like a good housekeeper, he was everywhere. He fussed about speeding taxis, the speed of welfare lines; he chased fires from the sidecar of a police motorcycle, usually out of office hours; at eight, he was coming downtown in his limousine from his small apartment in East Harlem, with a writing desk in the back to start on the letters, the memos, the fusillade of terse messages that his secretaries were expected to translate into flowing, grammatical and very nearly polite English. He dispensed with a bodyguard and packed his own gun. Asked what he did for relaxation, his secretary said: 'The Mayor's hobby is work.' Sickness was not a good enough excuse for any of his subordinates, and he did not understand vacations. He was always too busy to be friends with his commissioners, to allow the time to ease his orders into action. He instituted weekly lunches at which the commissioner who had made the most egregious boner of the past week was presented with an engraved ox-bone. He was punctilious; he fired a commissioner who had diverted sixty-five dollars worth of city gravel to his favourite Boy Scout troop. One visitor saw him punch at a buzzer in mid-talk, dictate a telegram and 'he seemed terribly high-strung and on edge – no repose whatever'.

But La Guardia was the man who understood New York's essence, who knew that his glorious city was his own particular dream. 'I dream! But my dreams rest me,' he said. 'Sometimes I see the City of Tomorrow, with marvellous parks and buildings, finer hospitals, safer and more beautiful streets, better schools, more playgrounds, more swimming pools, greater markets. There are fewer prisons, too, because in the city of tomorrow there will be less incentive to crime. I see a city with no slums and little poverty. It will be a reality some day.' If his concentration failed for a moment, then the city that he wanted would dissolve away, and become what it was to a man like Jimmy Walker: only bits of information, possibilities and problems. So La Guardia did what other mayors had never thought of doing, or dared to do: he invested his whole self, explosive, impetuous, difficult, egotistical, sarcastic. He took the public outrage at Seabury's revelations and attempted to impose a whole new administrative order. He brought in men with authority instead of party connections. His commissioner for public welfare was an expert on relief schemes. He put Adolf Berle in the fustian job of city chamberlain, so that he could help restore financial stability, act as point man in Washington and then abolish himself. He brought an authority on municipal purchasing from New York University to run municipal purchasing. His commissioner for health was hired away from New Haven because he had the reputation of being the best health administrator in the country. His administration, in the classic reform manner, was short of first-generation Americans; newcomers might still be on the make. La Guardia, the city's tiny, ferocious father, depended on patricians. Above all, he depended on Robert Moses, the tall, grey-eyed autocrat.

The Mayor wanted airports, bridges, art in the streets; 'the city,' as he said, 'could use quite a little beautifying.' But he was sick of the decorous Goo-Goos, the 'good government' campaigners, and their compromises. 'Why is it,' he asked, 'that every time you get to a point where you can do some good, the *nice people* get in the way?' He needed a fixer with immaculate credentials as a reformer, a scarce species: Robert Moses. And Moses, who had run against La Guardia and lost, needed a sponsor who could cope with the public political games that Moses played so badly. 'In exploiting racial and religious prejudices,' Moses wrote, 'La Guardia could run circles around the bosses he despised and derided.'

It was a perfect marriage, but only a brief honeymoon. La Guardia had a habit of summoning his commissioners and making them wait on hard benches outside his office; Moses sent a potted plant in his place. If thwarted, Moses would threaten to resign, knowing that he could never be replaced at $13,000 a year; 'I must insist,' he would say, 'otherwise, I cannot assume further responsibility for this work.' La Guardia heard this so often that he printed forms: 'I, Robert Moses, do hereby resign as ... ..., effective. ... .' Moses called La Guardia, among other things, a dago, a wop, a Guinea son of a bitch, that little organ grinder and Rigoletto. La Guardia, who had a sharper view of other people's aspirations, called Moses 'His Grace'.

For Moses was the grandest of the patricians. In the 1900s, he had been a junior member of the New York Bureau of Municipal Research, one of the reforming bodies which sought to make the city account-able, or at least to make it keep accounts. Cities did not have budgets at the time, nor did city departments. The Bureau read the notices of public contracts in the newspapers, went out to count the bags of concrete and found enough evidence in the difference to unseat the borough presidents of both Queens and the Bronx for corruption. 'Eager beaver amateurs,' Moses called them later, but for the moment their arguments for literally business-like efficiency quite neatly matched his own ideas. They were against the spoils system, against the politicians, against corruption; so was he.

His certainties were well-rooted things. Moses came from settled money, not a fortune made in America like the Guggenheims or Seligmans who started behind a peddler's cart, but capital brought from home and put shrewdly into property. Bella, his mother, busied herself with settlement houses for the newly landed Jews from Poland and Russia, and she taught her son public service by example. He was edgy at Yale, as Jews had reason to be, but when he came to Oxford he found a perfect fit for his values. He learned that gentlemen do not fuss about money, having enough; that gentlemen have a duty to the lower classes which the lower classes, being too poor or black or marginal, can never repay. For his D. Phil. he wrote on the British Civil Service, an admiring account of university men, the best of each generation, thinking a nation to glory while an army of clerks attends dutifully to business. For him, this was something like the dream of the Founding Fathers of America, betrayed by vulgar politics and 'government by the lowest denominator'; politicians simply stood in the way of enlightened, suitable government. He liked to quote Pope:

'For forms of government let fools contest;
Whate'er is best administered is best ...'

There were rather few experts on efficiency and administration at the time and, even if Moses's family joked that the six copies sold of his D. Phil. had gone to his doting mother and grandmother, his name was known; so when the Municipal Civil Service Commission wanted to plan reforms for the city, they turned to Moses. He was young, brilliant, sure; he strode into the quagmire of the city, on fire with the gospel of the British way.

He found a system in which nobody ever considered competence for a job, whether the job was needed, or how to run the city better. Instead, patronage gave jobs to relatives, to the errand boys of the ward bosses, to those who slipped cash to the right hands; only the examiner could see the dials when would-be firemen tested their strength, and the examiner's hand was open. Because of patronage, the same typist's job could pay $1,200 or $4,000 a year. At the highest level, Grade Five, a civil servant could double his salary by knowing the right people. Fifty thousand men and women took all this for granted, since they were in work. But Moses wanted examinations for competence, even for lift-boys; if anyone refused to take a test, he would be fired; the best examiners would be those who gave the most failing grades. Where someone was paid above grade, the pay would be cut back. Job and pay and rank would be meticulously described. Jerusalem would be built by civil service law.

Fifty thousand voters did not see it that way. Fifty thousand voters thought they should be exceptions to the rule; the man who ran the elevators at the Bronx Courthouse, for example, said his job was 'sensitive' and 'exceptional' because there were often convicted persons in his elevator. Tammany quickly understood the snobbery in Moses' zeal; the first time his name appeared in print, in the *Brooklyn Eagle*, the headline read: 'ONLY GENTLEMEN NEED APPLY: THAT IS MOSES' THEORY OF CIVIL SERVICE REQUIRE-MENTS.' Hard-luck stories multiplied. Moses would set out to defend his ideas, in his smart white suit, and he had to speak through catcalls and boos. He watched as his scheme was adjusted, diluted and, when 'Red Mike' Hylan was elected Mayor, abandoned. Moses went scrabbling for some low-paid bureau job. He stood on line in Cleveland, Ohio, looking for work. The bills were paid late, his wife and children cramped in their small apartment, his career stalled. It was the last time Moses would ally himself with the 'better class of person', the reformers whose power base was essentially their nuisance value. He had some appalling learning to do.

He went to school at the knee of Bella Moskowitz, a plump mouse in furs who would sit knitting in a corner of the office of the governor of New York State, unnoticed, until she said something sharper than any politician. Mrs M. was the only person who could change Moses' mind. She was invisible to anyone outside Albany, but indispensable to Governor Al Smith, a Tammany man who had somehow kept his honour and was thinking of reforms. The Governor listened to Moses, and Moses learned government from Moskowitz and Smith. He had no official position, but everyone knew he had access to the Governor. He understood fine print, how the machine worked. And unlike most apparatchiks, he had a vision. He went tramping the hidden parts of Long Island, where white sand and fine, grey reeds fringed the sea, where ponds with waterlilies swelled out of fast streams; much of the land already belonged to the state and city of New York, for its water supply among other things, and Moses wanted to give it to the people. Parkways, roads that run in an envelope of greenery, would link parks. Landowners would be dispossessed – grandees, Moses told Smith, although many were small-time family farmers. When local townships said they feared New York rabble, the Governor could be relied on to answer angrily, 'Rabble? That's *me* you're talking about.' The parks would be the kind of achievement you can photograph for the electorate, that flattered the Governor's taste for detailed plans and descriptions. But they involved using the state's one annual bond issue, putting parks above – say – hospitals or asylums. Smith approved that priority. He said to Moses, almost casually: 'Why don't you take the whole thing over yourself?'

As Parks Commissioner for the state, Moses bulldozed his schemes into being. He opened Jones Beach to the public, created the bath-houses and pools, made a park on Fire Island. Smith made him Secretary of State for this bulldozing talent, with instructions to push the state cabinet into action. Moses took the office next to the executive chamber, a sign that this unelected man was now the second power in the state after the Governor. He learned how to face down enemies. He clashed often with Franklin Delano Roosevelt, an upstate squire and, Moses said much too loudly, 'a poor excuse for a man' in his wheelchair. Roosevelt was chairman of the Taconic State Park Commission, with his own ideas for parks and parkways, and Moses would not tolerate a rival. He trimmed FDR's budgets. He blocked FDR's pet scheme for a Taconic Parkway. He refused to hire FDR's political secretary Louis Howe, snapping that Roosevelt could pay for his own valet. And, when Roosevelt succeeded Smith as Governor, he discovered the most galling fact of all: he could remove Moses as Secretary of State, but he could fire him as Parks Commissioner only 'for cause.' The two men had to co-exist. Before long, FDR discovered Moses' memory; if the governor wanted something that Moses disapproved, Moses would remember all kinds of patronage requests from earlier years, and threaten to publish them. Moses went on filing and knowing all his life. He became famous for getting things done, and being impossible to stop. But as President, Roosevelt forgot nothing, and he gained a clear advantage: to survive, New York City depended on the money that only he could grant.

La Guardia inherited the most famous city in America, its skyline honoured in dreams, and New York was many vital things: the port where newcomers arrived, the capital of the dollar, the emblem of the modern and streamlined city, the place where people came to change their lives. But New York was only a city, a marginal enterprise in American law, and the stepchild of the tax-gathering state and nation. At the International Conference of Cities in 1931, the United States delegation was the only one from a government which did not take direct responsibility for its cities. La Guardia, partly by rhetoric but mostly by cunning, helped to change all that.

In 1933, Chicago and Detroit as well as New York were broke. The crash, La Guardia told Congress, had 'put every municipality to the wall'. The cities needed help from Washington, because they knew they could expect no more help from the states, and they did not have the powers to help themselves. Even before La Guardia had been sworn in, he was organising schemes that would draw cash from the Civilian Works Administration, the New Deal's cumbersome machine for bringing work to the cities. He went to engineers, architects, experts; 'I come to you because I want . . . help from people who know something,' he said, 'rather than from the politicians.' He wanted labour-intensive schemes because Washington paid only for the labour. He devised schemes for clearing slums and schemes for building new homes on the cleared land. He wanted the parks disciplined and clean again, the docks saved from rot; he wanted shelter for the homeless. He wanted to build covered, secure markets for the street peddlers who were harassed by thugs and shaken down by city officials; in Walker's time, blind men and veterans had to find bribes of up to $7,000 for the privilege of selling on the streets. He was ready to such good effect that New York took one in five of all the jobs created with CWA money. The Works Progress Administration, another of the New Deal machines for putting people to work, announced in 1936 that New York, alone among American cities, would be allowed to administer its own federal relief operation. Other cities stayed on the margin, but La Guardia's New York was like the forty-ninth state, except when it came to fundamental questions of who had the last power.

His enemies saw La Guardia surrounded by Reds, a 'dictator', the 'Midget Mussolini', the 'Manhattan Messiah' who thought 'New York can be ruled by Proclamation'. His rule was as personal as his vision of a humane, workable city. He issued statements, paid for billboards, enlisted schoolchildren and formed committees for the quixotic end of making New York into a quiet place, free of sirens and klaxons and jackhammers and even conversation amplified by whisky; but all that happened was that one dairy, Borden's, put rubber mufflers on its horses' hooves. He went up against Ciro Terranova, the Mobster who monopolised the city supplies of artichokes and doubled their price, by a mayoral proclamation banning the 'sale, display and possession' of artichokes in all public markets. His authority, he said, was the mayor's power to quell riots. Within a week, the artichoke growers were talking directly to La Guardia and the racket was dead. But there were limits to what a man could do with talk. La Guardia also needed money. He wanted art in the city; he opened the nation's first municipal art gallery, free summer concerts, the High School of Music and Art. He wanted the apparatus of the public city to match the high claims made by all the new and shiny towers – the spire and gargoyles and eagles of the Chrysler Building which was 'dedicated to world commerce and industry', or the rentable practicality of the Empire State, or the blocks of Rockefeller Centre, started as a home for the Metropolitan Opera but completed as a particular family's notion of an unapologetic modern city. Such things could be done in the city, but not by the city.

La Guardia needed more taxes; after years of railing against sales taxes as a congressman, he imposed one on New York City to pay for unemployment relief and then, when the Governor decided that the emergency was over, howled with spirit to keep his city revenue. He faked budgets, so that the city's public plans and the city's actual spending were far apart; when Robert Moses wanted to make serious trouble, he only had to tell the story of his 'show' budgets for the parks departments, the ones La Guardia had demanded which were shams. The Mayor cleaned out Tammany hacks, but after three years, the city employed 9,609 more people than before. Not everything worked better; La Guardia could never clear the city streets of snow, nor stop the outer boroughs freezing into a kind of urban wedding cake, while Tammany at least put its friends and clients out on the streets with shovels and kept the city moving.

On the kind of project that Robert Moses understood, the visible and politically useful, the money arrived; and, thanks to Moses, it did not evaporate into Tammany pockets. Moses prided himself on cleaning the Tammany workers out of projects like the building of Jones Beach. A park engineer watched him clear six hundred bungalows, rented each summer by people with influence, out of the way of Orchard Beach; 'He just decides what he's going to do,' the man said, 'and it's done.' He fired the entire parks staff on his first day, kept an old lady on perpetual overtime until, at two in the morning, she admitted she was old enough to retire. His foremen were the 'ramrods', the toughest of them all. He cleared Tammany's men out of the Triborough Bridge Authority, which was still only a grandiose plan; but, with his political sense, he did not interfere with the Manhattan entrance, which had drifted twenty-five blocks north of its logical place for the honour of standing on land belonging to William Randolph Hearst. He began to reshape Manhattan physically, building a fringe of landfill on the East Side, hanging the FDR Drive ten feet over the East River, clearing out tenements and putting down highways: 'the most spectacular transformation that has taken place in Manhattan in this generation,' he said.

La Guardia depended on Moses to construct some of the city's most basic machinery – bridges, tunnels, expressways – but Franklin Delano Roosevelt had a long memory and a keen sense of timing. In 1934, Moses stood for governor and was trounced. The day after the election, La Guardia's administration was asking Washington for $8.1 million to finish the grandiose Triborough Bridge. The day after that, Washington answered: the money was, of course, available for a project that would employ so many men. But to get the money, one man would have to be fired: Robert Moses. No member of a public authority like Triborough could hold a paid job within the city where that authority operated. La Guardia realised abruptly what his colleagues should have known – the depth of feeling between the President, on whom Depression New York depended for funds, and the one man who could make that money work. 'Jesus Christ!' he bellowed, woundedly. 'Of all the people in the city of New York, I had to pick the one man who Roosevelt won't stand for and he won't give me any more money unless I get rid of him. Jesus Christ! I had to pick the one that he hated!'

Anyone but Moses would have faded from the Triborough project, a well-mannered appointee; but Moses himself had written the rule-book for the Authority, one of the services he did for Governor Smith, and he could be fired only after formal hearings had found him guilty of some specific charge. He was not going. If La Guardia tried to persuade him, he would tell the world how the Mayor had kow-towed to a President's whim, and dismissed a competent official. If La Guardia thought he could simply fire Moses as Parks Commissioner, the same threat applied. One reviewer giggled at Moses as a 'modern Horatius on another unfinished bridge'; but Moses had the number of every city editor in his pocket.

Months after the stand-off began, on 26 December 1934, when the city should not have been listening, with Moses retired to bed with a perpetual 'flu and La Guardia mortally affronted by everyone he needed, Roosevelt put his views into an administrative order. And Moses rose from his sickbed just long enough to make sure that every newspaper knew what he had done. Liberals saw their President interfering out of spite with thirty-one million manhours of work. Conservatives were ready to believe anything of Roosevelt. Privately, the lawyer C.C. Burlingham conceded to FDR that Moses was 'quite a blackguard'; but publicly he pronounced that 'Washington has taken the position the English king took towards the American colonies'. Letters to editors were furious about an affront to the 'sovereign state of New York'. It was left to La Guardia to slip out of town and board the presidential train at Philadelphia, to persuade FDR that exceptions had to be made to his new rule, and one of them must be the 'porcupin-ish' Moses. In Penn Station, in his own city, the shades of the carriage were lowered so nobody would know the Mayor was there.

Robert Moses held his job only at the pleasure of the Mayor, but he could face down the President. The Mayor teased him by delaying his reappointment to the Triborough Authority; Moses behaved as though the little man had dared lese majesté. The President, privately, called Moses 'the duc', but he acted more like a tidy-minded commissar. Once the Triborough Bridge was open, Moses had title to the Astoria ferry slip which stood at 90th Street in Manhattan. The ferry was hardly clear of the dock when his men arrived to tear down the pilings. La Guardia had it rebuilt; he stationed cops to protect the city docks from the city's Parks Commissioner. When the federal Works Progress Administration dared to take away 5,000 men who were working for Moses, he padlocked the parks; a skein of mothers knitted itself around City Hall in protest, on the side of a perfect aristocrat. For if his enthusiasm for public works looked somehow socialistic, that was an illusion. Moses denounced New Dealers, and anyone who mussed his careful nets of influence, as Bolshies, pinkos, commies; he slandered Frank Lloyd Wright, 'regarded in Russia as our greatest builder'; he rode the Red scares of the mid-1930s triumphantly, the man above politics, who knew what he was against. New York had thrown off the worst of machine politics for a while, but at the cost of acquiring its own unelected ruler: the man who, as we shall see later, came to shape even the physical boundaries of the city.

La Guardia's other revolution started with exposures of graft and incompetence. The city's Department of Accounts, which liked to sit over ledgers looking for the kind of fraud which shouts itself, now became the Department of Investigations and looked for subtler crimes. They found the Sanitation Department collecting fees for services that were supposed to be free, dealt with the thieves, and then La Guardia made the fees official so that the city could have the benefit of whatever people were prepared to pay. He fired those surgeons who insisted on being tipped before they would operate at city hospitals. His men raided the prison on Welfare Island and handed it back to the warden, who had been reduced to the errand boy of Irish and Italian Mobsters. The chief medical examiner inspected the teachers of New York City, and removed 1,500 who were either insane or mentally unbalanced. The old essay examinations in the civil service, where it was hard to dispute a passing grade because the marking was subjective, were abolished in favour of questions which had answers, right or wrong. The city began to define what its employees were supposed to do. In 1933, only 6,327 people thought they would take their chances at a civil service job, and everybody knew that almost every job down to the catch-all 'labourer' class was already sewn up; the safety the city offered was attractive, but unattainable without political connections. In 1939 a quarter of a million bright, well educated people applied to work for the city.

They were expected to be immaculate, for La Guardia could imagine a clean city. Adultery, for which Mayor Walker had been famous, became conduct 'prejudicial to the good name and interest' of New York. La Guardia warned motor vehicle inspectors: 'Beware of the nickel cigar. Accept no favours. . . . Oh, they will want to know if you're interested in fights or ball games. Look out. That's the preliminary necking. If you succumb to the preliminary necking, you're gone.' And without its perpetual ability to find people city jobs and take city graft, the awesome power of Tammany faded quite suddenly. In the 1940s, the bank foreclosed on Tammany Hall, and sold it to the International Ladies Garment Workers Union.

This meant the end of the Irish civil service. Tammany had been built on their special needs – their Catholicism, their schools, their need for work and shelter and help when they came off the boat. George Olvany of Tammany liked to say that 'even the Jewish districts have Irish leaders. The Jews want to be ruled by them.' But if this had ever been true, it was an absurd illusion in the Depression years. Jews and Italians easily outnumbered the Irish, and they wanted their say in city government. The changes in the city's population gave the Mayor a new coalition. The Mayor even stamped, unthinkingly, on Irish sensibilities; he appointed as medical examiner an Italian who had written meanly about them. He also appointed blacks to supervisory positions, something Tammany never tolerated, and that began the most heartfelt complaints about the sidelining of the 'natural leaders' of the city. The administration of New York had something to do with the city's peoples for the first time since the 1890s.

La Guardia knew he was doing good; he was fierce for the good, eyes blazing, fat little fists stamped down on the table. But sometimes, intentions were the only obvious difference between his ways and Tammany's. His relief programme was set up for the best of reasons, run by a man who knew how to plead for money for the poor, intended to make a humane life for women and men caught in an economic catastrophe; it only looked like the old-time ramshackle graft. Its managers took unexplained pay rises; the city claimed it had to pay more to keep staff; but where else in a Depression would all those clerks be working? La Guardia reversed the raises, but the political damage was done: his fusion administration looked inefficient, and city workers felt betrayed. The aldermen began a gleeful investigation of their tough, sharp-tongued and often self-righteous Mayor.

His relief schemes were full of waste, and a caricature of makework; the city paid for charts of early Chinese history, maps of Greek dialects, and a study of safety pins in Bronze Age culture. It also funded a door to door survey of how many ducks, chickens and eggs were eaten each week in New York, a survey whose methodology was seriously flawed: many housewives thought the pollsters were deranged, and slammed the door on them. Mr Robert Marshall was paid to teach 'boondoggling', by which he meant 'collecting odds and ends and making things out of them' (his job may have helped to change the meaning of the word).

La Guardia was thrown on the defensive, pleading that most of the money came from Washington, and putting a succession of tough-minded, but short-lived 'czars' in charge of making sure that relief looked both fair and sensible. He was attacked by revolutionaries who wanted no palliatives, and by conservatives who reckoned welfare only softened the soul in a most unAmerican way, and by Tammany hacks who thought they had caught him at last. He had to admit the scheme was a huge pot of money being carelessly tended. He also found his compassion, his decency was pulling the victims of Depression from across America. There was no work for them when they came, but there was relief. The indifference of other cities made New York's problems even greater. This problem of being the one great liberal city continued into the 1970s, when Southern states devised a simple welfare policy: handing out bus tickets to New York.

It was perhaps inevitable that La Guardia became distracted. He was Washington's favourite mayor, the spokesman for America's cities. Anything the city said, it said through La Guardia's office. He boasted about the bridges and roads that Robert Moses had built, much to the annoyance of Moses. He was a cover story, 'the busiest man in the world', who cleverly made interviews into such a privilege that reporters went away glowing with admiration. Naturally, he aspired to higher office. He could not forever will the city into life. Indeed, after his re-election he was absent from his office almost as much as Jimmy Walker, although he was away on national business, not pleasure trips. He grew more crudely political. In a way he mirrored the city itself, which had lost the old self-confidence of the glittering twenties and was now anonymous, careful, defensive.

The old La Guardia was on the workers' side; he briefly thought of himself as socialist. His police chief O'Ryan wanted all union officers to register their credentials and photographs, so the cops could track down agitators, and he planned a 'rifle squad' for strike duty; 'I don't believe in times of emergency in letting crowds collect,' he said. Striking cab drivers smashed and overturned the cabs still running, and only when some working cabbies were stoned and stabbed did La Guardia allow a full police response. The mayor was more concerned that the companies were paying 'starvation wages' and he insisted the violence was 'exaggerated'. He even fired O'Ryan.

But by 1940, when the three city subway companies were put together at last, the Mayor thought city workers should have no right to strike, and he opposed the closed shop. He began to put friends in high places, rather than recruiting the best technicians. He compromised with the local Democrat machine; 'He wanted their help to leave New York,' Thomas Kessler wrote, 'and they wanted him out.' The fearless La Guardia, who began by opening up the city, now told his staff he did not want to hear when he was warned that a commissioner was dabbling in drugs, hanging out with Mobsters and buying judges. He wanted reputation, which meant the city had to look calm and good. He was exhausted, his temper grown brittle, and he was frustrated at the failure of his city to live up to his expectations; his direct talk now became abusive, and sometimes he sounded off against targets, like boss rule, that he had the power to make into a matter of history.

In wartime, La Guardia's stock tumbled. Much of his success rested on federal funds, which were now diverted to the war. New York did not have the heavy industry which could boom in wartime. La Guardia was the first director of the Office of Civilian Defense. The old friend of labour now tried to persuade the FBI to infiltrate unions and look for subversives; Hoover himself thought that was beyond the bureau's powers. The Mayor who forbade city employees to take on other jobs was now doing two himself and, worse, he was not doing his national duties well. He would not delegate. He scampered around the country talking about imminent attacks, in which nobody believed. And in 1941, with a show of reluctance, he was persuaded to run again for Mayor of New York City and won by the second narrowest margin of the century. Six months later, a columnist in the *New Republic* wrote that La Guardia could no longer win an election in New York.

The Mayor would still not concentrate. He wanted to serve in the army; he wrote to Roosevelt that General Eisenhower could hardly do without him. He sent to Albany a cunning piece of legislation which allowed him to remain mayor even if he was serving overseas; after so long being everywhere, knowing everything, he thought he owned the city. But he did not escape. He stayed in the city, with its tensions now between anti-Semites and pro-Germans and pro-Italians, and the peoples of New York. He stayed while businessmen and the rich declined to pay the price of his kindness to others. There were thirty houses boarded up on Fifth Avenue now, where the rich had deserted. Businesses left in growing numbers, and La Guardia simply denied the fact: 'a malicious, deliberate lie, and the people who make it know that it is a lie, and anyone who passes it on must know that it is a lie.' The myth in a mobile society is that people choose their city; it was doubly upsetting that people could now be seen rejecting New York. La Guardia even denied that city budgets were growing. He used wartime changes – civil servants drafted into the army, projects held up for lack of supplies – to make the city look more solvent. But there was no money to maintain all those expensive gifts which La Guardia had extracted from Washington, the bridges and parks and roads, not even with his prodigious borrowings. When La Guardia left office, Rexford Tugwell, one of his admirers, said 'the whole of the City machinery was breaking down from sheer lack of funds'. La Guardia had built a modern New York, a generous place whose actions were properly considered, but he could not solve the problem of the city's limited powers to raise money, nor the paradox of the small government that had to manage a national asset. He bet on Washington's willingness to acknowledge what New York meant to the nation, forgetting that New York in some ways meant trouble, change, foreigners. He salvaged the city, but he also prepared its next bankruptcy.

The Mob slipped into the regular life of the city, selling not just vice and booze and gambling but concrete, garbage collection, children's frocks, justice and politics, taxing what was built, trucked or carted away as though it was a second government. The Mob threatened, and then protected; in this way, it came to license quite ordinary activities. It was officially invisible, a melodrama of an idea, and yet it was real enough to elect one mayor in the 1950s and make possible the career of another. For this, the remains of Tammany were essential.

When Tammany no longer had the graft that maintained its elegant headquarters on 17th Street, it moved in the early 1940s to three shaming rooms at 331 Madison Avenue. In place of machine Democrats who ran Tammany for profit, a more ominous class of gentry began to attend committee meetings. Some had grievances against the district attorney, Thomas Dewey, who was scrabbling furiously at the Mob's activities. Some had an interest in Tammany's traditional auction of judgeships – $100,000 could buy a man the nomination for the State Supreme Court until in 1939 the federal income tax was applied to judges, and the price dropped suddenly to $75,000. And many of them owed loyalty to Frank Costello, rum-runner and slot-machine king. In September 1943 Thomas A. Aurelio, a city magistrate, was phone-tapped as he offered Costello his 'undying gratitude' and 'loyalty'. Of course, Costello's helpfulness to a Tammany man was only proper; it was Tammany's complaisance which allowed him his slot machine empire.

This Frank Costello was fourteen when he committed his first known crime – a masked hold-up of his landlady who recognised him, but whose word could not count against Costello's carefully manufactured alibi. When he was twenty-four, the courts heard that he had 'the reputation of a gunman', and sent him to jail. He set up a business making punchboards, for games where you punch out a roll of paper and hope it will be the one that gives a prize, and the kewpie dolls to be won on the punchboards; he also organised its bankruptcy, and all the debtors somehow turned out to be East Side Mobsters. Such talent was rewarded. He was taught, and financed, by the great Arnold Rothstein, the tutor of a whole new underworld generation in the 1920s. Rothstein liked to bring the boys together; he introduced Costello to an extortionist called Dandy Phil Kastel, and together they formed the Tru-Mint Company. Tru-Mint ran the slot machines of New York, put them in speakeasies and candy stores, equipped them to hand out candy prizes as well as cash, which made them technically vending machines and supplied little ladders so that toddlers, too, could play. On this, and the liquor business, Costello made himself a power. But Rothstein also taught that a businessman needs friends in politics. Mayor Walker was always nervous when people said he was Rothstein's choice; he was out dancing when the news broke that Rothstein had been murdered, and he said only, 'That means trouble from here in.'

Rothstein knew many judges, and he was close to Jimmy Hines, the Harlem boss who let out the top floor of his Democrat club-house for Rothstein's gambling. Now Rothstein, the gangster, saw no clear line between a party boss and an underworld boss, and nor did the politician Hines. In 1933, Hines insisted on naming the next New York district attorney, and found a man so complaisant that grand juries could actually see how they were being steered away from the true rackets. Around the same time, Dutch Schultz met Hines to make sure that the cops laid off his policy banks, the illegal lotteries, and that the magistrates were reminded how to handle policy cases properly; Hines promised, took $1,000 in cash and $1,500 every week until in June 1935 the payments were cut in half because of 'hard times'. These connections were supposed to be confidential, but they were not entirely concealed. Anyone in the Drake Hotel in Chicago during the 1932 Democrat National Convention could have seen for himself the entwining of the Mob and the pols. In one suite slept Jimmy Hines and Frank Costello; in another, Thomas Farley, the sheriff with that magical tin box, and two known racketeers; Meyer Lansky and Lucky Luciano were down the hall.

Fiorello La Guardia took a sledgehammer to those slot machines of Costello's, had himself photographed breaking them into gaudy bits in a fine moral stew, but he could not break Costello's influence. By the winter of 1942, Tammany Hall was in its reduced circumstances and half its executive were Costello's men; he could elect a new county chairman, Michael Kennedy, and the party faithful knew who was the true boss. The style of the machine, which had never been gracious, became brutish. Warren Hubbard was forced to resign as leader of the Sixteenth Assembly District. 'The boys were in the clubhouse last night,' he told a friend, 'and stood me up against the wall, and for my own safety and the safety for my family, I am going to resign.' He said: 'I can't take it any more.' Hubbard's nominee for his successor was refused by Mike 'Trigger Mike' Coppola after a brief phone consultation with his boss. Kennedy put Thomas Aurelio on the Democrat ticket for the Supreme Court; Costello told Aurelio, 'When I tell you something is in the bag, you can rest assured.' But President Roosevelt himself had an alternative candidate, and Tammany weakened for a while on Aurelio's candidacy. A furious Costello confronted

Kennedy in his office and shouted the Tammany boss into defying the President. And the grateful Aurelio was elected, easily. Costello worked democracy well, for a man who never voted in his life.

In the middle of December 1942, he held a cocktail party. Tammany's men were there, and a crew of fixers, and William O'Dwyer, district attorney of Brooklyn and about to ship out for a distinguished war. O'Dwyer later claimed he was investigating Costello and a matter of air force contracts, but it was a curious way to question a man: the room was full of Tammany men and O'Dwyer never made an official report of his findings. It seems more likely, as Costello's lawyer claimed, that O'Dwyer had come to ask the blessings of his political godfather for a run to be mayor of New York. Of course, in wartime, anybody might talk to the wiseguys; Naval Intelligence made contact with Lucky Luciano and 'Socks' Lanza to ask them to discipline the waterfront so war work could be spared the usual gouging and beatings and conspiracy.

But when O'Dwyer succeeded La Guardia as mayor in 1946, he seemed edgy in office even when civic groups were praising him, reluctant to run for a second term as though questions might any day be asked about some cloudy bit of his past. He also seemed all too keen to impede any serious questions about gambling in the city, and police corruption. He almost wanted the city to remember how he had begged his first term as magistrate in a restaurant owned by the Mobster Joe Adonis; how his best friends went to the City Democratic Club in Brooklyn, along with Albert Anastasia and a crew of dock racketeers. He defended his buddy James Moran, who as first deputy fire commissioner shook down the city – charging anyone who wanted a new oil-burning boiler thirty-five dollars for the privilege, taking $55,000 in bribes from the head of a local of the firemen's union. Moran ordered the cops to take the 'Wanted' cards for the likes of Albert Anastasia out of the files. O'Dwyer himself had to explain why he had dropped what he called 'the perfect murder case' against Anastasia and Murder Inc., even though a grand jury thought there was a case. He said he did it only to protect a witness. He became so notorious, so sentimental and defensive all at once, that the White House intervened to remove him from office in the interests of the Democrat ticket at the fall elections in 1950. O'Dwyer was made Ambassador to Mexico, despite a barrage of objections. 'My country needs me,' he said, through sobs.

*

The rulebook made Vincent Impellitteri, President of the City Council, into Mayor until a special election could be held. It was assumed, by Costello's men, that Impellitteri was a nonentity who would step aside for the machine's next candidate; Carmine de Sapio, the new head of Tammany Hall, was certain he could not stay. Impellitteri had once been secretary to a judge, but that was the extent of his political career until he ran for City Council president. Even then, everyone knew the Democrats needed an Italian to balance their ticket, and fancied the party must have culled Impellitteri's name at random from the city's official directory, its 'green book'. They did not realise that Impellitteri had friends. Mayor O'Dwyer had nominated him as an obligatory favour to Congressman Vito Marcantonio. Marcantonio, in turn, had his own friends; he was close to Thomas 'Three Fingers Brown' Lucchese, one of Costello's rivals in the Mob. La Guardia had tolerated Marc's empire in Harlem, and Marc's word was what law there was. Marc knew all the bosses; he was an American Labor Party member, which at the time meant Communist, who also ran for office on both the Democrat and Republican tickets. Nobody liked to disturb this arrangement. In 1946, when a Republican did break ranks to run against Marc, a Republican party district captain and pollwatcher called Joseph Scottoriggio was walking to the polls in the faint Harlem dawn. He was caught, beaten too carelessly and left dying. It was the first election killing in the city for fifty years. Such friends brought Marc renewed respect. His man Impellitteri settled in the mayor's office and named a new police commissioner: Thomas Murphy, a friend for many years of Thomas Lucchese. To the fury of Costello's men at Tammany Hall, the Democrat mayor lunched once a week in an Italian restaurant with the police commissioner and with Lucchese, the Mobster rival of Tammany's Mobster boss.

Costello was deep into psychoanalysis now, and eager for the respectability which his record denied him. He tried charity work, but the guest list for each fund-raiser was reported as a scandal; nobody could be seen too close to him. He tried a little grand patronage, trying to make his dentist head of the US Government Assay Office in New York since the man knew gold, but he was detected. He tried to stop Impellitteri running for mayor in his own right, even sending out the same Mobsters who killed the pollwatcher Scottoriggio to threaten district leaders who dared change sides, but he failed. In 1952, he was summoned before the

Kefauver Committee of the Senate. He refused to be seen on camera, although the hearings were on national television; to America, Costello was a hand drumming nervously on a wooden table. He stalked out of the hearings and looked guilty. He was jailed for contempt of the committee. And yet he was able to win the next elections for mayor of New York. The Lucchese faction turned out to support Impellitteri, and Tammany sidled over to his side, unofficially, and still Impelletteri was defeated. The new mayor was Robert Wagner Junior, the protégé of Carmine de Sapio, Tammany's boss, who was himself the protégé of Frank Costello.

In the plodding business of two elections, the issue was which Mob faction would win: Lucchese from the garment trade, or Costello the slot king. Both men were of importance in their bloody world. Both were present, for example, at the summit meeting Meyer Lansky called in 1946 at the Hotel Nacional in Havana. Both had killed. They stayed in politics for the only kind of protection they needed. Their shadow is never far away from club-house deals – think of the friends of Meade Esposito, boss of Brooklyn, and Donald Manes, boss of Queens, and Stanley Friedman, boss of the Bronx. And New York has remained the stronghold of the Mob, even now that the older fashioned Cosa Nostra is in full retreat from the law.

The fall of Tammany can be briefly told. In 1961, Wagner revolted against the power of Carmine de Sapio, his backer in two earlier elections, and ran for mayor denouncing 'bossism' in all its forms. De Sapio was notorious enough for the message to work; he was a man who looked properly sinister, always in dark glasses, and men who could be mistaken for him were given the best tables in almost any restaurant, because he might well be dining under an assumed name. De Sapio himself lost the election for assembly district leader and was no longer eligible to be boss of Tammany. He was defeated by James E. Lanigan, a graduate of Harvard Law who had worked for Adlai Stevenson's presidential campaigns (De Sapio was defeated again in 1963 by Ed Koch, but by then the defeat was much less remarkable.) In 1971, De Sapio went to jail on bribery and corruption charges involving construction contracts for Con Edison. Tammany itself, the Manhattan Democrat machine, had no more hope of running New York. Instead, there was a loose conspiracy between the outer boroughs, the arrangements that made possible the careers of Donald Manes and Stanley Friedman.

The Mob remains, embedded in the life of the city. Walk into the stylish restaurant of the Sherry Netherland Hotel on Fifth Avenue, and at one time you would have been paying a tax to the Colombo family. The restaurant paid $7,500 a year to be free of labour troubles. Children ride on school buses run by the Mob, and at least one heating oil company is Mob-controlled; ARC Plumbing Company out in Ozone Park, Queens, has done business with New York City and State even though its principal salesman is the elegant, brutal John Gotti, *capo di tutti capi*.

The garbage trucks wake up the night with a racket of gears and grinders. They are great, square shapes, implacable as tanks, but painted fairground green and red. Their business is collecting the garbage from businesses, as the city collects from homes; it is worth more than a billion dollars a year. Everyone knows, as everyone knows things in the city, that the Mob somehow controls these fleets, and they are not to be challenged. Mr X went into the garbage business and undercut the competition. In a few days, there was a voice on the phone, saying he would not see his daughter again if he stayed in the business. The voice 'described the clothes that the man's ten-year-old daughter was wearing and that she was standing on such and such a street with a blue bicycle,' James Kossler of the FBI says. 'The next day, he sold his trucks.'

The United Nations, which pays carters more than $42,000 a month, does not even try to solicit bids for the work. Consolidated Edison once did, when its collector P & F Trucking suddenly wanted to renegotiate its almost new two-year contract; but nobody bid, and Con Ed agreed to pay what P & F demanded. This was particularly odd since the principals of P & F stood accused of helping Matty 'the Horse' Ianniello and his buddies in the Genovese crime family to stay in the carting business. Con Edison decided that a utility could not do business with a known gangster, and fired Ianniello's Consolidated Carting as 'part of an organised criminal network'. Court papers show that P & F took the job and three million in fees from Con Edison, but kicked half of it back to Ianniello and Consolidated. Nobody else bid for the jobs, of course. Patsy Serra of Village Carting had a contract, but Ianniello's associate Vincent Fiorillo terrified him into surrendering it. He did the same for John and Vincent Morea, whose Coney Island Rubbish Removal Inc. also had a deal with Con Edison. The practical results, so the New York State Organised Crime Task Force say, are poor service, and gross overpayments, as much as thirty-five to sixty-five per cent depending on which economist you trust: the city dependent on the Mob for protection against its own debris.

There are plenty of thin-ice businesses in New York, set up by new people taking risks – a restaurant, a clothes shop. They may suddenly run out of money when the bills come due, or have no way to talk a bank into letting them start on their own, but they have confidence enough that there will be money every week, or else they are truly desperate. Such people sometimes turn to 'Frankie the Hat' and Jesse David Hyman, otherwise known as 'Doc'. They see advertisements in the newspapers and go to the modern offices of Resource Capital; they are asked to sign the usual kind of papers. But then the loan is somehow delayed, and their need is urgent, and Resource is offering short-term money. There is no secret who is lending: a firm that has ties to organised crime, with principals who are senior wiseguys. Nobody should even think of failing to pay. So Donald Brindley took $330,000 at an interest rate of $6,000 a week, except that nobody said 'interest rate'; they said 'points' or 'vig', which is short for 'vigorish'. Champion Roofing and Siding needed money fast, was promised $12,000 but given only $10,500; the interest was $480 a week – four per cent a week. A restaurant called Wings on Wooster Street needed $125,000, at two per cent a week, and was bankrupted by it. A disco on 43rd Street called the Cowboy Palace needed $400,000; the Mob took ten per cent in 'fees', three per cent a week in interest, and twenty-seven per cent of the business. There were meetings at which the various Mob groups decided how to carve up the debt, and on what terms; before they started, the disco's owner, Thomas Duke, was beaten up as a reminder not to stall again. The disco never opened.

Thomas and Kasarmatee Rajkumar had a building at 2092 Amsterdam Avenue; they borrowed $30,000 from Resource Capital. For the money, Resource wanted fifty per cent of the profits from the building until the loan was repaid, a steady monthly payment of interest and capital, and, when the debt was finished, ten per cent of the profits forever. In December 1982, while the Rajkumars were still paying,

Resource wrote to the tenants demanding direct payment of the rent, because the building now had a new owner. The lucky ones, it seems, were those that Resource Capital never helped at all, who paid an advance fee and heard nothing more.

The city taxes change in Manhattan, living off the new property taxes; the shadow city of the Mob does just the same. Between 1978 and 1990, the Manhattan District Attorney's office reckons every major public and private contract in the city for windows, painting, dry walling, carpentry and concrete was rigged. In each trade, the Mob blesses a 'club' of contractors, and nobody else can compete. The Mob serves as a superior kind of consultant, able to enforce even their misjudgements, promising contractors that they can pay lower wages, avoid any squabbles between unions and pay off only once for each result. Their methods are sometimes traditional. 'Wild Bill' Cutola, a Teamsters Union official, disciplined one informant in the union with a shot to the head. The body was stuffed into a fifty-five gallon drum and dumped in the East River; but its gases made the drum come floating to the surface. 'Next time, I'll know better,' Cutola liked to joke. 'I'll cut his stomach open.' They meet, hugger-mugger, in some pasta importing business down on Grand Street, like their fathers and their Mustache Pete grandfathers might have done. But their racket now is policing the city's legitimate business.

The Colombo family has controlled concrete workers' locals of the Laborers International Union of North America, and locals of the Teamsters Union who deliver concrete to the sites; at one point Ralph Scopo, a 'made' member of the family, was president and business manager of the Concrete Workers District Council. Any time you fly Delta from La Guardia airport, remember Anthony Rivara who had to pay Scopo two per cent of his deal to build the terminal, because he didn't want 'to have to go down to Little Italy and sit with three or four guys with big necks'. The Colombo boys could bribe and cajole a sweetheart contract and they could menace and terrify the contractors to make sure they did not think of operating on their own. On some developments, like the Driftwood Landing Housing Development at Atlantic Beach, a Colombo crew were like hidden shareholders; Thomas Dibella, 'The Old Man', Dominic Montemarano, 'Donny Shacks', and Frank Falanga, 'Frankie the Beast' had to be paid $800 on each house sold.

The Mob controls the making of concrete, and pushed its price in New York City between ten and twenty per cent higher than in other cities, or out in the suburbs; it is another tax by the hidden government. The last company to dominate the market was Certified Concrete Company; in 1988 its owner, 'Biff' Halloran, was convicted along with Anthony ('Fat Tony', 'too fat to flee') Salerno of the Genovese family on federal racketeering charges. It seems that when Halloran went out to buy up his rivals, there was $800,000 in brokerage fees to Paul Castellano, head of the Gambino family. Certified went into decline and the upstart Valente Industries, selling five million dollars worth of concrete in a good year, suddenly expanded; in two years, Valente's sales were up to maybe fifty per cent of the $120 million worth of concrete sold in New York that year. A federal grand jury subpoena'd Valente's files.

There are Queens streets which look like empty store-fronts, the metal grilles pulled over the windows and rusted into place, old papers caught underneath them, and the windows black with paint and dirt. But the doors sometimes open. Inside, in dim and blue-white light, row after row of women sit cramped together at sewing machines. They are often newcomers, most without papers, and they work ten hours a day on a piece-work system that none of them quite understands; the money is never what they expect. The clothes they make go directly to jobbers in the garment district, who sell them on to stores. In this business, the truckers control everything. They find the money for sweat-shops, set them up and decide which ones get work. The jobbers pay them for every load that moves, even if someone else shifts the goods. Chinatown sweat-shops need a salesman who is Italian or Jewish, not just for reasons of language or culture. Listen to Ronald Borsack, president of a small-time manufacturer called Ragtime Ltd, talking to a detective. 'I have no choice who my truckers are, okay?' he says. 'I cannot stay in business without them. I do what I have to do.'

The largest of all the truckers is Consolidated Carriers. 'If you're with Consolidated or one of the others, you're protected,' a former prosecutor says. 'You don't have to worry about hijackings. They provide security. If you break off, however, then you're in real trouble.' Suppose Consolidated can't take a load, then a jobber calls 'this small outfit, just a coupla trucks'; but he still pays Consolidated. Truckers can sell accounts between themselves, although the Master Truckers of America assign all the trucking routes, and they take ten per cent of any sale; refuse the fee, and suddenly the International

Ladies Garment Workers Union, local 102, is out on strike. A jobber who changes truckers will probably have to take a few no-show workers on the payroll, or pay a fee. Jobbers aren't always sure which trucking firm will turn up to take a load and it costs money to the truckmen to get each load out of the building. 'With many loads a week, it adds up,' one says. 'This business is a jungle.'

Do business with K & K Garment Delivery, run by Vincent Aloi, a member of the Colombo family, and you do it for the long haul. Aloi found one owner of a shop in Queens who was griping about K & K's overcharging and having a friend shift small loads of dressing gowns at eleven cents a garment instead of K & K's thirty-six cents a garment. The owner was told he should not be making dressing gowns, anyway; he did not get the work through K & K. He was threatened with 'having the union come into my shop', with paying union rates, and union benefits. Days later, the federal Wage and Hour Division descended for an inspection and found major violations of the minimum wage laws. But a man can't pay union rates and attend to health and safety laws if he also has to pay the truckers their high, fixed fees and sell a pair of jeans out of his factory for a mere dollar fifty when it will retail at twenty dollars. He makes a political choice: whether or not he can afford the law.

'There is nothing nefarious about Mr Gambino,' his lawyer says. 'His trucks roll along the streets in full view and nobody is hiding anything from anybody.' Thomas Gambino controls 500 trucks – Consolidated Carriers, but also six more firms that fill up the side streets off Seventh Avenue with racks and boxes. Gambino has never been convicted of a crime; indeed, he was acquitted in 1989 on charges of obstructing justice. But he has a heady pedigree. He is the son of Carlo Gambino, who founded a Mafia family, and he is married to the daughter of Thomas 'Three Fingers Brown' Lucchese, the politician and the mobster. The Feds say he is a captain in the Gambino crime family. The Gambino family, it is said, controls what the whole garment district calls 'Greater Blouse' – the Greater Blouse, Skirt, and Undergarment Association. At various times, the Gambinos' *consigliere* Joseph Gallo has been in charge, and a Colombo soldier called James Clemenza was executive director. 'We have to join,' one jobber said, 'and we have to pay out $50 a month dues. If we don't join, we don't get any work.' The jobbers paid payroll tax to Greater Blouse, who held it a full quarter before paying the contractors, and took off their 'administrative expenses'.

The same gentlemen are in the meat market, sometimes on the fringes of the bond business, in the kind of stolen car business which, under the late Paul Castellano, required twenty-five murders; the fish market is as organised as it was in the 1920s. But they unsettle their own shadow city. They get too staid to be their own enforcers, and they bring in the 'zips', the Sicilian-born Mobsters who cling to the old-fashioned values of gun and boot. The 'zips' have no particular time for the sleek new Mob operations; they lack respect for the famous Mobsters like John Gotti. Listen to members of Gotti's crew discussing zips who run a 'gorgeous' café, a gambling front in Gotti's territory. Philip Cestero says: 'They said – who's a Johnna? I don't know no Johnna.' Peter Mosca says: 'Dom, I gotta ask you a question. Could they be that fucking dumb?' They do business in drugs, and sometimes they do drugs. John Lewis de Lutro tells Joseph Tuzzino on the phone: 'You're not my friend. You're just my worker. . . . You can't sniff with me no more.' Hear De Lutro say he can't come down to Caffe Palermo on Mulberry Street, not even for business, because he has 'pupils like a fucking ogre. My eyes are lit up.' And De Lutro is the son of a soldier, a soldier himself. They are as loose with the business as the bosses, as uncertainly competent.

30 June 1975. The teleprinters in city offices began to chatter. They carried orders to dismiss 19,000 city workers by midnight, because the alternative was declaring bankruptcy: an unimaginable confusion for a city with so many clients and dependents. Powers that the city had taken for granted were taken away so that New York could still raise money on the bond markets. The ever-expanding city budget finally had to take account of facts: that New York had lost 600,000 jobs, most of them in manufacturing industries, betwen 1969 and 1975. The economic base for a grand metropolis was fading. The city was a locus of need, rather than prosperity. There were fewer police; so there was nobody to bust the neighbourhood drug supermarkets, or the numbers games that posted yesterday's winners in a storefront window and offered doughnuts and coffee while you waited. Firefighters on Staten Island changed shift in gypsy cabs. Parks became wilderness. Subways broke down twice as often and ran more and more behind schedule. The City University, the resource for newcomers and for people determined to break out of poverty, ended its experiment in

open admissions and free tuition. Libraries were open only two days a week. The streets grew dirtier.

Within ten years, the city boasted of its recovery. But its economies and efficiencies were false. In the last half of the 1970s, the city budget rose at only sixty per cent of the inflation rate, even though the needs of newcomers and the poor did not diminish. Within another five years, the budget was visibly in deficit again, the cuts amounted to billions of dollars, the streets were again neglected and the libraries cut back and firehouses closed. The fiscal crisis and the recovery and the next fiscal crisis are not exceptional events; they represent a reality which La Guardia bequeathed, a gap between the city's own resources and the city's duties and aspirations which could not be permanently filled. New York City was so manifestly separate and independent in so many ways, even an outcast in the nation, except for its ability to pay and to make law; there, it was all too tightly integrated into the state. Its budget was a curious affair which did not even admit to an official surplus or deficit until 1975 and depended on debt to keep New York functioning; it barely connected with the real city costs, and those costs barely connected with need. The chatter of the tele-printers, all that sudden pain, was not so much an event as an illustra-tion of what was happening.

And in Minimum City, the fiscal crisis did not stop the alternative governments – the Mob, the city bosses – as they went about their schemes. The apparent prosperity of the 1980s only made them bolder. As Prohibition blurred the line between crime and opportunism, so the stock and bond market enthusiasms of the 1980s blurred the line between ambition and crime; not least because of the expectation that no corporate chief would ever do time for a crime committed by his company. A mayor who presided over a corrupt city could claim the most perfect innocence without, as in the case of Boss Tweed, irony.

Mayor Koch talked constantly about corruption in other adminis-trations, about how 'they were selling cadavers out of the morgue in the La Guardia administration'. He needed all the history he could muster. In his first eight years, in a city supposed to be so well run that it had come back from the brink of fiscal catastrophe in five years, 1,629 city workers were formally charged with corruption.

Party leaders and city officials no longer chatted casually and never mentioned favours. Commissioners assumed their phones were tapped. Democrat leaders in the Bronx became oddly shy in the presence of reporters; as one explained, 'My lawyer says that if we talk to the press, it wakes the Feds up again.' A City Council member who wanted to suggest a constituent for a job as deckhand on the Staten Island ferry was told the patronage route was closed, for the time being. By March 1986 there was talk of 'the paralysis factor', that decisions were stalled for the sake of appearances. A more stringent review process delayed the second phase of a hundred million dollar plan to build middle-income housing and froze the Board of Education's plans, already two years old, for modular school building. It was difficult to find persons pure enough and unconnected enough to sit in judgement on city projects; almost by definition, their names would not be known unless they were known to someone in the city, or doing business with the city. The corps of professional public relations persons was stymied, unable to use the access they were peddling; the doyen of them, Howard Rubenstein, dropped his clients Citisource and Datacom because he could do nothing for them except refer calling reporters to their lawyers. Indeed, the PR men, like the lawyers, now had clients with rather different needs: instead of pushing deals or laws, they were trying to make their past deals and laws look good, or at least legal. In summer, a certain class of city official took to carrying a raincoat because it served so well, in an emergency, to cover handcuffs.

And the Mayor, who kept saying that nobody ever called La Guardia corrupt, nobody, began to take a more finicky approach to his administration. Patrick McGinley, the city's chief investigator of wrong-doing, resigned because the District Attorney was asking about an incident in 1983 when a city worker came to McGinley's Manhattan apartment to install an air-conditioner for his asthmatic wife. The worker somehow injured himself, and claimed – twice – the pension of a man who has been injured at work. Propriety washed over the city. McGinley was reminded that he had called a previous schools chancellor unethical for using school employees to baby-sit for his children and to paint his house; that was 'vastly different,' McGinley said, because the chancellor had 'demanded' services, and he had only asked.

And still the embarrassments, the incidents continued. The new head of the Probation Department somehow failed to file state income tax forms for three years. The head of the Off Track Betting Corporation was forbidden to own horses, but his wife was trading them and owned one jointly with a gentleman who had been paid eleven and a half million dollars in OTB contracts in five years. The head of the Division of Real Property, who was supposed to buy and sell for the city, had taken on the side to buying and selling property for himself. The Mayor's chef used the Mayor's kitchens and city ingredients to make cheesecake for his private catering company and, when he was discovered, quit while the District Attorney carefully, lengthily decided not to prosecute. The Mayor's chef's dog was sent away for biting a garbage man, and a night-time TV comic said he was 'the only member of the Koch administration in recent years to leave without being indicted'. Mother Theresa called on the Mayor and the city knew at once she wanted a favour: a reserved parking space outside the Manhattan hospice she runs.

This Mayor had promised to clean up clubhouse dominance of patronage, and to allow commissioners to run their own agencies. Koch claims that at his very first meeting with the county leaders he told them that his government would not deal in patronage. But Koch was a reform politician, who had always kept his distance from the machine; he knew how to denounce it, but not how it worked. He seemed a little shocked to discover the county leaders, the easy demons in his early speeches, were nice enough guys. When he grew closer to them, the city understood that business would continue almost as usual; except that, since the Mayor was not involved, he could not limit what the party bosses did. Of course, the style of the operation changed. When Koch took an endorsement from Meade Esposito, the Brooklyn boss, he did not give specific promises; but as Esposito later said, 'Of course I expected something – I'm a county leader.' Out of kindness, Koch kept in his administration such Esposito cronies as Alex Liberman, who took $2.6 millions in bribes. He made Anthony Ameruso the Transport Commissioner, even though his own screening panel said the man was unqualified for the job. Ameruso was responsible for parking while owning a parking lot in partnership with a corrupt judge and a suspected Mobster. He was indicted for perjury when he concealed his million dollar interest in a company to which he awarded an unusually long franchise to run a ferry from New Jersey to Manhattan.

The machine attended quietly to its earliest habit: patronage. The Mayor had an assistant in charge of job referrals, Joseph DeVincenzo, who took Room One in the City Hall basement just under the Mayor's office and passed discreetly each day up the rear staircase to discuss matters with his superiors. Some former commissioners say they heard more from DeVincenzo as Koch grew more friendly with the county bosses. 'It didn't start to get sticky,' one says, 'until Koch lost the primary for governor in 1982, and got concerned that he might lose the mayoral race. It got stickier and sticker. We got more and more from Joseph DeVincenzo.' His formal title was 'special assistant to the mayor' but he was the gatekeeper: Joe D. had to approve new curtains for a city window, a new hatstand in the corner and, of course, any hirings or promotions. After 1983, he was in the business of social reform: he ran the Mayor's Talent Bank, which was supposed to bring more women, more blacks and more Hispanics into city government. The Bank did its work with a curious bias: the best-paying jobs, the desirable ones, went on the whole to the usual white males.

This situation was not easy to explain, but it went unexamined until Donald Manes cut himself. City Hall began to dread subpoenas, and some in the city hierarchy decided it was better to edit the files before the Feds could get to them. For a whole day and an evening, staff at the Talent Bank locked the doors and began tearing up their files, shredding them and carefully taking away their own notes. They sat at computer terminals and adjusted the city's memory. The point of all this was to erase all the messages from county bosses, all the suggestions that jobs be found for properly connected Democrats, all the patronage whose very existence the mayor would persist in denying. They also had to cover up a blatant racial bias. In this office supposed to help minorities, only one borough boss was kept out of the game: Denny Farrell, boss of Manhattan, who is black.

In these bothersome times, Joe D. decided that he was tired of city government. He engineered his retirement in February 1989 on a pension which could not be touched even if he was convicted of a criminal offence, and went bravely before a commission on the integrity of city government to forget every detail.

The Koch years are a scandal, but much more, they are a paradigm – the most recent tangle grown from the paradox of a grand modern city without the political means to run itself.

The single effective body which made real decisions was the Board of Estimate. That was declared unconstitutional, because it gave Staten Island and Brooklyn equal weight, despite their vastly different populations. More than a century after Boss Tweed tried to concentrate power on the mayor, a new City Charter does the same. The City Council is supposed to have new authority. But the city still has its alternative governments – the club-houses, the Democrat machine, the Mob and the pressure that financiers and developers can exert because the city is required to fund locally all its sensational ambitions; all these are better able to change the city, and administer it, than the official institutions. And the city depends on government – city, state and national. The government pay roll is $13.9 billion in wages a year; the biggest civilian employers on Wall Street pay out only $10.8 billion, and the construction firms only $4.2 billion. One job in six is in the public sector.

New York is a government town, without strong local government: a kind of colony, glamorous and dependent. It has no citizens because it is waiting to be invented as a political creature. That lack means New Yorkers belong first to their class, their job, their race or their family's country of origin; there is no political city to which everyone belongs and we are careless of each other. In the push and rush of the streets, where nobody minds, the lack can bruise you.

6
THE SKYLINE IS POLITICS

FROM THE AIR, Manhattan is an engineer's diagram, a fixed, hard-angled thing. There are no grand boulevards to remind you of a late Napoleon, as in Paris; there is nothing like the Imperial Forum, restored in Rome by Mussolini to justify his own attempts at empire. The villages of London still have their high streets, their churches and greens; the shape of the past persists. The merchant houses along Amsterdam canals may now be divided into apartments, but they still stand – palaces of virtue, their huge glass windows displaying how God has favoured the owner, their message intact.

New York has nothing like this. On its old streets, the clutter of fire-escape steel is just the exoskeleton of the building, to show how it stands up and how to get out: information in the present tense. The signs are shouts for shops and factories, not memos about events long past. Individual blocks may be boasts from corporations or families, but the avenues are not built to be a clear statement about power and authority – like the Mall that leads to Buckingham Palace, or the Champs Elysées, or the approach to St Peter's in Rome. Instead, the city has something in common with some Italian hill town from the Middle Ages, where clans built towers that filled whole blocks, and gave them the family name, just as Chase Manhattan and General Motors now give their names to 'plazas'. The towers defined the city's skyline, but each was the centre of a net of business and credit which connected much more with distant traders than with the immediate street. Their entrances were guarded and narrow, like the security forts at corporate doors. And the hill towns, like New York, often had to shout at the self-absorbed towers to remind them where they were.

Each block makes a point. The Woolworth Building is the 'cathedral of commerce', with gargoyles and misericordes; a dime store goes to glory. The downtown Federal Reserve is crenellated like a fort, to show security. The ground floor vaulting of the A T & T Building expects awe, but its Chippendale top is a badge of post-modernism, meant to separate it from the city around, which is famous for being only modern and may, therefore, be passé. It is braggadocio by that post-modernist master Philip Johnson, whom Hitler's architect Albert Speer once nominated as the perfect architect for any new Führer. The wasted pink marble of the Trump Tower atrium is all about spending, not taste; it is exactly right for a shopping mall. The doors to Brown Brothers Harriman on Wall Street, narrow and on an awkward corner, define a bank that is long established and does not encourage everyone to enter. Corporate buildings appropriate the sky with their glass and offer it to the street, second-hand; they give back atriums and courtyards full of glasshouse trees, as though rest and greenery were in the gift of a God-like IBM. All these things can be read on the streets of the city, but none of them is the city's own story.

From the air, you begin to see very different cities behind the noise of all this boasting. You see the grid of the city clearly, and the canopy of Central Park, the mid-town business district suddenly pushing up out of level streets, the wide tape of roads wrapped around the island and the clutter of bridges. These are the city's bones. Read them like an archive, and you see another story of the city: which is about its physical form, and how it was changed, and what that was all meant to mean.

A still street, a cold Christmas. There is an unfamiliar sound above the houses, and it takes a moment to think to look up to where birds sketch out on the grey cotton sky, snow geese beating south. Their wings make a curious music. For a moment, New York is not what we assume, not the 'factory of man-made experience, where the real and natural ceased to exist,' as Rem Koolhaas wrote. We stand shocked. This is the island that man broke to his politics, made into a fabulous machine; and wild things persist.

On fine days in late September, you can stand in the Bronx and watch the hawks, 12,000 of them jousting and bouncing south on the warm air. The northern finches pass overhead on an ancient flyway. A bittern falls from the air at 57th Street and Lexington; it is wrapped by a Spanish maid in a Bergdorf Goodman bag. There are twenty-foot worms, *Cerebratulus lactens*, that turn unseen in the mud of the East River. The Chinese praying mantis is common; John Kieran remembers knocking one from the shoulder of a woman who sat under the painted stars of Grand Central Station. Possums scat in Washington Heights when the cats, homely and feral, come after them. Woodchucks breed in Central Park. There is an alternative city, a kind of ecosystem which we hardly notice, in which southern flying squirrels glide like leaves to the bird tables of the Bronx and the big brown bat, which is not so ominously big, files itself for winter in the roof of the American Museum of Natural History. Dragonflies and damselflies shimmer in their shoreline club, on the north side of Belvedere Lake in Central Park. You can hear all thirty-seven species of American wood warbler in the city. North of the George Washington Bridge, in a bitter winter, you used to see the plumped up shapes of bald eagles on the ice floes; before they reached the bridge, they would tack back upstream. Now, they ride the air over Manhattan.

The city's supposed to be all laced up with cables and conduits, the works; but it is not perfectly controlled. There are eels in the piping of the subway men's rooms; 'Smelly Kelly', the trouble-shooter whose talent was his nose, found them. Rats in the subway tunnels grow so big that track crews know them as 'track rabbits'. Peregrine falcons used to bully guests at the St Regis Hotel, and now they swoop from cliffs of post-modernist colours to take pigeons outside the windows of startled office workers; they nest on church towers and in the high cables of the Verrazano Narrows Bridge. Daisies and common black mustard grow between cracks in parking lots, and tall, tart yarrow, and there is wild ginger in the Bronx woods. There are mink along the Bronx River; one zookeeper trapped eleven to make his wife a fur piece. Crawfish once dug up a golf course in the Bronx.

When a city is modern, nobody wants to see these things; what matters is the streamlining, the skyscrapers. Yet the rock of Manhattan is full of glittering things − garnets like stones in a field, rose and smoky quartz, amethysts found in Riverdale, an almandine garnet big as an egg discovered in the digging of the Brooklyn-Battery tunnel, black tourmaline dug when the rail tunnel was formed at Park Avenue and 96th Street, aquamarines in subway walls at 157th Street and Broadway, and golden beryl a block north. These things were made museum curiosities. Underground to us is the steel-plated trenches where the subways run, burrowing 200 feet under the ridges of Manhattan. It is steam pipes, 103 miles of them, that make the city seethe on a cold night with little dramas of hot mist; that usefully warmed the city when the blizzard of 1888 broke down lights and frosted the gas pipes and forced impatient office workers to wait until the tunnellers came to free them; that run the elevators and the air-conditioning that made skyscrapers possible. When steam hits water that has condensed in a cool pipe, in this old system, the 'water hammer' can burst out a geyser 150 feet high; which is what we expect, much more than the moments when the old Minetta Brook seeps back in an apartment house basement. Down deep in the rock, the Gaelic 'sandhogs' go to cut tunnels, suspended from cranes on barrel-sized platforms, finding forests at 200 feet that were calcified in some ancient mudslide; they cut the forest back with chainsaws. There is nowhere the city does not go. At 800 feet, as deep as the Woolworth Building is high, there are water tunnels for the next century. Down there, the sandhogs say, the air is so cold that it burns you.

But even the modern city has an odd relationship with the place it occupies. The grid of Manhattan looks burned on the land; but it depends on the natural as well as standing on it. If you look down at the shape of the Bronx and Manhattan, at where the skyscrapers stand and where the scale seems more human, you see the city's foundations. Up north is the Grand Concourse, the boulevard of the Bronx, built on a ridge of granite-like Fordham gneiss which dips under the Harlem River, makes the island which carries the Triborough Bridge and dwindles out in Long Island City. Broadway cuts on the bias across Manhattan; it follows a valley of dolomite. Over all this is Manhattan schist, a rock that is young in geological terms, a sunken mountain ridge rubbed down by glaciers, which carries New York County: the city and its skyscrapers. It runs from high points in the north at the twin bluffs of Fort George and Fort Washington, down to the north side of Washington Square; there it plunges hundreds of feet below the debris of the last great ice sheets that covered the island, the clay, sand, gravel and boulders which make an uncertain foundation for tall buildings. The guarantee of scale is rubble.

Then comes SoHo, which stands on flatlands which were marshes in colonial times, when a bad flood could cut Manhattan in two. Where Canal Street now runs, there was in 1809 a kind of drain across the island, with bridges to hold the bits of city together. The drain was planted with trees, and meant to be delightful; but it fouled, and the city fathers briefly considered pouring perfumes and essences into it, caught themselves considering, and quickly decided to fill it. Then comes Chambers Street, and the schist comes close enough to the surface to allow the twin towers of the World Trade Center, the shiny, boasting buildings that brokerage houses like, the fortresses of Wall Street. But the rock determines where all this can stand.

Water determined when it could grow. Even the horses turned away from Manhattan well water; Peter Kalm said so in 1748. Collect Pond, which lay to the south of modern Worth Street, had to be filled in 1796 because it was already stagnant and dangerous. You could make news in 1832 by drilling down 448 feet on Bleecker Street and coming up with the glitter of fresh 'rock water'; because the city was foul, dry and terribly afraid of fire that could make ash out of its planked streets and its wooden houses. The tree-trunk pipes of the Manhattan Company brought water that was 'poor and brackish'. Soda water sold on the corners. The groggeries could have floated the city on a tide of raw gin. To live, the city needed clean water from the country; in the early 1840s, an aqueduct was built up to Croton, on the Hudson River, which poured into the steep-sided fort for water which stood at Fifth Avenue and 42nd Street. Its opening was a glorious business. A city which hardly had monuments decided to spend $2,500 on a show-off fountain in City Hall Park. A hundred cannon and the bells of the island began at dawn. Water, the city's necessary condition, went up fifty feet in a column called the 'Maid of the Mist', then formed into a plume and then a fan; around it danced twenty-four other jets. It was a fantastical relief from the dust of Broadway, an adored celebration of the freshness and relief that the aqueduct brought down; until, in 1869, when the city fathers took water for granted, it was taken apart to make way for a new post office.

Tides saved the new city. Its waters were hardly ever frozen, and they were deep enough to take great liners; the city had a hem of docks and piers. It has a square mile of inland water for every five square miles of land. With Manhattan Island, and Brooklyn and Queens on Long Island, and the East River islands like Roosevelt and Randalls, and Staten Island, only an eighth of the city's surface area is even on the mainland of America. All this water pulls like an engine on the filth the city sends out, and dissipates the sewage of an extraordinary concentration of human beings. Somehow, it kept the famous oysters of New York harbour wholesome – 'Oysters we pick up before our fort,' Nicasius de Sille wrote home in 1654, 'some so large they must be cut in two or three pieces' – until, in 1916, the Department of Health finally forbade the harvesting of harbour shell-fish for fear of cholera, and in 1918, typhoid from Raritan Bay oysters killed 150 people. Caviar was a New York trade, from sturgeon pulled out of the harbour, until finally the waters grew too foul for the tides. Then, where the great fish used to run, ships were brought fifty years ago to New York Bay, because the water was toxic enough to kill the sea worms that bored into their hulls.

The city grew again, a tramp of a city with no cash to keep itself clean. Daily, until 1986, the west side of Manhattan poured 150 million gallons of raw sewage into the Hudson River. When treatment did begin, this man-made tide still overran the harbour tides. Something like 7,000 pounds of toxic metals settle each day in the sludge of the new treatment plants. Each time there is rain, the plants can't cope with the flow, so raw sewage has to be pumped directly into the rivers – 560 million gallons in an ordinary storm. Sewers flood into storm sewers, and take the city's waste out where the tides toss it around. There are plastics, wood, grease in a hundred forms, all bobbing in the harbour; seven million pounds of 'floatables' were recovered in the summer of 1989 alone. A junkie's needle, flushed in a Manhattan toilet, spikes up from the sand on a swimming beach. The city dumps its wastes in the ocean and claims the fish thrive, but the law says that must stop by 1992; the city piles its waste at Fresh Kills on Staten Island, building the tallest hill on the Atlantic south of Maine, stopping only when the weight of garbage would buckle the earth underneath. New York is to be ringed with incinerator chimneys, plumes of grey smoke that will take the evening light like monuments.

All this machinery is not enough. The city depends on grass, the spartina in wetlands at Jamaica Bay, the kidneys of New York. Spartina can resist the salt from icy roads, filter out pesticides and poisons which otherwise would make stagnant the waters which surround and cut into the city. What man can't manage, wetlands can. And yet in building the city, the wetlands were filled. At the height of his powers, Robert Moses brought rubble from blitzed London to fill in the Flushing wetlands and make lakes that now bloom with the acrid colours of algae. The island has grown with landfill, pushing Wall Street into the East River, hanging a highway there, making Battery Park City in the Hudson; as late as the 1980s, it seemed logical to line the west shore of Manhattan with a new six-lane highway, leading nowhere. And what's left, shoreline and wetlands, looks too empty; the city needs to fill it with new buildings to yield new tax dollars. Keeping the city solvent conflicts directly with keeping the city itself alive, and since bankruptcy is quicker and more visible than the ruin of a city, the tax issue often wins. But survival can be negotiated. See Parks Commissioner Henry Stern at a planning meeting. He thinks he is losing the case for a stretch of Jamaica Bay, where condos could be built. He pushes aside the practical, money talk that officials love, and he asks the presiding Deputy Mayor: 'You know what wetlands are good for?' There's silence; you can see the Deputy Mayor tasting tax yields. 'Peregrines,' Stern says. 'You know what peregrines are good for?' The Deputy Mayor says: 'What?' 'I tell you,' Stern shouts. 'They tear the head off of pigeons!' And the Deputy Mayor, who brings his car into Manhattan and tries to eat lunch outside in summer, says: 'Great, great!' The bay is safe, for the moment.

Some of the ways man changed the nature of Manhattan are obvious. Oil films have tamed the mosquitoes so children do not cry daily, as they did in the 1900s, at the bitter taste of quinine. The deer that fed the earliest settlers are now only rare strays from the north. Once there were wild pigeons 'shot by the thousands', according to de Sille, 'they taste like partridge'; gone. Traffic crushed the eastern box turtle. The pink ladyslipper orchid has to be guarded in tiny colonies in Bronx parks. The brown and garter snakes, common twenty years ago in Central Park, have vanished; and they are a test of the health of the wild city because they depend on insects, lizards, small mammals. We feel a familiar kind of horror at the way the city smothered out plants and animals as it began to fill the island. But it did not simply destroy; it changed. New York was colonised as much by leeches, roses, maples, starlings and sparrows as by man. The purple red spikes of purple loosestrife worked their way into summer marshes. Tiny scarlet pimpernel hugs the ground, there is thorny and indestructible multiflora rose, honeysuckles and porcelain berry vine and Norway maple; lovely, foreign things, making a new nature. The European medicinal leech – bigger and drabber than its American cousins, a functional grey ooze – inhabits city ponds. The northern fence lizard lives on Staten Island because once it was brought there to feed the snakes in a local zoo. The house sparrow came to America as a pet in 1852 and in 1890, for the sake of having all Shakespeare's birds in America, thirty were released in Central Park. They had a brief heyday while there were oats and straw for horses, and wooden

eaves to nest in; cars and concrete have cut them back. But the starlings, let out in New York on the strength of single Shakespearean
reference, did better. At night they roost in warm neon and in the
morning they flood out to the boroughs, a contrary parody of commuters.

Into the parks come boxed and antediluvian things, let loose by
people who can no longer bear them or care for them. There are
snapper turtles that scare any predator but man, that can crush the
head of a grazing swan. In season, the female hefts all twenty-five
pounds of her armour on to the land and frantically digs a flask-shaped
nest. She lays some thirty eggs and she tramples the ground; enough
young survive.

Passers-by call 911, for the cops.

The city used to lie at the very south of Manhattan, with a scatter of
farms and villages to the north. City Hall was built a mile north of
the Battery in the 1800s, and it was so remote that its builders reckoned
there was no need for marble on the north wall, because nobody
would ever see it. This city was a soft thing, never thoroughly mapped
and quite unplanned, its streets grown like branches and sometimes
twisted back in on the trunk. When the British held the city during
the war for independence, wooden streets were torn down for firewood. Fire caught up the city, and spoiled its familiar, provincial
shape. There is a pathetic sketch of Trinity Church, the city's monument, its roof and windows blown out with fire, a graveyard tree all
curled and black. A Dubliner who sailed into New York harbour in
1782 thought it 'a Pity to see such a fine City as this almost half
Burned to ashes, and to see now nothing rem[ainin]g but the bare
walls of fine Churches and other Public Buildings or to see those
rem[ainin]g Converted into magazines or other purposes for the use
of the army . . .' But once peace broke out in 1783, New York rebuilt
chaotically. Between 1783 and 1786, its population doubled to 23,614;
by 1800, it had 60,489 people, and by 1810 96,373. There were jobs
and markets and there was prodigious wealth. More, New York was
briefly the capital of the new nation, where the orderliness of streets,
the cleaning of gutters, the fact that three could walk abreast on the
sidewalks were meant to prove the value of the revolution. Brissot de
Warville saw the prodigious effects of liberty in the industrious streets,

where 'On all sides, houses are rising, and streets extending: I see nothing but busy workmen building and repairing.' Even when New York ceased to be the capital, and its arch-rival Philadelphia was appointed while the District of Columbia was made ready, there was no going back. The city did not rule the nation and, after the 1790s, it did not even rule New York State. But it could never be small or provincial again.

'The town had formerly been built without any plan,' the Duc de Rochefoucauld-Liancourt wrote in 1799. 'Except what has been rebuilt in consequence of the fire, the streets are small and crooked; the foot-paths, where there are any, narrow, and interrupted by the stairs from the houses.' Now there was open ground, and money to build, and the map of this hopeful city was up for negotiation. To open Greenwich Street meant dealing with Trinity Church, who owned the land. First Presbyterian Church in 1808 suddenly claimed the whole of Nassau Street. The street commissioners kept insisting they were the only people who could decide the line of a street, and nothing could be built until lots had been officially surveyed; they insisted, but nobody listened. Serious overcrowding and serious money complicated matters; landowners could block almost any civic scheme with their 'incessant remonstrances'. A modern city was waiting to be made, and it needed a plan 'to unite regularity and order with the Public convenience and benefit, and in particular to promote the health of the city.'

'Health' was not an afterthought. Too much of the soil on which New York had built itself was poison – landfill of garbage, offal, dung from the streets, dead horses buried where the docks were being filled. The spoiled ground was supposed to put out deadly miasmas. To be healthy, citizens would need to move north, into the blank parts of the island above Houston Street and Greenwich Avenue. Twice in the decade before the new city grid was commissioned, they had been forced to do so. In 1798, yellow fever broke out in lower Manhattan, and businessmen moved homes and offices into Greenwich Village. Again in 1805, post office, newspaper and business offices moved north when yellow fever broke out along the East River; the city put up temporary housing for refugees, but not in healthy districts because they might carry the 'fomites' or particles of the disease. The need to move north was something everybody understood, because they had seen the consequences of staying put. North was where the city had to be imagined out of the fields.

Commissioners were appointed in 1807 to make a plan, and four years later they delivered; their surveyor and draughtsman, designer of New York above Houston Street, was John Rendel Junior. His grid is a grand statement of intent; the Commissioners were half afraid they might be laughed at for allowing 'space for a greater population than is collected at any spot this side of China'. Where New York previously had grown with respect for hills and streams and ponds, the grid was forced on the land; hills had to be carted away, waters buried, to keep the streets in line. The plan was a boast in itself, of man's power over nature and the prospects for the city. But there were no boulevards or triumphal arches and very little open space; there was nothing aristocratic to offend a new democracy. Without palaces and monuments, the city seems to celebrate only itself; but it is egalitarian, homespun. Secretly, the Commissioners 'longed to lay out New York like Washington,' Edith Wharton says, thinking of temples and ornamental Malls, but they 'laid it out instead like a gridiron, lest they should be thought "undemocratic" by people they secretly looked down upon.'

There are no grand terraces or crescents. Blocks are straight-sided because 'a city is to be composed principally of the habitations of men, and ... straight-sided and right-angled houses are the most cheap to build and the most convenient to live in'. Nothing smacks of fine arts or other indulgences. The Commissioners laid out even what seemed unbuildable areas because leaving blanks 'might have furnished materials for the pernicious spirit of speculation'. Building plots, their heirs told Wharton, had to be 'exactly the same shape, size – and *value!*' This city was proper and republican, in a nation which was still caught up with Jefferson's dreams of rural virtue, of gentlemen leaders and honourable tenants – the blue mountain politics which made cities suspect for their trading and their unsettledness. This city is proud.

It lacks the parks that opened out London, and stood for the grace of royal power in Paris; they were not needed because, the Commissioners said, 'The large areas of sea which embrace Manhattan Island render its situation, in regard to health and pleasure ... particularly felicitous.' They could easily 'secure a free and abundant circulation of air,' as they had been told to do. But the city very soon filled up and stifled. You could walk among the ponds and the flowerbeds of Greenwood Cemetery in Brooklyn, thinking moral thoughts, but graveyards fill up with graves. On Saturdays, boys boated to the beaches and woods of Staten Island, but that took too long for an everyday expedition. There were steamboats up the Hudson, and no gentle person would think of living through a punishing city summer, but there was no break in the city for most people.

There were lovely curiosities, of course – Englishmen had land at Broadway and 21st Street where they made gardens of brilliant tulips, under white, light awnings of cotton. You could cross on the ferry to Hoboken, to the gardens of the Elysian Fields, but they soon developed a dubious reputation: too many ladies of the night working days. Mostly, escape was simply too expensive. 'Theatres, concerts and lectures were the only amusements within reach of the mass of the people,' Clarence C. Cook wrote in 1869; 'the sidewalks, the balconies, the backyards, the only substitutes for the Hyde Park or Tuileries of the Old World, or the ancient freedom and rural beauty of Young New York.'

What New York needed was a park. It was partly a matter of pride. New York didn't dream of being a great American city any longer; it measured itself by London and Paris, by the world. Its official faith was democracy and the republic; New York would have to show that good republicans could offer ease to their citizens as readily as any foreign king or count. The park would be the lungs of the great, stretched body of the city. It would be a taste of the calmer morals of the countryside; 'the great purpose of the park [is] to supply to the hundreds of thousands of tired workers who have no opportunity to spend their summers in the country, a specimen of God's handiwork,' as Frederick Law Olmsted, the maker of the park, liked to tell his commissioners.

And it would save lives. Since the park was built before the theory of germs was established, citizens fretted about miasmas and stenches held in tight streets; and about breaking God's laws and sanitary laws, which, since either sin was deadly, seemed much the same. The park was often mentioned in the same breath as the new aqueduct, which had helped clean the city and save it from fire and cholera. It would cost more than the city's entire income for a year, but the mass evacuations for yellow fever had been monstrously expensive, too; the city was used to spending on the welfare of its masses. The park, after long debate, was begun just after yellow fever very nearly did establish itself in New York City, when it broke out in Brooklyn and on Long Island and only quarantine kept it out of Manhattan.

The city found the wrong site, on the rocky spine of Manhattan where gneiss lies close to the surface and the scree held little organic matter at all. The trees were wiry runts, survivors of the building of the Croton reservoir. There were bone-boiling works and hog farms and swamps and stagnant water, 'wretched hovels, half-hidden among the rocks where, also, heaps of cinders, brick-bats, potsherds and other rubbish were deposited'; 'a suburb more filthy, squalid and disgusting can hardly be imagined,' the Park Commissioners wrote in their third annual report in 1860.

On this land, Frederick Law Olmsted dreamed. He was a literary man, not exactly an engineer, not even much of a farmer. Science he knew from a semester's lectures at Yale; he had once shared a house with a civil engineer; he had managed men on his Staten Island farm, bawling out the half-dozen day labourers who helped with the harvest. His notions of landscape came from family holidays and European tours in pursuit of 'scenery of a more domestic order', suitable for musing and loitering. But he brought to Central Park indispensible things: need and passion. 'A great deal of disappointed love and unsatisfied romance and down-trodden pride,' he wrote, 'fastened itself to that passion.'

In the summer of 1857, Olmsted had hidden himself in a Connecticut inn near New Haven, scribbling for money. He was shackled with debt. Money his father lent him for a publishing venture had all gone. He wanted to take his long campaign against slavery to the cotton barons of Manchester in the fall, to persuade them to buy raw material from free-soil settlements in Texas and not from the slave states, but he was not sure he would have the money for the fare.

He expected disappointment. He had wanted so much to have faith, and instead he grew up a rationalist. He loved one woman and she jilted him shamingly. His closest friend was the brother who died young of tuberculosis; out of a sullen kind of duty, Olmsted married his widow. He sat in the Mount Cove Inn without prospects, exiled from the writers' world he knew in New York, looking at the sea. Into his exile stepped an old friend full of New York talk, who told him the city needed a superintendent of the planned Central Park.

There were no Reptons or Capability Browns to jostle for the job, and the park was a writers' cause; Washington Irving, Olmsted's friend, was on the board. Faced with a job he could actually have,

Olmsted found a mission. Part of his distaste for slavery was aesthetic; he hated the South for having too many beasts and marshes, and too few shops and churches, and too little civility. 'Dame Nature,' he wrote, 'is a gentlewoman'; he did not forgive Southerners for keeping her ragged. The South was in 'an essentially frontier condition of society', he complained. He reflected on the city of New York and found the same wrong. 'We are too apt to regard the great towns in which so many newcomers are held as old towns – old settled towns,' he wrote, 'but we have nowhere on the western frontier a population newer to its locality and so little socially rooted and in which it is possible for a man to live so isolatedly from humanising influences and with such constant practice of heart-hardening and taste-smothering habits as that to be found in our great eastern cities.' Civilising the city was something like ending slavery. Frederick Law Olmsted was needed.

People, writers in particular, had been talking about a park for a decade. The poet and editor William Cullen Bryant came back from Europe full of the glory of the parks, and he thought he found a site: some 160 acres on the East River known as Jones's Wood, a ramble with glinting streams and old timber, with oak, tulip trees, liquidambar, hickory, cedar and birch. There were 'mansions', less grand than they sounded. But the city could think of its shoreline only for work and money, and the land was buildable; the city never bought it. Some supporters, like Andrew Jackson Downing, the landscape architect of the Hudson Valley, doubted if the woods were large enough for their vast purpose. Downing wanted at least 500 acres set aside before the city's growth pressed out all open space from its grid, and ruined its democratic meaning. A park, to Downing, would cut down the ever flashier plutocrats and grandees of the city, and the walls between them and the ordinary others: 'you would soften and humanise the rude, educate and enlighten the ignorant, and give continual enjoyment to the educated. Nothing tends to beat down these artificial barriers ... so much as a community of rational enjoyments.'

High minds were scarce in a city where politics was a grubbing business, all about contacts and bribes and treasury bill values, and everything run by party. The squires of the state legislature ruled in 1857 that New York was too venal to be allowed to govern itself. Olmsted could run Central Park because he was a Republican, like the squires, but not a threat to the city Democrats of Tammany Hall.

Next year, he put Greensward, the great design he made with the architect Calvert Vaux, into the competition to plan the park; all the Republicans voted for it. The first three prizes went to men the Commissioners already employed. But once you had power within this system, it was difficult for outsiders to question you; Olmsted could make the park like a scrapbook. There were parkways, separate roads for walkers, riders, carriages and wagons, because he remembered the Boulevard de l'Impératrice in Paris. But he allowed a continuous promenade because he knew that, in New York, pedestrians wanted 'ample opportunity to look at the equipages and their inmates'. He learned the principles of mass planting, a little late, from jungle visits, and re-imagined the pastoral he had seen in England. The sheep on the Sheep Meadow, dumb Southdown beasts, tended by a shepherd in quaint plaids with a defiantly picturesque crook, were an echo of the gracenote animals in English deer parks. In Central Park, Olmsted built his mind.

The same system that indulged him came close to killing him. Tammany saw the park as yet more outdoor relief for its ever-swelling list of clients; Boss Tweed, the fraudster and manipulator who gouged the city in the name of running it, ran an especially efficient welfare system for his friends. Olmsted did not have much time for the Park Commissioners, even the Republicans, consisting, as they did, 'of eleven New York lawyers and merchants ... unmanageable, undignified and liable to permit any absurdity'. And there was Andrew Haswell Green, a straight-arrow lawyer put in to bridle any expensive visions, who had often been to Sunday lunch with Olmsted's family but who quickly turned enemy. In 1859, he became treasurer of the park; and sanctimonious and parsimonious. 'Not a cent is got from under his paw that is not wet with his blood and sweat,' Olmsted complained. 'It was slow murder.'

The year the park was started, the city was in fiscal spasm. The Tammany crews on the park site, bottle-passing, shade-loving creatures, were mostly fired because there was no way to pay them. Olmsted could begin again. On the day set for hiring, twenty men were at his house before breakfast, applications in hand; four forced their way inside to the terror of his servant. There were 5,000 waiting in the park itself. There was a banner: 'Bread or Blood!' An alderman on a cart proposed that all men had a right to live, which meant they had a right to wages from the city, which meant Olmsted must give them work; Tammany's mob was easily roused to its rights. The alderman said that if Olmsted were backward in yielding work – 'and here,' Olmsted remembered, 'he held up a rope and pointed to a tree, and the crowd cheered.'

As for the Commissioners, Olmsted faced them down. They wanted a park full of stone testimonials to generals and aldermen; he promised that he would build a monument to commemorate 'some future historical event'. They wanted pavilions, an opera house, and he crammed all the invading elements – the arboretum, the formal gardens, the site for the Metropolitan Museum – into a kind of 'dress ground' along Fifth Avenue. The Commissioners, the banker August Belmont in particular, liked the notion of a wire suspension bridge over the lake, a steel climax to the park; Olmsted insisted he was building Nature. Where he was told to make a cricket ground, he made open meadow because, he said, ball-players were undemocratic; they could think of only one use for open space. Despite the Commissioners, he sank the obligatory roads through the park into cuts and tunnels. It was a model for humanising a city, picked up briefly in the American garden suburbs of the 1950s, but its cleverness was missed. The landscape, after all, did not look deliberate. 'Well,' as Horace Greeley said irritatingly in 1859, 'they have let it alone a great deal more than I thought they would.'

They had shifted ten million cartloads of earth to the clang of heavy metal wheels, and cut valleys with gunpowder. At times, the site was peppered with 'lakes without water, mounds of compost, piles of blasted stone,' as George Templeton Strong noted, and there were blasts like 'a desultory "affair" between advanced posts of two great armies'. The drains looked like some great industrial plant, settling purposefully into the soil; it took ninety-five miles of pipe to discipline the streams and open the great sheets of ornamental water where Olmsted wanted them. The trees were exotic, some brought from Scottish nurseries even though they might not take to the Manhattan weather; Olmsted was one of the first in north America to plant the gingko tree. And all this artifice vanished, like good stage machinery should. Within three years Oliver Wendell Holmes found 'an expanse of wild country, well crumpled so as to form ridges which will give views and hollows that will hold water.'

It was Olmsted's love, better than going home to the fragile, shallow life in his marriage. His partner Vaux used to tease him about the 'porcupine arrangement of Foremen's reports, ten to each pocket and one in your mouth so that you never had a word to ᵇy to a friend.'

With his army of park-keepers, his fastidiousness, Olmsted was turning into 'Frederick the Great, prince of the park police'. He believed the park was 'a democratic development of the highest significance ... on the success of which, in my opinion, much of the progress of art and esthetic culture in this country is dependent.' He also saw that the park would, in time, play the part of Memory. 'The time will come when New York will be built up, when all the grading and filling will be done, and when the picturesquely varied rock formations of the Island will have been converted into foundations for rows of monotonous straight streets, and piles of erect, angular buildings. There will be no suggestion left of its present, varied surface, with the single exception of the few acres contained in the Park.'

He was defending art, memory, democracy, a fearful load; he could hardly hold up his head for tiredness. The Commissioners tampered with his budget; they put his quondam ally Andrew Green to control the money and the paper. Green made Olmsted present himself, with an explanation, before paying out expenses of twelve and a half cents. The Commissioners saw Olmsted's exhaustion and sent him for six weeks on a European circuit, to look at parks. They thought they were giving him a respite, but he worked determinedly, on a racing schedule, seeing everything through a curtain of rain and mud. He came back to New York almost as tired as he had left. And then his luck came back, the evil luck. He was thrown from a carriage and splintered his leg so badly that he almost died. Within a week, his baby son John Theodore was dead of cholera. The Commissioners did not stop complaining; they took away clerks and then told him to control things better. He was carried on a litter through the park, grieving and cold with pain, holding the landscape together with his will.

He tried to quit in 1861. The Commissioners took six months to refuse his resignation, but removed the burden of managing the park's finances and left him the power 'to finish, plant and maintain' what he had begun. By then, America was at war with itself and Olmsted was chief staff officer of the US Sanitary Commission. He never again ran the park, although he did save it on occasions. Without Olmsted, Boss Tweed made work for his clients, shearing great trees into poles, smoothing anything remotely rugged, cutting back underbrush and digging suburban beds in what was meant to look like wilderness; a cartoon in *Harpers Weekly* shows axemen at the trees, kids disassembling benches, paper and cans strewn everywhere, a true Tammany ruin. When Tweed was sent to jail for all he did to New York City, Olmsted patiently restored the wildness of the park. He went on to make Prospect Park in Brooklyn, and Morningside Park on a sliver of Harlem too steep to build, and Riverside Drive above the rail tracks on the west shore of Manhattan. He always wanted kind, inviting views; he hated monuments; Grant's Tomb was put on the drive over his cross objections.

He saw his park diluted over time. It accepted presents – put up a big stone lady labelled 'Commerce', a bust of Schiller, a horrid bronze of 'Eagles Devouring their Prey'; it kept private a gentleman's present of 'the skeleton of a Negro'. Mary Duffus Hardy found 'great men of all nations . . . immortalised or libelled in stone'. The Commissioners put in a zoo. They thought of brick dinosaurs among the plantings, a World's Fair, a trotting speedway. But Olmsted's vision had the power to make other people see it, thousands of other people. The plan for a World's Fair was beaten back with demonstrations, and the law changed to ban exhibitions in the park. Demonstrations stopped the trotting speedway, even though a Belmont wanted it. The park was lively as a friend. 'I know that, on a bright winter's day, when the whole population seems to be driving out in sleighs to the great skating carnivals at the Central Park,' wrote Henry Dicey, sent to report the Civil War for the London *Spectator*, 'I have seldom seen a brighter or gayer looking city than New York.'

Olmsted did not stay with the city he helped to breathe. In 1887 he told Vaux he had grown tired of the Park Commission and 'its infernal underground politics.' He wrote: 'I left New York only because I was sick of it.'

The park stoppered Manhattan like a bottle. Nobody had wanted to build where Olmsted planted, but all around was a different story. Neighbours put up $1,675,590 of the $5,169,369 the city paid for the land, because they expected their own property to soar in value. It did. Most people could not dream of living near the park, and without rapid transport they could not live north of the park, not after a ten-hour working day. They could come up to breathe in Olmsted's order and then go back to streets that were awkward, cluttered, risky. Dung hung in dust from the horse teams in the avenues. Stagecoaches jarred on the split plank streets; there were vermin on the street railways and strap-hangers clung to the outside platforms of the street-cars, by 'eyelashes ... and toenails', as Mark Twain wrote. Drivers cut and whipped their horses and, in traffic jams, each other; men ran and horses screamed. And between the smart ladies passed the city pigs. 'Ugly brutes,' Dickens wrote, 'having, for the most part, scanty brown backs, like the lids of old horsehair trunks: spotted with unwholesome black blotches. They have long, gaunt legs, too, and such peaked snouts, that if one of them could be persuaded to sit for his profile, nobody would recognise it for a pig's likeness.'

New Yorkers dreamed of a new, improved street, like streets should once have been. A Broadway wine merchant called Alfred Speer devised a steam-powered promenade, an endless moving loop of speeded pavement raised above Broadway, with smoking rooms and withdrawing rooms for days that were rainy or windy, where passengers could travel at speed while they seemed only to stroll and chatter. The Arcade Railway suggested a 'scientific street' to run under Broadway; there would be sidewalks and stores underground, to the horror of established merchants, and all would be on foundations 'adamantine and everlasting', with 'indestructible' cars that were 'impossible to derail'. It would be nothing like the chaos of the streets. Of course, it would rival London's underground, but it would be sweet and airy, not the scalding, miasmic air of the tube, where young women, the papers gleefully reported, died suddenly from 'sulphorous and carburetted gases'. Even the phrase 'underground railway' suggested the covert ways that slaves ran north to freedom; newspapers toyed with the subway as freedom from the slavery of the streets.

But permission for such things would rest with Boss Tweed, the city's percentage man, who liked nothing new that he could not gouge. Having once been Deputy Street Commissioner and Commissioner of Public Works, he was already protecting the omnibus and street railroads. He had allies with property who hated the notion of digging and building that might spoil the value of what they owned. He could flatten dreams. To run around him required a special kind of rational passion, a man like Alfred Beach who was as habitual as the machines he sponsored; a patent broker, ally of Bell and Edison, inventor of the typewriter, publisher of *Scientific American*. Beach first thought of a subway which would be like Broadway, only the horse-drawn cars would run methodically, not in a wild race. And then Beach dreamed of a purer place, a countryside kind of city, where a train would run 'like a boat before the wind'.

He moved cunningly. He asked for a charter to build pneumatic tubes to the main post office at Liberty Street and, ingenuously, suggested one tube might be better yet than two small ones. He ran his gangs from the basement of Devlin's clothing store on Warren and Broadway, fifty-eight nights of tunnelling, the dirt tugged away down narrow streets on carts with muffled wheels. When the tunnel was made it was lit with brilliant zircon lamps and painted white; a fan with the power of a hundred fans was to draw or throw the single car along a tunnel of 312 feet. Air vents ran up into City Hall Park; each test run snatched the tall silk hats from the heads of gentlemen. Below, Beach put frescoes and damask, a fountain with goldfish, a grand piano in the ladies' section of the waiting room. The street became a salon.

On 20 February, 1870, Beach opened to the public: the *New York Herald* reported A FASHIONABLE RECEPTION HELD IN THE BOWELS OF THE EARTH. The next year, some 400,000 people came to ride the tunnel, at twenty-five cents a time (proceeds to charity). They were inspired by a street that worked with the wind, and resented the monotonous vetoes that met the scheme in the State Assembly. Boss Tweed felt obliged to have a vision of his own – a railway in the sky, racked up on forty-foot masonry arches, with John Jacob Astor, the city's landlord, and a Tiffany and the banker August Belmont on the board. Viaduct could break through any city block, commandeer what land it needed. But the vision was not as radical as it seemed. It was only, as a sober academic once called it, 'one of the biggest swindles of all time'.

For the city could no longer administer improvement; that was just not what its administration did. Betterment depended on reforming men like Beach, with ideal schemes but without official standing, who would resist the city machine; their natural enemies were men like Tweed, the gougers and schemers. And Tweed, in his way, was a genius. The Viaduct railway started with the city required to buy five million dollars worth of stock, the kind that operators watered down until it was almost worthless, ramped on rumours until they could get out at a monstrous profit, and then abandoned. Much of that five million would have stuck to Tweed's fingers; he was scheming sixty million dollars more. On the ground, his chums could buy and sell land depending on where the lines were to run and what damages would be paid for land compulsorily purchased and where the rail lines would make land especially valuable; it was their usual scam with public works but extended this time to all of Manhattan. Some landowners would certainly pay to be saved from Viaduct's plans. And that was before the Ring took their cut from the budget for building Viaduct – a budget so inflated there was serious question who would ever afford to ride the line. Out of the county courthouse budget of twelve million dollars, Tweed and his Ring skimmed a formidable nine million.

Beach's subway, Tweed's Viaduct bobbed through the State Assembly like corks on water. Viaduct fell because Tweed, unexpectedly, was exposed, tried and sentenced to life for fraud and grand larceny. Beach's scheme failed because, in the great railway panics of 1873, it was unfinanceable. But the very risk and scandals in railroad shares produced a building boom, because money had to go somewhere safer; the sheer force of dollars made the city grow. The need was immediate and the means were failing. In the autumn of 1872, the horses of New York went slack-necked with coughing; distemper rampaged through the stables, killing at least 2,000 horses, bringing out the ASPCA inspectors to turn back sick teams. The city stopped. Fashionable ladies lost their carriages, shops closed, fire engines could not move, workers walked. The need for rapid transit was obvious; 'absolute necessity,' the *New York Times* said. At 602 Sixth Avenue, an association met on Mondays to discuss ideas. The *Railroad Gazette* wrote: 'The number of people who think they know how to build a rapid transit railroad is, we believe, quite as large as those who are sure they could edit a newspaper. . . .' In a single session of the Assembly, twenty-seven different schemes were killed.

Only one machine kept moving: the crammed coaches of the elevated, the West Side and Yonkers Patent Railway, running now from the Battery to 30th Street. When it opened in the 1860s, it had seemed such a ridiculous thing – a trolley running over narrow iron columns, the cable-drawn track powered by steam engines under the street, its inventor, Charles T. Harvey looking vulnerable in a high hat. Tweed tried mobs and lawsuits to shut it down, a gold scam ruined its backers, but Harvey's line had permission to run to the northern tip of Manhattan at Spuyten Duyvil. The New York Elevated Railway Company was formed to run the road. By the summer of 1875, dummy locomotives were working the track to Central Park, disguised as cabins so as not to scare the horses. In 1876, Cyrus Field of Atlantic Cable bought the fragile survivor, doubled the fare to ten cents and pushed the lines north to 61st Street. The tracks helped define a whole new area of the city – the Upper West Side, where working people could live and move quickly enough to their offices.

The relief was minimal. New York was filling with new people, and two out of five of them found lodgings close to the Battery. You could tell by the peddlers jostling on the streets that people did not move far afield for food, chances, clothes. Each New Yorker took, on average, only 135 trips a year on the elevated railroads, the streetcars, the omnibuses and stagecoaches put together, which includes all those who commuted daily to Brooklyn or Hoboken by ferry, or took Commodore Vanderbilt's railroad to the north; and a double count every time someone changed from an avenue line to a crosstown coach. Too many people were fixed in a tiny space.

Rapid transit could help them escape. The issue had long been one of machines – how to build a better street. Now it became a moral cause, involving a profound change of mind. Cities were too important to be cut out of the ideal American life. 'The newspapers and poets are all busy painting the delights of the agricultural life,' wrote E.L. Godkin in *The Nation*, 'but the farmer, though he reads their articles and poems, quits the farm as soon as he can find any other way of making a livelihood; and if he does not, his son does.' America could not forever expand to some new frontier in the West, moving away from trouble; the cities had to be sorted out. All Godkin's complaints, which were many, implied that the city could be reformed. He worried that young men idolised stock-gamblers, that the wonder of the city was a dry goods store, that city bosses were professional gamblers, liquor dealers, keepers of 'dives' and, in one case, a convicted murderer; but he did not accept that this was all you could say about New York. Even charities that had once advocated sending the poor to the cleaner, more moral countryside now stayed to fight. Instead of blaming slums on feckless, workless, useless human beings, now crime, immorality and disease were often blamed on the slums. When cholera slipped into the city in the late 1860s, citizens campaigned for a Board of Health, and a tenement house act to change the lightless, fire-trap housing. Improvement was the issue.

This change of mind had unexpected consequences. It built the elevated railroads, defined the mid-town office belt, shaped the ziggurats of Park Avenue, made possible New York's Champs Elysées on the Grand Concourse in the Bronx, opened Queens and eventually created a Chinatown along the number 7 subway line; for it led to the subway system and the campaign for zoning laws and the shaping of the New York we know.

Dr Rufus Henry Gilbert was a Civil War hero, the man who performed the first surgical operation under fire at the battle of Big Bethel, the Director General of all US Army Hospitals. At the end of the war, he threw over medicine and took, with equal passion, to the issue of rapid transit. Such a change would seem bizarre now, some boyish taste for trains. But in its time, it was almost obvious.

While Gilbert was training to be a doctor, he did the rounds of tenements. He saw the way the poor lived and learned how to save them from cholera and typhoid, and he came to think of poverty as the worst disease. Its cause was the terrible congestion of the city; since 'congestion' was still mostly a medical term, meaning too much water in the lungs or heart, it took a doctor to play with its new, more general meaning. He also feared for the souls of the poor, and his qualms were shared. In the 1840s, the abolitionist Lydia Maria Child found loneliness in New York – enough people to hinder her, too many to know; she could not help all those in need, and she felt she was 'turning to stone by inches'. She feared for her soul, and she syndicated her fears nationally. In the late 1860s, the missionary J. C. Smith told his Scottish audience that the finer nature of tenement dwellers was lost because 'their eyes are downward, searching for coal in the refuse barrels of the street. . . .' On hot nights, all the sexes and ages mingled out on the sidewalk, catching the stray midnight breeze; which led 'to the excitement of the worst passions'. And crowding did not just irritate the nerves and temper. 'To be alone – that indispensable privilege to the Christian – is not to be thought of'. Congestion kept God out.

The solution was very Victorian: an inspirational machine. Gilbert won a charter in 1872 for an elevated railroad on Second and Sixth Avenues, and he drew double tubes which would soar above the street on Corinthian pillars and arches of filigree iron, like the bones of a fine church window. The cars would run by air, he thought, but when the panics of 1873 stymied him, other operators noticed the charter was not specific; a little money in the right pockets – $650,000 for the

State Assembly, to be exact – and Gilbert's New York Elevated could be converted into a rackety, steam-drawn thing. Instead of grace and air, the stations of the new elevated were gabled and finialed like some Swiss villa, and hunkered fatly over street junctions. The coaches were like boudoirs and the conductors, in 'smart-fitting uniforms', chosen for their looks, but there the glory ended. The Third and Ninth Avenue lines were built with more elegance, but they looped through Battery Park and spoiled its openness. Dr Gilbert found himself bamboozled out of his own company one day after the lines opened; he went away to despair. He was found unconscious a few years later, worldly goods strewn around him in a muddle of a room, sick with a bowel inflammation which had been made lethal with neglect; he had not eaten for six days. He died of exhaustion, another ruined improver.

His dreams of Gothick elegance were never honoured. The new 'el's were not quiet, subtle things; they were thieves of sun and air. Curious, cranking insect machines juddered along girders to lay the track. Shopkeepers found themselves troglodytes, broad avenues turned into tunnels; telegraph and telephone wires already made it seem 'you were looking through the mesh of a net', and now the remaining light was latticed with girders and columns. High trestles swept in an arc over 110th Street, bearing a storm of fire and shearing metal, 'an ever-active volcano over the heads of inoffensive citizens,' as an Australian visitor wrote in 1888. Sparks caught the awnings of shops. Oil was pitched through open windows. Whores took third floor windows to smile at the quickly passing trade, respectable matrons tried to look proper in their scanties and 'girls blushed and darted into closets' as the trains blustered by. *The Police Gazette* in 1882 showed 'a party of New York girls enjoying a little after-dinner pistol practice at the trains that rush by their windows of their hotel'; on the table is champagne.

The population of New York grew too fast for the 'el's to disperse; the new tracks simply spread congestion. New York in the 1890s was more crowded than Bombay. The most densely populated streets in Europe, the Josefstadt in Prague, had 485 people to the acre; parts of the Lower east Side had 986. The 'el's took population to the south Bronx; by 1905, the areas round the tracks had more than 600 people to the acre. They opened the Brownsville section of Brooklyn. In Manhattan itself, the balconies of Hester Street seemed to burst with bedding on a fine day. You shopped at the 'Pig Market' in the heart of what was variously known as the city's typhus ward or its suicide ward. Mortality was the worst in America outside the yellow fever belt. Since nobody could afford to live too far from work, rent was a kind of blackmail. Wives and children had to earn money, and still a roof cost half a family's income. Strangers came to board, despite fears about their morals. In unlicensed lodging houses, where a bed cost five cents a night, men and women crammed a dozen into a room barely thirteen feet by thirteen. Kerosene lamps spluttered all night for late-comers. The stove smoked by a jumble of drying boots. Possessions hung in bags on the wall. Heads poked out from the covers at disconcerting places.

In blind and airless rooms in the same tenement houses, there were fire-trap stores of rags. Wood construction stopped not because of the threat to life but because the insurance companies finally did their sums. Local butchers could still slaughter in their back yards, letting the offal trail on the stones. After heavy rains the sewers flooded on to swanky Broadway; but new sewers were reserved for newly built areas. The courts ruled that the usual limits to crowding did not apply in Manhattan; no property had automatic rights to the air and light it had enjoyed twenty years ago, because that could stem the city's growth.

The city was a crush of strangers – from southern Europe, from 'inferior' stock, rough, illiterate or too obviously Jewish. The settled citizens were not allowed aristocratic attitudes to the newcomers. On democratic principle, the masses had to be improved and made American. The masses, if child-like, needed the parental hand of the good middle class. And if nothing was done, then property and persons were at risk. The reformer Jacob Riis was horrified by the slums, and he blamed them for crime, as Dr Gilbert had once blamed them for poverty. Riis said eighty per cent of crime was committed by people who 'have either lost connection with home life, or never had any, or whose homes had ceased to be sufficiently separate, decent and desirable to afford what one regarded as the ordinary wholesome influence of home and family.' If duty did not mobilise the better class of person, as they called themselves, then fear would.

Out they came, merciless talkers, hunter-gatherers of reams of information, annoying enough to be placated by the city powers. They were never political; power was vulgar. Instead, they were right. They wanted to make sense of the city, beautify it and marbelise it,

standardise the height and scale of its buildings and hang it about
with monuments and watergates. They wanted public works without
involving the public city, because Tammany was sure to steal, and
'the opposition of Tammany to public art is simply a detail of the
opposition of Tammany to civilisation in general,' as *The New York
Times* observed. In the meantime, they reported potholes and held
teas for teachers and planned arcades and underpasses. They were
amateurs: 'the subject of municipal reform has been for some years
something of a hobby with me,' William G. Hornblower harrumphed.
They did what they did only because they could supply 'that element
of taste and reflection which the city lacks,' according to a founder of
the Municipal Art Society. And, since nobody makes a city except in
their own image, they meant to have monuments of their own. If the
Manhattan grid spoke of democracy, they would cut it up with avenues
on the diagonal, in the name of good taste.

The masses alarmed them, but the plutocrats were their natural
enemy. Cartoons showed Jay Gould, the stock wizard who chiselled
and cheated his way to control of all the city's elevated railroads, as
Satan's successor. Gould himself was a caricature of a robber baron,
the man held responsible each time the 'el's resisted paying up for
burning or wrecking property, the man who dared demand yet more
of the Battery to build a terminal for a third express track on the Sixth
Avenue line. The *New York Times* said he had 'an insatiable appetite
for grabbing everything in sight'. He even applied to build lines which
would criss-cross Manhattan, on routes reserved for the streetcar and
the omnibus; and here, at last, he overreached himself. He wanted to
pay taxes at only one third of the rate the city suggested. He did not
get his lines. And now the long debates about rapid transit had only
one serious possibility: the subway.

New York State set up a Rapid Transit Commission in 1891 for just
that purpose but, after two years, nobody bid to build the line. This
was curious, since, only a few years before, there had been two
subway companies wrestling their way through the judicial system
and the State Assembly, grunting out promises and counter-promises.
From the New York District Railway, the Commission plucked the
engineer William Barclay Parsons – a reticent, proud-faced man whom
some thought too young and untested for the job. He was set to
reform a system of streetcars and elevated tracks that already carried
more passengers than all the steam railways of north and south

America put together. His friends told him he was wasting his life on an unworkable dream, but, since nobody would pay to build a subway yet, he set out to master the subject. He learned the awesome deoxygenating power of a steam locomotive – eating the air 87,000 human beings could breathe; he observed the sulphur in steam, and the effects of humidity; he decided on an electric train. He had already published the definitive work on the maintenance of the permanent way. Now, he set out to learn the underground of Manhattan, the exact dimension of each little sewer leaching off into the rivers, the run of the drains and steam mains and the 'electric tubes'. He was entirely ready for his task; in a referendum New Yorkers voted three to one that he should get on with it; but the mayor remembered that the city's constitution limited how much New York could borrow. Parsons sailed away to a less arduous task: cutting a railroad through the 'closed province' of Hunan in China, where warlords were said to roam and foreigners had not yet explored. He was not expected to come back alive.

The reformers were beginning to accept that, however much they wanted their marble watergate, the matters of transport and housing had to come first. The changed scale of New York helped: in 1898, Manhattan and the Bronx married Brooklyn, Queens and Staten Island to make a single city. The reformers saw possibility on almost every acre. Staten Island was rural and a pleasure resort, with beaches and breweries, but the ferry journeys took too long for working men. Brooklyn could be opened beyond the merchant castles on the Heights and the slums of Brownsville, if only there was transport. And Queens, a patchwork of villages with broad streets and paling fences and ladies promenading under the trees, and parts which were wet and malarial, could be developed, once it was no longer a small fortune away from work in Manhattan. When the Tenement Commission heard evidence on this in 1903 – tenement reformers were subway reformers, of course – they found most workers did not even take a nickel ride on the horse-drawn streetcars; it was too much, and too slow. Commuting from Flushing cost five dollars thirty a month, and even twenty cents a day was too much.

A Mrs Miller came down from her 47th Street tenement to tell the Commission a thing or two. She said she'd much prefer living in Brooklyn, but could not 'because my husband works away downtown and I think he hadn't ought to live more than half an hour or three quarters at the most from his work. Just the same with any workmen.'

Before she married, she had been a working girl, and she'd seen how the bridges and trolleys let down the girls who came from Brooklyn, not to mention the ice and fog of the East River. 'If trains and boats don't run on time,' she said, 'you can't give that excuse too often. They can get men nearer home to work for them.'

The need was obvious and the means were found. The Tammany mayors of the 1890s were careful men, determined to do nothing new or clever which would revive the memory of Boss Tweed; but Mayor Abram Hewitt, who had no such fears, changed the city's constitution to enable it to borrow more, and carefully revalued the city's property so it had proper security. In effect, the city thought it was worth pledging its fabric to have a subway. The deal was that the city would pay for the tracks and own them, while the contractor owned the rolling stock and equipment, collected the fares and serviced the railroad's debt. A Tammany man put in the winning bid to build the subway and, since he bid too low, he had to be salvaged by August Belmont – son of the Rothschilds' man in America who had himself been a Tammany ally. Tammany, a plutocrat and reforming zeal were all aligned.

The city powers went on parade one brilliant March morning in 1900, to celebrate a 'new epoch in the development of their city', as the *New York Tribune* put it. Boys filled the trees, flag bombs each carried a gross of silken Stars and Stripes, the band was led by John Philip Sousa himself; fog bells and church bells and steam whistles and firecrackers and dynamite all sounded out. Everything became symbolic. Mayor Van Wyck turned the earth with a silver Tiffany shovel, whose handle was oak from the flagship of a fleet of 1812 and gum from a tree that Alexander Hamilton planted. August Belmont was saluted for rescuing the subway. The mayor declared New York an imperial city, more proud than Rome; its foundations were too solid to be shaken by the 'unjust attacks of the misinformed or misguided stranger'. The president of the Rapid Transit Commission boasted that the deal was good, not like the Ramopo Water Company – a scheme, newly nipped in the bud, which would have required the city to pay $200 million for water over sixty years to a company which didn't actually own anything. The mayor was so moved that he put the first shovelful of earth in his silk hat, and took it to his office. An onlooker was so moved that he tried to steal the hat.

Next day, the workers cut into Bleecker Street to lower a sewer pipe and there was a different kind of ceremony. Men rioted after the lifted cobblestones, because rumour said that a man with a stone would get a job – twenty cents an hour, ten hours a day, working with newcomers who had numbers and not names. City Hall soon looked like a mining camp, a glorious sight if you had just scuffed down the gangplank to some Bowery lodging house and were praying for work. 42nd Street, already chewed up to lay cable and trolley tracks, was cut in a chasm; houses emptied all around and the street began to change. Nearby, the *New York Times* established itself on Longacre Square, a cabbies' hang-out on the fringes of 'Thieves' Lair' and at the end of 'Soubrettes' Row', which was quickly renamed Times Square; the paper planned to speed the news by subway across New York. The avenues became trenches full of track and covered over with steel, with sunlight filtering down to the platforms. Kiosks appeared over station entrances, like pavilions from a country estate. City Hall Station was made with arches and vaults, a round and coloured crypt. The chaos of underground – pine-log pipes, inexplicable pipes, water pipes running through sewer pipes, old filled ponds and a subterranean Harlem lake; bones of a mastodon, the burned spars of a seventeenth-century merchantman, bits of the past – was tidied into order. The newspapers bragged about 'Harlem in Fifteen Minutes' and the police commissioner said he could 'have an armed force in Harlem in fifteen minutes'; 'This subway,' he said, 'is going to absolutely preclude the possibility of riots in New York City.' Abbey's Effervescent Salt advertised with cut-away drawings of the new marvel; Abbey's was 'The Rapid Transit To Health'.

August Belmont Junior built himself a private car for the subway, a glorious machine called the Mineola, which was to run on special tracks from the basement of Belmont's hotel on 42nd Street to the racetrack that bore his name in Queens. He had hot and cold water, leather chairs in the office, an oven, refrigerator, pantry, linen cupboard and an 'arched Empire ceiling'; he had, in effect, an ordinary plutocrat's railway carriage, just like the train he took each spring to South Carolina for the hunting. But the subway was not an ordinary railroad. It ran from City Hall to Grand Central Station, then cut across the island to the newly named Times Square and went north under Broadway as far as 145th Street in Washington Heights. The day it opened, it was mobbed; 'Indescribable scenes of crowding and confusion,' said the *Times*. It ran at capacity from the start. And just as the railroad had been the spine of development out in the country, so, in the city, the subway planned new districts just by opening; having created Times Square, it defined the mid-town business district, a rival at last to downtown. For the first time since the laying down of the stones that marked the Manhattan grid, the city as a corporation had decided on its shape; but unwittingly.

By 1904 the Municipal Art Society's committee on the city plan was no longer talking about 'the City Beautiful', that pompous fantasy of white stone and wide plazas that stole the mind of the American middle class at the World's Columbia Exposition in Chicago in 1893; the 'City Beautiful' was just embellishing a mess and helping the price of property. The serious middle classes were talking transit, on the grounds that without knowing where the tracks would run, nobody could tell where people would live; and planners could never put a park, a school, a public building in place. The enemy was still 'congestion', but the forces ranged against it were now powerful. At the Committee on Congestion of Population, Wall Street bankers sat beside workers in the settlement houses that tried to Americanise the new immigrants, and churchmen and trade unionists and William Barclay Parsons himself, who had survived China. Congestion was the 'ugly, demoralising and devitalising condition' that the poor faced and nobody, except the obstinate members of the Children's Aid Society, thought any longer that they could simply be shipped away from it to farmlands or the frontier. What's more, politicians were prepared to imagine that the law might help. Charles Evan Hughes, Governor of New York State, declared in 1908 that 'public regulation' was needed to maintain 'individual opportunity', just as the cops may be the price of freedom.

The better class of person was in politics now, on the Board of Estimate, which ruled any city project which cost capital, and on the state's Public Services Commission; they worked for grand ideas, for their certainties. They created zoning laws from the same notions that built the subway. Skyscrapers were beginning to rear up, vast and alarming; the city's light was being blocked. Zoning, to conserve sunlight, imposed the stepped-back ziggurat shapes of period apartment buildings. It defended the chic of Fifth Avenue against the garment district that threatened to encroach from the south. It tried to put family houses out along the subway lines instead of simply extending the tenement territory. The commercial was separated from the residential and it was assumed the industrial would fill the rest. There was even talk of a permanent planning commission for the city.

But the better class of person never did take permanent control.

The Interborough Rapid Transit and the Brooklyn Rapid Transit companies were contracted in 1913 to take new subway lines up the east side of Manhattan, creating the First Avenue tenement fringe to the Fifth Avenue mansions; and on, deep into Brooklyn, and through the fields of Queens and the Bronx. But they got pre-war prices for work done in the inflationary post-war years. The deals looked sweet enough at first for politicians to suspect the usual corruption, and turned out catastrophically. By 1918, the BRT was bust, and reborn in 1923 as the Brooklyn Manhattan Transit Company – the BMT of subway signs. Traffic on the subway grew, but at a flat five cent fare, reasonable in the stable America of 1913, but too low even in the 1920s. By 1937, it was clear the IRT would never catch up with the interest it owed the city, let alone redeem its bonds when they fell due. Yet the subway fare was sacred, a principle of city life. Politicians loved to bash the financiers who were losing money on the subways. They praised municipal ownership, which the city could not afford. And the ferocity of this talk owed much to one man: to Citizen Kane himself, the press mogul William Randolph Hearst.

Hearst was not yet the grotesque of San Simeon. He was a rich man in New York who wanted to be maybe mayor, or governor of the state, or president of the country, or something, anything more than the ink baron he was; his ambition grew with failure. In 1917 he very nearly managed to be the Tammany candidate for mayor, but even Tammany noticed that rival papers tended to label him 'spokesman of the Kaiser' while American boys were in Flanders. He left the race and threw his support to John F. Hylan, known as 'Red Mike' for his hair colour, a practical-minded one-time engineer on the 'el's who had been fired for taking a curve too quickly. Hylan advanced the Tammany way, to be an honest, if rather slow-witted judge, and then to be mayor of New York. He repaid a few favours – making the father of Hearst's mistress, the actress Marion Davies, into a city magistrate, for example. And then he set about repaying favours on a far grander scale.

Hylan wouldn't have anything to do with planning; he said he had no use for 'art artists'. He could easily make the whole process of zoning seem somehow middle-class and aesthetical which, indeed, it was; conveniently, anyone who wanted could buy land along the subway tracks, with nothing reserved for public spaces or public buildings. And Hylan had Tammany's clout, with the rather special kind of independence he owed to Hearst's money and influence. He ran against the subway barons and, to make his point, he committed the city to building and paying for a subway of its own – the IND or Independent system, with cars deliberately built too long to take the curves of the other companies' tunnels without sending up sparks. The IND took fifteen years to finish, went grotesquely over budget, was gouged by Tammany; the Depression put the city into such fiscal pain that the last tracks were not laid until America was marching into the Second World War. And if you ride it today, read the line carefully. There is an express stop at 42nd Street, one seventeen blocks north at the sparsely built Columbus Circle, and then the train runs without a stop to 125th Street; you may wonder why. It was another of Hylan's favours to Hearst, who had been buying land at Columbus Circle.

Thanks to Hearst, the brief enlightenment was over. The better classes had opened up the city, started to empty out the tenements and spread population out into the fields of the boroughs; but their subway suffered precisely because it was so essential and because it was so cheap and so well used. The same Civic Society which had helped engineer the system's pre-war expansion, now asked in 1927 that the subways be abandoned – 'in the name of New York's two million children', whose education could not be financed if subway spending did not stop. The five-cent fare, sacred to anyone running for election, and the assumption that the financiers were rolling in the profits from the misery in the tunnels made it impossible to make sense of subway finances. In 1940, the system went bust.

And the health of the city, the perfected street where trains would be borne by the wind, the underground railway that would end the slavery of the streets, were all forgotten. In Hart Crane's epic *The Bridge*, 'the subway yawns the quickest promise home'; but it is a moving Hades, where even the platform 'hurries along to a dead stop.' Machines, as Crane well knew, had already lost their 'sensational glamour'. The subway is a dark nightmare of gongs, guards, blank windows. It is the Daemon taking the 'wop washerwoman' home, the place of the dead where a spectral Edgar Allen Poe appears.

> . . . In the car
> the overtone of motion
> underground, the monotone
> of motion is the sound
> of other faces, also underground. . . .

There's no comfort as 'The train rounds, bending to a scream. . . .'
There are only 'interborough fissures of the mind'.

After work, the young Robert Moses used to walk the six wasteland
miles that were called, euphemistically, Riverside Park; a tall, athletic
figure with startling grey eyes, in among the tar-paper shanties and
the hillocks of raw garbage. He still saw things with an idealist's eyes.
He looked down on railroad smoke, the screams and stench of cattle
going slowly down to the slaughterhouses of lower Manhattan; he
heard the wrenching and shearing of the trucks; he saw the three
bridges which led to the waterfront over the tracks, but only if you
belonged to the right club. He watched as the trains left the 'park' and
cut into avenues, a horseman riding ahead with a red flag, traffic
stymied for half a mile. And once, when he was hanging on the rail
of a ferry across the Hudson, he turned to Frances Perkins, who later
became US Secretary of Labour. He planted a green parkland with
his words, set down basins for sailboats where everyone could go; he
planned even diaper-changing shelters, so mothers with toddlers could
go walking in his garden. 'Couldn't this waterfront be the most beautiful thing in the world?' he said. 'Isn't it a temptation for you?'

Robert Moses was not just Fiorello La Guardia's ally in the salvag-
ing of Depression New York. He became the city's master builder,
the one too clever to be confined by office or rank. He threw tapes of
expressway around Manhattan and across the Bronx and Brooklyn
and Queens, engineered great bridges and, unwillingly, great tunnels;
he made the city into motoropolis, scarred by the needs of drivers.
He carved out the land for the opera houses and the halls of Lincoln
Center, made parks, and stashed the poor away tidily in the red brick
towers of public housing. He started out thinking of humanity and,
as his power grew, he thought more about an orderly city, a homogen-
ised place. We owe him Riverside Park, the woods that now hug the
shore of the Hudson where the rail tracks used to run, and we owe
him a chronic shortage of housing for the people who need to live in
the city, and the planners' dream of making a city of movement,
migration and change into something neat.

Neither La Guardia nor Moses much approved of running a city
on laisser-faire, but while La Guardia was thinking of the cruelty of
the system, Moses was bothered by the inefficiency, by the obstacles

to doing what, he reckoned, was manifestly right. La Guardia created a City Planning Commission, a body to shape and civilise the city; Moses wanted to be commissioner. He wanted such complete control that the respectful La Guardia had great doubts since the planning commissioner, even on paper, had powers second only to the mayor. Instead of Moses, he appointed Rexford Tugwell from Roosevelt's brains trust, who set to imagining a better New York. Tugwell drew green belts and land use maps and planned to curb development in the interests of a more humane scale. But Tugwell did not have Moses' skill at in-fighting, or his knowledge of the system, or his files for blackmailing opponents. He had to depend on a La Guardia who had grown bored with dreaming a new city without the resources to build it. When La Guardia was denied his chance in Washington and realised he was confined to New York, he came to resent a man with powers close to his own. Tugwell, unable to make the city machine listen to a word he said, retreated to be Governor of Puerto Rico. His plans died. The Commission confined itself after 1942 to minimal matters – limiting the height of buildings, and the crowding of homes.

The vacuum was extraordinary: the political process was no longer connected to how the city changed, let alone to planning its mutations. New York's budget, chronically imbalanced, needed new buildings to tax; to make jobs, the city needed construction. Instead of considering and evaluating some new tower, the city had to have strong reasons to refuse it. The city's skyline became a matter of personal power – a commissar like Robert Moses or, later, the properly connected developers, the Trumps or Zeckendorfs, who can bamboozle and negotiate and bluster a building into being.

As it was, Moses had what La Guardia lacked: cashflow. In 1940, the capital budget of New York City was precisely one dollar; the city would be happy to build, but it could not spend. The same year, Moses was overseeing bridges and tunnels which brought in $4.5 million in tolls each year, enough to pay the interest on bonds for the construction that the city itself could never afford. But Moses could not be told to spend. He ran public authorities which were supposed to be proof against the corruption of politics, so he answered to nobody. He could force the sale of any land he needed. His authorities paid no taxes and never had to open their books. In effect, the city's capital lay in the hands of one man, and he could set his own agenda. He did not care about the city's hidden machinery, the schools and libraries and hospitals which had been neglected before La Guardia. He did not much care for the citizens, not the poorer ones, and certainly not the black and Hispanic ones whom he managed to exclude from the swimming pools in their own neighbourhoods; Frances Perkins said Moses admitted the public 'needs to be bathed, it needed to be aired, it needs recreation, but not for personal reasons – just to make it a better public'. He wanted to reshape the city with landfill, to remap it; he wanted to ring it with roads, to cut an expressway for motoropolis across the iron-frame streets of Soho, to wipe away tenements and build bridges.

By 1940, he had smashed tenements so successfully that the city's housing stock had seized up, a condition from which it never quite recovered; only three per cent of the city's apartments were vacant. He disapproved of money for the subway because it made losses. He valued the car so much – even his secretaries had chauffeurs on twenty-four hour call – that it came to dominate his thinking, from the early 1930s until he cut up the Bronx with roads in the 1950s. In a speech, he forgave the Commissioners who drew the Manhattan grid for their failure to anticipate the car.

La Guardia said he would keep that 'son of a bitch' off the newly formed tunnel authority; but, in the end, money made him give Moses control of every water crossing in the city. Moses now dreamed the finest of his steel follies: a bridge to span from the Battery to Brooklyn, which would steal the grand scale of the harbour and make it only a sideshow to motorists passing busily across Robert Moses' monument. Anyone who opposed him was talking 'the same old tripe'. A tunnel would be only 'a tiled vehicular bathroom smelling faintly of carbon monoxide'. Moses stood up against the men who had struggled to plan and salvage the city and he treated them with contempt. George McAneny, advocate of the subway, draughtsman of the zoning laws, spoke out, and Moses dismissed him as 'an extinct volcano', 'an exhumed mummy'. He walked out of meetings he was supposed to persuade. He attacked the men who had sympathised with him, admired him, and they saw suddenly a man with the power to freeze debate like ether. They were afraid of him. And they never quite knew that Roosevelt had his revenge at last, letting it be known that any bridge would be 'a very great hazard to navigation. In case of war, we can't have any bridges around there. They'll drop bombs and so forth.' The city saw only that the Defense Department quashed the project on strategic grounds, and Moses found himself presiding over a 'tiled vehicular bathroom' after all. It did not even look like a defeat.

Nothing now could stop Moses imposing his sensible city on New York. He tidied up reality; expressways were to 'weave together the loose strands and frayed edges of the New York metropolitan arterial tapestry.' Oppose him and you opposed history, so he said; the city had to cope with the car, the expressway, with progress. He ranted against anyone who dared make the city seem less perfectible. When Paul Kern, Civil Service Commissioner, suggested rewards for information on civic corruption, Moses told Kern to send the plan to Stalin's police 'whose American representative you seem to be'. If Moses could find no sin in his critic, he found it in the family – a brother-in-law's property deals, a father's long forgotten financial troubles. He expected to be obeyed.

He also knew how to sweeten deals for the Democrat politicians around him, how to engineer, for example, their profits from neglecting the Brownsville properties into which he decanted those he had moved in tenement clearance. Hot water and heat were not required; assorted insurance and legal scams made money; the only condition was membership of the proper Democrat club. The notion which Moses bequeathed to New York, of the financially autonomous public authority, was well learned by the likes of Nelson Rockefeller when he became governor. Rockefeller did not just borrow against the likely income of an authority; when it came to housing, where defaults were only too likely, he added a general obligation to dig into the general revenue of the state if necessary. These 'moral obligation' bonds allowed New York to spend wildly beyond its income, to leverage taxes almost indefinitely and to create limitless long-term obligations. Where Moses set public priorities by having the only cashflow in town, Rockefeller pursued his priorities by mortgaging all the public cashflow. Reality no longer counted.

When his speeches were collected into a kind of memoir in 1956, Moses boasted of holding state and federal purse-strings on projects like the Cross-Bronx Expressway and being able to countermand silly politicians who thought his plans could be changed. He told Mayor Wagner: 'If you try to move this Expressway, you'll never get another nickel from us.' The Mayor protested that he had made a promise to voters. 'You will just have to explain it was all a mistake,' Moses said. The city came to seem to Moses like an obstacle to the proper future, which was a future on the move in an automobile, not settled in companionable streets. His trick was to make movement seem like progress and to tap the New York addiction to change. 'There are people who like things as they are, ' he said. 'I can't hold out any hope to them.'

If you grew up in the Bronx, as Marshall Berman did, that sounded familiar. But Berman remembers watching the construction of the Cross-Bronx Expressway, which slammed through the city's one true boulevard, the Grand Concourse in the Bronx, and broke up its communities. The very recent dream of 'moderne' apartment blocks, showily elegant, was wrecked for the sake of Moses' modern notion: speed, the need to be part of a generalised world instead of roosting in a single neighbourhood and a single identity. The desirable Bronx became, with speed, the notorious Bronx. 'The Jews of the Bronx were nonplussed,' Berman writes. 'Could a fellow-Jew really want to do this to us?' But Moses had long ago given up being anything as specific, as constricting as a Jew; he had assimilated to a very rarefied kind of power.

He died without doubt, even when pushed out of office, even when named for corruption over the 1964 World's Fair. He kept his limousine, the last perk of office, and he liked to drive along the shore; he fancied he could see the longest bridge in the world between Long Island and Rhode Island. The city now seemed so intractable that he was a Lear up against the storm, except that he was convinced he could remake the storm. 'In the physical sense,' he wrote, 'there are no insoluble urban problems, once we get into the mood to be serious, honest, co-operative and unselfish about them.' He left extraordinary buildings – the white and glassy blocks at Lincoln Center, a cultural village that only he could have made; the careful wildness of Jones Beach; the road system on which the city stumblingly depends to this day. He made himself an empire – with its own palace tucked away on Randall's Island, its own troops and a phenomenal intelligence service that tried to know anything that one day might be used. And yet there was a fallacy in his thinking: faith. 'Even if Robert Moses rebuilt New York from end to end in the fashion he has already followed,' Lewis Mumford wrote, 'it would still be a doomed city.'

Forty-Second Street, the Deuce, became a kind of ruin, a scuttle between hissed promises of sex and drugs, its little shops selling beer and sandwiches, and Vaseline and crack vials and bongs and rubbers and poppers. The hookers with their high shrieks of hair moved west on their heels, leaving only the men, who duck like fighters as they walk because they are among men. The street has buildings low enough to show the sky, and everyone watches the sidewalk. 'Police arrest the dealers by the dozens,' said William H. Daly, head of the Midtown Enforcement Office which tries to make the law stick on the street. 'It doesn't have a major effect. There's been an army of police out there for years and people are still getting stabbed, killed. It's just incredible.'

The ruin once was 42nd Street, the 'naughty, bawdy, gaudy' street, and the block between Seventh and Eighth Avenues was its core. It spilled into Broadway at Times Square, the city's heart, its symbol. 'Broadway is a great place of health,' Stephen Graham wrote in 1928. 'It is a free electric ray treatment. It is a tonic light bath. . . . Almost everyone in the world feels better in health when he leaves the cross-streets and the inferior avenues to bask in the great, open space in front of that New York temple, the Times building. Here voices are clearer, eyes brighter and the whole body more vivid than anywhere else in New York.' When BOAC in the 1950s made posters for its various destinations, most showed idylls and trees and old things, but America is New York and brown derby hats and streamlined cars, and the lights of Times Square, the modern already faintly nostalgic. But all that glory dissipated into anarchy. The city surrendered all the powers to save its heart, and the story of Times Square is the story of the city, limelit.

It was once Longacre Square, a hang-out for cabbies, fragrant and dark like a stable. Streetlights stopped at 42nd Street; to the north lay 'Thieves' Lair', a refuge rather than a workplace for the city's pickpockets, since the gentry never ventured there. There were homes along 42nd Street. The first Oscar Hammerstein had gone bust building 'the greatest amusement temple in the world' at dark 45th Street, too far north of the true Broadway strip. But in 1899, he had money in his pocket again and he built at the corner of 42nd Street and Seventh Avenue, first the Victoria theatre and next the Republic. He had a troupe of one-legged acrobats, naked ladies as 'reproductions of famous statuary'. On the roof he made the Paradise Gardens, whose glass roof was constantly cooled with streams of water, which had swans in ponds drifting under rustic bridges; people could eat, drink, dance and glory in the sheer unlikelihood of such a place. This city was a spangled thing, offering everything marvellous.

Across the avenue, the *New York Times* built its tower, with a station for the new subway set in its foundation. The *Times* took a risk in moving from the newspaper village at Park Row, but the new site had advantages: once the subway was embedded in the *Times* building, it was easy to persuade Belmont's IRT that the station should be called Times Square, and the whole area followed. Times Square became the focus of the subway system, the start of mid-town. The building of the subway, after years of streets ripped for cables and tracks, drove away many of the old residents. The success of Hammerstein's new theatres in 1899 opened 42nd Street as a theatre district. The New Amsterdam had its thin, tall entrance on 42nd Street for the sake of the address, even though the theatre proper backed onto 41st Street. For years, you could climb to the roof-top Ariel theatre, where swells drank absinthe and over-cold champagne, and listen to Fanny Brice. When D. W. Griffith wanted prestige for the opening of *Birth of a Nation* in 1915 he hired the Liberty Theatre on 42nd Street. In twenty years, the street had gone from quiet houses to the flourishing notoriety of the theatre.

It had become a place without names. Sailors coming up from the docks where the great liners moored would find their first warmth on 42nd Street. Commuters and tourists came in by Grand Central Station, or the All-American, Dixie, Consolidated or Mid-town bus terminals, all within a block. When the new subway lines were built, Times Square was an interchange much more than a destination, a place of transit. Everyone was visiting, pushing through Rectors' famous revolving door to dinner, going to Ziegfeld's new show at the New Amsterdam, looking for a dime-a-dance palace; or staring at the gaudy walls of neon light that surrounded Times Square, a cage of brightness.

Prohibition began its ruin. Without the subsidy of the Champagne Charlies in the roof-top clubs, the theatres were quickly in financial trouble. Some became movie houses and for a while the movies kept the Square brilliant; Paramount built its flagship theatre on the square, where a chamber orchestra played as you waited for a seat. In others, when Depression New Yorkers no longer had five bucks for a play, burlesque rushed in. In the Republic that Hammerstein built, the Minskys presented the clever, thin Gypsy Rose Lee, and the 'cyclone of sex', the piston-hipped Georgia Sothern, who most embarrassingly turned out to be only fourteen, but with a travelling case of neatly faked birth certificates. For a quarter, you got four hours of fun, sex and movies and, if you caught a pin that the Gypsy threw into the air, a free ticket to see it all again.

It was a carnival, possible only because the Depression had stopped short the various plans to make 42nd Street respectable. In 1931, the publishers McGraw-Hill built headquarters of blue-green terracotta and glass just across Eighth Avenue, because they needed to be in an area with industrial zoning, so they could manufacture and ship books. It seemed 42nd Street was going to the skies like the rest of New York, with the print all around and the garment district butting up from the south; but the car park across from McGraw-Hill has been vacant now for half a century. The financing simply stopped. The street itself began to slide. La Guardia in a fit of puritan anger shut down burlesque and the shows for sailors and businessmen went around the corner and turned raunchier. The live theatres in wartime turned into movie houses; in some, the men strolled with their hands behind their backs, the way to parade for other men's attention. The street was already an issue in the 1950s, famous for perverts and monsters and hustlers. There was talk of making a kind of urban theme park, to show what it once had been; but nobody could find a use for it.

In the 1970s, the 1930s happened again. Developers assembled sites for towers on 42nd Street, but the city went into fiscal spasm. The property man Mark Finkelstein complained: 'How can I afford to stay in business without collecting rents?' He rented to pornography shops because nobody else would move in. 'If the mayor will clean up the area,' he said, 'we will rent to someone else.' Finkelstein served on the Midtown Citizens Committee, lobbying enthusiastically to clean out his own tenants. Sol Goldman and Alex di Lorenzo, who defaulted on their mortgage on the chrome and neon wonders of the Chrysler Building in 1975 and still remained the city's largest landlords, had a tangle of small companies which owned properties with dubious tenants; it looked uncommonly as though they were putting distance between – say – Princess Books at 138 West 42nd Street, the Avon Corporation that owned the building, and their own interests in Avon. Many of the landlords had comfortable links to the Democrat club-houses. They reckoned to subsidise a whole building from what a porn shop would pay for a single floor. But nobody wanted to be beside the sex shops, and, worse, they were often 'bust-out' operators, ready to move on at the drop of a summons, so the face-saving rents often remained theoretical, and the area declined. In this mess, club-house politicians had no interest in denouncing their allies; the landlords were innocent victims of their own leases, apparently. Nobody had zoning control of 42nd Street to block either the spread of sex shops or the dereliction they were supposed to patch temporarily. If a building went somehow wrong, the city's only interest was in making that property earn taxes as soon as possible. The street was out of control.

The nickelodeon machines arrived, hand-cranked blue movies in a row, and the women scuttling from massage parlour to massage parlour, and sometimes a building went up in blazes because a parlour had dared to drop its prices. The street was lawless with dealers, first of pot and sometimes oregano and seeds for the tourists, then with crack cocaine. The street's people changed; most were black, young, full of a restlessness that could topple into a game or a fight or a crime. Having neglected the street, a horrified New York City now felt the need to bribe developers to clean it up. Zoning laws were changed to encourage development on the west side of Manhattan; a clutter of anonymous towers began to push up around the northern edge of Times Square. The state's Urban Development Corporation, itself one of those bodies taught by Governor Rockefeller to issue 'moral obligation' bonds, issued a plan for Times Square and 42nd Street.

In the shelter of the UDC's powers to buy property by fiat, gentlemen with connections also began to buy. The grimed white flanks of the Candler Building, a twenty-five storey monument from 1914 to the fortune made by Asa Candler selling Coca-Cola to the nation, was bought in 1980 by Michael Lazar. Very soon, it became conveniently clear that the Candler would survive the remaking of the Deuce. The lack of tenants on 42nd Street was solved; Lazar had once been chairman of the Taxi and Limousine Commission, which now rented four floors of the building. In 1985, Lazar sold the building on, for a profit; in 1986, he was indicted for racketeering.

Around Times Square, the Republican Party financier George Klein became the favoured developer. Klein was promised breaks on property taxes – between $300 million and $600 million, depending on how you do the sums – to build four towers around the Square, the single most important change in the Manhattan skyline since the 1930s. Such tax breaks had become the ordinary way of doing business, what developers expected from the city before they would condescend to make their profits; the city, hot for tax dollars, gave them away to keep the illusion of change. City and state subsidy promised profit at rents one-third less than in rival buildings. The state's powers to buy land meant the developer did not need to use his own expensive money to assemble a site. And George Klein, 'a very private man', according to his office, was a man with connections. He knew President Reagan. He knew Alex Liberman, the city's Director of Leasing, well enough to pay him a cheque for $5,000 to his synagogue's funds just after Liberman had leased three floors of a broken-down Klein building in Brooklyn which had not seen a tenant in a decade. And he knew the mayor, Ed Koch. In his memoirs, Koch is proud that he faced down developers who came kvetching to him about their losses in mid-town ('I do what I have to do, and you do what you have to do') because Klein, along with Donald Trump, 'was at the very top of my list of campaign contributors'. It was under Koch that Klein's Park Tower Realty was assigned the lucrative Times Square project.

At the start of 1991, the wreckers were due to put the first ball through the site of Nathan's Famous Hot Dogs and the next-door porn theatre. In place of a jazz of a square, there would be fortress towers, each with the outline of a smaller, neater tower picked out in stone on its bossy glass flanks; or glass towers stuck tastefully with bits of neon razzamatazz for old time's sake; but always there would be great slabs of glass and concrete cutting down the sky. There would be 4.1 million square feet of new office space in a city which was losing jobs in a recession and had already given away enough tax dollars to ensure that mid-town was in perpetual, lifeless shadow. The place of transit became a destination, a place of identity cards and guards, no longer the anonymous Deuce. Leases had to require shops to stay open into the early morning, in case they preferred to keep suburban hours. In the end, to salvage the street, men like George Klein had to be paid by a struggling city to kill it.

The sexshops prepare to close. 'The Macdonalds of sex,' Mid-Town Enforcement call them, policed by the smell of carbolic and men with mops, shilled by guys who hiss 'Puss-eee, puss-eee, puss-eee', but who also clock in for shifts and note each punter on a sheet headed: 'Always Be Courteous to the Customer'. Off the Deuce, in a little tower above the Show World palace of porn, lives the man who owns all this: Richard Basciano. He is a considerable man; his boxing gymnasium fills a floor of his building; he cannot be faulted by the cops, except on the matter of his friends. His partner Robert di

Bernardo left home in 1986, and has not yet returned; the police say he features in their file on the Gambino crime family. Basciano sits waiting for the wreckers, not much concerned.

He likes to put his girls and his neon where developers do not want to see them. In the late 1970s, he opened where Citicorp was putting up its prism of a headquarters on East 53rd Street. 'Girls! Girls! Girls!' the sign said, winking at corporate propriety (times change; Basciano now owns theatres for girls, boys and transsexuals). The bank finally broke and bought him out – four million dollars for his share in three run-down buildings. At the west end of the Deuce, he has property which the state will have to buy to complete its grand redevelopment. He paid maybe ten million dollars, a stake he earned back years ago; he can expect at least twice the price. And he is left with his honky-tonk Show World, exactly opposite what's planned to be a tourist hotel. He has only to wait.

In New York, the real dirty story is always real estate.

7
THE SIEGE OF MRS ASTOR'S BALLROOM

T HE CITY IS full of furious signals, enough to disorient people, even panic them. There is neon, gilded statues, flyposters, street signs, banners that hang along the iron fronts of SoHo like some mediaeval market. There is the suit on a man's back, the way that woman walks to make sure you know she's executive class, the way homeboy swaggers in alien territory. The city is various to the point of hysteria, and insistent you know who each person is. To avoid ambiguity, or even unpleasantness, everyone signals – class, tastes and standing all set out in a way of dress or accent or a style of holding yourself. This is something beyond the obvious thought that you can't teach graduate school in a suit or take a deposition in a T-shirt; you also signal political correctness, your admirable income, when you are at large and anonymous in the city. Without the signs, people disappear. The signs are so powerful that they even open the hope that you could be someone else: lawyers playing clarinet in Bohemian drag or stepping out in black leather.

You could be diminished by being with the wrong sort; you could be at physical risk. And yet you're surrounded by newcomers who have not yet settled their social standing, unless they can be categorised by race or colour or fame. Ambitious people want recognition, but nobody recognises them, so they signal their standing to the streets; 'yuppies' in trainers and navy blue, their almost unconstructed suits, are making sure everyone knows they are young, urban and professional. Go back fifty years, to when Simone de Beauvoir came to New York expecting free, sporty women; instead, she discovered that 'a woman's social success is closely linked with the richness of her appearance; it is a terrible handicap for poor people'. Go back to the turn of the century, when poor Lily Bart in *The House of Mirth* explains, 'A woman is asked out as much for her clothes as for herself.'

Thirty years before that, middle-class New Yorkers were afraid to live in apartment buildings in case they lived among the wrong people and lost social standing; they had begun to realise that appearances might be misleading, or faked. A letter in the *New York Times* in 1873 says it is sometimes safer to stay in a boarding house, which avoids the possibility that friends will be obliged to cut you for living at the wrong address. New Yorkers were horrified to find, in the Parisian originals of their 'Paris' flats, a jumble of classes arranged by floor; they wanted clear separations that everyone could understand. Their snobbery was about defending their position, avoiding confusion, in a city where everything had become uncertain. Other cities suffered the same crisis; in Paris, the vertiginous changes in street names, the laying of the new boulevards, the experience of revolution all made the city an unfamiliar landscape. There were Parisian jokes that husbands returned from abroad, unable to find their homes and their wives. But New York was the extreme case of change, and it created an extreme kind of Society, which rested on an awkward foundation. It was snobbery, exclusiveness, discrimination which ultimately depended on public approval, as we shall see. It was as baffling as an elected Versailles.

Consider the complications in defining Society. On the Upper East Side, a lady with an old Quaker name is taking tea with a gentleman with an old Scottish name. Both are patricians; both qualify for the Blue Book, the Social Register. 'We,' says the lady, sipping the good Assam, 'are Society.' But the gentleman disagrees. 'Society,' he says, 'is what's in the papers. You have to be social to be Society.' He remembers in the 1920s being poor and newly married, and wondering if a Connecticut hotel would even cash his cheque; but finding the next day that his overnight stay was in the New York papers because his name was in the Social Register. He remembers being 'in Society' a few years, the dinner parties on the gilt-edged china, the ladies who sent the driver to collect you and those who never would, but just as distinctly he remembers checking out of Society as though it was a resort. For New York Society lacks the continuities of land, political clout, a deferential tenantry or obvious arbiters whose word is law. Society is more like a show.

The tabloids print the guest lists, the frock lists, between headless bodies and drug-war shoot-outs. Publicists fax the details of a party before it happens. The columnist Suzy in the *New York Post* once reported guests who never did turn up. Publicists organise who should be invited to newcomers' parties and fix invitations to the right charity balls. Their clients include grand names: Sonny and Mary Lou Whitney, whose family fortune was based on Manhattan street railways, keep a regular man who makes sure we know when Mary Lou wins the owner-dog look-alike contest at Saratoga in a tutu ('best tutu look-alike in the senior citizens' class'). Other countries, more robustly, like to read about adultery and catastrophe; New Yorkers read about thirty-dollar tulips, the Louis XVI barstools in Donald Trump's apartment, the parties in cultural temples like the Metropolitan Museum, what a Mrs Kempner wore last night. Mrs Kempner, wife of a Wall Street power, is so assiduous at putting herself before the cameras that she gets her frocks at special rates, and *Women's Wear Daily* refuses to photograph her. Some of this is a sideshow, vicarious living, even a shared ambition to be rich enough to be frivolous; but that is not where its interest lies.

The whole melodrama of the city's wealth – sudden money, sudden ruin, crooks and grandees and high-wire financiers – is encoded in what look like social games. So is what we think about being worthy, and being worth a lot, and the possibility that the two are different; and about the signs on which we depend to know strangers, and the possibility that they are lies.

On the face of it, Society is not much fun. The right names assemble purposefully, never just dining, but dining for a good cause. A new disease is best. It is not an efficient way of raising money. The CREO Society staged the musical *Hair* in the General Assembly Hall of the United Nations, on behalf of children with AIDS and UNICEF in general; its sponsors included William F. Buckley and other social lights. They had late-model hippies skipping down the aisles and asking the black-tie regulars to dance, and sold $829,667 worth of tickets. When the accounts were done, there was only $74,000 left for charity. CREO closed down after the State Attorney General suggested they were more interested in organising society parties than in helping charity. But going to a CREO event was still obligatory. The banker Felix Rohatyn suggested good-hearted socialites should simply write cheques for charity. His wife found herself doing verbal battle with her social friends in the middle of 72nd Street. She was, as it happens, on her way to have a dress fitted for another charity event.

At the World Financial Centre, Society is 'raising money for AIDS'. It is worthy, worth half a page in the *New York Times*. The limos let out the charitable and they have to scuttle past bars full of mocking yuppies on their way to the high, cool amphitheatre of the Winter Gardens. Society does not always get respect. The ladies teeter down marble steps, surprisingly awkward, and they pose. Contact is an air-kiss, talk is all introductions. 'My family's foundation bought the tickets'. Pause. 'We just bought a little castle in Ireland'. Pause. Nobody talks to strangers, for fear of somehow losing status. Newspaper columnists sit at the top table and are called 'friends'. The guests scent cameras like dogs sense the wind. Elizabeth Taylor is here, and those who pay court to her also work for her, because Ms Taylor implies a daunting standard of fame outside Society. 'I am a close friend of Ms Taylor,' says someone at the wrong table.

Men look abstracted, or downright resentful, except for the handful of 'walkers', the escorts who are never too threateningly sexed. Walkers defend women, walkers say; 'a best woman friend will do her in, whereas the best man friend won't,' says Jerry Zipkin, the most famous of the breed, buddy to Nancy Reagan and a Harlem landlord in real life (which does not intrude here). The women are dressed as matrons, since this is a social conscience night. At ten there are speeches. Elizabeth Taylor drops her lovely voice to tell us we are all, yes all of us, citizens of the world. John Kluge signs a million-dollar cheque and is introduced as the richest man in America; just for a moment, the room ripples with involuntary applause. Very soon after that, the limos call. Duty is done. On the dance floor, six tall drag queens erupt suddenly, playing and swaying to everyone's alarm. Drag queens, too, used to be ordinary, and only aspiring to be fabulous; like the other guests, who do not care for reminders.

The money in the room could be Texas oil, or California, or business with no headquarters in New York or with no precise location in the taxable world. Money comes to New York to make a point. Its owners could stay in the mansions of Dallas, or the disposable palaces of Beverly Hills, but only one city – the inconvenient, filthy, crime-ridden, unstable New York, quite devoid of mansions – will do.

Other cities are just as snobbish. San Francisco has a tribal pecking order, and an Opera with the nineteenth-century function of exhibiting a social hierarchy while other people sing. Fords in Detroit can put their names on anything, because their workers owe them loyalty at least as deep as their mortgages. Other cities have sudden money; Michael Milken saturated the country with junk bonds from an office in Los Angeles, and Chicago has the commodities exchanges. Other cities are more obviously comfortable, and allow for more spectacular display; there is nothing in New York quite like the Atlanta mansions, set in manicured lawns, that Coca-Cola built.

But New York is April, May, October, November and December on the smart calendar, including Christmas for the nice chic whiteness of the city. Paris matters in February, but only for frocks; couturiers sit the key wives on the front gilt chairs in the hope they will take away and display the product in Manhattan. Otherwise, socially ambitious Americans go to New York or they go 'away'. March is skiing, in Switzerland; June and July are for Maine or perhaps the Bahamas; August and September are country tours, villa to villa in Switzerland, France or even Chiantishire. And January is a sleepy month.

This world is rarefied, but not remote. The need for display produces charity, and charity builds all manner of monuments which in time become the institutions and the culture of the town. In the flashy 1980s, it seemed shocking that anyone with $30,000 for Metropolitan Museum funds could throw a party in the Temple of Dendur or the Mediaeval Hall. A public, scholarly, proper institution was disgraced by show-off socialites; it was 'the nadir of the museum', according to the critic Hilton Kramer. The parties were often business affairs, quite unconnected to art. Carolyne and Henry Kravis, frockmaker and buy-out banker, sat there listening to the violin, rapturous and spotlit. Sid and Mercedes Bass, oilman and new wife, gloried in raucous Texan yahoos. Laura Steinberg, daughter of a corporate raider, was married in the Great Hall on 18 April 1988; the museum earned only $30,000, but the guests sat among a half-million dollars worth of flowers. Social columnists counted the parties, and called the museum 'Club Met'.

But the Met, like other city institutions, was entangled with Society from the beginning. It belonged to grandees, not to scholars and critics, and certainly not to the masses. Joseph C. Choate, an early trustee of the Metropolitan, liked to address himself to the 'millionaires of many markets'. He urged them to turn 'railroad shares and mining stocks – things which perish without the using, and which in the next financial panic shall surely shrivel like parched scrolls – into the glorified canvas of the world's masters, that shall adorn these walls for centuries'. The names of the artists were almost as prominent as the millionaires'.

The Met hardly dared to quarrel with its patrons. It touted Cornelius Vanderbilt's gift of 700 Old Master drawings, every one of which is a copy or a school study. In 1884, the museum bleakly records its gratitude for 'an Oil Painting, artist and subject unknown'. In 1896, an enormous varnished canvas of Washington crossing the Delaware arrived, of which Mark Twain said that it 'would have made Washington hesitate about crossing, if he could have foreseen what advantage was going to be taken of it'. Catherine Lorillard Wolfe, heir to the Lorillard tobacco fortune and the Wolfe hardware fortune, presented acres of sugary Salon pictures along with a cash endowment of $200,000. The trustees would later use the money to buy pictures that Ms Wolfe would have thoroughly disliked – a Goya, a Renoir, a Daumier and a Delacroix – but for the moment they had to provide a 'suitable well-lighted, fireproof apartment, gallery or separate space' for pictures they did not want, and name it for Catherine Lorillard Wolfe. In the 1920s the grandest families began to move into apartments rather than mansions, and the Metropolitan acquired very big art – too big for the new walls. Later, the same patrons who paid for new wings were also in the auction houses bidding up prices for paintings far beyond what the Metropolitan could afford. The Steinbergs, whose daughter was married in the museum, needed a curator to catalogue the thirty-seven rooms of their apartment, and hired one from the Met.

The museum was a beacon lit by an élite, or so the élite said; it took Tammany pressure to open its doors on Sundays, the one day when working women and men could visit. It was a very public boast that New York was the equal of London or Paris, that no student of art could pass America by. But it celebrated the power to acquire, not to discriminate. Millionaires wanted goods with a reliable value, and they insisted museums take them at that value. Sometimes their influence came surprisingly cheap. The great J.P. Morgan was inclined to make a brief loan look like a generous gift. He clawed back from museum funds the cost of building shelter for museum archaeologists in Egypt; overnight, when the trustees saw what had happened, they turned 'Morgan House' into 'Metropolitan House'. He munificently bought out a gloomy hotel on Lake Geneva so its owner, a collector of armour and a potential benefactor, should not be distracted from his giving; but Morgan charged the ramshackle venture to the Metropolitan.

Usually, as the museum's first director complained, millionaires 'will give money for buying collections, and for building purposes, because both remain visible monuments of their generosity ... while endowment funds are invisible and remain unknown to the general public'. There was money for display, but not for thinking about it; and, without income, an institution is always the supplicant. The museum had only one sizeable endowment in the early years, and that came from Jacob Rogers, a manufacturer of railway locomotives, a petulant man who particularly wanted to leave nothing to any human being, much less his relatives, and therefore gave five million to the Metropolitan. He would not have been amused by the elderly lady who arrived on the museum's doorstep, claiming that she was the Metropolitan Museum that Rogers had meant.

Until the late 1970s, the museum's board had a seat reserved for a Morgan; and for an Astor, a Whitney, a Rockefeller and (such is the power of the *New York Times*) a Sulzberger. The spirit of William Cooper Pine, a Victorian trustee, survived. Pine once said the public 'must stop thinking they support the museum and be compelled to see what *we* own and support the museum and give it in pure charity for public education'. The museum had been a spit-shined place, where the public was required to behave; it demanded respect for the institution, and the powers that funded it. When the bands and the caterers came in the 1980s, the notion of pleasure arrived for the first time.

The grand institutions are not the only places where Society, and particularly its gilded age, persists. The newest, glassiest monuments draw on what everyone remembers of the past. When the apartments at Trump Tower were first on the market, the prospectus crowed that it had been fifty years since anybody had been able to live at that address, and those anybodies were somebodies: Astors. 'And the Whitneys lived just around the corner,' it read. 'And the Vanderbilts across the street.' For a price, newcomers could be slipped into the past as if it was a club. All the excess and wonders of the 'gilded age' – the Russian punch, the diamond stomachers, the live swans swimming at the dinner table – survive as a city rumour.

For a saga of change, of robber barons and unimaginable fortunes and sudden ruin, it has one curious continuity. A hundred years ago, a Mrs Astor dominated New York Society. In 1991, a Mrs Astor still does, although she is no longer the law-maker and the keeper of the Social Register, simply the doyenne. We begin, therefore, with the world in which the Astors made their fortune, and the Society they helped build to defend it.

The Astors came lumbering into New York during the Revolutionary War, big-shouldered butchers from Heidelberg who dealt in confiscated meat. John Jacob set up shop next to the Friends' Meeting House on what is now Pearl Street. He married a poor relation of the Brevoort family who brought him a $300 dowry. He sold musical instruments 'for very low terms for cash' and he bought and sold raccoon blankets and muskrat skins and beaver. His dealings reached up the Hudson and, with the aid of guns and booze, deep into Indian territory. He dreamed of opening the whole American North West as Astoria, a republic of the skin trade. He chartered the first great American trust, the American Fur Company, which controlled the skin game east of the Mississippi – anywhere there were people to buy as well as animals to kill. The smell of skins clung to his money, long after he had left the trade. The frontiersman Davy Crockett came to stay in the grand Astor House Hotel; 'Lord help the poor bears and beavers,' he said, 'but they must be used to being skun by now'.

John Jacob's story later became a city fable, how the poor boy came with only seven flutes and his wits and made an inconceivable American fortune. In the fable, Astor sails for London on business and meets an old school friend who now has risen to be Governor of the East India Company; for old time's sake, the friend gives Astor a talisman – permit 68 to trade with any port the Company monopolises. That permission was worth a half-share in any voyage, even though Astor had no ships. He went into the China trade, and his talisman duly brought him treasure. The crew cut firewood on a Pacific island and stashed it in cords on the deck. When the ship docked in Canton, they discovered it was sandalwood, worth a fortune. For seventeen years Astor kept the trade to himself, never saying where the woods grew. Astor ships always sailed, even during the 1808 embargo on foreign trade; Astor claimed that some tea-sipping longshoreman in a forward cabin was really a Chinese mandarin, in immediate need of passage home.

John Jacob took his brother Heinrich's advice: 'Buy land'. He liked
to ride the rough tracks of Manhattan on his own, and he knew by
instinct how to turn his trading income into the perpetual institution
of a fortune. 'Had I the money to invest,' he said, 'I would buy every
foot of land on the island of Manhattan.' For a century, the grand
proprietors of Manhattan had treated land like a store or a show of
wealth, not expecting to earn money from it. The island was dotted
with country houses and estates with fancy names – the Louvre, the
Hermitage or Bellevue, some named for half-remembered London
pleasure grounds. But the city was changing, and the patricians began
to see that tenants were coming in their thousands. One copper-
bottomed loyalist, James de Lancey, had already mapped a square and
streets on to the old Dominie Farm, between what are now Houston
and Division streets (Delancey Street, the frontier of the Lower East
Side, lies half-way across the farm). De Lancey lost his lands after
the revolution and asked the English for compensation, not because
he had lost a farm, but because the land 'was extremely valuable for
its contiguity to the Town of New York, there being no other way
of extending the Town but by building upon this Land'.

John Jacob saw a chess game opening; he could buy and trade to
be always in the way of the city. He traded, as he traded in fur or
sandalwood. Five years after he landed, he did his first deal: $625 for
two lots on Bowery Lane. He bought the Bayards' hayfields on lower
Broadway, and the city caught up. He sold a Wall Street house for
$800, fashionable as it was, and put the money into eighty lots above
Canal Street, where the city hardly reached. He watched for opportunity. When Vice President Aaron Burr needed to skip the country
after a murderous duel, Astor bought his leases in Greenwich Village
cheap. His obituaries still disapproved of his moves in the financial
panic of 1837, when 'he was a willing purchaser of mortgages from
needy holders at less than their face; and when they became due, he
foreclosed on them, and purchased the mortgaged property at the
ruinous prices which ranged at the time'. He bought Medeef Evans'
mortgage for $25,000 and it gave him control of the land between
Broadway and the Hudson River, from 42nd to 46th Street – the
modern theatre district. He bought underwater lots that were to be
filled. He lobbied to make the line of Broadway cut across his land,
so meadows became frontage on a grand avenue.

And always, he put the burden of developing land on to his tenants.
They had twenty-one year leases; they had to level, improve, build,

manage, pay taxes and assessments as well as rent, and then hand everything back to Astor. He even made the tenant of the Vauxhall Gardens pleasure grounds pay for the cutting of streets and the creation of building sites which ruined his business, until the courts, after long appeals, suggested that Astor make some contribution to his own fortune. The *New York Herald*, reporting his death, said that 'one half of his property – ten millions at least – belongs to the people of the city of New York . . . the farms and lots of ground, which he bought forty, twenty and ten and five years ago, have all increased in value entirely by the industry of the citizens of New York'.

In Astor's lifetime, New York became unrecognisable. He landed in a homespun town. John Adams complained in 1774: 'I have not seen one gentleman, one well bred man since I came to town.' Bostonians or Virginians, Henry Adams testified, 'visited and admired, not New York but Philadelphia'. 'The people of Philadelphia are stiff in their manners and not so hospitable,' the Scots traveller J.B. Dunlop wrote in his diary for 1811; New York was cheerful and open-hearted alongside Philadelphia, Frances Wright wrote in 1821. New York, in other words, was provincial. An anonymous, bilious French traveller complained that New York lacked 'the pleasures of the great capitals'. The women had a 'haughty, tough and masculine air'; they were 'thin and plain, with enormous feet, a sign of low birth which riches cannot change in one or two generations'. He was bored with all the high-minded talk about 'temples, sects, sermons, religious fervour . . . revolutions, patriots, insurrections, American achievements, their superiority over the English, the French, their creators, over the whole world'.

Abram Dayton was an old-guard New Yorker, a true Knickerbocker, who remembered the days when a man could put his whole credit at risk if he was observed riding during office hours. An aristocrat was designed to be idle, but in New York occupation was essential. De Tocqueville found that 'the families of the great landed proprietors are almost all commingled with the general mass'. The great landowners of colonial New York were often the great merchants, or else married to the great merchants. Gentlemen took up law; it was the profession of the richest students at King's College, later Columbia, from the middle of the eighteenth century; Ludwig Gall counted the town directory, found 171 lawyers in just the first half, and was appalled. The families from colonial days, the Knickerbockers, kept out anyone who sold retail, but their snobbery was otherwise about the quality of men, not just their occupation. Philip Hone, founder of the grand Union Club, waxed nostalgic in 1847 about the city of his youth: 'The president and directors of a bank were other sort of people from those of the present. Proud and aristocratical, they were the only nobility we had, and now we have none'.

This kind of snobbery depended on knowledge, not deliberate social signalling, on knowing everyone, and every pedigree. Marriage announcements showed how closely the city's patricians clung together; money married money, names married names. Van Rensselaers, from the patroon family, married Stuyvesants, descendants of old peg-leg Petrus, and the immensely rich Delafields; Stuyvesants married Livingstons, the first true dukes of the new world; the Morrises of the Bronx married Van Cortlandts and Gouverneurs. Schermerhorns married Bayards and, later, Astors, because the Astor fortune was becoming visible. Philip Hone, in his diary, notes that Lispenard Stewart married not a daughter of the Salles family, but '2 or $300,000'. Charles Astor Bristed, a British satirist, wrote that he 'used to think that in your unsophisticated republican country, people married out of pure love, but now it looks as if the fashionables, at least, marry for money as often as we do'.

Since everybody knew everybody's standing, there was no point in display. Restaurants were regarded as 'creations ... of a foreign element in the city'. The town's dowagers stopped public dances at the City Hotel despite the decorous sponsoring committee; waltzing was thought to inflame the young and make them liable not to impropriety, but to colds. A gentleman could go out to the Castle Gardens for music and sponge cake and lemonade, or take a sherry cobbler or a mint julep on the roof of Rabineau's swimming bath, moored off the Battery; but what mattered were private invitations. You might take tea. You might 'spend the evening', which meant arriving at seven in your frock coat and leaving at ten, the hour when a decent Knickerbocker house was locked tight. Young bloods who wanted to visit the serving girls at the Apollo Ballroom had to make sure a basement window was left unbarred.

This lack of ostentation made the town look almost classless. De Tocqueville was struck by dining with lawyers and bankers and men of business instead of the titles and minor officeholders of a Paris salon, and even more that the ordinary sales clerk did not have the 'bad form' of the French lower classes. When Ludwig Gall fled the confusion of the Napoleonic wars, he found that in New York 'the home of a rich merchant differs from that of a craftsman in almost nothing but size'. On the river-boat he thought everyone was upper class because their behaviour was so free, until he realised he was travelling with the keepers of country stores.

Even in the 1820s, each house was a tiny factory, not a showcase of wealth. In the grandest federal home, the water still came from the street pump, and there was an open hearth for cooking. Light came from candles or kerosene lamps. The house slops had to be emptied into the gutters because street sewers had not yet been built. Nothing about the house could be taken for granted. Each household quite usually made its own soap, its own candles. A prosperous wife would come back from the country in September to supervise the making of jams and head cheese and sausage for the winter.

But these things changed quickly. In the growing city, you could buy goods and services easily. It became a matter of pride not to work in the house; 'women might work,' a contemporary wrote, 'but not ladies; or when the latter undertook it, they ceased to be such'. Even for a middle-class woman like Julia Lay, wife of a head bookkeeper in a bank, class was no longer a simple issue. Lay writes in her diary how the buying of clothes and furniture bolsters her shaky sense of being, properly, a 'lady'. The plan of houses changed, so the mistress was in the parlour and the servants down below, made to climb up for orders or complaints; and to climb further still to their own quarters. By 1840, a middle-class parlour suffered an 'epidemic of humbug and sham finery and gin-palace decoration,' as George Templeton Strong said. This decoration was a woman's job and much of her identity, and she was required to pour effort into it.

She might well see frightening signs on the street that her social standing would not always be obvious. The Knickerbockers gave their servants cast-off clothes, because a well turned out servant was a credit to his master. The new middle-class were made nervous, even angry, by the stylishness and the spending of their servants. A gentleman found it necessary to complain that 'The washerwoman's Sunday attire is now as nearly like that of the merchant's wife as it can be, and the bootblack's daughter wears a bonnet made like that of the Empress of the French'. For the Knickerbockers grew nervous behind their apparent arrogance. They had reason to fear the slightest accident could topple a family into obscurity or bring up some other tribe of millionaires.

They were used to having some connection with the labourers and artisans around them, but they no longer knew everybody. Landlords like the Goelets did service in fire companies and militias; civic duty made a man's name, even if he was rich. The city was organised by wards and local communities. The rich still collected door to door for the relief of the poor, and, more remarkably, went door to door handing out that relief; in 1839, perhaps one out of ten home visitors doing charitable work could be called genuinely wealthy. But more and more, they felt mobbed by newcomers. 'We shall be over-run with vagabonds,' the *New York Minerva* complained in 1797; Humanitas, a columnist in the *Commercial Advertiser*, wrote that 'a large number of vagrants are suffered to wander about our streets, many of them in a state of drunkenness ... and in the practice of every vice'; George Templeton Strong, more directly, denounced the booming city as 'one huge pigstye'. By 1817, poor relief was the largest single expenditure of the city of New York.

The Irish arrived in force, and the Germans. There were strikes, food riots, nativist campaigns against the Irish. The city was losing its peace. Thuggish gangs strutted the Bowery, where the poor once walked easily. Broadway, with its fashionable stores and its ladies wearing silk even in November, was also open to the working classes and to a sizeable number of bosomy tarts, cruising like frigates in the armour of their stays. Visitors noticed that on Sunday morning, many of the promenaders were black. In Mitchill's 1807 guidebook, the Battery is 'open to all citizens', for 'the fresh breezes from the bay and the shade of the trees, every afternoon of summer'. But Asa Greene in the late 1830s reports that, in the alarming new city, some people 'are particularly offended that the common people should presume to appear on that delightful promenade. ... "It is so very vulgar," say these aristocrats, "to be seen walking in the same grounds with mechanics, house servants and the labouring people."' When abroad, even the newcomers who had just jumped class liked to talk of being 'the few select' of the 'large Augean stables' of America.

The poor were not even the main problem. James Fennimore Cooper, in 1828, thought 'Society in New York is rather in a state of effervescence than settled'; and when he returned from Europe in 1833 he found the old guard eclipsed by a chaos of new men. He complained of the newcomers' 'greedy rapacity for money ... the vulgar and indiscriminate expenditure'; 'the desire to grow suddenly rich has seized on all classes'.

For the Knickerbocker provincials had lived on into the trading capital of America. Abram Dayton was smugly proud that 'the mysterious ways by which fortunes are now gained without visible continuous labour had not been discovered'. But when European war gave neutral America a sudden bite of the world's seaborne trade, it was New York which in 1797 became the busiest port in America. It was the home of the American Stock Exchange. The British decision to dump cloth in the city at the end of the War of 1812 gave the city a virtual monopoly of the trade. There was an auction system, regular ships to Europe, the start of exchanges where men could make huge profits without stepping on a ship or handling a bale. You could buy and sell the world on paper. The Erie Canal took New York's empire into the Midwest, while Boston and Philadelphia were left with only overland routes.

All this furious activity had come to the town which the Knickerbockers still tried to keep sober and quiet. New York was a turntable of trade, a place where people took profits from the relationship between prices, not just from making goods and selling them for a price. Cooper walked down Wall Street, he said, and touts promised six thousand per cent returns on farms, streets, towns. The city's mood swung on its paper markets. Captain Maryatt arrived during the Wall Street slump of 1837. 'Suspicion, fear and misfortune have taken possession of the city. Had I not been aware of the cause, I should have imagined that the plague was raging.'

All this was sudden money which needed a social role to match its bank balance. The new rich could not be aristocrats, like British lords who had political clout and the power to nominate to the bureaucracy. Politics carried no status in New York. Men could vote without owning property from the 1820s. In 1833 the mayor was first elected by a direct vote of all the citizens. Some of the wealthy remained party stalwarts: Hamilton Fish for the Whigs, and the store tycoon Alexander Stewart, William B. Astor and even August Belmont, Rothschilds' man in America, in unlikely alliance with the Tammany Democrats. But fewer and fewer wanted to be chairman of the ward committee of a party, or to run for office. A rough check shows that thirty-two grandees stood in elections between 1828 and 1840 while only 12 stood between 1850 and 1863. The rich did not come back to city politics until the 1870s, after the fall of the Tweed Ring, and then they were not hoping to establish their status. They hoped to take back the city from immigrants and thieves.

There was not much comfort in buying grand estates. Riot ran around the countryside in the 1840s, with rent strikes and murder, and made the great landowners nervous about their almost feudal tenure. Nor did sudden money have a captive audience – no forelock-tugging masses who had to buy their jobs with respect. The city rich were generally as far away from the mundane source of their money as the nobles of Versailles had been. Except for their servants, nobody they passed on the streets would feel dependent on them. And yet they were drawn to New York, because it was a lesson in how to be urbane, but much more because it was the mother of markets. Even Southerners who thought that manners and virtue stopped at the Mason–Dixon line were aware that 'all the profitable branches of freighting, brokering, selling, banking, insurance, etc., that grow out of the Southern products, are enjoyed in New York'. Gazaway Bugg Lamar, from Augusta, Georgia, made his money in the South as cotton factor, commission merchant and general speculator; but he dreamed of going north to the 'commercial emporium of the Western World'. His life was broken when his wife and six of his children went down with the exploded wreck of his own steamship, the *Pulaski*. After a time of introspection, Lamar married again, found a house in Brooklyn and plunged into new speculations – cotton, wheat, apples and pig iron, for a start. He founded his own bank, dealing mostly with Southerners; he bought muskets for Confederate Georgia, and for South Carolina just before the Civil War. To be a truly rich man, even to be a good Southerner, Lamar had to be in New York.

Slowly, such men began to build a social world which ignored the Knickerbockers; or, as the Knickerbockers thought, defied them. The first great costume ball in New York was given in 1830 by Mme Charles Brugière, wife of an exile from the Haitian revolution. The new style became notorious when the *New York Herald* gave its front page on 2 March 1840 to the ball held by Henry Breevort Junior at his house on Fifth Avenue. The reporter William Attree had to infiltrate, disguised as a knight in shiny stage armour. He found frocks that cost more than $800, a would-be bloodhound whose dog-skin breeches had burst, a fist-fight, a Katherine of Aragon under a tiara of real diamonds, a man dressed as a Chinese mandarin who ate with chop-sticks, and a six-foot man in a schoolgirl's short white frock. All this was pardonable, if startling; but at four in the morning, a Persian princess slipped away with a Southern gentleman, and the princess turned out to be the daughter of the British consul. The elopement was blamed on all the opportunities of masked parties, which were banned from the city for the next fourteen years.

Society's doings were suddenly a public matter, to be regulated and reported. The *Herald's* circulation soared. It devoted a column to the comings and goings of the gentry at the Astor House. It went on to sex scandals, to social absurdities, sometimes leaving out the names and sometimes including them. This mockery and exposure had a secure foundation: on democratic principles, it was for the people to decide who had truly arrived in Society, and who should be asked to leave.

Among the dancers at Breevort's ball was August Belmont, the social monster that the dowagers most feared. He was new in New York, and that was part of the problem. He landed during the panic of 1837, bound for Havana to investigate the Cuban economy for the Rothschilds. On Wall Street, he found the Rothschilds' agents were among the many firms that had suddenly failed. Even their new, unfinished office building had fallen in on itself. Belmont gambled on the Rothschilds' good will, and asked to promote himself from their secretary to their agent. He imported the Rothschilds' sense of the great nets of business from capital to capital, port to port; he could think abstractly about cash and commodities.

In three years he had made himself one of America's richest men, mostly by arbitrage – buying cheap in one market and selling dear in another. He looked around for a social life. He was a Jew with 'liberal views regarding religious beliefs', but he was not at home with the settled and snobbish Sephardim, who were already disconcerted by the arrival of thousands of Ashkenazim from Eastern Europe. The Ashkenazim struck him as uncivilised. The Knickerbockers held him out because they regarded money as vulgar, since they had only enough of it. All that was left for Belmont was the company of a handful of wild boys, the sons of Knickerbocker families, with a taste for drink and women and racing horses furiously on the macadamed surface of Third Avenue.

To them, he introduced serious cooking, and the art of kissing a lady's hand. He drove a four-in-hand in a city where a carriage was not yet essential for a gentleman. He had the credit of the Rothschilds, almost the only credit which could impress a circle of provincial merchants and survive the scandal of his extravagance. He gave grand dinners, and although he was rarely invited back, the Knickerbockers came, and giggled. He was European, after all, and therefore every-thing a Knickerbocker girl could dream of, so much more sophisticated than the local boys. They had only just discovered perfumed pomades and were inclined to ask their sweethearts to smell their hair. But most disconcertingly for the dowagers, who knew all the cousins of all their cousins, he seemed to have invented himself on landing in New York. He was the first man they could not judge by his family, and still could not ignore. 'He taught New Yorkers how to eat, how to drink, how to dress ... how to live generally according to the rules of the possibly somewhat effete, but unquestionably refined, society of the Old World,' as the *New York Sun* wrote in 1877. He might even be slightly diabolic; the dowagers' husbands said he could arouse a woman sexually just by looking at her.

Belmont forced the Knickerbockers to be openly snobbish. They organised a City Ball, held at the City Hotel in January 1841, with 800 registered gentlemen and registered ladies of long Dutch and English descent, turning in the radiance of diamonds and candles in a mirrored room. The committee, some 150 young men who resented the new people and their money, intended a statement: this is Society, and our Society is brilliant. The Knickerbocker style changed to encompass a series of Assembly Balls at Delmonico's Restaurant. Their descendants delighted in the cleverness of it all. Mrs John King Van Rensselaer still told in the 1920s how Belmont had confronted members of the committee; 'I can assure you,' she said he said, 'that either I get an invitation to the Assembly this year, or else the day after the Assembly each of you will be a ruined man.' He was duly invited, and arrived – spruce, starched, arrogant – to find he was the only guest. After that, the committees for old guard dances were usually secret, to avoid the pressure of the social-climbing 'bouncers'.

Belmont could not care less. He invented his own society, his own class; he up-ended every assumption that made New York a quiet, provincial town. He married brilliantly: Caroline, a Botticelli girl and daughter of Commodore Matthew Calbraith Perry who would later take gunboats and begin prising open Japan to the world. Belmont was disowned by the grander New York Jews when it became clear that he would baptise his son and raise him in the Episcopal Church. George Templeton Strong thought him 'a mere successful cosmopolite adventurer and alien'. Patrician merchants, no longer secure in their wealth, had great doubts about his exuberance. They feared that New York, America, the market, the world were all growing too fast and must inevitably splinter.

The merchants needed a mask of seriousness. Downtown at 142 Fulton Street (Rear Building), Freeman Hunt worked 'to raise and elevate the commercial character', because 'worth' still had a moral dimension. His monthly *Merchant's Magazine and Commercial Review* first appeared in 1839 with clarion calls on the Rise and Progress, the Advantages and Benefits of Commerce, and 'Leisure – Its Uses and Abuses'. Hunt's narrow columns were filled with a head prefect's ideal of the trading life, in which the merchant is dutiful to family, generous to charity, inclined to small profits and slow accumulation, a patron of the arts and plump with decorum. He deplored 'the fashionable demeanour of the present day: which, in attempting to be easy, often overlaps the bounds of propriety and decorum'. 'The rich and prudent are plain men,' the magazine declares. 'Rogues usually dress well'. He celebrated merchanting, which was 'quite as honourable as the inglorious ease in which so many of the nobility and gentry of the old world wear out their unprofitable lives'. He was harsh on landlords whose credit was 'part of that ancient prerogative which the domineering lords of the soil exercised during the dark ages on the continent of Europe'. It was inexplicable, the sermon continues, that 'the character of an American merchant is not highly respected abroad' on account of their slow settlement of bills, and a certain casualness about bankruptcy.

Hunt's propaganda was on serious issues. America still listened to Jefferson, and thought itself the land of rural gentlemen. The merchant class needed dignity to justify their power. The city itself was still suspect. In his unfinished history of Manhattan, written in 1851, James Fennimore Cooper writes that 'it has long been a subject of investigation among moralists, whether the existence of towns like those of London, Paris, New York etc. is or is not favourable to the development of the better qualities of the human character'. Cooper finally decided: 'If there be incentives to wrong-doing in the crowded population of a capital town, there are many incentives to refinement, public virtue, and even piety, that are not to be met with elsewhere.'

The *Merchant's Magazine* was torn between asserting the worth of the city's dealers, and persuading them to mend their ways. For Hunt was afraid he could hear the tyro merchant: 'Do you suppose I am induced to lead this slavish life, buried in a small counting room, among brick walls, two thirds of every day, amid smells and odours altogether disagreeable and indescribable, suffering in health for want of pure air – do you think I endure all this for any prospect of good to my fellow creatures? Believe it not! I am bent on making a fortune in the shortest possible time, and then I shall retire and enjoy my leisure.'

Business divided New York into a woman's city and a man's city. The magazine reports that husbands and wives live almost apart, the man engrossed in business from sunrise to sunset, the women left 'to seek her own enjoyments'. 'How much excuse is to be found for the lavish habits in the wife, when she is deprived of the concert and companionship of the husband! How much for waste of time in empty frivolities, for the final concentration of her thoughts and feelings upon the nothings of fashion!' Wives of the upper classes had acquired a kind of leisure which horrified purposeful, work-hungry men, and spawned an ostentation which Hunt associated with slack morals and speculation. 'The larger speculator must keep up appearances; he must live in a large house; give expensive entertainments; his wife and children must dress in the richest fashions. And why? Oh, to show that he is confident of success. . . .' He proposes a certain Colonel Beers, who gives his daughter Emily a birthday party among paintings 'of the Italian masters . . . choice specimens of American genius'; in an over-stuffed house with several lovely statues, superb sofas, ottomans and divans, rich carpets, glittering chandeliers and French pier-glasses. 'Should we fail, Emily,' the Colonel is saying, 'who would yield us respect and sympathy after such scenes?'

'This aristocracy here is itself nothing but a wealthy, overgrown bourgeoisie, composed of a few families who have been more success-ful in trade than the rest,' Francis Grund wrote in 1839, 'and on that account are now cutting their friends and relatives in order to be considered fashionable.' Cabin passengers never talked to steerage; in *Martin Chuzzlewit*, Martin is put out of a dinner party when his host discovers that he did not sail first class to America. Dickens claims that 'men were weighed by their dollars, measures gauged by their dollars; life was auctioneered, appraised, put up and knocked down for its dollars,' an indictment which would be more sharp if the Duke of Westminster had been honoured in London mostly for his soul. Dollars were admired, as Calvinists saw wealth as proof of God's favour. Chuzzlewit is told that America does have an aristocracy: 'Of intelligence, sir . . . of intelligence and virtue. And of their necessary consequence in this republic. Dollars, sir.'

The Knickerbocker ladies were shocked that wives now wanted carriages of their own, parties 'to which they invite people they have never met before and from which they exclude their friends and nearest relations'. The newcomers did the round of the upstate springs in summer, spent at least one winter in Washington. Their lives depended on credit. The very bed on which they slept was quite usually bought on a six-month note. If 'in spite of their scrambling after fashionable society, they do not obtain access to the very first of it, the men are teased and tormented until they . . . seek in one of the numerous "growing places" of the West an asylum in which they cannot be outdone by the *old families*'.

The Knickerbockers were not yet interested in assimilation, so the survivors of the social wars had to shout their status. L. Maria Child, in New York since the early 1840s, complained that 'the number of servants in livery visibly increases every season'. In 1851 J.H. Ross observed that children 'are first taught in the nursery for show. Then they are taken to church for show, sent to Madam *******'s boarding school for show, to the milliner, mantua maker, musician, parlor, party, promenade for show; taught to speak and act and think and live and die for show'.

The First of May, the day that annual leases fell in, was a 'day of horror', the *Evening Post* declared. It was a mad moving day, everyone jockeying for the next best place; streets crowded with 'carts over-loaded with furniture and hand barrows with sofas, chairs, sideboards, looking glasses and pictures, so as to render the sidewalks almost impassable,' as John Pintard observed in 1832. Whole houses were shifted on rollers when long leases ran out and aldermen complained of the nuisance. A rainy May Day was miserable, fuelled with booze and disrupted with brawls, since old tenants were sometimes unwilling to move. John Jacob Astor, the city's landlord, went down to City Hall Park each year to watch the multitude waiting among their worldly goods. He could see for himself the crowding, the competition and the snobbery that were making his fortune. For an address was already life itself. William Bobo noted: 'The first rage was to get on the Eighth Avenue; it was gotten up on legitimate circumstances, that of the pretty locality, sites etc. The next was the Fourth Avenue; because some leading man happened to locate over on that street, property was enhanced by ten per cent in ten days; the street was settled up, when another "great" man made a purchase on the Fifth Avenue, and forthwith the rage was the Fifth; and this happening when nobody but the first class merchants and brokers could raise the wind to get out; therefore the Fifth Avenue was settled up by the rich nabobs, consequently it has kept up pretty well ever since.... The rage is now Stuyvesant Square, immediately in the neighbourhood of Hamilton Fish. His fine house and his money is enough'.

Later, Henry James in *Washington Square* has the irritating fiancé of Catherine's cousin insist: 'That's the way to live in New York – to move every three or four years. Then you always get the last thing. It's because the city's growing so quick – you've got to keep up with it. It's going straight up town – that's where New York is going.' He says he would move to the very north of Manhattan, and wait ten years for the city to reach him, but his fiancée wants neighbours: 'She says that if she's got to be the first settler she had better go out to Minnesota.'

The city had shifted from a placid hierarchy to an open and furious competition. It lacked the social giants of the 1880s and the 1890s, the Astors and the Vanderbilts of the gilded age. Old man Astor was only a city sight, the miser huddled over a table in his offices on Prince Street behind barred windows. He was famous for a memory printed with rent rolls, and he knew what was due to him any hour, any day. When he died, he left twenty million dollars, which seemed to the newspapers 'incomprehensible as infinity'. His will disposed of the equivalent of one fifteenth of all the money invested in America in sugar, ships, candles, cotton, furniture or wagons. But he was not honoured for it. He was 'Old Astor', 'Old Hunks', 'The Old Skinflint', 'Miser Astor', and, without compliment, 'the richest man in the country'. He gave $400,000 to build a library, and $60,000 for the site, and he was still thought mean. The settled wealthy of New York saw charity in the old colonial way, involving people, not just bank drafts.

His children married up, but to those whose European credentials Astor could understand. When his daughter Eliza wanted to marry a dentist, Astor cut the man and provided instead a count who was Minister of the German Free Cities at Paris. And riches were not enough sign of God's favour, not to the comfortable Knickerbockers. Philip Hone went to dinner with old John Jacob in October 1844. 'His life has been spent in amassing money and he loves it as much as ever,' Hone wrote in his diary. 'He sat at the dinner table with his head down upon his breast, saying very little and in a voice almost unintelligible, the saliva dropping from his mouth, and a servant behind him to guide the victuals which he was eating, and to watch him as an infant is watched ... the machinery is all broken up, and there are some people, no doubt, who think he has lived long enough.'

In his fine Greek house on Staten Island, Cornelius Vanderbilt had fallen in lust, this time with the governess. To simplify his life, he sent his long-suffering wife Sophia on a trip through Canada. He sat looking out at Manhattan – already a steamship millionaire, buying into railroads, set on course to be the world's richest man but still a rank outsider. His first attempt on Society had been a catastrophe. His conversation bristled with dockside words. He spat out tobacco on fine carpets. He fingered the bottoms of the prettier maids. He was, as Henry Adams said, 'not ornamental'. He retreated to the house that Sophia loved, and to the town where he had owned his first ferry-boat, a flat-bottomed periauger that plied from Staten Island to New York. But his business now was in Manhattan, and he wanted to be back at the heart of his business. In Sophia's absence, he began work on a brick and brownstone house at 10 Washington Place, between fashionable Broadway and Washington Square. When she returned, she refused to leave her comfortable life and her friends. Vanderbilt decided that the change of life had made her mad. He had her committed to the Bloomingdale Insane Asylum for not wanting to move to Manhattan. Even when the doctors refused to keep her, Sophia knew she had to bend to her husband's will.

In time, these two fortunes – the Astors' land, the Vanderbilts' railroads and steamships – will make possible the first Society wars.

It is four in the afternoon. The gaslights bend the air in some Midwestern hall. The band plays. The curtain parts. Behind the proscenium is a picture – more than half a mile of painted canvas, unrolling from one cylinder to another, the product of Lavish Spending and Seven Years' Toil: Mr Otis A. Bullard's Moving Panorama of New York City. More than a million people paid to see it on its tours in the 1850s, and paid more than $250,000 for their tickets, a quite astonishing hit. The tour was extended for another full decade. What happened in New York was brought to all America – as a show and an example.

Before your very eyes, Manhattan passes in the brilliance of fresco and the kind gaslight. A lecturer explains what you see. It is as though you are on a ferry boat slipping past the docks of West Street, or an omnibus that magically could move in the traffic jams of Broadway;

for two hours in the theatre, you take a walk that takes only three on the streets ('a little too long to be all viewed at one exhibition,' a Portland critic thought). You wonder at steamships and barges ('more than one mile of shipping!'), the floating baths and chapels; the Battery; the churches and the famous hotels and shops of BROADWAY, as the posters printed it, all excited, in THE GREAT COMMERCIAL EMPORIUM. The papers say it is certainly 'true'; you can 'trace out ... every house, sign, stall, hotel, church and public [or private] building ... from the moving throng of men, brutes and vehicles, to the stationary trees, paving stones and lamp posts'. You can recognise even the horses. But although the realism is remarkable, it is not the point; a picture teaches lessons. 'Joy of all beholders/ Bullard's panorama,' said the posters in Worcester, Mass., 'With its welcome lesson/ Truthful as a drama....' In those stuffy halls, the crowds learned pride in an all-American artefact (but made 'expressly for exhibition in Europe', to give it credentials of taste). They learned pride in the city which even the Governor of rural Vermont acclaimed as 'the great metropolis of this great Republic'.

Of all American cities, only New York sits among Bullard's catalogue of inspirational subjects. Before the Panorama, he painted Emily Dickinson, among 900 other portraits, and grand patriotic themes – 'The Last Blanket', offered by a poor widow for the cold soldiers of the Revolution – and religious themes that lent themselves to blood and chiaroscuro, like 'Judith in the Tent of Holofernes'. The National Academy showed his pictures of American manners ('John, I've Got The Rooster') and the American Art-Union gave away as a national lottery prize his picture of Ethan Allen's daughter, begging her father on her deathbed to follow her mother's Christian ways. It seems there was only one city which could follow child saints: a city worth hagiography, and a genre in itself. But New York was no national capital, full of monuments which serve as stone memos of the nation's history, presidents and wars. In New York, the show taught nothing patriotic, nothing historical; the show was the immediate life of the city. Its life was laid out to be admired as though on the rosewood and marble counters of some department store.

Reports of the city crossed the nation. The very idea of a sensationalistic newspaper was born with the city's loose women, dreadful murders, sudden fires, suicides, executions and riots as its subject (and a few curiosities; in its first two weeks in 1835, the *New York Herald* also covered kangaroo hunting). Midwestern newspapers carried more news of New York than of any other city in the nation; reporters found 'everything connected with the "London of America" fraught with interest'. California's despatches went weekly by way of steamer to Nicaragua, train to the Pacific, and steamboat again to the waiting presses.

Elizabeth Barstow Stoddard made an arrangement with the *Alta California* newspaper in San Francisco for a weekly column by 'Our Lady Correspondent'. This was remarkable since the paper specialised in dry business talk, and the occasional stolen verses, but New York life was also a serious subject, showing how to be urbane, worldly, civilised. Stoddard wrote of men who had to go East from the gold-fields of California to build status in New York on their money. The first were crude and bearded, she wrote, toting nuggets of gold and settling their bar bills in gold dust. Now they knew enough to dress finely, to wear diamonds and costly watches. When there were bills to settle, they wrote 'clean, big' cheques. They had grown almost civilised in the city. 'While [a] fight was going on, the yelling and pistol firing in the street aroused a returned Californian. . . . He got out of bed, opened the window, thrust out his head and cried: "Go it, old boys! go it; that puts me in mind of Sacramento." Whereupon he went back to bed and his innocent dreams.''

By mid-century, New York had grown big enough not just to provide a steady supply of copy, but also for its citizens to take a keyhole interest in the many parts of the town they would not dare observe for themselves. They mobbed the theatre to see *A Glance At New York in 1848*, sketches in which firemen and butchers went out spoiling for a *muss* (or fight) and city sharks set baited traps for country fools. The species of the city could be visited, as in a zoo, and observed by outsiders. Knickerbockers fretted that there was now a public arena which could judge a socialite, a patrician or an actor with equal rigour. Opinions differed on Society, whether it was a glory of the republic, consisting of the only ladies and gentlemen fit to represent America abroad, or else a undemocratic scandal. Either way, it had become a most public and political issue. Everybody watched. 'Social movement and life yesterday in the fashionable districts of the city was a little more noticeable and pronounced than on Thursday,' says a *New York Times* Society column of 1900, 'This was due to the warm weather, the passing of the rainstorm'. Outsiders were as involved as insiders.

'Self-advertisement,' Mrs John King Van Rensselaer sniffed of

1920s' Society. She quite mis-remembered that 'years ago, it also stood for breeding'. But breeding was never the point of Society, as opposed to the Knickerbocker social round. Visibility was. Money, charity, glamour, status had to stand a very public test, since there was no other available – no king, no court, no Versailles. This notion confused outsiders. Salomon de Rothschild wrote home in the 1850s that 'this country is too much in love with great names, lofty titles, decorations – in a word, everything that glitters to the eye – to be able to keep its democratic government for long'. He discovered 'the strangest and often the most unjust social system possible'. 'I have seen few countries,' he wrote, 'where society is more exclusive, and this exclusiveness is founded on nothing at all. Wealth, political position and education are not the keys that provide admittance. One is fashionable or one is not, and the why of it is completely unknown to those who are the object of this preferment and to those who confer it'. New Yorkers suspected only a lack of subtlety. 'It's hopeless,' as a dowager says in an Edith Wharton novel, 'to expect people who are accustomed to the European courts to trouble themselves about our little republican distinctions.'

Yet taste and status were most reliable when imported. A title was a sure thing, and to be accepted by someone with a title was security. Royalty, of course, was even better. De Rothschild describes the 'frenzied "hurrahs" of the good republicans' when the Prince of Wales arrived at the Academy of Music one October night in 1860. New York gave 'the greatest ball ever' for the Prince, an event which quite scuppered Knickerbocker reticence and upstaged the still small scale of the new men's parties. 'By ten o'clock, people were stationing themselves along the curbstones of Broadway ... one long dense mass of impatient humanity,' George Templeton Strong wrote in his diary. 'Great care had been taken,' De Rothschild noticed, 'to leave out all the authorities, so as not to give the young Prince any sight of the "aldermen and common men of the council."' Instead, the grandees paraded, wonderfully dressed. Nathalie Dana's mother remembered 'a young lady's hair adorned with a pair of antlers from whose points shot flames fed by a small tank concealed in the vast folds of her hoop skirt'. Even Ward McAllister, later the chamberlain at the court of the great Mrs Astor, made social *faux pas*, trying to crash the supper room; 'the vigilant eye of John Jacob Astor [III] met mine. He bid me wait my turn'. Starch and skirts rustled into silence; the band played 'God Save the Queen' and 'Hail Columbia!' 'The last note had barely died,' De Rothschild wrote, 'when the floor, over-loaded with the enormous crowd that had pushed forward to see the Prince, collapsed'. It took an hour and a half to repair the floor, but the crowd was as decorous as a congregation. 'After the first cry,' De Rothschild wrote, 'not a word was uttered.'

Outside this Society, William Backhouse Astor, heir to the first John Jacob, left his tenants to operate upon the city. Newcomers poured into New York and tenements were thrown up roughly and people made what life they could there. On some slums, Astor earned fifty per cent a year. On most he made fifteen to twenty per cent, which was twice what a lot on the middle-class West Side brought him. Astor always profited. If buildings began to decay, then poorer tenants and many more of them could be crammed inside, even dere-licts curled out of the cold in the hallways at three cents a night.

When he was sixteen, in 1853, John Pierpont Morgan went to London, the gentleman's city. He heard a sermon at St Paul's. He went to Buckingham Palace. At the Bank of England, he ran his hands over a million pounds in gold bullion. He was inducted into all the right attitudes for the model of a Knickerbocker survivor. Old Money still clings to his memory.

The true sign of Morgan's authority was his nose. It was bloated and ribbed with acne like some ruined fruit. In photographs it was almost always air-brushed. 'I have never met anyone so attractive,' his last mistress, Lady Victoria Sackville-West wrote in her diary, adding inevitably, 'One forgets his nose entirely after a few minutes.' Only great power could overcome such a handicap because, as Edith Wharton observed, 'In that simple society there was an almost pagan worship of physical beauty, and the first question asked about any youthful newcomer on the social scene was invariably: "Is she pretty?" or: "Is he handsome?" – for good looks were as much prized in young men and maidens'. 'A homely man had no chance of being selected a Morgan partner,' one of his earlier biographers wrote. His partner Robert Bacon was known on Wall Street as 'the Greek God', and the Street said Morgan had 'fallen in love' with him. Sickness and imperfection were not tolerated. Grand New Yorkers were sent abroad to die; 'the Protestant grave-yards of Rome and Pisa were full of New York names'.

Otherwise, Morgan fitted. He was the descendant of a Welshman who landed in America only a decade after the Mayflower, and spawned a hymn-singing, Gospel-hungry line of gentry. J.P. Morgan grew up a decorous Episcopalian, a true son of the church that cut the vulgar bits from the marriage service, but also believing every word of the Bible. He startled fellow travellers on the Nile by pointing out the exact spot where Moses had been plucked from the bulrushes. His grandfather left the family farm and founded the Aetna Insurance Company. His father set up in the kind of dry goods business which, because it had to finance producers and sometimes buyers, turned logically into a merchant bank. Junius Morgan came to the attention of old man George Peabody, an American banker in London, and became his partner and his heir.

Business went easily. The Crimean War forced up the price of American wheat and American railroad shares; in a decade, investors found a billion dollars to build new track, investment on a scale nobody had imagined before with extraordinary risks and returns. The railroad business changed New York. It brought authentic riches made in stock markets, and fortunes made from laying track. At the heart of all this was J.P. Morgan – for thirty years, his father's man in New York City.

Capital flooded from Europe to America for the rest of the century; the Morgans advised it, represented it, dispersed it and took their great authority from it. They were translators – turning European funds into American cornfields and railroads and corporations, old money into new, and the rough process of making money into something clubbable and gentlemanly. If Morgan later had to seize control of whole railroads, or act as a central bank, or single-handedly salvage the gold standard (as he did in 1895) it was always for some high professional purpose and not just for a profit. If America went into a slump, as in 1893, and there were riots in the streets and a line of failed corporations, Morgan took on the duty of salvage and just happened to acquire perpetual clients; General Electric was tied to Morgan's by a rescue.

He profited when family fortunes turned into public companies – when the Vanderbilts were bullied into selling more shares in their railroads in 1879, and Morgan placed a quarter of a million without spoiling the price; and, much later, when Carnegie's steel companies and the others were put into the great paper empire of US Steel. Morgan, like a lawyer, used who he knew and what he knew to make the deals. Only the young men about town, flush from the dealing, called themselves 'financiers'. He made money professional, which sat well with Old New York which had, as Edith Wharton reported, 'a tranquil disdain for mere money getting'.

His alchemy began with the Civil War. The dollar sank and, with it, the fixed incomes of Old New York. Edith Wharton's father leased his country and town houses to the next wave of new men and went away to a life in hotels. The war had stopped the effects of the panic of 1857, and it produced the bull market of 1862 – when brokers could earn from $800 to $10,000 a day in commissions, and it sometimes seemed as though 'the entire population of the country entered the field'. Prices of any stock could be massaged or ramped or collapsed. The Common Council of New York went short of some 50,000 shares in the Harlem Railroad, anticipating their own decision to take away its franchise.

Such markets produced extraordinary fortunes, which seemed to rise overnight and to operate at one remove from economic reality; so that the quick expansion of railways turned into corners in railway shares, and bear raids and manipulation. But the money, while it lasted, was real. The old guard were forced to acknowledge interlopers rich enough to replace them. 'When I was a girl,' says Mrs Archer in *Age of Innocence*, 'we knew everybody between the Battery and Canal Street; and only the people one knew had carriages. It was perfectly easy to place anyone then; now one can't tell, and I prefer not to try'.

Families that were famous in the 1840s seemed to disappear within fifty years. The webs of cousinage were lost – the bonds between clans, and between clans and their legendary founders, the one who signed the Constitution or settled in New Amsterdam or was granted a county or two in the seventeenth century. The new men began to assume other people's history. Wharton was dining at a nouveau table when she was offered some of 'the famous Newbold madeira' as a kind of trophy. She was a woman of manners and she did not say that the wine came from her own late father's cellar.

To rich New Yorkers, the Civil War was about keeping the wide American market open for them all; they opted for the Union because the Union was the best hope of peace and money-making, and being on the right side had its privileges. They were nicely detached from duty. Years later, some of the 'better' families would shuffle their feet embarrassedly if asked what their young men did during the Civil War. They ran the insurance companies which prospered, or the banks which paid dividends of seven per cent and more. They dealt in grain and flour that were still going abroad. The cotton trade was closed, but they took over the tobacco business; the Dukes of Durham came to New York to make the first, experimental cigarettes. J.P. Morgan's main contribution to the war effort was the six-fold profit he took on buying Union guns, having them rifled and selling them back to the Union.

When the war was done, financial power had slipped to New York from Boston and Philadelphia, even the specialised business of raising cash for the government. The Philadelphia Drexels came asking to marry Morgan's firm, because they needed him. Morgan bustled into the rambunctious age of railways and the property boom they spread across America, mile by iron mile. He was a fine robber baron, big-fisted and alarming, and when he ceased taking any exercise at all on doctor's orders, he filled out to a sleek and ominous tycoon. He kept the cloak of a gentleman. He stayed obstinately in Murray Hill, while the newcomers dashed to Fifth Avenue. By the 1870s, he was stranded between 'Aristocracy to the south, and Money to the north' and he did not care. He found the new social whirl rather prissy and pretentious. He liked provincial grandeur, not city chic. A deliberately dowdiness was a sign of status, just as much as a choker of diamonds. The old Opera House was preferred to the new precisely because it was small and inconvenient, and kept out newcomers. A woman wore her wedding dress to the opera for the first few years of marriage, because it was far too expensive to be set aside. Paris dresses were tugged from the tissue paper in the trunk that arrived once a year, but then set aside for a season – two, if your family was from Boston – so as not to appear excessively fashionable. Only Caroline Belmont had the clout to defy the rule.

Yet dress always mattered. In an unstable city, it was proof of willingness to follow the rules. 'It's their armour,' Newland Archer thinks in *The Age of Innocence,* riding at the side of his rather unsatisfactory wife, 'their defence against the unknown and their defiance of it.' The look of everything mattered. The ancient gag about ladies who draped the naughty legs of their pianos probably began with a wit called John van Buren in New York; Mrs Cruger did make aprons out of pocket handkerchiefs for the Diana, Apollo and Venus in her salon. Society withdrew for the summer to Newport, and in the afternoons ladies with card-case in hand went the rounds of fashionable houses, asking for each other. By the 1880s, younger women simply drove around leaving their cards, the upper left-hand corner properly turned down, without bothering whether the hostess might be waiting in her drawing room or not. These senior ladies made their servants list those 'who did not ask', and struck them from the next season's invitation lists; which was no bother, since they were always the duller hostesses.

Grief and love were policed with rules laid out in Edith Wharton's novels. Widowhood meant black, as long as 'the most intolerant censor in the family decreed'. Any death invoked 'inexorable laws ... three crepe-walled years for a parent, two for sister or brother, at least twelve solid months of black for grandparent or aunt, and half a year (to the full) for cousins, even if you counted them by the dozens. ...' It was scandal if a sister's veil, worn for a lost brother, was shorter than those which hid her sisters-in-law. As for love, it was organised as soon as it became official. A couple might have played as children, and been born to parents who played as children, but once the engagement was announced, they did not know each other. Headlong engagements were never known, let alone runaway marriages. These were people who 'dreaded scandal more than disease, who placed decency above courage, and who considered that nothing was more ill-bred than "scenes", except the behaviour of those who gave rise to them'.

The city was set up for discretion. J.P. Morgan lived his life in his seventeen gentlemen's clubs. He had yachts always called *Corsair* for entertaining offshore ladies. He liked the company of sharp-witted, lively women, especially the swan-necked actress Maxine Elliott. He was once the rival of Diamond Jim Brady for the favours of the great Lillian Russell. There is a Street joke of the 1900s in which a chorine, thinking of Morgan's vast and acneous nose, says she thinks it's nothing to find a pearl in an oyster: 'I got a whole diamond necklace out of an old lobster.' But this life was private. Charles Schwab of US Steel went on a very public racket in the South of France and, on his return, boasted to Morgan that he had never been hypocritical, or done things behind closed doors. 'That,' Morgan snapped, 'is what doors are for.'

Old New York never did too much good. They liked Morgan's air of being habitual with money, but they were doubtful of his flamboyant spending on art, and sometimes charity – sweeping into a Harvard meeting, demanding to see plans for a medical school, pointing to the three buildings he would finance for a million and sweeping out. Old New York thought charities rather a bore and the Society for the Prevention of Cruelty to Animals, for example, much too new to be respectable. Edith Wharton observed that 'they viewed with instinctive distrust anything likely to derange their habits, diminish their comfort, or lay on them any unwonted responsibilities, civic or social; and slow as their other mental processes were, they showed a supernatural quickness in divining when a seemingly harmless conversation might lead them into "signing a paper", backing up even the mildest attempt at municipal reform. . . .' The charity and responsibility of newcomers like the Rockefeller clan were as disturbing as their obstinate shabbiness. Power, to Old New York, could not wear suits as shiny as John D. Rockefeller, nor dine on bread and milk. The narrow Rockefeller brownstone had only one extravagance – a yard that could be flooded in winter as a skating rink, where Rockefeller took his early morning turn on the ice, under the new-fangled blue-white of electric light, in greatcoat and silk hat.

Knickerbocker families were lucky that the city produced newcomer generations in need of mansions and homes. In the 1880s, just when the newcomers might have swamped them all, there was a convenient surge in property prices which made the smallest of Manhattan country estates into a fortune. New men were ready to learn the old guard's ways, and to marry for the sake of a solid social foundation. 'The daughters of his own race,' Ralph Marvell observes in *The Custom of the Country* from the heights of his old colonial lineage, 'sold themselves to the Invaders; the daughters of the Invaders bought their husbands as they bought an opera box. It ought all to have been transacted on the Stock Exchange.' The banks remained almost incestuous in their shared directorships, as endogamous on the board as in the marriage bed.

But even J.P. Morgan found someone to fear: the Jews. He proposed a merger with Barings in London to bring two Protestant houses together, 'the only two,' as he thought, 'composed of white men in New York'. He would have been furious to know that the people on the streets, if they thought about it at all, assumed that since J.P. Morgan was a rich banker, he must also be a Jew. Grand gentiles shared Morgan's nervousness. 'The Crowd', the Strauses and Loebs, Goldmans and Sachses, Schiffs, Lehmans, Lewisohns, were rich and cultivated, able to challenge the Morgans and their friends on matters of art, patronage, manners or cash. Indeed, the congruity between Knickerbockers and the great German Jewish families only made the separation of the two seem more essential. In the eighteenth century, Abigail Franks' best friends were Fanny Moore, wife of the merchant and politician Colonel Johnson and Fanny Riggs, daughter of the Commissioner of Indian Affairs. She dined with the Governor and Mrs Cosby. One of her nine children married a De Lancey, and another an Evans of Philadelphia. By every important Knickerbocker test – the family alliances by marriage, the social circle, the easiness with rulers of the colony and the time spent living there – she was an insider. Yet she did not have to be, as did some twentieth-century Jews, unJewish in order to be accepted; she was actively involved with Jewish education in the town.

This ease disappeared by the late nineteenth century. In summer, at Saratoga Springs, the rich stayed only at the United States Hotel or the Grand Union; Elizabeth Drexel Lehr remembered placards at both doors which read 'No Jews or Dogs Admitted Here'. Joseph Seligman was a serious candidate for the Cabinet, and one of the most powerful bankers in America; but he was refused a room in Saratoga because he was a Jew. Anti-Semitism concentrated not on the very obvious newcomers on the Lower East Side, but on men and women who were not different enough to be pushed away on account of dress, manners, talk or connections. 'The Crowd' cared generously for their own community, just as Old New York once did for theirs. The Temple worship of the most successful German Jews became churchified in America; men prayed bare-headed, which was unthinkable in Europe. Temple Emmanu-El on Fifth Avenue is like a cathedral with a fine rose window. Its rabbi was imported to preach in correct British tones. Reform Judaism abolished in America the old-fashioned notion that a rabbi should rule a congregation. As for the armour of Society, 'the Crowd' told their girls to avoid gaudy dress, which looked too 'ethnic'. They handed their children to German nannies for a regimen of cold baths, shame, and belts and restraints to keep eyes on homework. The townhouse of Ben Guggenheim looked like some Adirondack lodge, its gloom shadowed with stuffed things, including a bear whose startling red tongue sometimes fell to the floor.

But 'the Crowd' was still limited to a specifically Jewish world, concentrated on making clothes, running stores and finance. On Wall

Street, gentile and Jewish firms had quite different politics. Kuhn Loeb, under the stiff-necked Jacob Schiff, financed Japan against Russia in 1904, remembering the pogroms and calling the Czar 'the enemy of mankind'. Jack Morgan gave credit to the Romanovs. Morgans had financed the French against the Prussians in 1870, and refused to do business with the newly united Germany. Schiff, the grandest of the Jewish bankers, raised money for the Germans until war broke out in 1914, when he dutifully stopped speaking German to his family in public. Society itself was a gentile show. The social life of 'the Crowd', one insider observed, was 'based only on family and on a quiet enjoyment of the people we loved'. Astors, Vanderbilts and such were known for 'publicity, showiness, cruelty and striving'.

One family did cross the line: the Guggenheims. They were richer, Swiss and not German, manufacturers and not rivals to the Wall Street gentiles, although old man Meyer kept an office at Albert Loeb's finance house. 'The Crowd' had reservations about the 'Googs'. Meyer was always dusted with cigar ash, his wife Barbara was never chicly dressed, and their entire dinner talk seemed to consist of little Swiss-German proverbs ('Roasted Pigeons,' Meyer would say, 'Do Not Fly Into Your Mouth'; it was not a kind conversational opening). Their boys, though, came to know the Whitneys and Roosevelts and Harrimans and Lindberghs; one of their grandsons, Harry, was even elected to the New York Jockey Club. Had others tried to bridge the gap between Jewish and gentile society, most likely there would only have been more pointed talk about Jewish social climbing. This myth sounded particularly hollow on the tongues of social Alpinists. Even the sympathetic Edith Wharton singles out a Jew in *The House of Mirth* for playing precisely the game that all of sudden money was playing. Sim Rosedale puts 'Wall Street under obligations which only Fifth Avenue could repay'. He is on charitable boards, at banquets for distinguished strangers; 'his candidacy at one of the fashionable clubs was discussed with diminishing opposition'. 'All he now needed was a wife whose affiliations would shorten the tedious steps of his ascent' – Lily Bart, a Protestant and an Anglo-Saxon with a remnant of the right connections.

But Wharton is shrewd. A real-life Sim Rosedale would have had the same marriage problem. Well brought-up girls from the grand Jewish families dreamed of foreign suitors, preferably dukes with cash; Eleanor Guggenheim married the son of the Earl of Castle Stewart, and everyone approved. But they more usually married into the cousinage of German Jewry, a limited circle. What they could not do respectably was marry down, to a new man like Sim Rosedale. Alva Bernheimer married Bernard Gimbel, of the store-owning family, and was considered déclassé, unable to raise her husband's chances. The attitude exactly reflected Old New York's horror of the retail trade.

Society did worry at the change in the city, the alien faces on the streets – Italian or Jewish or other. When Henry James came home from his English exile, he was horrified by the Lower East Side, a 'Jerusalem disinfected'; he feels 'at the bottom of some vast sallow aquarium in which innumerable fish, of over-developed proboscis, were to bump together, for ever, amid heaped spoils of the sea'. He feels, in short, drowned. Because he writes of 'a Jewry that has burst its bounds', he shows that he thinks the newcomers should be confined, and their settled cousins, too.

There is a monument to this panic in a most surprising place. Walk through the New York Zoological Society in the Bronx, and you walk through the fears of Old New York in the 1890s. The zoo was a notion of Theodore Roosevelt's hunting buddies in the Boone and Crockett Club. All the original animals of Manhattan were to roam there, with elephants standing in for mastodons. The zoo was America on an island, free from the vulgar commerce that had cut down the buffalo herds, culled the beavers, poisoned the wild where Roosevelt liked to test his mettle, and, worse yet, imported the cheap foreign labour that now crammed the tenements. These newcomers were the zoo's enemies. Its first director, William Hornaday, battled neighbourhood Italians, who liked to shoot the song-birds and take firewood. He cursed 'the low-lived beasts who appreciate nothing and love filth and disorder'.

The more the threat, the more imperial grew the zoo's exaltation of an old America. Wild meadows were planned, but a Court of Honour was added, based on the 1893 Columbian Exposition in Chicago, the plasterboard show which glorified the first, white Europeans to arrive in America, and taught their descendants a taste for marble and Beaux Arts columns. The wild was boxed up to show man's superior ways and, by extension, man's superiority to other men. Later, the zoo-keepers would spell all this out, praising the 'Nordic' tradition of America – which oddly included Jesus, the French Huguenots and the Irish – and suggesting a bar against 'worthless race types' and mass sterilisation for those already arrived. For the moment, the zoo simply imported Ota Benga, a pygmy, in 1906 and put him in the monkey house with a specimen card. You could go to see humans in fairgrounds – at Dreamland on Coney Island you could meet a Filipino village, imperial tribute brought back from a new American colony, and an Eskimo village; in Barnum's museums, fifty years before that, you could pay to see a live Chinese family – but here in the zoo, Ota Benga was a specimen whose standing was enforced by science and taxonomy. There were passionate black protests. The zoo, shamed, took to saying that Ota Benga had been 'hired' because he was so good with the chimpanzees.

William Backhouse Astor died in 1875, the last Astor who was all wrapped up in leases. One son, John Jacob III, was a beanpole of a man, not clever, who fussed over the books and edited telegrams for the sake of saving pennies; but even he was becoming a touch aristocratic. 'Work hard,' he once said, 'but never work after dinner.' William Backhouse Junior, the other son, was brighter, but he was an indeterminate sort; he had the physical clout of his family but none of their drive. John Jacob kept him out of the office and William Backhouse did not complain. He did not even like the city. He had an estate up the Hudson at Rhinecliff, and he spent his time there among his racing horses and his green conservatories. But William Backhouse changed Society in his absence. He married a Schermerhorn, and that marriage gave Society its most solid institution: *the* Mrs Astor.

Nobody was ever quite sure if Caroline Schermerhorn married William Backhouse or his fortune, but it was a persistent marriage. She heard talk of William's showgirl lovers, and the wild parties on his yacht, and politely said only that she was so sorry to be such a bad sailor. She had a clear sense of her own worth: as a Schermerhorn, from an old Knickerbocker family, it was she who brought glory to the Astors, and they must never forget it. She would sail in Society as an agent of the old guard, but spending the newcomers' money. August and Caroline Belmont had lost their daughter Jeannie and both of them were distraught. Caroline Belmont abandoned public life. There was no more Queen of New York Society. Sensible Caroline Schermerhorn, with her ski-slope nose and her thin lips and her plumply reassuring bosom – 'really homely, no looks at all,' said a disloyal niece – was a quite different presence from Caroline Belmont, but she stepped in.

She invented a role much needed by those who could never tell if they had properly arrived, or had some way to go, or what rules applied. Even those excluded by Mrs Astor were grateful to know where they stood. Invitations to her annual ball were essential; if the card did not arrive, doctors suddenly diagnosed a need to be out of town, the telegraph office delivered news of a dead relative, anything for an alibi. Nobody who worked for a living could expect to be invited nor any of the new millionaires who made their money from railroads. Ladies vied for a seat on the red silk divan from which Mrs Astor watched the dancing. A Drexel ran sobbing from the room when she did not find a place-card with her name on the divan. One matron could never be told she was excluded, and socially ruined, just for the regal scale of her hips.

The divan was 'the Throne'. Mrs Astor's dinners were 'state dinners'. Mrs Astor's presence was as thunderous as royalty's. She was never seen in a hotel until she was seen sensationally at the Bradley Martin's costume ball, in white satin and her famous pearls. 'I never dreamed,' wrote one columnist, 'that it would be given to me to gaze on the face of an Astor in a public dining room.' There was even a role for a 'Mrs Astor' when the real Mrs Astor would not think of being present. At the notorious, promiscuous masked ball at Madison Square Gardens, a woman sat in the Astor box. She sat unmasked, wearing black satin and gloves to the elbow and crusted with diamonds, accepting the formal homage of hundreds of men. The 'Mrs Astor' was otherwise Miss Western, one of the town's more elegant madams.

In all this, Mrs Astor had an ally: a dumpy, balding man with a brambly moustache and a bright, fake English accent, who made a career of ingratiating. Ward McAllister had only a million in capital, and considered himself among the genteel poor. He had no intention of losing his social standing. He climbed by the side of Mrs Astor, helping her winnow her guest lists, proposing protocols and manners, acting as a chamberlain and a secretary and an advisor. He was also the publicist who made sure everyone knew that Mrs Astor mattered. He was so useful that Mrs Astor failed to notice that her prime defence against social climbing was himself a quite spectacular social climber, a man reporting what he could remember of French and English manners. He had once, he said, seen the dining table laid at Windsor

Castle. He laid down his habits as social rules: serve champagne with flecks of ice in it, serve hot salmon only in spring, hire only Swedish cooks (cleaner, more economical), consider the first offers of marriage because they are usually the best, avoid conspicuous jealousy and do not cut a shabby man with a pedigree – 'it is better to cross the street and avoid meeting him'. He elevated soup to a weapon of social war – 'I myself once lost a charming friend by giving a better soup than he did' – although he also had to acknowledge that soup had its practical difficulties in rough New York: 'Our servants are oftentimes unskilled, and have a charming habit of occasionally giving ladies a soup shower bath'.

Mrs Astor had the income to hear only his compliments. She was his 'Mystic Rose', an extraordinary title usually reserved for the Virgin Mary. She was 'a great personage (representing a silent power that had always been recognised and felt in this community, so long as I remember, by not only fashionable people, but by the old quiet element as well)'. She agreed with him that men should dominate Society, but only if she could dominate the men. When the first guests arrived at a party, Mrs Astor set McAllister aside like a servant.

She shared one of his principles: that her Society would be defined by exclusion. He trimmed her guest list to four hundred names – the famous 400 of the Social Register – on the reasonable argument that 'outside that number, you strike people who are either not at ease in a ballroom or else make other people not at ease'. Mrs Astor's ballroom was big enough for a thousand on a crowded night, but in legend it held only 400 and every socialite was required to lay siege.

You qualified by being qualified, nothing else; there had to be consensus. McAllister ruled that you could safely invite someone you had met in four good houses; 'then you can make advances to them without the danger of making a mistake'. But he was always concerned to control 'the money power', the Astor in Caroline Schermerhorn Astor, that might otherwise cut out the McAllisters of New York. In his memoirs, he writes that in 1862 'there were not more than one or two men in New York who spent, in living and entertaining, over sixty thousand dollars a year. There were not half a dozen *chefs* in private families in this city. Compare those days to these and see how easily one or two men of fortune could then control, lead and carry on society, receive or shut out people at their pleasure.' When McAllister devised the Patriarchs' Ball in 1873, for twenty-five grandees and their guests, the secret was 'making it extremely difficult to obtain an invitation', so that 'one might be sure that anyone repeatedly invited to them had a secure social position'. But the Patriarchs could no longer exclude the moneyed, as the City Ball had tried in 1841. McAllister reckoned it took four generations to make a gentleman, but there were two third-generation Astors among his twenty-five.

He tried to make his world important by shouting about it. 'The surprise to me,' Ward McAllister wrote, 'is that in this city our clever-est men and politicians do not oftener seek society and become its brilliant ornaments. They should know that there is no power like the social power; it makes and unmakes.' He saw the city changing around him, and he set out to recruit for his Society. He courted families that Mrs Astor flatly rejected. He gave dinners for the rough old Commodore Vanderbilt, announcing that he was 'one of America's most noble and cultivated men', a startling thought, as well as 'the richest man in the United States if not in the world'. McAllister wooed with good soup and canvasback ducks and fine wines; he remembered Vanderbilt saying, 'My young friend, if you go on giving dinners like this, you need have no fear of planting yourself in this city.' Mrs Astor intensely disliked the Belmonts, even standing godparent to the child that Oliver Belmont disowned, but McAllister cultivated August. It was a basic miscalculation. McAllister thought sociability and social climbing were the same thing. When McAllister wanted support for a ball that would spite some social faction, Belmont sniffed, 'I certainly prefer their good will to McAllister's.'

Newcomers were arriving in the city, steel magnates and railroad kings who had piles of cash from selling shares in their plant and tracks and engines. They respected Mrs Astor because she was there; but they reckoned she was not very much fun. Dinner was as formal as a service. You arrived ten minutes after the appointed hour, which usually would be 8.30. In the gentleman's cloakroom each male guest was handed a stiff envelope containing a card, with the name of the woman he would take into dinner. If he knew the lady, he would ignore her studiously, and if he did not, he would frantically try to identify her. At table you could discuss books, provided you kept to plot and character, or paintings or the opera or even politics, at least as far as politics affect stocks. At the end of dinner the ladies retreated to the drawing room to smoke cigarettes and talk frocks, the gentle-men to the library for cigars and sudden, winey gusts of eloquence inspired by winning or losing in the stock market. A man and a woman could not talk unless assigned to one another. When the sexes reunited, the drawing room was full of fortune tellers and negro minstrels and mind-readers; or, on more elevated occasions, singers from the Opera and a crowd of new guests who were invited only for the music. Abruptly, the footman called for grooms and chauffeurs and the party was over.

Monday night was Mrs Astor's night at the Opera – the old, exclusive, inconvenient Opera. The audience came at eight, the overture began at 8.30 and, towards 9.15 or so, Society began to settle in the horseshoe of grand tier boxes, always before the end of the first act to cause the greatest stir, its rubies and diamonds and satin and pearls signalling to the unsocial below and the box curtains opening and closing like lighthouse beams. Any music-lover in Society took seats in the stalls. The gentlemen visited, box to box; the ladies, whose realm this was, looked on the horseshoe as a kind of social barometer – here a minor dame had captured a genuine earl that she had not paid to import, there a husband sat a box away from his newly remarried wife. It was obligatory to leave just as the hero died and it seemed all too likely the heroine would sing. 'The opera,' Ralph Pulitzer wrote, 'gives Society a point of contact, and thus of contrast with that horde against whose incursions it is its mission to defend itself'.

At a dance, each social hostess could judge, could signal promotions and subtle losses of standing, could invite some possible and worthy outsiders; even the timing of the invitations, sent out only a week or five days before the event, was a statement that this great lady feared no rivals. The first guests came at 10.30, most at 11.30; they climbed between rows of plush footmen up the grand sweep of the mansion staircase, to the stiff, straight, lacquered hostess, stuck with jewels. Beyond lay general dancing in a ballroom heavy with flowers, a hefty supper and the cotillion, a dance mercifully staggered to help the digestion. The ballroom was ringed with light chairs, each numbered, and the leader of the cotillion – the married daughter of the hostess, most times – handed slips of paper to the women to show which post they had been assigned. The most prominent chairs went to those the hostess most wanted to cultivate. Some men noticeably retreated to the library at this point, for rye or Scotch or champagne.

At each dance, the choice of partners was political, a question of which invitations might be expected. A plain girl had many partners, since no man wanted to be stuck with her. But the true ritual was the handing round of favours, pretty things whose cost was a statement of the hostess's standing; a man could give his to a woman, or a woman to a man. They left at four in the morning, with gold match-safes, jewelled scarf-pins, hand-painted fans, Dutch tiles, silver trumpets, and their precise social and sexual standing to be tallied in the carriage home.

At the heart of this world Mrs Astor stood four-square and established, a fortress to be fired on. Mrs Ogden Mills, married to a Western mining fortune but born a Livingston of grand colonial stock, fought with scorn. She invited only 200 to her dances, to prove she was the more exclusive. She said, 'There are really only twenty families in New York,' but would never give their names. The more serious threat to Mrs Astor's queendom came from the Vanderbilts, whose vast fortune eclipsed even hers, and from Alva Vanderbilt in particular. Alva came from Mobile, Alabama. During the Civil War, her parents escaped to Paris and then moved to New York with neither cash nor standing: Alva's father traded cotton with only moderate success and Alva's mother ran a boarding house. But Alva was lucky to have social friends like Consuelo Yznaga, who launched her in a rich set. She met William Kissam Vanderbilt, the Commodore's handsome grandson, and married him a year later. Even for a poor girl, it was a daring marriage. 'The Smiths of Alabama cut me dead for marrying W.K. Vanderbilt,' she said, 'because his grandfather peddled vegetables.'

Like Mrs Astor, Alva planned to live up to every cent of her husband's income. She was proud when dear Consuelo married into the English nobility, and became Lady Mandeville; she set out to live like a lady herself. She ordered a mansion on Fifth Avenue which would be 'a little Château de Blois', its white limestone glimmering among the drab, chocolate brownstone façades. Noble families across Europe were salvaged by selling her their armour, art, floors and alabaster bath-tubs. It was a monument to Alva's presence; but it could be nothing more, while Mrs Astor disapproved. Mrs Astor had a proper brownstone, which was therefore enough for a lady. Mrs Astor was a Schermerhorn, and no parvenue from Mobile could buy her way into her Society. Mrs Astor, plump and pompous, was Mrs Astor, and she had no need to deal with the likes of Vanderbilts. She did not invite them to her annual ball. When little McAllister dared to take Alva and Willy to the Patriarchs' Ball, she refused to meet them; 'People seem to be going quite wild,' she said, loudly, 'and inviting all sorts of people to their receptions.'

Mrs Astor misjudged her strength. Alva Vanderbilt retired with

Lady Mandeville and calculated the housewarming party for her new palace – 26 March 1883, because Lent was over; a fancy dress ball because society dinners were dull and windy, and Mrs Astor's own ball was never all that much fun; a party in honour of Lady Mandeville, because even the most arcane New York snob could not argue with an English title; and a Monday night, because Mrs Astor thought she owned Mondays. It was a formal challenge. She knew that Mrs Astor could defend herself. Others had been left humiliated, alone and expectant with the flowers, the band, the footmen and the red carpet. But she knew the power of publicity; after all, Mrs Astor's power and Ward McAllister's rule book were famous from the daily papers. The success of Mrs Astor's ball rested on everyone knowing that it was hard to be invited, and on the willingness of a crowd to brave the January cold and stand outside to witness Society walking the red carpet to her door. Alva understood that anyone might be curious about her new palace. People might come out of curiosity, but they would come. She read that the tailor Lanouette put 140 dressmakers to work on the costumes. She read that New York puzzled publicly over whether to appear as Marie Antoinette or Mary Stuart or Electric Light. A thousand invitations went out, and redrew the boundaries of Society; especially since Mrs Astor was not invited.

McAllister played diplomat, charming Alva, telling her how his daughter had been practising the star quadrille with Mrs Astor's last unmarried daughter. Alva listened, and regretted that the girls should have been to such trouble, and been fitted for such frocks; for she could not invite them. She had never been received by Mrs Astor. McAllister could only acknowledge that Alva knew Mrs Astor's rules. He found his Mystic Rose all red and angry. She, the arbitrix, had been humiliated. Worse, she knew she would have to capitulate. Young Carrie Astor could not be kept out of such an event. The Astor carriage was despatched to 660 Fifth Avenue; a footman took in the card, inscribed only 'Mrs Astor'. The next morning, Alva delivered invitations to the Astor mansion. Mrs Astor acknowledged that 'it was time for the Vanderbilts', that America had made them, and provided they were mannerly, they had better be accepted. But Alva Vanderbilt had done much more than infiltrate. She had scuppered any one woman's pretensions to hold Society in her gift.

On her night, there were swords clanking on the stone steps and chandeliers brilliant in the great hall, and a tropical forest of ferns and palms in the great gymnasium of the house. Joan of Arc followed

Mme le Diable, trimmed with the heads and horns of demons; there was a King Lear and a Christopher Columbus, a sheik, a Dutch maiden and Mary, Mary Quite Contrary, all careful not to arrive too early or seem too eager, and jammed in the crush of carriages waiting their turn at the long red carpet. It was a procession of ghosts, of the rough bits of what every educated American could remember of the past, of books, of other countries, all gloriously jumbled; the limits of imagination went dancing together. It was proper, because it could be judged against a European standard; nobility was there. And finally, there was Mrs Astor, dressed as a Venetian princess and 'borne down by a terrible weight of precious stones'. Mrs Astor and Mrs Vanderbilt met as equals, and in dauntingly similar frocks.

After that moment, there would be other leaders of Society, but they could never legislate for Society; usually, they were the relicts of a faded way of doing things, still respected, but not obeyed – a Mrs Vanderbilt in the last Fifth Avenue mansion when the other grandees had retreated into apartment blocks that could be defended, a Mrs Astor in the 1980s who generously found newcomers 'fun', and was herself regarded by socialites who looked at bloodlines rather than fortune as a social climber.

The Mrs Astor smiled, and a queendom fell.

Society needed Stanford White. He was a rush of a man, risky in his ways and given when thinking about some architectural problem to such eager twisting of his red moustaches that junior draughtsmen had to brush away the bits of broken hair from their drawings. The moralist Anthony Comstock once thought he could seek out vice by renting an apartment close to White's. For Sunday dinner at Sherry's, White was 'outrageously badly dressed, his untidy shock of red hair looking as though it had not had a comb passed through it for a week. . . . "It never takes me more than five minutes to dress," he remarked.' He was the licensed genius. He built the mansions that spelled out who and what Society was.

White was not unlike the clients for whom his firm, McKim, Mead and White, built fine houses. He had to jump classes to join Society. His father was an Anglophile academic, shabby genteel, a man who spent his life in search of proper deference and found it only from porters at English railway stations. White started work at sixteen. He was a clubman, his real life organised around companions and shared adventures – sprees in Paris, or some dinner where a girl of sixteen sprang naked from a pie, a stuffed blackbird on her head. He was never rich enough to have a yacht like J.P. Morgan or William Backhouse Astor, but he had hidden cabinets of memories and photographs, discreet rooms scattered round the city for assignations. He also had the grand estate, the townhouse on Lexington Avenue, and the official wife: Bessie. On his design for the Washington Square Arch, the figure of War has Bessie's features.

His job was building histories for his clients. Robber barons filled their dark halls with the dull shine of proper baronial armour. There was a craze for job lots of English portraits that, hung together, could almost make a family. August Belmont had been able to re-invent himself when he landed in New York, but that was long ago, and besides he had the credentials of Rothschilds' man. Credentials now had to be bought. In J.P. Morgan's art collection were a bit of Napoleon (his watch), Leonardo (his notebooks), George Washington (a five-page letter), Shakespeare (the first folio), eleven of the Caesars on coins, and jewels that once belonged to the Medici. The more circumstantial detail, the better: 'There can hardly be too much in a room,' wrote one decorator of the 1880s, 'granted that it is possible to move about.'

White, too, was a kind of collector – he brought back a 'mosque full of tiles' from Istanbul, 'broken china' from Rome – but his true claim on the past was the new houses. They have the didactic purpose of those exemplary antique torsos beloved of Florentine dukes; put together, they claim a Renaissance is happening, and its taste is certified by being old and proper. White bought the ceiling of a Venetian palace and adjusted Henry Poor's house on Gramercy Park until it fit. He built a whole 'palace of the Doges' for the bile-tongued, imperious Mrs Stuyvesant Fish, who married a railroad and wanted a house which would be 'an uncomfortable place for anyone without breeding'. It was as though the Doges had commissioned Titian and Veronese just to camouflage the roots of their fortune in something as mundane as double-entry bookkeeping.

White built the Italian Renaissance for the Pulitzers, who had to rebuild because poor Joseph Pulitzer, the newspaper magnate, needed absolute quiet for sleep and could not tolerate the noise of a sump pump and an elevator. For some younger Vanderbilts, he recreated a miniature French château. For the king of street railways, William

Collins Whitney, he built 'a veritable patchwork of European castles'. The great rival of White's firm was Richard Hunt, who had studied at the Ecole des Beaux Arts in Paris and was drenched in a proper historicism; he had even finished Lefuel's design for the Pavillon de la Bibliothèque of the Louvre. He had proper European credentials; he could sing all the words of the 'Marseillaise'. White, on the other hand, was a showman with a library, who could put together enough that was recognisable from the past to make a point. His own entrance hall in Manhattan held four sarcophagi and an antique altar, pieces which had lost all their meaning except for being old.

These houses were a woman's domain. 'To a woman a home is a necessity,' *the* Mrs Astor once wrote, 'not so for a man, whose life is so free and independent.' Mrs White mostly stayed at home, flanked by the wide, completed lawns of Box Hill, and she had time to make useful lists in the hope of self-improvement – bleak lists, to be learned by heart, of the Kings of England, the Presidents of the United States, the signs of the Zodiac, the 'Best Books in Chronological Order'. Other ladies used a little hashish to pass the day or prepare for a ball. When drink was barred from Newport, the wives still had their chosen comforters – chloral hydrate or, better still, chloroform. The gentlemen had their clubs and yachts and business. The ladies needed a little comfort.

Harry Lehr was perhaps the first great 'walker', full of breathy admiration for the social ladies, mother-fixated and willing to live off his wits. He came to New York from Baltimore, toting scrapbooks filled with glowing reviews for his soubrette roles in amateur operetta. He was a meticulous charmer and he very soon discovered a whole career in being noticeable. Because his guests were grand and famous, Delmonico's and the Waldorf never charged him for a meal. Wetzel made his clothes, to dress the man who 'sets the fashion for American manhood'; Kaskel and Kaskel provided shirts and pyjamas, while asking him somehow to work into conversation the provenance of his knickers. People thought it original that he sent telegrams and not letters, but the truth was that stamps cost money while he knew the wives of the cable magnates. He travelled always by rail, on the lines owned by the husbands of Mrs Fish, Mrs Vanderbilt or Mrs Gould. For pocket money, the wine merchant George Kessler paid him $6,000 a year to sell his champagne. He filled up the Astors' cellars.

When he decided to marry, he needed a woman that Society could approve. He chose Elizabeth Drexel of the Philadelphia banking family. He investigated her money meticulously. He laid siege to her. Before he would commit himself, he took her to lunch with Mrs Astor, Mrs Stuyvesant Fish, Mrs Oerlichs and Mrs Oliver Belmont, the dragons of the social world. He was happy only when Mrs Oerlichs whispered: 'We four are going to take her up. We will make her the fashion. You need have no fear. . . .' As for Elizabeth Drexel herself, almost an afterthought in this marriage, she was both dazzled and amused. Harry was wonderfully direct. He said out loud how he made his living, and he said he would need an allowance once he was married. 'There seems to be every chance of our combined happiness and peace,' she wrote. On her wedding night, she dressed beautifully, diamonds on her rose brocade. She ordered a supper of caviar, quails in aspic, champagne. 'I wanted us both to remember this evening all our lives.' But her maid came in and said that Mr Lehr had ordered dinner in his own room.

A few minutes later, Harry stomped in, pale and unsmiling, like a man who has been disturbed in his bath by a salesman. He laid out his terms. He promised only to be respectful, attentive and seemingly devoted in their public life. 'When we are alone,' he said, 'I do not intend to keep up the miserable pretence, the farce of love and sentiment.' She asked why he had married her, and he said: 'I married you because the only person on earth I love is my mother. I wanted above everything to keep her in comfort. Your father's fortune will enable me to do so.'

Elizabeth Drexel suffered her *mariage blanc* for twenty-eight years, smiling always, for fear of the social dragons. If she crossed Harry Lehr, they would surely turn her out of Society. If she divorced him, she thought she would be finished. Alva Vanderbilt managed to divorce Willie and marry Oliver Belmont, but she had the temperament of a pioneer; 'I was the first girl of my "set" to marry a Vanderbilt,' she once said. 'Then I was the first society woman to ask for a divorce, and within a year ever so many others had followed my example. They had been wanting divorce all the time'. Elizabeth Drexel only persisted. She knew everyone, went everywhere, engaged in 'deadly earnest business', as Ralph Pulitzer said, like those women and men 'who make of Society a responsibility from which there is no relaxation, a pastime from which there is no leisure'. She presided over dinner parties for 150 at the St Regis Hotel – 'a record, even for New York!' – where waiters needed telephones to co-ordinate the service. Each July and August, the Lehrs went to Newport, where Harry was amusing and inventive, and Elizabeth wrote cheques. 'The only thing that you can do,' Harry bawled at her, 'is to provide me with money, which I at least have the taste to spend properly'.

Society existed only in the round of its social functions. They might look like the rituals of some deeper system, but in reality, they were Society itself. Yet this Society was taken seriously; its sophistication put New York on a level with London or Paris, and its travels made the fact visible. There were always Americans in Melton Mowbray for the English hunting season, ever since James Gordon Bennett of the *New York Herald* took Hamilton Lodge in 1877, and one of his guests announced that the town was a lunatic asylum in pink coats. The Americans were welcome for actually paying their fifty pound assessments for the Quorn. Vanderbilts stayed overnight at Blenheim Palace and deplored the plumbing. There were Americans in Paris, buying dresses at Worth in early spring, coming out as formally as they would do in New York. Society was a diplomatic fact. One night, Harry Lehr promised that a Corsican prince was coming to dinner with Mrs Stuyvesant Fish, a rather wild prince and not used to drink. At eight that evening, the doors were flung open and the guest of honour arrived: a small monkey, immaculate in evening dress, who sat between Mrs Fish and Elizabeth Lehr, who thought his manners 'compared favourably with those of some princes I have met'. But newspapers resented the ridicule – on Society's behalf, and a little on America's. 'New York society represents America in the eyes of the foreign world,' said one columnist, 'and we should behave with a becoming sense of dignity.'

Ward McAllister disapproved of foreign marriages. He preferred 'native stock' to 'importing, from time to time, various broken-down titled individuals from abroad'. But money sought titles, ruthlessly, and titles seemed to seek money, blindly. The Duke de la Torre of Spain, tall, distinguished, barely able to speak English, came visiting America on his tiny income of $4,000 a year to study military installations, so he said. Within weeks, a half-dozen heiresses were supposed to be marrying him, even Sylvia Green, daughter of the richest woman in the world, the stock market matriarch Hetty Green. The *New York World* ran pictures of all the English dukes, outlined those still available and captioned them: 'Attention American heiresses. What will you bid?'

Around the end of the century, one in ten noble marriages in England involved an American partner. Not all the wives were rich or the husbands indigent, but land reform had tampered with noble incomes, and a duke no longer always wanted a duke's daughter. In 1895, nine American fortunes married peers of the realm: a Whitney whose money came from the New York street railroads, a LaRoche, with drug money, a Rogers who was an oil baron's daughter and, most famously, Consuelo Vanderbilt. In Consuelo's case, snobbery was a prison. She was deeply in love with another man, but she took the orders of her mother Alva to marry the ninth Duke of Marlborough. Everyone knew the marriage was forced. Alva became 'perhaps the most hated woman on earth', threatened with bombs and death. A *Life* cartoon shows tall Consuelo and the tiny Duke kneeling on Cupid's coffin. The idea that dynasty should overcome romance was shocking. And when Consuelo was taken to the 'land of half-tones and shades, of mists and fleecy clouds, of damp and rain', the results were predictable. Her husband spent gloriously to establish the point of the marriage, insulted Consuelo and announced that she was 'physically repulsive to him'. After eleven years, the couple separated. By now, Alva was ready to think that perhaps she should not have forced Consuelo into marriage, but lovelessness or the wrong choice of man or the hunger for aristocracy were not the problems. Alva had become a suffragette and disapproved of any marriage at all until the sexes had been made equal.

Stanford White built both the mansions and the clubs, the women's and the men's domains. Himself, he belonged to more than fifty clubs. He was elected to the cultural Century Association which the publisher Henry Holt found full of 'simply colossal' fun, and Mark Twain called 'the most unspeakably respectable club in the United States, perhaps'; it was an honour. He built the Century a handsome, Palladian club-house, cool and elegant, on West 43rd Street. He built the Metropolitan Club, which was J.P. Morgan's answer to the blackballing conservatives of the Union Club; 'Build a club fit for gentlemen!' Morgan said, 'Damn the expense!' The Metropolitan opened during the depression winter of 1894, when the expense could not be mentioned for fear of riots.

White built the Players' Club on Gramercy Park, Edwin Booth's attempt to 'incite emulation in the "poor player" to lift up himself to a higher social grade than the Bohemian level'. He built for the theatrical Lambs, and was elected a life member. He built the Brook, named for Tennyson's brook ('I go on for ever') and intended to answer the Century's unsocial habit of sending members out into the cold streets at midnight; it was to be, White wrote to his beloved Augustus Saint-Gaudens, 'not all society men, like the Knickerbocker, or men of the world, like the Union and Metropolitan, or a degenerate lunch club like the Players, or one where mainly bum actors congregate, like the Lambs, or a Sleepy Hollow, like the Century'.

When the first women's club, the Colony, was planned for New York, White built it; and when the Harmonie needed a new building, the second for the most exclusive of Jewish clubs, he built it; and he built the Freundschaft Society, for rich families of Germany ancestry. He belonged to the Restigouche Salmon Club, which leased miles of Quebec waters; there, he built for William K. Vanderbilt one of those chiselled, raw-looking lodges, like an enlargement of a log cabin, which allowed rich men to claim the pure old and simple virtue that they usually despised. Stanford White could live all the exact little details of a man's life in his own buildings.

He even built the circus, the red and white and gold amphitheatre at Madison Square Garden, with its elegant terracotta'd tower of apartments and its very golden and very naked Diana standing on top of a shining crescent moon. In Diana's honour, Madison Square filled up with men who liked art, some with binoculars. At night, she was bathed in golden light and she could be seen from Connecticut, the first sure sighting of the city from so far. The Gardens had basement stables and an arena that could be flooded – to simulate the canals of Venice, for example, with small gondolas; the Garden was a kind of imperial Colosseum built to please imitation Medicis, as though those instructive tours of Italy had been taken at rather too sharp a pace. It was supposed to be democratic, but actually it imposed a hierarchy of fame and cash. There was the annual Chrysanthemum Show where Mrs Astor herself 'sniffed the fragrant atmosphere from a box' while Mr Morgan 'strolled around in the crowd'. There was the annual horse show, where a box and a mention in the programme cost $550 and the ladies paraded in brilliant new frocks at each performance; in the streets around the Garden all the shop windows suddenly turned blue and yellow, the show's colours, and hotels and restaurants were full of violets and chrysanthemums, the show's flowers.

In the middle of all this, the tower had rooms for artists, sculptors and Peter Cooper Hewitt, who experimented there on wireless, X-rays and the Mercury vapour lamp. White took a studio for his Manhattan *pied à terre*, which 'turned out a great success. Indeed I don't know of anything so "chic" or like it in the world,' as he told a friend. He could look down on the city and the fountains and shrubs of the roof gardens, strung at night with Chinese lanterns and electric lights: 'Fairyland,' he said.

He was murdered there.

Stanford White loved young women. He sent cabs to pick them up and took them to discreet dinners, far from the limelit lobster palaces of Longacre Square. He collected photographs and paintings of young girls. He arranged a little privacy from Colonel Mann's notorious gossip sheet, *Town Topics*. The Colonel was prepared to accept 'loans' when those involved had 'checked the galleys', and nothing, not even the Colonel's usual calculated innuendo, appeared about his creditors. White was settled in the 'ruling set', too visible for his own liking; he was working ferociously; he was deeply in debt after stock market catastrophes. He was hungry for a bit of innocence.

He met Evelyn Nesbitt, one of the famous girls from the *Floradora* show – fresh-eyed, fragile, lovely and, although she was sixteen, told by her mother to dress like a schoolgirl of thirteen. They met at the apartment he kept above the toy shop FAO Schwarz. She thought White 'splendid . . . thoughtful, sweet and kind'. He could make love to her, and he could play with her, all at once. She would sit, naked, in a red velvet swing under a painted paper parasol, and he would push her back and forth until she was soaring towards the ceiling and her bare feet broke through the paper. He was even jealous of her. 'Evelyn plays with me as a kitten might,' he told a friend. But she did not like jealousy; she had a public life and there were other men. One was Harry Thaw. The two men disliked each other at once. White was self-made, working for his living, making a life by Society's rules. Thaw was the brutish and cocaine-bright heir of a speculator in railroad and mining stocks. White had a professional position and a marriage to protect. Thaw liked to claw and whip both boys and girls, but he paid them off and avoided any consequences. Yet Thaw could marry Evelyn, and White could not. Evelyn went away to Europe with Thaw and he would cherish her and then tear her clothes and beat her and then doggedly apologise. When she came back to New

York, White was waiting. One night, he went to the Madison Square Theatre to meet her, and discovered she had already left with Thaw. At the stage door he pulled a revolver from his pocket and went into the alley bellowing: 'I will find and kill that bastard before daylight.'

Stanford White was out of control. He was heavy with debt; he collected everything he could sell in a 30th Street loft, but it burned before it could be auctioned. His friends rallied round a man who had lost both money and the lovely objects which gave him pleasure and made his name. Yet on the surface, White was as grand and as success-ful as ever. He put up elegant *palazzi* for the jewellers Tiffany's and Gorhams, and plotted a skyscraper sixty storeys high for Grand Central Station, the tallest building in the world with a folly on top: a jet of steam, lit red at night. He was commissioned by Gordon Bennett, the newspaper man, to build a bronze owl 151 feet high – a megalo-maniac mausoleum which paid homage to the line of owls with wink-ing eyes along the cornices of the *New York Herald* building; perhaps it was lucky for White that he died before the sketches could be cast. It also seems he wanted Evelyn back, a solace in his frantic life. His secretary kept a scrapbook with every story about her.

Society, like Stanford White, was unsure. There was a curious passion for Louis XVI, for the defiance and the style of a court about to be wiped away by revolution. The famous stomacher, the jewels every-one waited for *the* Mrs Astor to wear, once belonged to Marie Antoin-ette, and so did the rubies which Mrs Bradley Martin flaunted. For his notorious costume ball, James Hazen Hyde commissioned a Louis XVI Versailles in the ballroom of Sherry's restaurant. White laid a garden in the supper room, with a lawn of rose petals, and orchids and statues in the niches of the walls. Hyde brought in a theatre company, and the orchestra and *corps de ballet* from the Metropolitan Opera.

In a city of depression, torn up with violent social rifts, Hyde claimed a particular kind of social privilege. He was a prickly, domi-neering young man who cared very much about his standing. He expected his dance to cost $200,000 and Harry Lehr warned him, 'Don't let that get into the newspapers. . . .' Stanford White, looking sober and distinctly tired, found it 'a great sight, the finest and most complete thing that has ever been done here'. It was 'complete' because it made a protected world on a few floors of a Fifth Avenue building that White himself had built; it was like the apartments which soon would replace the bombastic mansions of the rich – as close to invisible as extravagance can come. Through its lovely artifice could pass Mrs Mackay, dressed in gold and silver as Theodora, her ten foot train attended by two tiny Numidians, a figure who might quite reasonably have been stoned on the streets.

It was also a miscalculation, an anachronism, but not because of what the public might think. Hyde was the son of the founder of the Equitable Life Assurance Company, which to him was as personal as a kingdom; but Equitable had become a public company, and Hyde had responsibilities, not just powers. There were rumours that Equitable paid for part of the great evening. Company officials demanded Hyde's resignation, New York State began to examine the workings of insurance companies and within a few years of his social triumph, Hyde was forced into rather royal exile in France. He did not quite grasp the change in money: that now wealth rested on papers and shares that could be traded, rather than directly on the surplus that a business makes.

And this new money, even Vanderbilt money, was risky. The great railroad fortunes, the foundation of the gilded age, were vulnerable to panics and stock deals and rambunctious, suicidal competition. Stanford White built a courtyard of austere mansions on Madison Avenue for Henry Villard of the Northern Pacific Railroad; but Villard lived there for only three months in 1884 because he could not afford both his house and the struggle to shore up the railroad. Money from gold and silver mines had to be carefully protected when it came back east. Banks could fail, and your sole protection was the conscience of bankers. Shares brought each shareholder an obligation to settle the company's debts, or pay for the restoration of some flooded mine. Such obligations helped to ruin White.

Once the great house of Morgan sold shares in US Steel, there was a huge speculative market in shares which meant fortunes could dissolve as well as accumulate, even if the usual suspects were not ramping or going short. Panic and boom were as nerve-racking as an ill-kept rollercoaster. The gentlemen of Wall Street schemed to help the pain or the profit. Wall Street rivals spent not less than $50,000 trying to upset William Guggenheim's divorce after he had remarried, according to Guggenheim's lawyer; they wanted to shake down the clan.

Gentlemen went nervously to prophets. William Waldorf Astor spent his life in fear after a gypsy said he would be murdered. J.P.

Morgan, the Titan, consulted the astrologer Evangeline Adams about the markets and elections, and his son's future. Even Morgan, the law-maker, had reason to fret. Each spring, his European banks waited nervously to see if his balances could cover his spending on fine art. When Morgan died, the steel mogul Andrew Carnegie, master of the largest company in the world, was not at all ironic when he sighed, 'And to think he was not a rich man. . . .'

Stanford White died in the old world – before Morgan died and before the crash of 1907. On the night of Monday 25 June 1906, the Thaws were at dinner at Martin's restaurant on Fifth Avenue, and White walked in. Evelyn passed Thaw a troublemaking note, 'The B. was here a minute ago, but went out again.' The B. was the 'beast', Thaw's name for White since he discovered who took Evelyn's virginity. After dinner, the Thaws went with friends to the roof garden at Madison Square Garden to see a show called *Mamzelle Champagne*, and Thaw paced the room, a little drunk, as though he was waiting for someone. Stanford White dined and went to the show in the roof garden at the New Amsterdam theatre, and had a drink at the Manhattan Club, and then came alone to Madison Square Garden, to his 'fairyland'. He sat alone, elbow on table, chin in hand. A tenor was singing, 'I Could Love a Thousand Girls'.

The Thaws, Evelyn and Harry, were about to leave; they had reached the elevators when Harry turned back. He had the collar of his overcoat turned up like a detective or like an assassin. He looked stark white. He pulled a revolver, walked into the gardens until he could stand a couple of feet from White's table and fired three quick shots. White slid to the floor, his neck and head black with powder. *Vanity Fair* wrote this headline for his death: 'Stanford White, Voluptuary and Pervert, Dies the Death of a Dog'.

And now the sense of falling, the constant terror of the gilded age, became a rout. Evelyn testified at her husband's trial, and her story was thought too indecent to print. Harry Thaw, a sadistic junkie, was cheered on his way to the lunatic asylum as though he had avenged his wife's honour. The public approved the killing of a social hero. The underpinnings of White's gorgeous world began to crack. Throughout 1907 there were rumours of trouble; half the bank loans in the city were secured against stocks and shares, which is a shaky basis for a business in which the customer can arrive and demand cash. The banks had distaste for their rivals in the trust companies, but even they were alarmed when the Knickerbocker Trust Company, 'distinctly and distinctively the Society bank of New York', tried to corner shares in United Copper. They knew that the Morgans and the Guggenheims, in unlikely alliance, were planning to open rival copper mines in Alaska. When the news broke, the price of United Copper slumped, and depositors became anxious about the Knickerbocker. 'The consternation of the faces of the people on the line, many of them I knew, I shall never forget,' Benjamin Strong of Bankers' Trust said. The bank had to close its doors. Its president, Charles Barney, shot himself, and some of his depositors took the same way out. The city waited for J.P. Morgan, who happened to be attending an Episcopal Convention with someone else's wife. He came back to New York for his final grand performance.

It took two weeks to calm the city. Tellers at the trusts were told to count money in slow motion. A man could earn ten dollars a day keeping someone's place in the line of anxious depositors. People waited overnight in the February damps. Wall Street – the fount of the fortunes on which all Society rested – was a mass of dark and sober men. Trading was almost halted on the stock exchange because nobody had cash, and if they could borrow it, they might have to pay 150 per cent. J.P. Morgan brought the city's bankers together to his library, trust men in the West Room with Madonnas, commercial bankers in the East with the Seven Deadly Sins. He locked the tall bronze doors. He waited out the night, and at a quarter to five in the morning he had his deal.

The trusts were set up to handle the wills and estates of the rich; if they failed, nothing was sure any more. Government began to edge out the patriarchal Morgan as the source of order in the markets. William Rockefeller was on the lam for seven months in 1912 from a Congressional committee that wanted to discuss 'the money trust'. Teddy Roosevelt had preached against 'the malefactors of great wealth'. Letters in the *New York Times* railed against the idea that 'any offence against public justice and public morality' could be wiped away with large enough donations. The courts even ruled that too much money was corrupting; James R. Roosevelt Junior, nephew of John Jacob Astor III, had his allowance halved by the New York State Supreme Court on the grounds that all children, however rich, should be brought up in prudence and moderation. When money went wrong, the poor milled in the streets. The newcomers talked Bolshevism. White's Fifth Avenue mansions were sold off and built over in the 1920s precisely for the sake of discretion. When the Great Depression came, there were bulletproof steel shutters on the surviving houses, hoards of coffee and canned meat in the country estates, and in 1931, the rich lingered in Newport to be close to yachts which, Neil Vanderbilt wrote, were 'kept under steam, day and night, ready for a three-thousand mile jump on a second's notice'.

The 'gilded age' died of fear. But the tension within Society remained – the knowledge that public acclamation made a socialite important, but that public judgement could bring him or her down. Stars come front and centre, like players, to be pelted, applauded or ignored.

When Truman Capote gave the Black and White Ball, the party of the year in 1966, the *Washington Post* announced 'a social happening of history-making proportions'; but then their proprietor was the guest of honour. 'Boy, is this town full of phonies,' one bell captain whispered on the night. 'Do you know there are people hanging around here in black-and-white clothes who ain't even going to Truman's?' And Society had a curious new element: the social success as promotional expense. Capote could write off much of the $16,000 bills for his party against tax. What a Mrs Astor did on principle, he did for business. The new rich of the 1980s saw the point. They were promoters, men with bright ideas to absorb the vast impersonal surplus of pension funds and other fiduciaries; they bought equity in huge deals by having ideas about where that pool of unused dollars might be put to work, and where it might make a quick turn that would look good to the shareholders or the pension trustees. The needs of a Henry Kravis, persuading others to buy companies on borrowed money that was secured against the assets of the company they planned to buy, were very different from those of the gentleman banker of Wall Street. Kravis dealt in deals, not long-term relationships; he wanted equity, not just fees; he needed to be noticed for his ingenuity and his sharpness, not just for his steadiness and care. He chose to buy respectability as a cultured person, string quartets after dinner, parties where everyone was given a forty-five dollar book on Degas, a reputation for exquisite manners. He wooed his wife by investing in her company.

More boorishly, Donald Trump's Louis XVI barstools, his marble dining table for seventy-five, his bedroom painted, he said, 'with the quality of the Sistine Chapel' are exercises in promotion as well as excess. In Queens the Trumps rent middle-income housing to ordinary Joes, but in Manhattan they sell hotel rooms and apartments to people who need proof that they have chosen right. The more ink the Trumps acquired, the more they were models of richness and success, the more certain people wanted to live in Trump Tower, where there is a dearth of captains of industry and powerbrokers, but a number of California absentees including the TV talkshow host Johnny Carson, and a certain notorious Madam. You could see the Trumps' social existence, even their claims of billionaire status before the fall, as the promotional expenses of the more sober investors – in the case of Trump Tower, the Equitable Life Insurance Company – who could not overprice the property on their own.

But to maintain the illusion takes real money; Society still rests on stock markets and business cycles. When anyone forgets that, when they imagine they are aristocratic and that privilege attaches to them whatever happens, then there are morality stories. Consider the Gutfreunds.

John Gutfreund is a stocky, squashed figure, powerfully bland, the head of the investment bankers Salomon Brothers. In the Wall Street revolution of the late 1970s, when traders simply swamped the old boys by making more money and thinking more clearly, Gutfreund was the star. He schemed for business, instead of acquiring it from fellow gentlemen over the cabinet pudding at some club like the Downtown Association. He grabbed. He married money – Joyce Low, daughter of a partner at Bear, Stearns and Co. The marriage went sour because there was no fun in it. Gutfreund took the limo to the office at six each morning; at 7.30 he was on the trading floor, watching, growling, almost never sequestered in his private office. Gutfreund made himself head of the firm. He dreamed of power in Tokyo or London, anywhere the dealing rules were changing. But when the markets shut each night, and he had to leave the roar and the clash of the trading floor, John Gutfreund shifted miserably. At one Paris party, he went to an old friend and said, 'Do you remember me? I'm John Gutfreund.'

Before he iced his patron, Billy Salomon, out of the firm, the old man considered him frugal and conservative; 'I thought that was a good example for the boys.' Gutfreund was 'King of Wall Street' on the magazine covers, ruler of an equity portfolio worth thirty-eight billion dollars which was four times the worth of his nearest rival.

Then, he met Susan Penn, and they wholly misjudged Society; they thought it could be personal, and private, and fun.

Susan Penn is a woman who invented herself from scratch. She said she was born in some thatched, middle-ages manor house some-where in England, but her air force father says she was born in Chicago. She was a stewardess for Pan Am in the days when the job still had a ring of fantasy – for girls, for the gentleman travellers. She took such good care of passenger John Roby Penn, a Texas property merchant, that she married him. When the marriage went wrong, she stayed in Fort Worth; one society columnist says, 'She was out to catch a rich husband.' But Texas was too small for her ambition. She graduated to New York, engineered a dinner invitation to meet the 'trader king' and the two were smitten at once.

At their first Christmas, the tree was surrounded by empty blue Tiffany's boxes, nothing else – a statement of intent. Susan insisted her new name was pronounced 'the English way', which is 'Good-friend'. John assumed a vaguely British accent. Susan greeted Nancy Reagan with 'Bonsoir, Madame' and demanded a *fumoir* in her new apartment. But her social progress was not easy. John found a way to cash out of Salomons while keeping control of the firm, and he took home thirty-two million dollars. But this did not count as auth-entically rich, since Gutfreund made money for other people, cutting deals instead of cloth but as much a tradesman as any tailor. Susan had to manufacture her standing.

She went to the couture weeks in Paris, which is a little showy, but she knew to say that she went only because there was this wonder-ful Chanel show at the Opera and she so loved set design. Her taste for clothes placed her socially; as Nelson Aldrich shrewdly wrote, 'Fashion is appalling to so many Old Money beneficiaries because it carries with it a dreadful reminder of the incredible force and fluidity of the marketplace.' She hired decorators who performed the secret task of society decorators, which is to introduce their clients. She bought frocks from the designer Bill Blass, clear, unequivocal signs of her new status, and Blass in return brought the Gutfreunds to the attention of John Fairchild, the publisher of *Women's Wear Daily*, the accidental Baedeker of visible New York.

Frockmakers understand such things; they need to know those women, perhaps twenty of them in the world, who are photographed enough and known enough to show off their clothes. On this display depends the frockmaker's profit; it makes his name, and names can be licensed. So frockmakers advise; when ex-Senator Abe and Casey Ribicoff were nervous about buying an apartment on Sutton Place South because the building had a particularly formidable board of owners, Blass told Mrs Ribicoff to shut up and wear a bow in her hair, and the grateful Ribicoffs were housed. In Susan Gutfreund's case, there were headlines in *WWD* about Nouvelle Society, a shiny new set, and Susan Gutfreund was its leader. Blass went to her Proustian party, where there were roses twined round each chair ('the thorns stuck in your back,' he complained).

Susan was lavish. She went to her exercise class by limousine, as the thin, rich gentry of the Upper East Side go three blocks to dinner by limousine. She turned half a floor of a large apartment in the grand River House into a bathroom and dressing room, installed a refrigerator so that her perfumes could be chilled. Her invitations were hand-delivered, each pinned with a yellow rose. She threw a sixtieth birthday dinner for Henry Kissinger himself, and served green apples of silken sugar, blown like Venetian glass. She employed the decorator Henri Samuels to collect her antiques, and took compliments on them personally; 'Thank you,' she would say, 'I've had it for ages.' She liked to point out the million-dollar rug, the double marble jacuzzi, and to let her staff be counted by the magazines; but 'I don't want publicity,' she said, 'whenever you see photographs of me, I'm not looking at the camera.'

But like the heroine of some fairy story, she had fatally missed the point. She existed only in the social arena, and there she existed because she commanded attention. New York ladies are supposed to use this visibility for some charity work, but Susan Gutfreund would never join a committee. Her work was her private world, a mansion suspended in an apartment block at 834 Park Avenue, with a leather-lined library, a Hollywood staircase, and Monet waterlilies. For just as long as the boom years continued, her indulgence was almost reassuring; everything must be well on Wall Street.

When the boom stopped, people grew scared and then judgemental. Salomon Brothers was New York's single largest tax-payer, after all, and the main underwriter of the city's struggle up from bankruptcy in the 1970s. Finance companies doubled their payrolls between 1977 and 1987, and the city depended on jobs in the securities business. Those jobs made possible the sharp clubs, the *nouvelle* restaurants, the new office towers and the high cost of those city apartments with natural light. Thousands of people shared, and more aspired to share, some tiny part of what Susan Gutfreund had to spend. But John Gutfreund was a trader, not a long-term strategist. Salomon's spending was out of control, its worldwide expansion misfired, and Gutfreund quit the municipal bond and commercial paper markets overnight, an exit which some considered brutish and amateur. The firm was split over junk bonds, a market which Salomons discovered late. Gutfreund abandoned his plan for great office towers at Columbus Circle that would throw Central Park into shadow for ever, a mark on the city as deliberate as any in his favourite book, Ayn Rand's *The Fountainhead*. Salomon shares rose on rumours that he would quit.

New York read about all this avidly; it was a public issue. Susan Gutfreund should have done some public duty. John Gutfreund should be successful, not just moneyed, because success is a sign of worth – of God's favour, even, as a Calvinist might have thought. Their social standing depended on public approval, in the democratic way. The city felt implicated in their troubles. Susan Gutfreund sensibly took herself to a *hôtel particulier* in Paris where her grand dinners, her decision to dig up the courtyard to build an underground car-wash, were American oddities. She was not expected to know the rules perfectly. She could even be forgiven her usual lavish attempts to make friends; she bought letters of Marie Antoinette for Liliane Rothschild, who promptly sent them back, perhaps not knowing New York's odd fellow-feeling for a defiant royal court.

A writer of fables would put a moral at this point. In New York Society, the moment is everything; there is nothing in Society except the consistent attention of other people. Society makes nobody secure. There is nothing as persistent as a title which can compensate for being in financial trouble, or even being poor. The most solid thing is sudden money, which is hardly solid at all.

8
TAKING LIBERTIES

HOW ONE WOMAN came to the city, and learned to use it: Lauren Hutton came up from crackerland Florida in the 1960s, from the fringe of the South, with thirty-seven dollars and friends who thought she could pick up all the bills; 'I looked,' she says, 'like a big basket of fresh vegetables.' First time in the city, she knew you had to tip a cabbie, and she handed out a dime; 'I left the cab and I heard a word I never heard before, no idea what it meant, some part of the female anatomy. Something hard hit me and hurt me in the back of the head at the same time.' The second time, she was already twenty-two and she said she wanted to be an artist, or go to Africa, to be away; she knew the friend of a friend, and the name of a tramp steamer sailing in three months. 'But I was really climbing the beanstalk,' she says.

She couldn't explain to her family that she was moving. 'My family had only ever been to New York for war – Civil War and world wars. They didn't know that people went to New York to live. My stepfather suggested I pin my money to my underwear. He didn't know that by then I had stopped wearing underwear. I was told I would die. But I wanted choice and I wanted to know something in order to be able to choose.

'I was a very lovely, attractive country girl, coming from a place where if someone smiled at you, you smiled back. I was swinging down Madison Avenue at twenty-two and a gentleman in a three-piece grey flannel suit with a briefcase smiled at me – this was before I started modelling – and I smiled back. I had to stop at a phone booth and the next thing I knew the doors were being pushed open and this man put his hand on my thigh, and with the other hand he was pressing a card on me. My friend on the phone says I kept saying, "Please. Sir. Please". Today, I'd say things to wither his timbers.' She learned to negotiate the streets – to put on speed so people didn't think she planned to Mau Mau them, to look into the faces of thousands of people a day to winnow and grade what she found there, city skills. 'If you can live here,' she says, 'you truly can live anywhere.'

She wouldn't be a waitress in a costume; 'in those days, if a woman wore a costume, you were a hooker'. She was told to look in the *New York Times* and she found a job modelling for Christian Dior. 'You suddenly are this commodity,' she says, 'everybody comes up and stares at you and often they reject you. That's shocking. You'd have five or six people touching you at the same time – hairdressers, make-up people, stylists – and you'd go to five places the same day'.

But she learned, very quickly, that she could negotiate. 'I chose my society. I had the opportunity to get into just about any damned society I wanted. It's stunning now when I think back. I was getting first-class tickets from South America, jewels being sent from people I didn't know. The first man I ever slept with, I lived with for several years, so I didn't go out on a single date for the first seven months in the city, although an awful lot of people were hitting on me. I would arrange to have tea, and since I was only making fifty dollars a week and I was paying for my own tea, I would meet them at Chock Full O'Nuts because they had fifteen cent coffee, cheapest in town. There were these guys with Rolls Royces pulling up at Chock Full O'Nuts. . . .'

Imagine Walt Whitman, not in that workman's shirt he wore for the first edition of *Leaves of Grass* but as a man who wore 'a frock coat and high hat, carried a small cane, and the lapel of his coat was almost invariably ornamented with a boutonnière'. This is Walt Whitman the editor and politician: who signed up to campaign for Van Buren in 1840, who shouted at mass meetings for Tammany Hall in 1841, who even flirted with Nativist parties that hated the newcomer Irish Catholics until he decided it was better to fight the coalition of politics and religion. This is the man who had serious reasons when he called New York a 'city of orgies'.

'As I pass, O Manhattan, your frequent and swift flash of
    eyes offering me love,
Offering response to my own – these repay me,
Lovers, continual lovers, only repay me'.

In his New York diary for 1862 we find 'Dan'l Spencer . . . told me he had never been in a fight and did not drink at all gone in 2d New York Lt Artillery deserted returned to it slept with me Sep 3d'; and again: 'David Wilson night of Oct 11, '62 walking up with Middagh – slept with me. . . .' Whitman built his Manhattan on desire. There is an element of guilt, perhaps, in the way he refuses to be better than tarts or felons: 'You prostitutes flaunting over the trottoirs or obscene in your rooms/ Who am I that should call you more obscene than myself?' But there is also a cry of affirmation: body, sinew and come, Whitman falls into the city in a kind of delirium. He desires the insistent, democratic crowd – 'O an intense life, full to repletion and varied!/ The life of the theatre, bar-room, huge hotel for me!' He is fascinated by Broadway – 'What hurrying human tides, or day or night!! . . . What curious questioning glances – glints of love!/ Leer, envy, scorn, contempt, hope, aspiration!' He celebrates the 'City of the world! (for all races are here/ All the lands of the earth make contributions here)'.

Everything that stalwart, middle-class, anxious people feared – the muddle of peoples, the newcomers, the busyness of the city, the swagger of the streets with none of the ingrained shame that creates decorum – was sheer glory to Whitman. His poetry, he wrote, springs from 'sixty or seventy millions of equals, with their lives, their passions, their future – these incalculable, modern, American, seething multitudes around us, of which we are inseparable parts!' Whitman wants to absorb and be absorbed by the multitude. He demands his freedom in the crowd just as urgently as moralists and reformers, old Comstock and his rat-hunters, knew they had to dam up desire if they were ever to control the city. He is canny enough to be unspecific, but he notices the thighs of the firemen.

The city is sexual, a sexual market, but also a space where anything is possible and everything, including the rules, could be negotiated on the street, where desire was a matter of choices and not obligations. In the city, there was an obvious sexual politics. The streets were supposed to permit anarchy. The *Journal of Public Morals* complained in 1833 that half of New York's vice was down to 'men who at *home*, under the restraint of village life, maintain a credible character'. Once in Brooklyn, in 1847, an Irish crowd came to yell and groan and hoot, play 'cowhorns, marrow bones and cleavers, tombstone fiddles, tin kettles and thundermugs' before the house of a famous seducer and adulterer who was being married; but they had been organised by the man's political enemies, not out of their own moral fervour. The moralistic Committee of Fifteen complained in 1900 that 'the main external check upon a man's conduct, the opinion of his neighbours, which has such a powerful influence in the country or small town, tends to disappear'. But without constraint, Whitman sees the city's crowds, and the city's setting as one magnificent being: 'A million people – manners free and superb – open voices, hospitality – the most courageous and friendly young men/ City of hurried and spark-ling waters! city of spires and masts!/ City nestled in bays! my city!' His city is a moral place, of fine mothers and good leaders. It is the city Whitman wants, quite as much as the city he saw: 'Proud and passionate city – mettlesome, mad, extravagant city!' More, it turns New York upside down, making everything alarming into a cause for joy' including the glances, the bright eyes that used to bring the streets to life. In times of sexual caution, the city dulled down.

Doctor Destouches found the city less lovely in 1926: commercial, anonymous, ruthless. When he used the city in fiction – in *Journey to the End of the Night*, written as Louis-Ferdinand Céline – he was horrified by the way each 'el' train seemed to smash into the city from a distance. He saw skyscrapers as a frozen deluge of matter, 'an abominable system of constraints, of corridors, locks and spyholes'. He found humanity only in underground lavatories, caverns of feculent marble where the men took off their jackets and cheered each other 'in a joyous shitting communism', in 'such free and easy intimacy . . . and up on the street such perfect restraint'. He looked down on 'the great stewpot of people in a city', and 'Help! Help! I shouted, just to see if it would have any effect on them. None whatsoever.' But in amongst this horror passed the women: goddesses, he wrote in his letters, with 'prodigious legs'. He stood still in wonder. He loved their feline quality, their 'divine, winged gait'; he found them healthy and joyous, with 'the appeal of youth, even extreme youth'. As Céline, he sang their supple grace, their sense of triumph – 'every conceivable promise of face and figure ful-filled!' They lived in a city that was not languid like European cities that 'recline on the landscape, awaiting the traveller' but 'absolutely erect. New York was a standing city.' Inside this machine, all steel and stone, anything as personal as desire is amplified: as the whisper of silk thighs shifting against each other or the click of high heels on the sidewalk.

You need warmth. 'Their rooms are fit only to sleep in; close friends they have few or none,' George Kneeland wrote of the clerks among the working girls in 1917. 'You can watch them on the streets any evening. Hour after hour they gaze at the passing throng; at length they fling themselves into the current – no longer silent or alone.' But everything is risk, and risk amplifies the senses. Anything can be negotiated, including the rules. The power to look belongs to everyone. A tenement city is full of vantage points, to handle passers-by with the eyes. You look out to lit windows across courtyards or alleys or streets, an involuntary voyeur; you take this liberty whether you want it or not. You are anonymous, and if you are known, you need only move a few blocks or change quarter to be nameless again. Nothing keeps the alarms and obsessions quiet. 'Obsession of all the beds in all the pigeonhole bedrooms,' John dos Passos wrote in *Manhattan Transfer*, 'tangled sleepers twisted and strangled like the roots of pot-bound plants. Obsession of feet creaking on the stairs of lodging houses, hands fumbling at doorknobs. Obsession of pounding temples and solitary bodies rigid on their beds. . . .'

This is also perverse. Only a sadist finds it easy to put the brute facts of the city together with the desire that is supposed to transcend them. For a sadist, the sheer nervousness of the city is erotic – the street threat, the underground squalor, the sense of anonymity which allows the most gratifyingly horrid act to be performed without consequences. In Alain Robbe-Grillet's *Project for a Revolution in New York*, the city has almost been levelled; but once the physical city is cleared away, we are trapped in the idea of New York, where there are no cops to call. The novel proceeds like a porno loop, sometimes breaking and needing repair, circling the same carnal actions – the hurting, slicing, piercing and binding of women, imagined to test what the reader can bear and, suppos-edly, to brace him and reward him for some kind of revolution (the women simply die). In this city, the subway punks, the muggers in the park, are only playing their part in a most elaborate sexual game; crime is remade for the author's pleasure as a simple lack of limits. The city's part-time secretaries and shopgirls offer themselves up, deprived even of the dignity of victims because they are bound by the nature of the city to do as they do.

The filthy city, jittery and violent, where people can step outside the systems of a small town and make a little space for their own warmth and love; and where there are always police.

When the American republic began, everyone knew about virtue. It was very male and Roman: *virtus* – plain, disciplined and unsensual. Women of the republic claimed virtue from being the mothers of virtuous men, and while evangelicals found virtue in running a plain and disciplined household, daughters and wives were subject to their men. It had to be so. Women were too much tangled with the senses and amusements and indulgences; they were not serious like the republic. It followed that a woman on her own could not be virtuous. The rake on the street could block her way, jostle her and bother her, talk dirty in her ear; he took his manners not from republican pamphlets but from what he thought he knew of Regency London. The courts believed a female had all the lusts of Eve, at almost any age. Counsel for the weaver Richard Croucher, accused in 1800 of raping a girl of thirteen, argued that 'the passions may be as warm in a girl of her age as in one of more advanced years'.

But in the city, the women tasted a little freedom. A cotter's daughter, out of Ireland, was no longer her family's domestic serf; she could sew for a living or work as a maid or go on the streets; she could choose. A woman wrote home to County Cork in 1850: 'Oh how happy I feel ... as the Lord had it not destined for me to get married to some Loammun or another at home.' There were thousands of single women, five for every four young men in 1840; the Irish Famine brought whole families to America but in 1860 there were still five women for every four young men. In part, that was because they could not go away after labouring jobs like the men; their chances were limited to the city. The men, in any case, were exhorted out of New York.

Many of the women who stayed were living beyond the control of their families; Christine Stansell found more than half were living independently in 1855. They could sometimes defy the cantankerous, nosy discipline of neighbours. By mid-century, many were factory girls, sociable and robust, and out in the world. They mixed with men, moralists complained. They encouraged each other in a taste for fashion, way beyond their means. It was usual enough for a couple to make love before being married, but it was done as a proof of betrothal, and on the parents' terms, and quite often in the parents' house; these girls could take their sexual pleasures without asking their parents. When married, they stayed independent. James Burn, an English hatter who lived in New York during the Civil War, found 'one of their common remarks to each other when speaking of their husbands is that they would like to see a man who would boss them'. They were crammed into garrets and dormitories, and they had nothing to wait for, and nothing to do but make a life.

One widow's little shop, maybe started with a five-dollar grant from the Society for the Relief of Poor Widows, was set respectably in her rooms and sold candy, fruit and cake. Another widow's shop was 'a disorderly house', what everyone knew as a 'bawdy house', where there was cheap booze for a rough clientèle – apprentices and sailors, free blacks and women who were not cosily confined in a family. They were prostitutes, some of them, but also runaway wives and girls out courting, and some who simply wanted a bright, ginny night out. Some of the bawdy houses were tame as coffee houses; some had rooms for sex. The court records show that neighbours disapproved of the 'dancing, kissing, cursing and swearing' and the raucous crowds who shouted and brawled around their steps.

A man's authority only lasted as long as his wages, and most could not earn enough to keep a family. Women and children also had to work. Marriage was often an economic contract, a pool of two incomes that did not have to involve affection. Indeed, the first trades unions called for a family wage so women could stay at home and do their old domestic duties, and be safe from their own fallen natures. The dangers began where men did what they could to maintain their authority. A Mr Twomey beat his wife to death for buying a turkey without first asking him. Patrick Carroll kicked his wife senseless when she complained that he'd brought home only two salt shad for dinner and a half-pound bag of broken candles. Neighbours would come to a woman's help, but there were rules: she first had to cry 'Murder!' and be serious about it.

There was a catch in the way women controlled, for the most part, the trade in women; they were always subject to these tides of rage. It was doubtful, by 1831, if a woman could walk safely after dark; 'There are strange things said of attacks upon females in the streets of New York . . . if alone,' reported Niles Register. After 1830, the courts began to hear about gang rape – 'getting our hide,' one rapist called it. Mary Galloway, a seamstress, was walking home from work one evening when six men attacked her, shouting: 'Choke the god-damned vagabond'; but she did not look like a vagabond, only a woman out on her own. Men took to booze in a new way, and together they went rampaging; a 'spree' could be playful (throwing mud at a brothel door) or brutal (stealing the drink and beating the madam) or worse – throwing vitriol, blinding Amanda Smith in her house on Franklin Street and beating her crippled son, taking a sword to Sarah Smith's face; and there was always the prospect of rape, often meant to punish a woman for daring to think she could set the terms of a sexual transaction.

Where there's riot, especially drunk and self-righteous riot, there is immediately protection. The law sometimes helped; a prostitute could prosecute a man for an unwanted kiss on the street (but she might drop the charge if the man apologised). The watch would come and save a bawdy house from attack, even though the attackers would say it was a damn shame that watchmen should protect whorehouses. Madams expected such protection; they were figures in society. Eliza Bown Jumel put the world between her thighs until in 1804 she married a grand wine merchant; and since social New York knew all too much about her past, he had to put his grand mansion at a distance, in Harlem Heights. She outlived him by forty years, now one of the wealthiest women in America, living in one of the most gracious houses. Aaron Burr, a former Vice-President, was happy to marry her briefly. But from the 1830s, madams had to buy their safety, and, by the 1850s, they paid pimps, not simple guards. On the corner of Broadway and Broome stood the 'Broadway statues', men waiting for the working girls to hand over the take and go out to trawl up more custom.

While republican virtue was the standard, any independent woman – factory workers or servants or the women who sewed – fell short, just like the whores. But these Bowery girls, flocking in bright colours, were quite different. On a good day, they could go carriage riding, or on a steamboat 'on a party of pleasure'; sometimes they sponsored dances, where they brought the booze and the food and the men made the music, and sometimes they went to Tammany Balls and sometimes they were content with oysters, at six cents for all you could eat. They went 'walking out' where the neighbours could never catch up, on Broadway or in City Hall Park or on the Bowery, flirting while they did their errands and chores. They hung on the arms of the Bowery B'hoys, the flashy lads with their glassy, greased hair and their cigars and their rings and their shirt collars turned down to show off a labourer's strong neck. They had their own style – 'an intolerable glare of crimson and scarlet shawls, ribands and faded bonnet flowers, with a sultry sense of yellow calico past all endurance,' as George Foster found in the 'intelligence offices' where girls went to look for servants' work. Unlike prostitutes, they wore hats, but the kind that showed off the face; unlike wives, they went without veils and their dresses clung a little at the hip and thigh, not just at the ominous and plated middle-class bosom. They feared nobody. This was their world; they would see off any uptown visitor thinking to amuse himself, with scorn or with fists. Their 'very walk has a swing of mischief and defiance in it,' George Foster wrote.

There were no rules for such women; everything was negotiated by a glance, a chat, a little time together. Taking a man's help when looking for lodgings could be risky, since he might take a simple request for directions as an invitation to some house of assignation for a hot time. The same houses that served streetwalkers also served lovers, by the hour – grog shops for the sailors, houses where young men could keep their working-class mistresses, Broadway brownstones where ladies could make love in the afternoon while their friends went promenading by the shops. Everything was a matter of degree. These Bowery nights did depend, for women who earned a dollar a week making shirts, a dollar and a half as a tailor, on a kind of 'treating' – a little sex in return for the booze and the company and the dinner and the dancing. One victim of rape had to defend herself in court by saying that 'I never went with him to any place of public amusement. He never made me presents of the value of anything.'

It was quite a small move for a girl to decide she would rather sell herself than any other labour; it might be her only way to a room of her own, to a little space in the city. Servant girls had a harder time by the middle of the century; they had to bargain for time off, and sex might give them a more leisurely life. Some country girls were lured to the city; Joe Farryall went three or four times each year to the villages of Vermont, promised a girl she would be a lady and brought her back to his brothel. But some chose the streets. Susannah Bulson of Albany made love to a young cabinet-maker and came with him to New York. They lived together for a while in a boarding-house, but Susannah liked the free comings and goings of the street-walkers and she left her man for their independent life. Months later, he was still begging her to come back.

The girls who ran errands for the grog-shop and dance-hall tarts down at Corlear's Hook were tempted to seize independence, even if they had a job, a home, a family. One girl of thirteen told the warden of the House of Refuge in the 1830s that she'd sell herself for a shilling – what a seamstress then earned in a day – rather than scrub public houses in return for food for her family. Eleven-year-olds hung around City Hall in the 1840s; the flower sellers, apple sellers, match sellers on the street would add some lewd suggestion to their talk. When families needed money, they did not ask too many questions, and when children were hungry to get through the week and survive, they sold what they could. 'I am only fourteen, but I am old enough,' Mary Ann Pitt said. 'I have had to take care of myself ever since I was ten years old, and I have never had a cent given to me. . . . The rich do such things and worse, and no one says anything against them. But I, sir – I am poor – I have never had anyone to take care of me.'

By the 1850s, George Templeton Strong complained that 'no-one can walk the length of Broadway without meeting some hideous troop of ragged girls'. Horatio Alger, who lost his ministry because he loved boys too much, came down to the city and roamed the docks, looking for friendless urchins, handing out candy and money and making friends; his biographers think he was a good man, determined not to sin. There was a fine line between play and rough-housing and fumbling and rape. Children were in the sexual market. Around a third of the cases of rape prosecuted in New York City from 1790 to 1876 involved victims under twelve. But a soldier charged with rape on a five-year-old in 1842 said: 'I lay the child in the Bunk as I often have done before as well as other men in the same company'; he saw nothing wicked in what he did, provided he stopped short of 'violence', which meant full intercourse. Candy for a fumble was an ordinary trade for children, and it was a short step from taking a present and keeping quiet to taking cash for pleasuring a man. Older women acknowledged the taste; in the late nineteenth century there were 'buzzards in doves' plumes' on Sixth Avenue, women disguised as schoolgirls, toting satchels.

The city made a business out of warmth, poor women and lonely or hungry men, thrown together in a strange place. There were sailors in port, immigrants newly arrived and visitors; as early as 1835 the leading hotels of New York counted 60,000 signatures a year on their registers. Since it cost either marriage or money to buy private relationships, commercial sex was actually more practical for many people. It took a J.P. Morgan to maintain yachts, and an apartment in Westchester County for his ladies. The sexual trade had a geography. At the start of the nineteenth century, 'idle and disorderly loose women' pestered sailors on 'Holy Ground' behind St Paul's Chapel, owned by the Episcopal Church. In the taverns by the East River docks, the women paid four shillings for each customer they took to the back rooms. A Chapel Street house, close to Columbia College, served only men under twenty-one. There were whores in the bustling dance palaces of Greenwich Village, where fine carriages waited, and close to the houses of the rich. 'Rotten Row' was three blocks of Laurens Street North of Canal, with fancy brothels and houses of assignation; there were frequent riots and calls as early as 1834 for the city to buy the street or close it down; men went to find heat among 'filthy pools of stagnant water, and heaps of garbage and offal. . . .' Yet 'Rotten Row' was only blocks away from mansions. In 1859, the Stadt Theatre resounded to the awful din of *Tannhäuser* – under the direction of Carl Bergmann, conductor of the Philharmonic Society – in a district famous for other theatres where the third tier was prowled by commercial ladies, and hungry men, who got to know each other well for cash.

In the disorderly docks by Water and Cherry Streets, Walt Whitman found 'women half exposed at the cellar doors as you pass. Their faces are flushed and pimpled. The great doings, in these quarters, are at night'. At the east end of Grand Street, at Corlears Hook, the streets sold cut-rate sex, the fiddlers playing rowdily before 'coarse, fat, vulgar-looking women . . . calling each other *sisters* and affecting bright red or yellow dresses' as Thomas Butler Gunn found. In the toilet room at the Fulton Street ferry house, you might find thirty working girls, in among the decent ladies; three ferries came into 'the Hook', and five into Water Street, and the bustle of passengers was perfect cover for a man with an afternoon itch. The 'Hook' was considered more rough even than Five Points, the slums where taverns clustered on alleys crooked and soiled. Deckhands from the steamboats, oystermen and whalers congregated there; 'it was a jubilee, indeed, to the landlords of the Points when the crew of a United States ship of war got paid off,' Florry Kernan remembered. The stench and the crowding were famous, and the ragged creatures nestled in straw on shelves; some tarts worked where 'there is not a door and floor, nor roof to the house they live in'. Whites and blacks mingled, and made sex, to the horror of those who feared the mixing of races; a raid in 1830 found 'several well-dressed white men, found in the hovels of negroes'. People mingled across frontiers of class and income, and this was extraordinary even in a city which fancied it had a single middle class without undue snobbery. In the sex streets, this social order was apparently, shockingly suspended by contact with the poor. But some things do not change. The poor sold their labour. The rich rigged the market.

Since private space was so expensive, and this kind of sexual pleasure was taken away from home, it was likely to be quite public and communal; although 'a great mob' collected when Isaac and Rebecca Davis stripped and attempted carnal connection, which suggests that actual sex on the streets was more an event than a backdrop. But the city's few public spaces were crissed and crossed in pursuit of sex. At night on the Battery, down on the Bowery, or among the gaudily dressed 'cruisers' on Broadway corners, bare arms and jewelled bosoms glinting in the night light, the streets were alive with desire. And desire transforms the city, makes the drab electric, as it transformed the women that Whitman's disinterested eye found pimpled and ugly; a spell of glamour rests on the streets for a man, at least until he comes.

The 'whorearchy', the street children and the independent Bowery girls all distressed the genteel – who imagined women could stay home with their children, and visitors could stay happily in the 'Grahamite boarding houses', named for the inventor of Graham crackers, which meted out chastity, bathing, bread and vegetables. A woman, by definition, had a home; being homeless was vagrancy, the same charge brought against prostitutes. Women who worked the streets rag-picking, coal-picking, swill-gathering were assumed to throw away their modesty because they were seen too much, and they had too much freedom of movement. A German father told his daughter, when she lost her job as a drudge at fourteen: 'I don't want you to be a rag-picker. You are not a child now – people will look at you – you will come to harm.' Girls who sold flowers were suspected of selling themselves, or working the 'domestic lay' – accusing men of fumbling them, whether they did or not. All this was a deep offence to the evangelicals and the prophets of a 'Christian Sparta' in New York.

These gentry hardly knew whether to worry more about blood and thunder dramas at the Tivoli, or girls walking the streets brashly without veils, or all the vulgar public amusement, or the presumption and the cheek of the troublesome, menacing working classes, or the evils of the police courts; they were as offended by the disorderly brats on the street as by the notion that children might have to sell their bodies to eat. Behind vice, they rightly smelt politics. The city marshal, in 1810, was arrested for running a disorderly house. The city watch went dancing with the common girls. A brothel-keeper in good standing with the watch could arrange that girls who left inconveniently would be arrested for stealing. William Lowe, in the 1800s, claimed the Mayor himself had given him a licence to keep a public whorehouse, and to whip or 'cowhide' the girls. And this was in the days when politics was still an occupation and a cost for richer men.

When Tammany began to take power, career politicians needed cash; the simplest way to raise it was to protect the houses from the drunk, violent Tammany men that might otherwise come to bother them, and to make sure the Tammany authorities were selectively tolerant of brothels and saloons and gambling hells. The watch, and then the city police after 1844, served two years at a time, depending for their jobs on city politicians. The politicians and the ward bosses could make sure the bribes flowed easily from the houses to the cops to the political machine. Police commissioners could never quite control the force; Theodore Roosevelt in 1896 said the police were 'a business of blackmail and protection'. The cops worked their neighbourhoods like local bully-boys, quicker with a nightstick than a warrant, and it was hopeless to remind them about legal niceties. They might well think prostitution was only human nature, and would simply move elsewhere if they took action. Captain Alexander Williams in 1887 told a complaining reverend that 'suppose you succeed in expelling them, then all these houses will be empty, for more than twelve years no honest people will occupy them but Negroes'. And besides, the fine for failing to close a disorderly houses was five days' pay – twenty to thirty dollars in 1895; but a single house on Bleecker Street would pay that much a month and in the Tenderloin it could rise to a hundred dollars. After two years service in the 1890s, a Greenwich Village cop had enough for a $10,000 house; his boss, Captain James Brogan, was supposed to make at least $700 a week from all the business he ignored. And if the cops were told to close the brothels in some access of municipal purity, they simply demanded higher fees to allow them to re-open – $500 from Charles Priem's Bayard Street house in the 1880s. One anonymous Madam claimed that she could not earn enough to pay her protection when trade was dull. 'As I could not pay it,' she told Abram Hewitt in 1887, 'I sold my furniture and am now destitute'.

The cops sometimes lived with working girls; Officer John J. Miller's wife was accused of running a brothel herself. Their captains sometimes visited working girls. The captain's assistants, the ward-men or 'fly cops' knew every Madam. When Sarah Myers was tried as a madam, her counsel was an ex-mayor; later, Matilda Street was defended on the same charge by an ex-judge. 'Madame Restelle', who advertised for 'ladies who have been unfortunate' and who built a fine Fifth Avenue mansion on the profits of abortion, was defended in 1847 by a Tammany leader who had been district attorney. Tammany workers claimed a share of the business: a court interpreter kept a low house on Broadway and Charles 'Silver Dollar' Smith, boss of the Third Assembly District, was also the owner of a choice house on Sixth Avenue at 31st Street. Philip Wissig, once an Assemblyman, introduced brothel-keepers to the wardmen, kept a tavern for the girls; his son owned two brothels. Martin Engel, the poultry butcher who ran the Lower East Side, bought up Allen Street houses and concert halls and hotels; his room house on East Sixth Street was both a brothel and a Democratic club-house.

The reformers knew the law had been bought and sold, and their opinion of the most worthy sounding politicians was not high. Fernando Wood was elected mayor in 1855 on promises of cleaning up prostitution, gambling and Sunday drinking; but his police force arrested only the streetwalkers, not the indoor girls, ignored the fashionable gaming houses and even the policy or lottery shops and somehow contrived to turn a state Prohibition law upside down with a quibble about imported liquor that made it more than a policeman's job was worth to challenge a drinker. Wood went on to stuff the force with Democrats who campaigned for him, and to make one saloon-keeper, famous only for having bitten off a man's nose in a bar-room brawl, into a precinct captain.

Such things were done by the brief, bright hope of the middle-class reformers. Yet all around them they could see the city going to hell. Edward Winslow Martin wrote, in *The Secrets of the Great City*, that streetcars were packed with the all too visible lower classes 'in search of what they call enjoyment. At night, all the places of amusement are open, and are crowded to excess. ... People have no idea how much of the charity they lavish on street beggars goes in this direction. The amusement offered at these places ranges from indelicate hints to the grossest indecency.' 'The steady advance of business and trade,' stalwart middle-class virtues, 'has broken up many of the vilest dens' in areas like the slums of the Five Points, but still there is disorder and vice. All that sexual possibility, those choices being made by people who should not make choices, that hissing and turning that disturbed the proper streets were corroding city and nation.

So reformers went outside the law: vigilantes for God and clean living. Anthony Comstock pursued obscenity as a special agent of the US Post Office. He truffled up dirty shows in brothels, and wrote down each licking, each unusual use of a cigar. He hounded vice wherever he could find it; everyone was suspect. His Society for the Suppression of Vice said obscenity required lynchings, since trials only gave the pornographers dignity. 'You must hunt these men,' Comstock wrote, 'as you hunt rats, without mercy.' By the 1890s his society stopped issuing reports because a true account of their actions might have landed them in court.

The Reverend Charles Parkhurst, the Presbyterian leader of the Society for the Prevention of Crime, thought the police were 'organised municipal criminality'. 'Every effort to make men respectable, honest, temperate and sexually clean,' he preached, 'is a direct blow between the eyes of the mayor and his whole gang of drunken and lecherous subordinates'. Parkhurst's followers hired Pinkerton detectives to sniff out vice. They sent out men with sledges and hammers to batter down gaming houses and dubious cafés; they set up traps for seducers, claiming they simply did work 'which naturally might have been passed over to the Police Department'. They fought against child performers, but not simply to enforce the law; they wanted to define the proper relations of parent and child. They helped shut down the dime museums, because they admitted children, and theatres with blood-and-thunder dramas, because boys might steal money to go there and then become vagrants, and concert halls because of the pretty 'waiter girls' who might turn to immorality. They wanted to build some orderly, mannerly city where proper middle-class folk would set the standards and define the culture. The concert halls, one place where labouring men and clerks and lawyers all met together, were shut down in 1886 at just the time that the city fathers were frightened of anarchists and socialists and four bloody strikes by streetcar workers in a year, when labour demonstrations were banned with limp excuses, police first began breaking up picket lines and boycotters were sent to prison. The newspapers suggested a nation at risk from ungrateful newcomers, rampant socialism, bombs and strikes. The reformers wanted control, and the easy camaraderie of the concert hall came to seem like a threat.

You could tell who the reformers were. At one meeting of the City

Reform Club, thirty-eight members present, thirty-six carried canes, thirty-six wore their hair parted in the centre, and fourteen were in full-dress suits. They were the middle class in the armour of their clothes, dressed to show their propriety and standing. Dr Parkhurst spoke to 'self-respecting' men, to 'tax-paying citizens', to college graduates who were the 'chieftains of events'. They were divided between wanting a city clean enough for the Chamber of Commerce, and wanting the Kingdom of God on Earth, but at least they had chosen their enemies: newcomer Jews and Italians, who did not keep the Sunday Sabbath, who voted for Tammany men and not for the 'best persons,' who refused to listen to insistent evangelicals, whose casual ways were offensive. The rumour that Jews had some special role in the white slave trade started only as Jews became an important constituency by sheer force of numbers: one quarter of the population of New York City by 1910. Reformers knew that prostitution was the most public issue, because it offended many and because it subsidised Tammany and might subsidise other of their political enemies and because it represented choice – economic choice, sexual choice.

In their eyes, each step away from decorum turned Manhattan into an anarchy of loose women and vice, just as each boatload of new-comers transformed the city they thought they knew. The two fears ran together easily. Respectable families liked to live as far as they could from the smoke and the oil and the falling coals of the elevated tracks, which left the avenues for newcomers and whorehouses. Each new nationality and race brought its own kind of vice. There were few Irish whores, as even Theodore Roosevelt, no lover of the Irish, had to admit; but there were black whores on Seventh Avenue, and down in 'Coontown' in what is now SoHo, and up in Harlem; French whores on 43rd Street and around New York University; whores around Columbia University who danced with the white college boys in rathskellers like the College Inn on 125th Street and whores on the Bowery who promised to do 'an immodest and indecent dance known as the Zulu'; white whores for Chinatown, Italian whores on Mulberry Street in the heart of the slums, and Jewish whores on the Lower East Side. Michael Gold remembers them 'sprawled indolently, their legs taking up half the pavement. People stumbled over a gauntlet of whores' 'meaty legs'.

The sexual trade permeated the neighbourhoods. After 1880, mass-age parlours opened, and the 'magnetic water treatment' shops and the nail-polishers and hair-cutters who could front for prostitutes.

Cigar shops on the Lower East Side, long narrow stores where only men went, had curtains 'from behind which emerge half naked women, whenever a customer enter'; they sat at windows, their breasts bare, in one Delancey Street store. The wholesalers of cigars would suggest that shopkeepers 'take in some women'. Soda water stores and cider *stubes* wanted fifty cents a drink or two dollars a visit, and if a man did not complain, they knew what he really wanted. Café Tortoni on Lexington at 30th had private wine rooms, with beds. At Owney Geoghegan's rowdy Bowery saloon, gaudy and loud, there were women boxers, who left with the customers. And when drink reformers forced through the Raines Law, which confined Sunday drinking to hotels, a hundred bars and roof gardens acquired some cubicles at the back – suitable for new-met couples, by the hour. Luchow's famous restaurant maintained twenty-five bedrooms.

Since it was simple to find a bed, the girls no longer needed the brothels. They could go out and work the streets as they wanted, or as they had to. Even Emma Goldman, the anarchist, went out to work Fourteenth Street to raise money for her lover Alexander Beckman, in 1912. She 'felt no nervousness at first, but when I looked at the passing men and saw their vulgar glances and their manner of approaching the women, my heart sank. . . . I wanted to take flight, to run back to my room, tear off my cheap finery, and scrub myself clean.'

The reformers had made themselves a kind of purity police, because they judged the public authorities were too deeply corrupted. Middle-class conviction overrode the scrubby, compromising business of democracy. This conservative social agenda involved not just an end to prostitution, but limits on the social and sexual freedom of anyone who worked for a living. It was a model for later surveillance of other deviancy, political, sexual or social. By 1910, the fear of sexuality on the streets was the engine of twenty-six organisations to keep women off the game, thirty clubs offering 'friendship, recreation and training' for young women so they would not choose the wilder pleasures of the Bowery girls, and at least fourteen groups trying to reform prostitutes.

A silent policeman helped their cause: the spirochaete. Syphilis was not just a disease, but a judgement. In the early part of the nineteenth century, men with syphilis were always turned away from New York Hospital. A hundred years later, a schoolma'am acquired a chancre on the lip and no respectable hospital in the city would treat her. Syphilis was a disease of cities, another consequence of the massed millions in the streets. 'Its frequency,' Dr L. Duncan Bulkey reported, 'is commonly seen to diminish in a pretty direct ratio to the suburban or rural character of the people'. It was considered a disease of the foreign-born – of course – because most prostitutes were foreigners and prostitutes were the great reservoir of the sickness; reformers were sure of this. Italians, Chinese and Negroes, a New York doctor insisted, tried to cure themselves by having sex with a virgin. The disease was everywhere; you could be infected, Dr Bulkey said, by a whistle, tattoo, toothbrush, pen, pencil, toilet or even a doctor.

This 'insontium' – infection of the innocent – was a notion whose power was hard to confine. It explained the incidence of venereal disease in children and excused the doctors from thinking too hard about child abuse. It made a bridge between the social evil of the underworld, and everyone else; any appetite, not just the sexual, could ruin an innocent person. The women's magazine *Forum* carried in 1912 the agonising story of a woman whose doctor said she had caught syphilis from a drinking fountain. She was, she wrote, always so careful about things like that, but 'after recalling a number of times when my thirst had forced me to go to the public fountain, I came to realise that what he had told me was true'. Since we now think that syphilis and gonorrhea are almost always transmitted by sexual contact, these easy diagnoses are most interesting: it's as though doctors were exaggerating the public danger in order to impose control of private behaviour. Prince Morrow, who founded a society against the social evil, put the issue alongside such very public matters as the honesty of the banks.

The first of New York's commissions on vice, the self-appointed Committee of Fifteen, acknowledged in 1900 that 'the effect of vice upon the physical health of the community is receiving at present more attention than any other feature of the problem'. The spirochaete was the reliable spy, the good policeman. Its agents were lovely women, not yet marked; each sexual possibility was a risk of death. It controlled behaviour in a crowded tenement with thin walls, and in a boarding-house where the sexes jostled together. It gave evidence long after the crime, as when syphilis appeared in a respectable marriage bed. It marked out sinners. It discouraged immorality; reformers agitated against the Page Law which ordered medical examinations for any woman found soliciting, followed by detention for the infected until they were no longer contagious, because sex must never be safe.

In 1911, doctors banded together to oppose municipal clinics in New York to treat venereal disease because they did not want to lose lucrative patients; in the 1930s, the weekly, year-long shots of arsenic and bismuth could easily cost $380 and sometimes $1,000, and four out of every five patients never finished the course. Because nobody would speak directly about it, or pass out condoms that might break the chain of infection, and because moralists saw the power of death as their friend, the spirochaete spread. Public health officials claimed that one American in ten was infected.

The Commission on Training Camp Activities in the First World War laid out the choices – purity or death – in a melodramatic flick called *End of the Road*. Two girls come to New York City to seek their fortunes. One becomes a nurse, helps the war effort, goes to tend the troops in France. A soldier boyfriend asks 'a memory I can never lose' on the night before shipping out, and good Mary flares her eyes. 'Paul,' she says, 'how could you suggest such a thing?' In a rare spare moment, she marries a doctor. Meanwhile her friend Vera is not in a decorous, disciplined, private occupation, following the rules. She is seen in public, serving at a counter in a Manhattan department store. She smiles at many men in her line of work. She meets rakes, goes to bed with one who promises marriage – never trust a man – and catches syphilis. *End of the Road* is exact and graphic about the lesions.

Consider this story: a claim on freedom that became all muddled up with the business of sex, and ended in petrified respectability because of a disease. Something like it will happen again.

Murray Hall was a poker-player, gruff and connected, with a big black cigar and a taste for whisky, who served Tammany and knew all the political gentry; when the cops said Hall claimed far too many assets as a professional bondsman, it took only a brief stop in Skelly's bar at Tenth Street and Greenwich Avenue to round up a posse of politicians to buy Hall out, even of the charge of beating up the cop who tried to make the arrest. Hall stomped around New York, hat crammed down on a bushy head of black hair, coats always a size too large but still not concealing the narrowness of shoulders, the tininess of polished feet.

In the 1870s, Hall opened an employment bureau on 23rd Street and lived with the first Mrs Hall; until Mrs Hall complained that her husband was much too friendly with the clientèle, and any woman on the street, and went away. A second Mrs Hall appeared from nowhere and the couple settled at 145 Sixth Avenue with their adopted daughter, Minnie, until the second Mrs Hall also began to complain of flirtatiousness. Hall was left cold, going down to the Jefferson Market to play poker, sinking a diet of beer that would have felled most men, playing politics. And then, in 1901, Hall died of a cancer that had eaten from the skin to the stomach and a doctor discovered that Murray Hall was a woman. She was afraid to show any doctor her cancered breast. She was afraid to lose the self she had made in New York, the power to go roaring and scheming that she held for thirty years. In the city, nobody knew her history. Even her birthplace was doubtful, although probably it was Govan in Scotland. Since people knew only the story she told, nothing was out of place. Her adopted daughter said she never had any doubt that her father was a man. She died for the sake of being the other sex.

A visiting German homosexual in 1871–72 was startled to find his tastes 'more ordinary' in America than at home. Simple sodomy was almost never punished; according to the 1880 census, there were only five men in jail in the whole of New York State for the 'unspeakable crime against nature'. In Dutch times, there are very few such offences, and none where both partners were adult. Sometimes, a man was indiscreet; an Irish cop called Edward McCosker happened on Thomas Carey pissing in Cedar Street in 1846, told him there was a 'great deal of grinding going on in that neighbourhood'. Carey asked where, and McCosker made a pass, for which he was put out of the force. But mostly the law was indifferent. The friendships of women, however romantic, were only rarely considered sexual. Men had business to be out and around in the streets, and together. One wonders about John Halstead, a tea merchant who left his half-million fortune to the new Cooper Union, a 'confirmed woman-hater' according to his adopted sister; 'I know of a score of instances where he has set young men up in business, and I am sorry to say that he lost a considerable fortune at the hands of men whom he befriended'. Or about Altman, the department store king, who made a ribbon clerk his heir and died unmarried.

The real offence was being a shape-changer, a witch, someone who was brazenly not of the right sex when arrested. Stephen Crane was alarmed and sickened by a waterfront boy who came tugging after him, 'painted, with big, violet eyes like a Rossetti angel'. The *American Journal of Psychology* discovered the 'fairies of New York', who met to knit, gossip and crochet. In the 1880s, gossip began to suggest that the notorious Edward Hyde, Lord Cornbury, who was Governor of New York in Queen Anne's time, wore women's clothes because he was a lover of men; until then, the startling portrait of Cornbury in white gloves and a décolleté of cornflower blue, occasionally shown at the New York Historical Society, had been taken simply as a sign of eccentricity. In a time when taxonomy was fashionable, it was wicked to muddle the settled category of gender.

But the city was a cloak for the shape-changers, a place to lead a doubled life, to find quick, sharp pleasures on the street. Earl Lind was a literate man who had sorrows and knew his Goethe; he passed as Ralph Werther. He also passed as Jenny June. He published a medical autobiography in 1918 and he lies on the frontispiece, fat and bare, legs crossed, buttocks up, emphasising discreetly a distinct pyramid of white tit. He was, he wrote, especially proud of his calves. In September 1891, he came to Columbia University, and discovered that 'in a great city, the temptation to a double life is exceptional'. He could pull on a suit so shabby he had to leave his lodgings without being seen, and walk over to the steam-sour streets of Hells Kitchen, with nothing to say who or what he was. He said he was a baby, and needed a big strong fellow to pet him; he came back with a bloody face. He tried Mulberry Street between Grand and Broome, talking to all the young men, especially the ones with muscles. Here, in the disorder of the lives of first-generation immigrant kids, he served a purpose. He felt 'a non-sensual, wifely love' for the boys he serviced, he bought the three-quart pails of beer that made their parties go, and sometimes they protected him, sometimes they raped him.

He was exiled in the suburbs for a while, but came back hungry. He began to patrol 14th Street; now, instead of playing poor boy, he made himself flashy. He wore a blue suit, Norfolk style, and white gloves, patent leather shoes, and the red tie which Havelock Ellis reported was the badge of the male tart or the amateur enthusiast. He took himself through the bar-room at 392 Bowery, or else through the side entrance with its spyhole, and went upstairs to leave all his maleness in a locker. He paraded down to the bar called Paresis Hall, a fairyland of curious tourists and cruising men, and men who for the moment were 'Princess this and Lady So and So and the Duchess of Marlboro' [sic]. The Bowery, Lind wrote, 'was the wide-open red light district for the un-Americanised labourer, and for the common soldier or sailor'; and he was in the window, smiling.

Like Murray Hall in Tammany, only a few yards from the bars where Lind held court, the androgyne Lind needed the city. He writes that 'a sense of gladness would spring up that in the great metropolis, I was lost to all who knew me'. The excitement was not always the possibility of living a double life, since Murray Hall lived only one. It was the chance to remake yourself, to undo any of God's little errors, to slip from under the social pressures to be what was expected. This was not always easy. When Lind went to a doctor to ask advice, he was immediately reported to Columbia, which cost him his job and his degree. When his millionaire employer discovered his second existence in the city, Lind was fired. At twenty-eight he decided he was not really a man, and had himself castrated. But if you were quick enough, and went to places far away from your assigned rounds, you could be wild in the second life: 'If a street car conductor happened to be youthful and good-looking,' Lind wrote, 'I became almost irrational. . . .'

We know men waited for each other in cars on Riverside Drive in the 1900s, and there were already notorious bath-houses like the Everard Baths, and the Mount Morris in Harlem. A German searched the advertising columns of the *New York Herald* for a whole year, and could find only two advertisements which seem to be from men seeking men; one of those is for a 'Friendship Club' based in Cincinnati. He remarked that such advertisements were far more common in Berlin or Munich. Probably New York papers were finicky, and there were enough alternatives to advertising. Elsie de Wolfe, the woman who invented the job of interior decorator, lived very publicly with the mannish Bessie Marbury, play agent to Oscar Wilde, from the 1890s; the ladies were known as the 'Bachelors' and people conspired for invitations to their Sunday salons. Other lovers were protected by other people's inability to imagine what they might be. One man remembers from 1920s' New York: 'It was much harder to find gay life then. But once you did, you were relatively safe, since no-one knew anything about it.'

But the rumour spread. Federico Garcia Lorca came to New York in 1929, because 'I think it's a dreadful place and that's why I'm going,' and because he hoped to have a very good time; America was an erotic ideal – young, simple, strong, masculine, companionable, available – and New York was where it could be met. The same dream still haunts all those European bars and baths called the Bronx or the New York. Lorca was in love with Whitman's ideal of comradeship – something between true men that was wholly uncompromised by money or drink; Whitman was 'Enemy of the satyr/enemy of the vine/ and lover of bodies beneath rough cloth'. But he found, instead, men perhaps too much like him: only homosexual, not ideal. A friend took him to meet Hart Crane at a party; the two poets spoke very briefly and then divided the drunken sailors between them. In his *Ode to Walt Whitman*, Lorca pours out not so much his anxiety at always hiding his lusts and loves, but his bitterness at travelling so far and finding the same imperfections. He imagined the queens pointing out Whitman, claiming 'He's one, too', on penthouse roofs, in bars, coming up from the sewers, trembling between the legs of chauffeurs 'or spinning on dance floors wet with absinthe'. He seems terrified that lovely, rough bodies should somehow be confused with

> '... urban faggots,
> tumescent flesh and unclean thoughts.
> Mothers of shit. Harpies. Sleepless enemies
> of the love that bestows crowns of joy'.

The city offered him a kind of liberation, and only confirmed his self-disgust.

Visitors came for the sexual epiphany; residents got on with it. The poet Harold Norse remembers the streets of the 1930s: 'You stood absently gazing into a shop window, and if they stopped, you asked for a light or the time; the signals were understood. Sex was usually conducted in secretive silence; even on parting, we rarely spoke....' It took war to break that secret open, to marry the city's glamour and its possibilities. War sent men and women away from home, muddled them promiscuously, let them discover themselves perhaps in a 42nd Street movie house, or on a walk in Prospect or Central or Fort Greene parks. At weekends, the uniforms filled up the YMCAs, the bars in Greenwich Village and the raw spaces of Times Square.

Being gay already had an official geography: the painter Robert Motherwell was exempted from military service because, being in Greenwich Village and an artist, the draft board assumed he must be homosexual. It also had a secret geography: the 'bird circuit' of bars in the East 50s, George's Tavern a block south of Sheridan Square on Seventh Avenue, a basement restaurant with pine tables on Greenwich Avenue near Tenth Street, Central Park if you entered at 72nd Street and Central Park West, the steam-room of the Hotel Shelton, the Dizzy Club full of 'tight boys in tighter pants,' as Harold Norse said; Mary's on Eighth Street where sometimes the Bleecker Street Goths strayed, the young Italians who would beat up any man who wore glasses or carried a book; and later the San Remo bar at Bleecker and MacDougal, in Goth territory. Women, or so *New York: Confidential!* insisted, hung out on Third Street for their 'purple parties . . . within draped walls, in musk-heavy air' ('recently,' the *Confidential* writers go on with a wonderful indifference to words, 'there has been some Negro penetration'). The hurly-burly of the war spread the knowledge of this geography – specific places to meet other men who liked men or women who liked women. Besides, Depression and war had held up marriages, and there was nothing odd about being seemingly unattached; the city was an erotic circus, full of fear and need.

When peace broke out, almost everyone conformed. People married, at last. They went out to live in suburban ranch houses, among people of the same race, age and class. Everyone seemed to agree that strikes were terrible, and communism worse. In the middle of all this order, Kinsey went out to the Eighth Avenue bars that sold guns and drugs and men, and to Village parties which his associates improved with a little experimental booze, and revealed that the order was not what it seemed. There was variety in sexual practice and inclination. The exact boundaries between queer and normal were elastic at best. He imagined, as a good taxonomist, that he was merely reporting; but he alarmed an America already alive with suspicions about anyone different.

The old-established gay culture depended on invisibility but now mayoral elections brought raids on bars, arrests on the beaches, cops chasing men away from the river at Sutton Place where they said they were watching the twilight. The Quakers set up organisations to help, insisting they were not homosexual organisations. The Veterans Benevolent Association, whose meetings could draw 400 or 500 friends, divided and died in recriminations about cissies and behaviour 'in bad taste'. 'The League' was a discussion group of gay professionals whose comings and goings at night in the warehouse district of the Lower East Side made a neighbour suspicious; when a polite note arrived from the local police precinct, there was panic.

There was the Mattachine Society, modelled on Alcoholics Anonymous, with speakers who thought the problem with queers was that they would not acknowledge they were sick; it printed buttons with a lavender equals sign, just as CORE had buttons which showed black and white equals, but they were never worn in public. Newspaper columnists could always make an issue out of the very existence of gay bars; Lee Mortimer of the *Daily Mirror* used to blast the laxity of the cops. The *New York Times* announced in December 1963 that 'the city has what is probably the greatest concentration of sexual inverts anywhere in the world'. Its front page headline read: 'Growth of Overt Homosexuality Provokes Wide Concern'.

Like the Bowery girls, homosexuals were alarming because visible, making a public claim on life and pleasure and freedom; it was a change when people were most afraid of change. You could define a way of life by your sexual preferences alone, a way which had its own rules and pressures, and its own institutions; Edmund White remembers the sheer civilising thought of being able to go to a gay restaurant, somewhere for gay men that did not serve only their sexuality. The city allowed you to keep this separate from work and your economic life. Nobody expects workers in the same Manhattan office to live in the same suburb, have the same friends; each has a journey, perhaps a long one, to their homes and they can travel also to a different life. White in the 1960s was writing for *Time* all day, eating and going straight to bed in order to up again at eleven for the bars. His colleagues were always incurious.

The city also allows for specialisation, erotic or social; you can assemble a gay, deaf baseball team. It could support bars or bath-houses because there was enough casual traffic, and so gay men, however discreet and doubled their lives, acquired places where they did not have to be masked – where they were not a minority. Both cops and gays knew the Mob was interested in running what it contemptuously called 'fag joints'. In the 1960s, the police hired 'actors', cops whom they thought could pass for queer, a curious acknowledgement that the law and the outlaws had much the same blood. They were sent to check the carefully guarded back rooms where men and men danced; then the light that warned the cops had arrived would flash just too late.

In the course of closing thirty bars in 1984, when much more went on in backrooms than simple dancing, the State Liquor Authority found the same names over and over again as doorman, bartender or manager. They suspected the influence of Matty 'the Horse' Ianniello, who owes his nickname to the 300 intimidating pounds of muscle that hang from his CinemaScope shoulders. 'The Horse' is an underboss in the Genovese crime family, wily enough to stay one step ahead of the law, who specialises in the carting of garbage and in midtown bars of all inclinations. His control is usually indirect, by way of payments for – say – installing vending machines or hiring dancers. His empire grew to include the lease of the Mine Shaft sex club in the meat market of the West Side, and the hustler bar the Haymarket on Eighth Avenue, among some eighty others. He had muscle enough and the police contacts to buy some quiet as gay men on their own could not; he sold a kind of protection. The more public, commercial gay life was made in the spaces between enemies: the Mob and the cops.

New York never changed with the beat culture that helped to radicalise San Francisco, nor the scandals which could make gay men angry. In 1965, Mayor Lindsay probably won gay votes by promising a civilian review board for the police. The board could have helped to curb the harassment of the bars and the entrapment practised by duty cops 'in tight pants, sneakers and polo sweaters' at the 'meat rack' on the Western fringes of Washington Square. But a year later, Lindsay ordered sweeps of Times Square to wipe away the 'honky tonks, promenading perverts ... homosexuals and prostitutes'. On summer evenings, the cops were everywhere in Village streets; a gay man hardly dared dawdle. And even when the cops were told not to lure gay men into offences, the threat did not diminish; one off-duty transit cop went down to the waterfront and shot two unarmed gay men who were only strolling there, in hopes. When Howard Brown became health services administrator for the city, he never talked to other gay administrators on any phone, because phones can be tapped and secretaries pick them up unexpectedly, or in official cars because the drivers might hear. He asked his lover of five years to move out of their house, to avoid talk.

But there were enough gay people concentrated in some New York districts in the early 1960s to form a voting bloc, even a movement – Greenwich Village, where one management company with eighteen buildings reckoned a quarter of its tenants were gay; the shabby, comforting West 70s, where all-night cafés on Broadway sheltered the all-day queens; the 'A' list East Side from the upper 40s to the 70s. 'A Third Party For The Third Sex?' the *Village Voice* suggested. The civil rights movement taught that no minority had to suffer in shadows. And the sheer numbers of gay men and women in New

York – perhaps 600,000 by the late 1960s – meant that homosexuality was suddenly a public fact and not, as a law of 1927 had laid down, something that must not even be mentioned on the New York stage. It was only a matter of time before such a substantial minority realised they had power.

The night of Friday 27 June 1969 was hot and kind. Two detectives from the Sixth Precinct assembled a team of cops and went off on a routine raid: a bar called the Stonewall, on Sheridan Square. It was the middle of a mayoral election campaign, and a new commander at the Sixth Precinct had started a purge of the gay bars. The Stonewall was known to have Mob connections, to have no liquor licence and to have go-go boys. Besides, its patrons were not always white, and some of them were drag queens from that little ghetto of runaways in the East Village. It was a raid that everyone would approve.

The cops blocked the doors, and released the customers one by one as a crowd on the street watched. There were jeers as a paddy wagon cruised off with a bartender, a bouncer and three drag queens aboard. The officers tried to steer the last lesbian from the bar to a patrol car, but she fought them back from car to the bar to the car.

And suddenly, the impossible happened. The victims forgot to be victims. Beer cans and bottles and coins rained down on the cops; a parking meter was torn up and used as a ram to batter the bar doors; there was a blaze of flame in the window of the Stonewall. Overnight, 'Gay Pride' graffiti appeared. The queens moved no longer like anxious creatures; they were restless and angry. When they saw officers clubbing a young man, they saved him. They made taunting chorus lines and high-kicked at the cops' faces, dodging round blocks to come up mocking at the cops' backs. And when Allen Ginsberg arrived on Sunday evening, he saw something much more remarkable than the trash fires and the mob movements of the past forty-eight hours, something which made a street riot with a couple of thousand queens into a political fact. He said, 'They've lost that wounded look the fags all had ten years ago.'

I see José in a white room, a view of trees, a curtain half-closed around his bed. He looks brittle and blank. The kid who comes to fix the TV in the corner wears a kind of spacesuit, although he smiles sweetly enough through the visor screen. The nurses have latex hands. José isn't funny, as he used to be, or bright or full of blood. The IVs leash him, the virus makes him suspect his mother is stealing from him, he is settling ill-temperedly into death.

It's too early to write dispassionately about AIDS – the virus which, like the spirochaete before it, took the bright life out of the streets and policed sexual behaviour with terror; and, much more importantly, is the leading killer of young men in New York City. Disease forces controls – the closing of sexual arenas, clubs, baths, dance halls with planetarium skies, movie houses, the playgrounds that were open for those gay men that wanted them – and in so doing makes the state control sexual behaviour. Babies who are born infected with HIV become the symbol of the innocent sufferers; for many people, just as syphilis was what the underworld visited on respectable homes, so AIDS is what homosexuals have unleashed on babies. Those who thought homosexuality somehow infectious now had a perfect metaphor for their fears.

But a virus is a virus, nothing more; it significance lies only in its ability to make cancers, or blood disorders, or to eat away the immune system. A virus has neither morals nor a policeman's badge. And its consequences are not predictable. AIDS has already stretched the hospitals of New York City beyond their capacity. You hear doctors complain that AIDS cases are blocking 'their' cases from hospital beds, as though sickness was proprietary; of course, New York doctors did regard syphilis as proprietary. The Chamber of Commerce worries about the dying homeless, 'a new Calcutta'; their predecessors in the 1890s worried that vice itself would make the city an impossible place for business. There are homeless people on the streets who have full-blown AIDS, who huddle on corners out of the cut of the wind. Tuberculosis has returned to Manhattan, perhaps because of immune disorders associated with AIDS. AIDS is spreading most quickly among junkies, mostly black and Puerto Rican, and their sexual partners. Women and men who go to crack houses for a hit like to make out there, kiss the smoke from mouth to mouth to save it and then fuck while the brief high is in their lungs; the fucking is also spreading AIDS.

Then there are the children born HIV positive, some of them addicted to cocaine. They were supposed to be the throw-away generation. But listen: the throw-away generation is bustling down the hall – gun in the hand of Santos, cowboy hat on Josue, and a sweet and slightly worried smile on his younger brother Pedro, huge dog twisting in among them and a cat keeping careful distance. They're quiet with strangers after they've shot you once or twice. Pedro, who's two, with a head of Botticelli curls, comes up and looks into your eyes. 'He doesn't know what being well is,' his foster father Carlos says, matter of factly. 'How can they tell you when they're sick?'

All three children were born HIV positive, infected with the AIDS virus, to mothers who used drugs. Santos, who's six, takes hospital for granted; he was there with pneumonia last December. Josue has some development problems, a speech impediment, which have to do with the infection. And Pedro is something like a miracle. Often, children born HIV positive are carrying antibodies from their mother's blood but they do not carry the virus itself. Up to fifteen months, they may suddenly sero-convert; that is, tests consistently show they are free of the virus. Pedro will not get AIDS. It's the best of news in what long seemed a hopeless calamity.

All three live now with a gay couple – David, who's part-black, part-Italian, a private man who always wanted to have children; and his lover Carlos, manager of housing in a run-down neighbourhood on New York's Upper West Side, the kind of guy that everyone talks to on the streets. Santos, a dark boy with a long, serious face, is their child – adopted, formally, by David. The other two are the subject of a grumbling court dispute, in which their grandfather wants them back; 'but their mother,' Carlos says, 'is a junkie. She prostitutes herself. She couldn't do anything else. This man made a mess of bringing up his daughters, and now he wants our boys'.

At the start Carlos wasn't keen on having children, but 'in seventeen years together,' he shrugs, 'David worked on me.' They saw reports about AIDS babies stranded in hospital – sick, alone and seemingly hopeless. A fostering agency, Leake and Watts, was beginning to break the usual limits on who could foster these children. Carlos remembers going to the hospital, wearing gloves. There were six kids on a square of linoleum; hospitals were never built to be nurseries. Pedro and Josue had been there four months, abandoned. Pedro was ten months, and he'd hidden himself under a cot. Josue was a year and nine months, terribly responsible for his younger brother. Give Josue a cookie, he'd want one for Pedro; or else he'd hide the cookie and give it to Pedro later. When David and Carlos took them home, they had no coats to go outside. Between them they had one toy: a pencil-sharpener.

Carlos and David knew that they might have to mourn their new family within a few years. 'But we talk about our life now,' Carlos says, 'and we're not going dancing, we're waking up when we think a child might be sick, like a parent does. Our life is the five of us, not just the two of us. From the start, David said to me – We're going to get a child. We are going to love him so much, and he's going to love us so much, that he's going to want to live.'

THERE ARE THREE locks on the door, this being Manhattan, each to be closed and checked: the Medeco, the Police Lock, the Union. Each falls into place. I am leaving the city.

Things fall together here in patterns which are not known elsewhere – money, death, the love of children. Differences collide with each other. The city is violent, sexual, corrupted, extravagant, ambitious, pretentious, full of foreigners and newcomers and strangers; all those familiar things. But when you examine how each works, and what each means, you find both the hurt and the satisfaction which come from being no longer able to evade issues. The city is risky and edgy for that reason. The New York paradox is that it is shiny and distracting, full of glamour and specious things, and yet the city is uncomfortably alive with ideas. Issues like worth, identity, freedom, democracy are what you have to live out and question, not just polite abstractions.

I am leaving New York, but it will not be for long.

SOURCES & BIBLIOGRAPHY

B OOKS LIKE THIS are a ledger of debts to other people's work. Besides my own reporting and research, I have depended on hundreds of earlier studies. Without the luxury of academic footnotes, it's hard to acknowledge this debt properly. The problem is compounded when it comes to sources – court records, for example, or newspaper accounts of trials and hearings – where a half-sentence may well depend on a dozen or more references. Since a full apparatus would either edge the book off its own pages, or make a second volume like a raggedy kind of encyclopedia, these notes are meant only to single out the most important sources from the bibliography that follows.

The most extraordinary resource for the history of New York is I.N. Phelps Stokes: *The Iconography of Manhattan Island 1498–1909*, with its chronology of the city's life and its *catalogue raisonnée* of papers and documents. It is wonderful, and in its ambition and doggedness, almost appalling. The best single volume on the history of New York, told chronologically, remains *Mirror for Gotham*, Bayrd Still's formidable collection of contemporary observations of the city. John A. Kouwenhoven edited *The Columbia Historical Portrait of New York*, which shows the past of the city in engravings, maps and photographs.

In what follows, NYH means *New York History* and NYHSQ means the *New York Historical Society Quarterly*, both of which combine scholarship and remarkable accessibility.

Warnings to Travellers: New York's nickname, and its origins, are finally sorted out by Gerald Cohen in *The Big Apple: A Preliminary Study* in *Comments on Etymology* XVII 2, 5 and 7. On Daniel Denton's marital troubles, see Gerald F. Rooney: *Daniel Denton, Publicist of Colonial New York* in NYHSQ 1971 55:272–276. Paul Marx's 1983 PhD *This is the City: An Examination of Changing Attitudes Toward New York as Reflected in its Guidebook Literature 1807–1860* is an excellent survey and interpretation of the first forms of the New York myth. On the career of 'Gaslight' Foster, see George Rogers Taylor: *Gaslight Foster: A New York Journeyman Journalist' at Mid-Century* in NYH 1977 58:297. Richard Alleman's *The*

Movie-Lover's Guide To New York is a very useful reference. Peter Conrad's *The Art of the City: Views and Versions of New York* is often perverse and always mannered, but it ranges from high art to film noir with authority.

The Manitou: The essential source for New Amsterdam is, of course, the seventeenth-century Dutch records. Some historians have preferred to tell the story from an English point of view, but this is misleading. It may not be much worse than some of the translations from the Dutch which are available – selective, and unreliable on names and places. Of the early translators, A. J. F. van Laer is to be trusted. The publication of the *New Netherland Documents*, under the editorship of Charles Gehring, is making the American sources available in reliable translation and an excellent edition. The most purely readable of the surviving first-hand accounts is *Voyages from Holland to America AD 1632 to 1644* by David de Vries. The archaeological record is particularly important for imagining the life of the settlers, as in the work of Paul Huey. The late Simon Hart, municipal archivist in Amsterdam, opened up the notarial records there which show who came to New Netherland, and often why; since the records of the Dutch West India Company were auctioned for wastepaper on 27 November 1821, having 'by dampness, vermin and repeated removals ... been considerably damaged and become defective and useless ...', the notarial records are even more important. Oliver Rink synthesised this material in *Holland on the Hudson*, which is the most reliable account of New Amsterdam to date. On the secular nature of New Amsterdam, see George L. Smith: *Religion and Trade in New Netherland, Dutch Origins and American Development. A Sweet and Alien Land: The Story of Dutch New York* by Henri and Barbara van der Zee is almost puzzlingly detailed.

For Henry Hudson's voyages, see Henry C. Murphy's *Henry Hudson in Holland*, based on documents he collected while American Minister at The Hague; and *Henry Hudson the Navigator* by G.M. Asher. Later works tend to be imaginative and symphonic. The Mohican account of Hudson's arrival was collected around 1760 by a Moravian missionary, John Heckewelder, and presented in a letter to Dr Samuel Miller; see the *New York Historical Society Collections, new series* vol I. On Amsterdam's curious 'modernity' and values, see *Capitalism in Amsterdam in the Seventeenth Century* by Violet Barbour. This is another excellent excuse to re-read Simon Schama's *The Embarrassment of Riches* on Dutch attitudes and styles of the seventeenth-century Golden Age. On points of detail: Samuel Oppenheimer's *The Early History of the Jews in New York 1654–1664* puts Joseph Barsimson in New York before the Brazilian refugees. Linda Biggs Biemer's *Women and Property in Colonial New York* sets out the role of the great women merchants. I have used Mary Weatherspoon Bowden's analysis of Washington Irving's various targets in *Cocklofts and Slang-whangers: The Historical Sources of Washington Irving's Salmagundi*, in NYH 1980 61: 133.

Frontiers: On Elias Neau and his melodramatic life, see *Elias Neau, Instructor to New York's Slaves* in NYHSQ 1971 55:7–27. On the slave insurrections, see *The Slave Insurrection in New York in 1712* by Kenneth Scott, in NYHSQ 1961 45:43–

74. Daniel Horsmanden's *The New York Conspiracy* is the basic text on the 1741 events, best read in Thomas J. Davis's edition. Davis also wrote *Rumor of Revolt: The 'Great Negro Plot' in Colonial New York*, a first-rate questioning and retelling of Horsmanden's material. On events at the turn of the nineteenth century, see *Mobocracy: Popular Disturbances in Post-Revolutionary New York City 1783–1829*, Paul A. Gilje's PhD thesis. Douglas T. Miller examined *Immigration and Social Stratification in Pre-Civil War New York* in NYH 1968 49:157. On the draft riots, see Iver Bernstein's extraordinarily intelligent study. On attitudes to newcomers, see David Ward's *Poverty, Ethnicity and the American City 1840–1925* and *Reconstruction in the North: The World Looks at New York's Negroes, March 16 1867* by David P. Thelen and Leslie H. Fishel Junior in NYH 1968 49:405.

Rocco Corresca and Sadie Frowne told their own stories to Hamilton Holt of the weekly *The Independent*, who published them in 1906 in a collection called *The Life Stories of Undistinguished Americans, As Told By Themselves*. William Loren Katz and Jacqueline Hunt Katz collected these stories for *Making Our Way*. Richard Sherard's account of coming to America needs the additional detail in Thomas M. Pitkin's *High Tide at Ellis Island* in NYHSQ 1986 52:311 and *A Modern 'Black Hole of Calcutta'? The Anglo-American Controversy over Ellis Island* by Benjamin D. Rhodes in NYH 1985 66:229.

Peter Kwong's *The New Chinatown* is brief, but useful. Loren W. Fessler edited *Chinese in America: Stereotyped Past, Changing Present* a collection of documents and testimony. The single most fascinating book on Chinatown is the sympathetic Louis J. Beck's *New York Chinatown* published in 1898. *Chinatown Inside Out* is a snappy 1936 account by Leong Gor Yun. The 1984 hearings of the President's Commission on Organised Crime dealt with *Organised Crime of Asian Origin*.

I have drawn on Suzanne Windholz Model's PhD thesis *Ethnic Bonds in the Work Place: Blacks, Italians and Jews in New York City* for evidence of how newcomers found jobs, and which jobs they found. The real estate history of Harlem is in two papers: *The New York City Negro and the Tenement, 1880–1910* by Seth M. Scheiner in NYH 1964 45:304 and *A Decade of Urban Tragedy: How Harlem Became A Slum* by Gilbert Osofksy, in NYH 1965 46:330. On the Harlem Renaissance, see David Levering Lewis: *When Harlem Was In Vogue* and Kathy J. Ogren's essay on *Jazz Performance as Theme and Language in the Harlem Renaissance*. On the Lubavitcher Hasidim, the essential book is Lis Harris: *Holy Days*.

Audition City: Some of the material on the street-corner hiring markets is from *New Yorkers at Work*, a tape compilation prepared by the Robert F. Wagner Labor Archives.

It would be a pity not to read William Dunlap's 1832 memoirs, which come disguised as his *History of the American Theatre*, and the theatre biographies listed in the bibliography; but for stricter truth see the theatre histories of Garff B. Wilson, Thomas Wood Stevens and *A History of the Theatre* by George Freedley and John A. Reeves. Jared A. Brown wrote *A Note on British Military Theatre in New York at the End of the American Revolution* in NYH 1981 62:177. On the life of Union Square, see *Actors and American Culture 1880–1920* by Benjamin McArthur.

John Tebbel's *Between Covers: The Rise and Transformation of Book Publishing in America* is the standard work, but Henry Walcott Boynton's *Annals of American Bookselling 1638–1850* and Sheila McVey's paper on 'Nineteenth Century America: Publishing in a Developing Country' in the collection *Perspectives on Publishing* are also essential. The jolliest book on Bohemianism is *Garrets and Pretenders: A History of Bohemianism in America* by Albert Parry. The Oscar Wilde dinner is from *Oscar Wilde: Interviews and Recollections* edited by E.H. Mikhail. On literary salons, see Charles M. Lombard in NYHSQ 1971 55:38 and on the Authors' Festival, see Warren G. French in NYHSQ 1955 39:357.

On the development of the art business, see *The Artist in American Society: The Formative Years 1790–1860* by Neil Harris. Rita Susswein Gottesman wrote on *New York's First Major Art Show* in NYHSQ 1959 43:289, and R.L. Stehle on *The Dusseldorf Gallery of New York* in NYHSQ 1974 58:305. John Ferguson Weir's memoirs have been edited by Theodore Sizer: I quote from the Tenth Street episode in NYHSQ 1957 41:351. See Richard Cox's *Coney Island, Urban Symbol in American Art* in NYHSQ 1976 60:35, especially on Stella's paintings. Robert C. Vitz's paper *Struggle and Response: American Artists and the Great Depression* in NYH 57:81 was useful. Dore Ashton's *The New York School: A Cultural Reckoning* is a thoughtful, elegant account of a movement, lit up by personal knowledge. Calvin Tomkins's *The Bride and the Bachelors* is useful on Duchamp and Rauschenberg in particular. Serge Guilbaut's *How New York Stole The Idea of Modern Art* is a cross, stimulating and political study.

The Skyline is Politics: The essential reference books on city buildings are the *AIA Guide to New York City* by Elliot Willensky and Norval White, and Barbaralee Diamonstein's catalogue of *The Landmarks of New York*. Rebecca Read Shanor's *The City That Never Was* catalogues those fancies, visions and atrocities that were never built, and in so doing clarifies the development of the real city. Norval White's *New York: A Physical History* is valuable. John Kieran's *Natural History of New York* is essential. On reptiles as a test of the health of the city, see Michael W. Klemens: *Survivors in Megalopolis: Reptiles of the Urban North East* in *Discovery* 1985 18 i p.22. My account also draws on the Natural Areas Management Plans drawn by the Natural Resources Group of the city's Parks and Recreation Department.

On Central Park the best source is Olmsted himself; *The Papers of Frederick Law Olmsted*, vol. III, 'Creating Central Park 1857–1861' have been edited by Charles E. Beveridge and David Schuyler.

See Maury Klein's *The Life and Legend of Jay Gould* on the robber baron's interest in the 'el's. Mrs Miller's testimony is in *The Tenement House Problem* edited by Robert W. de Forest and Lawrence Veiller. There is a general book on subway systems, Benson Bobrick's *Labyrinths of Iron*, but remarkably little in print on what the subways meant. Wallace B. Katz's paper *The New York Rapid Transit Decision of 1900: Economy, Society and Politics* is buried in a mimeo'd government research report. Peter Derrick's very important PhD *The Dual System of Rapid Transit: The Role of Politics and City Planning in the Second Stage of*

Subway Construction in New York City, 1902 to 1913 is sadly unpublished, although some of Derrick's ideas are in *Catalyst for Development: Rapid Transit in New York* in *New York Affairs* 1986 9.iv:29. On the 'better classes' see Richard Skolnik's *Civic Group Progressivism in New York City* in NYH 1970 51:411.

Robert Moses published a self-defence, *Working for the People: Promise and Performance in Public Service*, but it was not enough. Robert A. Caro's *The Power Broker: Robert Moses and the Fall of New York* is a perfectly astonishing feat of research, animated by apparent loathing of its subject. It's helpful to read it alongside Thomas Kessner's no less monumental, but rather less bilious *Fiorello La Guardia and the Making of Modern New York*.

On 42nd Street: Patricia Robin Klausner has a useful account of some of the shenanigans on the Deuce in her PhD *The Politics of Massage Parlor Prostitution: The International Traffic in Women for Prostitution into New York City 1970-present.*

Minimum City: The essential books on the workings of modern New York are Jack Newfield and Paul du Brul: *The Abuse of Power: the Permanent Government and the Fall of New York* and Jack Newfield and Wayne Barrett: *City for Sale*. Both books develop the brave and sharp city reporting of the *Village Voice*. For the Manes affair, and for the corruption of modern New York, I have drawn mainly on trial reports appearing in the *New York Times*, especially on the trial of Stanley Friedman and others at New Haven; and the trials of Mario Biaggi, John J. McLaughlin, Judge William C. Brennan. The litany of corruption in the years before Manes fell is based on trials in which the defendants were convicted for the offences mentioned. Two pieces by Nicholas Pileggi in *New York Magazine* are especially helpful: *The New Corruption* 11 November 1985 and *The Mob and the Machine* 5 May 1986. The reporting of Andy Logan in the *New Yorker* is always valuable, especially his *Around City Hall* columns of 30 June 1986; 3 November 1986; 5 January 1987; 14 September 1987; 26 September 1988. On Roy Cohn and his ways, see Nicholas Hoffman: *Citizen Cohn*, but also Sidney Zion: *The Autobiography of Roy Cohn* for some of the man's political *obiter dicta*. Edward Koch's *Mayor* is a self-serving eulogy that now seems rather sad.

The history of New York as a legal idea is discussed in Hendrik Hartog's PhD thesis *The Properties of the Corporation: New York City and Its Law, 1730 to 1870*. Amy Bridges in *A City in the Republic: Antebellum New York and the origins of machine politics* connects the machine with ideas and with class and conflict. The origins of Tammany and the later debates about the machine are discussed in Thomas Bender's *New York Intellect*. See also NYHSQ 1971 55:52 *E.L. Godkin* by Diana Klebanow. For the history of fire companies, see Stephen F. Ginsberg: *Above the law: Volunteer Firemen in New York City 1836–1837* NYH 1969 50:165; and *The Police and Fire Protection in New York City: 1800–1850* in NYH 1971 52:133. Ivor Bernstein in *The New York City Draft Riots* has a brief but brilliant analysis of the politics of the Tweed Ring. See also Alexander B. Callow Junior in NYHSQ April 1965 54:171 *'What Are You Going to Do About It?': The Crusade against the Tweed Ring* and John W. Pratt: *Boss Tweed's Public Welfare Program* in NYH 1961 42:396. My account of the Ring is based directly on the reporting of the *New York Times* from 1870 to 1872, which is the source for verbatim quotes and descriptions.

The aftermath of Tweed and the consolidation of Greater New York are discussed by David C. Hammack in *Power and Society: Greater New York at the Turn of the Century*.

The early promise of Jimmy Walker is noted in articles collected in *The Best in The World*, edited by John K. Hutchens and George Oppenheimer. On Prohibition manners, see Stephen Graham: *New York Nights*. On corruption under Walker, see *Stand and Deliver* by E.H. Lavine. The fall of Jimmy Walker is taken from contemporary reporting in the *New York Times*, which published full transcripts of the Seabury hearings. Thomas Kessler's *Fiorello H. La Guardia and the Making of Modern New York* is the essential biography: sharp, exhilarating and full. See also Arthur Mann's *La Guardia Comes To Power* and Leonard Chalmers's essay *Fiorello la Guardia, Paterfamilias at City Hall: An Appraisal* in NYH 1975 56:211. On Mob involvement in Tammany, see Virgil W. Peterson: *The Mob: 200 Years of Organised Crime in New York*, a sober account by the one-time head of the Chicago Crime Commission; and the rather thin, but first-hand *The Last of the Big Time Bosses: The Life and Times of Carmine de Sapio and the Rise and Fall of Tammany Hall* by Warren Moscow. Original sources for the discussion of the Mob as an alternative government include these documents filed in the Southern District of New York, United States District: (on trucking) Indictment 85 Cr. *United States of America v. Matthew Ianniello et al* and US Attorney's press release of 19 February 1985; (on loansharking) Indictment S 84 Cr. 479 (LBS) *United States of America v. Vincent Joseph Rotondo*; (on construction trades) Department of Justice press release 25 October 1984 and Indictment 84 Cr. *United States of America v. Carmine Persico aka 'The Snake' et al*. On the garment business, see various reports from the office of State Senator Franz S. Leichter, who continues to take an interest in the subject, but especially *Sweatshops to Shakedowns: Organised Crime in New York's Garment industry* (mimeo: 1982). Direct quotes from Mobsters come mainly from Government's Memorandum of Law in Opposition to Defendant's June 28 Motions in *United States of America v. John Lewis de Lutro et al*. 84 Cr. 664 (MJL) also in the Southern District.

The Siege of Mrs Astor's Ballroom: Manhattan anxieties about what an address can mean are laid out in *Alone Together: A History of New York's Early Apartments* by Elizabeth Collins Cromley. Attorney General Robert Abrams's statement on the Creo Society was reported in the *New York Times* 22 October 1989. Calvin Tomkins's history of the Metropolitan Museum, *Merchants and Masterpieces* is especially valuable on the early years.

On early attitudes to land, see Elizabeth Blackmar: *Manhattan for Rent, 1785– 1850*. On the founding of the Astor fortune see *John Jacob Astor, Landlord of New York* by Arthur D. Howden Smith and *The Golden Earth: The Story of Manhattan's Landed Wealth* by Arthur Pound. Attitudes to homes, and to politics and charity are discussed in Christine Stansell's *City of Women* and Amy Bridge's *A City in the Republic* respectively. On the travelling show of New York, see Joseph Earl

Arrington: *Otis A. Bullard's Moving Panorama of New York City* in NYHSQ 1960 44:309. On the origins of the New York Zoo, see Helen L. Horowitz: *Animal and Man in the New York Zoological Park* in NYH 1975 56:426

The literature on the grand New York families is exhaustive, as the bibliography suggests, and sometimes numbing. I owe a special debt to Ron Chernow's magisterial *The House of Morgan: An American Banking Dynasty and the Rise of Modern Finance*, David Black's fascinating *The King of Fifth Avenue: The Fortunes of August Belmont* and Arthur T. Vanderbilt II's *Fortune's Children: The Fall of the House of Vanderbilt*. I also draw on Paul R. Baker's *Stanny: The Gilded Life of Stanford White*. Elizabeth Drexel Lehr's memoir, *King Lehr and the Gilded Age*, is a tragedy disguised as a gossip column. The novels of Edith Wharton and her autobiography *A Backward Glance* are indispensable sources for nineteenth-century and turn-of-the-century New York attitudes, although she is less sure about the city of the 1920s. Of all the satires and denunciations of New York Society, which now have a history of at least a century and a half, the most informative on its times is Ralph Pulitzer's *New York Society on Parade* of 1910. For the world of 'nouvelle society', see John Fairchild's *Chic Savages*, an anthology of frockmakers' gossip.

Taking Liberties: Christine Stansell's *City of Women: Sex and Class in New York 1789–1860* is a quite extraordinary study of working women, on which I have drawn heavily; along with Timothy J. Gilfoyle's encyclopedic 1987 Columbia PhD *City of Eros: New York City, Prostitution, and the Commercialisation of Sex 1790–1920*. See also Claire Marie Renzetti: *Purity v. Politics: The Legislation of Morality in Progressive New York, 1890–1920*. Ianniello's empire is detailed, in part, in Indictment 85 Cr., Southern District of New York, United States District Court: *United States of America v. Matthew Ianniello etc.* Jonathan Katz's *Gay American History* remains a most remarkable sourcebook, to be supplemented by John d'Emilio's *Sexual Politics, Sexual Communities: The Making of a Homosexual Minority in the United States 1940–1970* and Edward Sagarin's unpromisingly titled *Structure and Ideology in an Association of Deviants*.

On Walt Whitman as politician, see *Walt Whitman, Politician in New York* by Stanley J. Idzerda in NYH 1956 37:171. Earl Lind's bizarre *Autobiography of an Androgyne* was republished in 1975. The geography of gay New York in the 1940s is derived from the many confessional memoirs of the 1980s. The *New York Times* headline on the growth of 'overt homosexuality' ran on 13 December 1963, and includes some detailed reporting. The *Village Voice* pieces ran on 27 September and 11 October 1962.

BIBLIOGRAPHY

Actors Equity Association. *Equity News* vol. 73 New York, 1988.

Ades, Dawn. *Dali*. London, 1982.

Aldrich Jr., Nelson W. *Old Money. The Mythology of America's Upper Class*. New York, 1989.

Alexander, H.M. *Striptease: the Vanished Art of Burlesque*. New York, 1938.

Alexander, Shana. *When She Was Bad. The Story of Bess, Hortense, Sukhreet, and Nancy*. New York, 1990.

Alger Jr., Horatio. *Ragged Dick and Struggling Upward*. Harmondsworth, 1985 [1890].

Alleman, Richard. *The Movie Lover's Guide to New York*. New York, 1988.

Altbach, Philip G. and Sheila McVey, eds. *Perspectives on Publishing*. Lexington, 1976.

Amory, Cleveland. *Who Killed Society?* New York, 1960.

Anderson, John. *Box Office*. New York, 1929.

Anderson, Samuel K. 'Public Lotteries in Colonial New York' in *The New York Historical Society Quarterly*. vol. 56, 1972, (133–146).

Andrews, Charles H. *Narratives of the Insurrections 1675–1690*. New York, 1915.

Andrews, Wayne, ed. 'A Glance at New York in 1967. The Travel Diary of Dr Benjamin Bullivan' in *The New York Historical Society Quarterly*, vol. 40, 1956, (55–73).

Andrews, Wayne. *The Vanderbilt Legend. The Story of the Vanderbilt Family 1794–1940*. New York, 1941.

Anon. *Voyage de New York à la Nouvelle Orleans*. Paris, 1818.

Armstrong, William M. 'The Godkin-Schurz Feud,1881–1883, over Policy Control of the *Evening Post*' in *The New York Historical Society Quarterly*, vol. 48, 1964, (5–21).

Arrington, Joseph Earl. 'Otis A. Bullard's Moving Panorama of New York City.' in *The New York Historical Society Quarterly* vol. 44, 1960.

Asbury, Herbert. *The Gangs of New York. An Informal History of the Underworld*. New York, 1989 [1927].

Asher, G.M. *Sketch of Henry Hudson the Navigator*. Brooklyn, 1867.

Asher, G.M. 'Henry Hudson the Navigator.' in *Halyut Society Works* vol. 27 London, 1860.

Ashton, Dore. *The New York School. A Cultural Reckoning*. New York, 1979 [1972].

Astor, Brooke. *Footprints: an Autobiography*. Garden City, New York, 1980.

Astor, Michael. *Tribal Feelings*. London, 1963.

Astor, William Waldorf. *Silhouettes*. London, 1917.

Auchincloss, Louis. *The Vanderbilt Era. Profiles of a Gilded Age*. New York, 1989.

Auster, Paul. *The New York Trilogy*. London, 1988 [1985].

Baart, Jan M. 'Dutch Arts and Culture in Colonial America 1609–1776' in *New World Dutch Studies*. Albany, 1987.

Babcock, Richard, ed. 'Our World. How Bad is New York's Environment?' in *New York* April 1990, (28–46).

Baker, Paul R. *Stanny. The Gilded Life of Stanford White*. New York, 1979.

Balmer, Randal. 'Religion Dimensions of Leisler's Rebellion.' Paper presented at the 12th Rensselaerswyck Seminar, 23 September 1989.

Barbour, Violet. *Capitalism in Amsterdam in the 17th Century*. Ann Arbor, 1963 [Baltimore, 1950].

Barlow, Elizabeth, and William Alex. *Frederick Law Olmsted's New York*. New York, 1972.

Barnes, Djuna. *New York*. Los Angeles, 1989.

Baromé, Joseph A. 'Fernando Palmo – Pioneer Impresario of Grand Opera in New York' in *New York History* vol. 45, 1964, (59–76).

Beaton, Cecil. *Cecil Beaton's New York*. London, 1938.

Beck, Louis J. *New York's Chinatown*, New York, 1898.

Bender, Thomas. *New York Intellect*. New York, 1987.

Bender, Thomas. 'James Fenimore Cooper and the City' in *New York History* vol. 51, 1970, (287–305).

Bennet Jr., Lerone. *Before the Mayflower*. Harmondsworth, 1988 [1962].

Berman, Marshall. *All That Is Solid Melts into Air. The Experience of Modernity*. Harmondsworth, 1988 [1982].

Bernstein, Ivor. *The New York City Draft Riots. Their Significance for American Society and Politics in the Age of the Civil War*. New York, 1990.

Berrol, Selma C. 'School Days on the Old East Side: The Italian and Jewish Experience' in *New York History* vol. 57, 1976 (201–213).

Berthoff, Rowland T, trans. and ed. '"Life in America" A Disillusioned Welshman in New York.' in *New York History* vol. 37, 1956 (80–84).

Beveridge, Charles E. and David Schuyler, eds. *The Papers of Frederick Law Olmsted, vol. III. Creating Central Park 1857–1861*. Baltimore, 1983.

Bianco, Anthony. 'The Decline of the Superstar. Recent Debacles Have Wall Street CEOs Struggling to Show Who's Boss' in *Business Week* 17 August 1987, (190–198).

Biggs Biemer, Linda. *Women and Property in Colonial New York*. Ann Arbor, 1983.

Bigland, Eileen. *The Indomitable Mrs Trollope*. London, 1953.

Black, David. *The King of Fifth Avenue. The Fortunes of August Belmont*. New York, 1981.

Blackburn, Roderic H. 'Remembrance of Patria' in *De Halve Maen* vol. 59, 1987, (1–7).

Blackmar, Elizabeth. *Manhattan for Rent, 1785–1850*. Ithaca, 1989.

Board of Commissioners of Central Park. *Third Annual Report*. New York, Jan. 1880.

Bobrick, Benson. *Labyrinths of Iron. A History of the World's Subways*. New York, 1982.

Bolton, Reginald Pelham. 'The Scene of the Purchase of Manhattan Island' in *Indian Notes* vol. 5 no. 4, 1928, (364).

Boyer, Lee R. 'Lobster Blacks, Liberty Boys, and Laborers in the Streets. New York's Golden Hill and Nassau Street Riots' in *The New York Historical Society Quarterly* vol. 57 1973 (281–308).

Boyton, Henry Walcott. *Annals of American Bookselling 1638–1850*. New York, 1932.

Brandt, Alan. *No Magic Bullet. A Social History of Venereal Disease in the United States Since 1880*. New York, 1987.

Bridges, Amy. *A City in the Republic. Antebellum New York, and the Origins of Machine Politics*. Ithaca, 1987 [1984].

Brogan, Hugh. *The Pelican History of the United States of America*. Harmondsworth, 1986.

Bromwell, William J. *History of Migration to the United States 1819–1855*. New York, 1969 [1855].

Brown, Jared A. 'A Note on British Military Theater in New York at the End of the American Revolution' in *New York History* vol. 62 1981, (177–187).

Brown, Mary M. *Amazing New York*. London, 1913.

Brownlow, Jack. *Melton Mowbray – Queen of the Shires*. London, 1980.

Bryant, Edward. *Pennell's New York Etchings: 90 Prints by Joseph Pennell*. New York, 1980.

Buranelli, Vincent. 'Governor Caby's Hatchet-Man.' in *New York History* vol. 37, 1956 (26–39).

Burgess, Charles O. 'The Newspaper as Charity Worker: Poor Relief in New York City, 1893–1894' in *New York History* vol. 43, 1962 (249–268).

Burnhands, Alan. *New York Landmarks*. Middletown, Conn., 1963.

Cayo Sexton, Patricia. *Spanish Harlem. Anatomy of Poverty*. New York, 1965.

Calder, Jenni. *Robert Louis Stevenson – A Life Study*. London, 1980.

Callow Jr., Alexander B. *The Tweed Ring*. New York, 1966.

Callow Jr., Alexander B. '"What Are you Going to Do About It?" The Crusade Against the Tweed Ring' in *The New York Historical Society Quarterly* vol. 49 1965 (117–142).

Camus, Albert. *American Journals*. Translated from the French by Hugh Levick, New York, 1987.

Caro, Robert A. *The Power Broker. Robert Moses and the Fall of New York*. New York, 1975 [1974].

Carpenter, Humphrey. *W.H. Auden – A Biography*. London, 1983.

Cashman, Sean Dennis. *America in the Gilded Age. From the Death of Lincoln to the Rise of Theodore Roosevelt*. New York, 1988 [1984].

Céline, Louis Ferdinand. *Journey to the End of the Night*. Translated from the French by Ralph Manheim, New York, 1983 [1934].

Cellis, Maurice. *Nancy Astor*. London, 1959.

Cerillo, Augustus, Jr. 'The Reform of Municipal Government in New York City. From Seth Low to John Purroy Mitchell' in *The New York Historical Society Quarterly* vol. 57, 1973 (51–71).

Chalmers, Leonard. 'Fiorello La Guardia, Paterfamilias at City Hall: An Appraisal' in *New York History* vol. 56, 1975 (211–225).

Chalmers, Leonard. 'The Crucial Test of La Guardia's First Years: The Emergency Economy Bill' in *The New York Historical Society Quarterly* vol. 57, 1973 (235–253).

Chern, Kenneth S. 'The Politics of Patriotism. War, Ethnicity, and the New York Mayoral Campaign, 1917' in *The New York Historical Society Quarterly* vol. 63, 1979, (291–313).

Chernow, Ron. *The House of Morgan. An American Banking Dynasty and the Rise of Modern Finance*. New York, 1990.

Christman, Henry M., ed. *Walt Whitman's New York. From Manhattan to Montauk*. New York, 1963.

Christoph, Peter R. 'The Freedman in New Netherland' in *Journal of the Afro-American Historical and Genealogical Society* vol.5 nos. 3 and 4, 1989 (109–118).

Churcher, Sharon. *New York Confidential*. New York, 1986.

City of New York, Mayor's Office of Midtown Enforcement. *Annual Report 1987*. New York, 1987.

Clarke, Gerald. *Capote. A Biography*. New York, 1988.

Cohen, Arthur A. *A Republic Apart. Hasidism in America*. New York, 1970.

Cohen, David S. 'In Search of Carolus Africanus Rex' in *Journal of the Afro-American Historical and Genealogical Society* vol. 5 nos.3 and 4, 1989 (149–162).

Cohen, David S. 'How Dutch Were the Dutch of New Netherland?' in *New York History* vol. 62, 1981 (43–60).

Cohen, Gerald. 'The Big Apple: A Preliminary Study, part I' in *Comments on Etymology*. vol. 18 no.2 1988. Part II vol. 18 no.5, Feb 1989. Part III vol. 18 no.7 April 1989.

Cohen, Ronald D. 'The New England Colonies and the Dutch Recapture of New York, 1673–1674' in *The New York Historical Society Quarterly* vol. 56, 1972 (54–78).

Cohen, Sheldon S. 'Elias Neau, Instructor to New York's Slaves.' in *The New York Historical Society Quarterly* vol. 55 1971, (7–27).

Colbertson, Judi, and Tom Randolf. *Permanent New Yorkers. A Biographical Guide to the Cemeteries of New York*. Chelsea, Vermont, 1987.

Coleridge, Nicholas. *The Fashion Conspiracy*. London, 1989.

Collier, John Lincoln. *Duke Ellington*. London, 1987.

Collin Brown, Henry, ed. *Valentines Manual of Old New York*. New York, 1926.

Comley, Elizabeth Collins. *Alone Together. A History of New York's Early Apartments*. Ithaca, 1990.

Condon, Thomas. 'Political Reform and the New York City Election of 1886' in *The New York Historical Society Quarterly* vol. 44, 1960 (363–393).

Conrad, Peter. *The Art of the City. Views and Versions of New York*. New York, 1984.

Cooper, Diana. *Autobiography*. Salisbury, 1979.

Corliss, Richard. 'Welcome to Harlem' in *Time* 24 April 1989 (68–74).

Countryman, Edward. *The American Revolution*. Harmondsworth, [1985] 1987.

Cowles, Virginia. *The Astors*, London, 1979.

Crane, Hart. *The Complete Poems and Selected Letters and Prose of Hart Crane*. Edited by Brom Weber, Garden City, 1966.

Crouthmel, James L. 'James Gordon Bennett, the New York Herald, and the Development of Newspaper Sensationalism' in *New York History* vol. 54, 1973 (294–316).

Crouthmel, James L. 'The Newspaper Revolution in New York, 1830–1860' in *New York History* vol. 45, 1964 (91–113).

Crouthmel, James L. 'James Watson Webb: Mercantile Editor' in *New York History* vol. 41, 1960 (400–422).

Current Biography Yearbook. 'Brooke Astor' in *Current Biography Yearbook, 1987* (22–25).

D'Emilio, John. *Sexual Politics, Sexual Communities. The Making of a Homosexual Minority in the United States 1940–1970.* Chicago, 1983.

Dana, Nathalie. 'The Municipal Art Society. Seventy-five Years of Service to New York' in *The New York Historical Society Quarterly* vol. 51, 1967 (161–183).

Dana, Nathalie. 'Farm to City – A New York Romance' in *The New York Historical Society Quarterly*, vol. 49, 1965 (217–225).

Dana, Nathalie. 'Lenox Hill in the 1880s. A Girl's Memories of Saint James Parish. Part I: Our House on East 71st Street' in *The New York Historical Society Quarterly* vol. 46, 1962 (171–217). 'Part II: Our House on East 69th Street' in *The New York Historical Society Quarterly* vol. 46, 1962 (245–279).

Danielson, Michael N. and Jameson W. Doig. *New York. The Politics of Urban Regional Development.* Berkeley, 1982.

Davis, John H. *The Guggenheims (1848–1988). An American Epic.* New York, 1988.

Davis, L.G. *Paul Robeson: Research Guide.* Westport, 1982.

Davis, Thomas J. *A Rumor of Revolt. The 'Great Negro Plot' in Colonial New York.* New York, 1985.

Davis, Thomas J. 'These Enemies of Their Own Household' in *Journal of the Afro-American Historical and Genealogical Society* vol. 5, nos.3 and 4, 1984 (133–148).

Davisson, Willian I. and Lawrence J. Bradley. 'New York Maritime Trade: Ship Voyage Patterns, 1715–1765' in *The New York Historical Society Quarterly* vol. 55, 1971 (309–317).

Dayton, Abram C. *Last Days of Knickerbocker Life in New York.* New York, 1897.

De Beauvoir, Simone. *America Day by Day.* Translated from the French by Patrick Dudley, New York, 1973.

De Forest, Robert W. and Larence Veiller, eds. *The Tenement House Problem.* New York, 1970 [New York 1903].

De Jong, Gerald Francis. 'The Siekentroosters or Comforters of the Sick in New Netherland' in *New York History* vol. 53, 1972, (339–359).

De Jong, Gerald Francis. 'Dominie Johanes Megapotensis: Minister to New Netherland' in *The New York Historical Society Quarterly* vol. 52, 1968 (7–47).

De Roever, Margriet. 'The Fort Orange "EB" Pipe Bowls: An Investigation of the Origins of American Objects in Dutch Seventeenth-Century Documents.' in *New World Dutch Studies,* 1986 (51–62).

De Vries, David Petersz. *Voyages from Netherland to America.* Trans. from the Dutch by Henry C. Murphy. New York, 1853.

Degles, Carl N. 'The West as a Solution to Urban Unemployment' in *New York History* vol. 36, 1955, (63–84).

De la Court, Pieter. *The True Interests and Political Maxims of the Republic of Holland.* New York, 1972 [London, 1746].

Delgado, Karla. 'Robbing Two Neighborhoods Together' in *Village Voice.* October. 31 1989.

Denton, Daniel. *A Brief Description of New York: Formerly Called New Netherland.* London, 1670.

Derrick, Peter. 'Catalyst For Development: Rapid Transit in New York' in *New York Affairs* vol. 67, no.4, 1986 (29–59).

Derrick, Peter. 'The Dual System of Rapid Transit: The Role of Politics and City Planning in the Second Stage of Subway Construction in New York, 1902–1913.' PhD dissertation, Department of History, New York University, 1979.

Diamond, Sigmund, ed. *A Casual View of America. The Home Letters of Salomon de Rothschild 1859–1861*. Stanford, 1961.

Diamonstein, Barbaralee. *The Landmarks of New York*. New York, 1988.

Dickens, Charles. *The Life and Adventures of Martin Chuzzlewit*. Harmondsworth, 1986 [1843–4].

Dickens, Charles. *American Notes for General Circulation*. Harmondsworth, 1987 [1842].

Dinnerstein, Leonard. 'The Impact of Tammany Hall on State and National Politics in the Eighteen Eighties' in *New York History* vol. 42, 1961 (237–252).

Dorwart, Jeffery M. 'The Roosevelt-Astor Espionage Ring' in *New York History* vol. 62, 1981, (307–322).

Dos Passos, John. *Manhattan Transfer*. Boston, 1976 [1925].

Driberg, Tom. *Ruling Passions*. London, 1978.

Duffy, John. 'An Account of the Epidemic Fever that Prevailed in the City of New York from 1791–1822' in *The New York Historical Society Quarterly* vol. 50, 1966 (333–364).

Dunlop, William. *History of the American Theatre*. New York, 1963, [1872].

Dunnings Thomas J. Jr. 'Minutes of Oceanus Engine Company No.11, 1780–1819' in *The New York Historical Society Quarterly* vol. 53, 1969 (78–81).

Durden, Robert. *The Dukes of Durham 1865–1929*. Durham, 1975.

Eerdams, Martha. *Peter Stuyvesant: An Historical Documentation*. Grand Rapids, Michigan, 1957.

Ellis, David Maldwyn. 'Rise of the Empire State, 1790–1820' in *New York History* vol. 56, 1975, (5–27).

Ellington, Duke. *Music My Mistress*. London, 1977.

Ellington, Mercer. *Duke Ellington in Person*. London, 1978.

Ellis, C.D.B. *Leicestershire and the Quorn Hunt*. Leicester, 1951.

Ellis, David. '"Upstate Hicks" versus "City Slickers"' in *The New York Historical Society Quarterly* vol. 43, 1959 (202–219).

Emmer, P.C. 'The West India Trade Company, 1621–1791: Dutch or Atlantic?' in Blusse, Leonard and Femme Caastra, eds., *Companies and Trade*. Leiden, 1981.

Emmer, P.C. 'De Slavenhandel van en naar Nieuw-Nederland' in *Economisch- en Sociaal-historisch Jaarboek*. n.d. (94–147).

Epstein, Perle. *Pilgrimage*. Boston, 1979.

Ewen Frederick. *Bertold Brecht: His Life, His Art and His Times*. New York, 1967.

Exman, Eugene. *The House of Kasper*. New York, 1967.

Fairchild, John. *Chic Savages*. New York, 1989.

Farnan, Dorothy J. *Auden in Love*. New York, 1984.

Fay, E.S. *Londoner's New York*. London, 1936.

Federal Writers Project. *The WPA Guide to New York*. New York, 1982 [1939].

Fester, Loven W. *Chinese in America: Stereotyped Past, Changing Present*. New York, 1983.

Fido, Martin. *Oscar Wilde*. Harmondsworth, 1984.

Fisher, Clive, ed. *Anecdotes, Sayings and Impressions of Sir John Gielgud*. London, 1988.

Fisher, Joel. 'Urban Transportation: Home Rule and the Independent Subway System in New York City, 1917–1925' (mimeo) PhD Dissertation, Department of History, St John's University, 1978.

Fisher, Margaret. *John Masefield*. London, 1963.

Fitzgerald, F. Scott. *The Beautiful and Damned*. New York, 1986 [1922].

Fleming, E. and H.S. Kates. *New York*. London, 1929.

Foner, Nancy, ed. *New Immigrants in New York*. New York, 1987.

Foner, Philio J. *Paul Robeson Speaks*. London, 1978.

Fox, Joseph. *Rabbi Menachem Mendel of Koch*. New York, 1988.

Fox, Kenneth. *Metropolitan America. Urban Life and Urban Policy in the United States, 1940–1980*. Jackson, 1986.

Frazere, M.P. *Mrs Trollope and America*. Caen, 1969.

Freedley, George and John A, Reeves. *A History of the Theatre*. New York, 1955.

French, Warren G. '"Honor to Genius" The Complimentary Festival to Authors' in *The New York Historical Society Quarterly* vol. 39, 1955, (357–367).

Frost, James A. 'The Home Fronts in New York During the Civil War' in *New York History* vol. 42, 1961 (273–296).

Gammond, Peter. *Duke Ellington*. London, 1987.

García Lorca, Federico. *Poet in New York*. Translated from Spanish by Greg Simon and Steve White. New York, 1988 [1940].

Gates Raddin, George Jr.. *Hocquet Caritat and the Early New York Scene*. Dover, NJ, 1953.

Gehring, Charles T. trans, and ed. 'Curaçao Papers 1640–1665' in *New Netherland Documents* transcribed and ed. by J.A. Schiltkamp, Interlaken, NY, 1987.

Gehring, Charles T. and Robert S. Grumet. 'Observations of the Indians from Jasper Danckarts's Journal, 1679–1680' in *The William and Mary Quarterly* vol. 44, 1987 (104–120).

Gehring, Charles T. 'Material Culture in the Seventeenth-Century Dutch Colonial Manuscripts' in *New World Dutch Studies*, 1986 (43–50).

Gehring, Charles T. 'Dutch Manuscripts relating to New Netherland in US Repositories' in *New Netherland Studies* nos.2–3 1984–85, (136–141).

Gehring, Charles T. 'New York's Dutch Records: A Historiographical Note' in *New York History* vol. 56, 1975, (347–355).

Gehring, Charles T. and William A. Sharna. 'A Case of Fraud: The Delacroix Letter and Map of 1634' in *New York History* vol. 66, 1985 (224–261).

Gehring, Charles T. and Nancy Anne McClure Zeller, eds. *Education in the Netherland and the Middle Colonies*. Albany, 1985.

Gibson, Ian. *Federico García Lorca. A Life*. New York, 1989.

Giddings, T.H. 'Rushing the Transatlantic News in the 1830s and 1840s' in *The New York Historical Quarterly* vol. 42, 1958 (47–116).

Giffin, Fredrick C. 'Leon Trotsky in New York City' in *New York History* vol. 49 1968 (391–403).

Gifford, James P. 'The Celebrated World of Currier & Ives. In which Heroic Fire Laddies Raced to Battle Conflagrations While Police Disappeared in the Most Amazing Way' in *New York Historical Society Quarterly* vol. 59, 1975, (348–365).

Gilbert, Douglas. *American Vaudeville. Its Life and Times*. New York, 1963 [1940].

Gildje, Paul A. 'Mobocracy: Popular Disturbance in Post-revolutionary New York City, 1783–1829' PhD dissertation, Department of History, Brown University, 1980.

Gilfoyle, Timothy J. 'City of Eros: New York City Prostitution and the Commercialization of Sex, 1790–1920.' PhD dissertation, Graduate School of Arts and Science, Columbia University, 1987.

Ginsberg, Stephen F. 'The Police and the Fire Protection in New York City: 1800–1850' in *New York History* vol. 52, 1971 (133–150).

Ginsberg, Stephen F. 'Above the Law: Volunteer Firemen in New York City, 1836–1837' in *New York History* vol. 50, 1969 (165–186).

Goldstein, Israel. *Jewish Justice and Conciliation*. New York, 1981.

Goodfriend, Joyce D. 'Black Families in New Netherland' in *The Journal of the Afro-American Historical and Genealogical Society*. vol. 5 nos.3 and 4, 1979 (95–108).

Goodfriend, Joyce D. 'Burghers and Blacks: The Evolution of a Slave Society at New Amsterdam' in *New York History* vol. 59, 1978, (125–144).

Gor Yun, Leong. *Chinatown Inside Out*. New York, 1936.

Gordon, Harry A. *Subway Nickels. A Survey of New York City's Transit Problem*. New York, 1925.

Gordon, John Steele. *The Scarlet Woman of Wall Street*. New York, 1988.

Gottesman, Rita Susswein. 'New York's First Major Art Show as Reviewed by Its First Newspaper Critic' in *The New York Historical Society Quarterly* vol. 53, 1959 (289–305).

Graham, Stephen. *New York Nights*. London, 1928.

Greenfield, Haskel J. 'From Park to Mutton: Urban Subsistence and Bone Taphonomy in Colonial New Amsterdam and Early Historic New York City' (mimeo) Department of Anthropology, University of Indiana, 1988.

Green, Stanley. *The Great Chorus of Broadway*. New York, 1984.

Green, Martin. *New York 1913. The Armory Show and the Paterson Strike Pageant*. New York, 1988.

Greenberg, Douglas. 'Patterns of Criminal Prosecution in Eighteen-Century New York' in *New York History* vol. 56, 1975 (133–153).

Gribbin, William. 'Divine Providence or Miasma? The Yellow Fever Epidemics of 1822' in *New York History* vol. 53, 1972 (183–148).

Grigg, John. *Nancy Astor*. London, 1980.

Grund, Francis J. *Aristocracy in America*. New York, 1959 [1839].

Guilbaut, Serge. *How New York Stole the Idea of Modern Art*. Translated from the French by Arthur Goldhammer, Chicago, 1983.

Gwyn, Jullian. 'Private Credit in Colonial New York: The Warren Portfolio, 1731–1795' in *New York History* vol. 54, 1973 (269–293).

Haberly, Lloyd. 'The American Museum from Baker to Barnum' in *The New York Historical Society Quarterly* vol. 43, 1959 (273–287).

Hamlin, Paul M. ed. 'Money Circulating in New York Prior to 1704. A Report Submitted by Cadwallader Colden, M.D.' in *The New York Historical society Quarterly* vol. 40, 1956 (3610167).

Hammack, David C. *Power and Society. Greater New York at the Turn of the Century*. New York, 1982.

Hanpf, Helen. *Apple of My Eye*. Mt Kisko, NY, 1977.

Harris, Lis. *Holy Days*. New York, 1985.

Harris, Neil. *The Artist in American Society. The Formative Years, 1790–1860*. New York, 1966.

Hart, Simon. 'The Dutch of North America in the First Half of the 17th Century. Some Aspects.' Paper Presented at the Colloque International, University of Ottawa, Nov. 1969.

Hart, Moss. *Act One: An Autobiography*. London, 1987.

Hartnoll, Phyllis. *The Concise History of Theatre*. New York, 1968.

Hartog, Hendrick. 'The Properties of the Corporation: New York City and Its Law, 1730–1850.' PhD dissertation, Department of History, Brandeis University, 1981.

Harvey, George. *Henry Clay Frick, the Man*. New York, 1928.

Hasidic Corporation for Urban Concerns. *The Study of Poverty in the Jewish Community: City of New York*. New York, 1972.

Hay, Robert P. 'Britons in New York on Brother Jonathan's Birthday' in *The New York Historical Society Quarterly* vol. 53, 1969 (273–282).

Hayes, John D. and Doris D. Maguire. 'Charles Graham Halpine: Life and Adventures of Miles O'Reilly' in *The New York Historical Society Quarterly* vol. 51, 1967 (326–344).

Heffer, F.H.M. *New York is Not America*. London, 1927.

Hershkowitz, Leo. 'The Troublesome Turk: An Illustration of Judicial Process in New Amsterdam' in *New York History* vol. 46, 1965 (299–310).

Hertzberg, Arthur. *The Jews in America. Four Centuries of an Uneasy Encounter*. New York, 1989.

Historic American Engineering Record. 'Interborough Rapid Transit Subway' (mimeo) Washington, 1979.

'Hollandse Huizen, Gebouwd in de 17de Eeuw in Amerika (Part.I)' in *Amsterdamse Monumenten* Nummer 3, Oktober, 1987. Part II in *Amsterdamse Monumenten* Nummer 4, December, 1987.

Holbrook, Stewart H. *Dreamers of the American Dream*. New York, 1957.

Hood, Glifton Dodds. 'Underground Politics: A History of Mass Transit in New York City Since 1904' PhD Dissertation, Graduate School of Art and Sciences, Columbia University, 1986.

Horowitz, Helen L. 'Animal and Man in the New York Zoological Park' in *New York History* vol. 56, 1975 (426–455).

Horsmanden, Daniel. *The New York Conspiracy*. Boston, 1971.

Howard-Howard, Margo (with Abbe Michaels). *I Was a White Slave in Harlem* . New York, 1988.

Howe, Irving. *World of Our Fathers*. New York. 1989 [1976].

Hueguin, Charles A. 'Macmonnies' "Civic Virtue".' in *New York History* vol. 37, 1956 (17–25).

Huey, Paul R. 'Old Slip and Cruger's Wharf at New York: An Archaeological Perspective of the Colonial Waterfront' in *Historical Archaeology*, vol. 18 no date, (16–37).

Huey, Paul R. 'The Archaeology of Colonial New Netherland' in Nooter Eric, and Patricia U. Bonomi eds. *Colonial Dutch Studies: an Interdisciplinary Approach*. New York 1988, (52–77).

Huey, Paul R. 'The Beginnings of Modern Historical Archaeology in the Northeast and the Origins of the Conference on Northeast Historical Archaeological' in *Northeast Historical Archaeology* vol. 15, 1986 (2–15).

Huey, Paul R. 'Reworked Pipe Stems: A 17th Century Phenomenon from Site of Fort Orange, Albany, New York' in *Historical Archaelogy* 1974 (105–11).

Humphrey, David. 'Urban Manners and Rural Morals and Ritual Morals: The Controversy Over the Location of King's College' in *New York History* vol. 54, 1973 (5–23).

Hutchens, John K. and George Oppenheimer, eds. *The Best in the World*. New York, 1973.

Hyman, Harold M., ed. 'New York and the Civil War Draft' in *New York History* vol. 36, 1955 (164–171).

Idzerda, Stanley J. 'Walt Whitman, Politician' in *New York History* vol. 37, 1956 (171–148).

Irving, Washington. *Diedrich Knickerbocker's A History of New York*. Tarrytown, 1981 [1854].

Jacobs, Jane. *Cities and the Wealth of Nations. Principles of Economic Life*. New York, 1984.

James, Henry. *The American Scene*. London, 1987 [1907].

James, Henry. *Washington Square*. Oxford, 1986 [1880].

James, Robert Rhodes, ed. *'Chips' the Diaries of Sir Henry Channon*. Harmondsworth, 1970.

Jameson, J.F. *Narratives of New Netherland*. New York, 1909.

Jardin, André. *Tocqueville: A Biography*. London, 1988.

Jewell, Derek. *Duke*. London, 1977.

Johnson, Herbert A. 'English Statutes in Colonial New York' in *New York History* vol. 58, 1977 (277–195).

Johnston, Herbert Alan. 'Magyar-Mania in New York City. Louis Kossoth and American Politics' in *The New York Historical Society Quarterly* vol.48, 1964, (237–249).

Johnston, Johanna. *The Life, Manners and Travels of Fanny Trollope*. London, 1980.

Jones, Wilbur Devereux. 'Made in New York: A Plot to Kill the Queen' in *The New York Historical Society Quarterly* vol. 51, 1967 (311–325).

Jordan, Jean P. 'Women Merchants in Colonial New York' in *New York History* vol. 58, 1977 (412–439).

Joyce, Donald Franklin. *Gatekeepers of Black Culture*. Westport, 1983.

Judd, Jacob. 'Gleaning from a Captain's Letters' in *The New York Historical Society Quarterly* vol. 52, 1968, (270–274).

Juvenal [pseud.]. *An Englishman in New York*, Adelphi, 1911.

Kafka, Franz. *Amerika*. Translated from the German by Willa and by Edwin Muir, New York, 1962.

Kalm, Peter. *Travels into North America*. Translated by J.R. Foster, Warrington, 1770.

Kamen, Robert M. *Growing Up Hasidic: Education and Socialization in the Babover Hasidic Community*. New York, 1985.

Kammen, Michael. 'The Rediscovery of New York's History, Phase One' in *New York History* vol. 60, 1979 (373–405).

Katz, Jonathan. *Gay American History*. New York, 1976.

Katz, Stanley N. 'Newcastle's New York Governors. Imperial Patronage During the Era of "Salutary Neglect"' in *The New York Historical Society Quarterly* vol. 51, 1967 (7–23).

Katz, Wallace B. 'The New York Rapid Transit Decision of 1900: Economy, Society, Politics' in Historic American Engineering Record 'Interborough Rapid Transit Subway' (mimeo), Washington, 1979.

Katz, William Loren, and Jacqueline Hunt Katz, eds. *Making Our Way. America at the Turn of the Century in the Words of the Poor and the Powerless*. New York, 1975.

Kavaler, Lucy. *The Astors*. London, 1966.

Kelly, Arthur, ed. *The New York City Transit Authority's Facts and Figures 1986–87*. New York, 1987.

Kerber, Linda K. 'Abolitionists and Amalgamators: The New York City Race Riots of 1834' in *New York History* vol. 48, 1967 (28–39).

Kerkkonen, Marthi. *Peter Kalm's North American Journey*. Helsinki, 1959.

Kerouac, Jack. *The Town, The City*. London, 1973 [1950].

Kerouac, Jack. *Lonesome Traveler*. New York, 1960.

Kessler, Henry H. and Eugene Rachlis. *Peter Stuyvesant and His New York*. New York, 1951.

Kessner, Thomas. *Fiorello H. La Guardia and the Making of Modern New York*. New York, 1990.

Kieran, John. *A Natural History of New York*. New York, 1982.

Kissaloff, Jeff. *You Must Remember This. An Oral History of Manhattan from the 1890s to World War II*. San Diego, 1989.

Klaunser, Patricia Robin. 'The Politics of Massage Parlor Prostitution: The International Traffic of Women for Prostitution into New York, 1970–present.' PhD dissertation, University of Delaware, 1987.

Klebanow, Diana. 'E.L. Godkin, the City, and Civil Responsibility' in *The New York Historical Society Quarterly* vol. 55, 1971 (52–75).

Klein, Carole. *Gramercy Park: An American Bloomsbury*. Boston, 1987.

Klein, Maury. *The Life and Legend of Jay Gould*. Baltimore, 1986.

Klein, Milton M. 'Why Did the British Fail to Win the Hearts and Mind of New Yorkers?' in *New York History* vol. 65, 1984 (357–375).

Klein, Milton M. 'From Community to Status: The Development of the Legal Profession in Colonial New York' in *New York History* vol. 60, 1979 (133–153).

Klein, Milton M. 'Politics and Personalities in Colonial New York' in *Hew York History* vol. 47, 1966 (3–16).

Klemens, Michael W. 'Survivors in Megalopolis. Reptiles in the Urban North East' in *Discovery* vol. 18, no.1, 1985.

Kluger, Richard. *The Paper. The Life and Death of the New York Herald Tribune*. New York, 1989 [1986].

Koch, Edward I. (with William Rauch). *Mayor. An Autobiography*. New York, 1985.

Kwong, Peter. *The New Chinatown*. New York, 1987.

Kranzler, George. *The Face of Faith: An American Hasidic Community*. Baltimore, 1972.

Kuwenhoven, John A. *The Columbia Historical Portrait of New York*. Garden City, NY, 1953.

Kupp, Jan. 'Aspects of New York-Dutch Trade Under the English, 1670–1674' in *The New York Historical Society Quarterly* vol. 58, 1979 (139–147).

Labor, William. *The Social Stratification of English in New York City*. Washington, 1982 [1966].

Lapham, Lewis H. *Money and Class in America*. New York, 1988.

Launitz-Schurer, Leopold S. Jr. 'Whig-Loyalist: The Delanceys of New York' in *The New York Historical Society Quarterly* vol. 56, 1972 (179–198).

Leder, Lawrence H. 'The Politics of Upheaval in New York, 1689–1709' in *The New York Historical Society Quarterly* vol. 44, 1960 (413–427).

Leder, Lawrence H. ". . . Like Madmen Through the Streets." The New York City Riots of June 1690' in *The New York Historical Society Quarterly* vol. 39, 1955 (405–415).

Leder, Lawrence H. 'Dongan's New York and Fletcher's London: Personality and Politics' in *The New York Historical Society Quarterly* vol. 55, 1971 (28–37).

Lee, Henry. 'Blood of the Flower – When the Streets of Chinatown ran Crimson. In the Crossfire of the Great Tong Wars' in *Daily News Magazine*, New York, Feb. 5, 1989 (8–9).

Lehr, Elizabeth Drexel. *King Lehr and the Gilded Age*. Philadelphia, 1935.

Leonard, Ira M. 'The Politics of Charter Revision in New York City, 1847–1849' in *The New York Historical Society Quarterly* vol. 63, 1979 (7–23).

Leonard, Ira M. 'The Politics of Charter Revision in New York, 1845–1847' in *The New York Historical Society Quarterly* vol. 62, 1978 (43–70).

Levine, E.H. *Stand and Deliver*. New York, 1931.

Lewis, David Levering. *When Harlem Was in Vogue*. New York, 1982.

Lewis, R.W.B. *The Poems of Hart Crane, a Critical Study*. Princeton, 1967.

Lind, Earl. *Autobiography of an Androgyne*. New York, 1975 [1918].

Lockwood, S.M. *New York: Not so Little, Not so Old*. Garden City, 1926.

Lombard, Charles M. 'An Old New York Salon-French Style' in *The New York Historical Society Quarterly* vol. 55, 1971 (38–51).

Lubavitch News Service. 'The Lubavitcher Rebbe Menachem M. Scheenerson. A Brief Biography.' Brooklyn, 1990.

Luftman, Herbert R. *Albert Camus*. London, 1979.

Lum, Joann, and Peter Kwong. 'Surviving in America. The Trials of a Chinese Immigrant Women' in *Village Voice*, 31 October, 1989 (39–41).

Lunt, Jack, and Lee Mortimer. *New York Confidential!* Chicago, 1948.

Mabee, Charleton. 'Long Island's Black "School War" and the Decline of Segregation in New York State' in *New York History* vol. 58, 1977 (385–411).

Mabee, Charleton. 'Charity in Travail: Two Orphan Asylums for Blacks' in *New York History* vol. 55, 1974 (55–77).

MacColl, Gail, and Carol McD. Wallace. *To Marry an English Lord*. New York, 1989.

Maestdagh, Robert. *Manhattan People and Their Space*. London, 1981.

Maika, Dennis. 'New York City Merchants in the Age of Leisler.' Paper Presented at the 12th Renseelaerswyck Seminar 23 September 1989.

Mandelbaum, Seymour J. *Boss Tweed's New York*. New York, 1965.

Manhattan, Frank. *The Upper Ten Thousand*. London, 1852.

Mann, Arthur. *La Guardia Comes to Power, 1933*. Westport, 1965.

Marshall, F. *An Englishman in New York*. Margate, 1944.

Martin, Edward Winslow. *The Secrets of the Great City – Virtues, Vices, Mysteries, Miseries and Crime*. Philadelphia, 1868.

Marx, Paul Alan. 'This is the City: An Examination of Changing Attitudes Toward New York as Reflected in its Guidebook Literature, 1807–1860' PhD Dissertation, Committee on Higher Degrees in History of Civilization, Harvard University, 1983.

Mathis, Robert Neil. 'Gazaway Bugg Lamar: A Southern Businessman and Confidant in New York' in *New York History* vol. 56, 1976 (298–313).

Matlack, James H. 'The Alta Califonia's Lady Correspondent' in *The New York Historical Society* vol. 58, 1974 (280–303).

Matson, Cathy. 'Commerce after Conquest: Dutch Trade and the Goods in New York City 1664–1764. (Part I)' in *De Halve Maen* vol. 53, no. 4, 1987. Part II, in *De Halve Maen* vol. 60, no.1, 1987.

Mazzei, Filippo. *Researches on the United States*. Trans. and edited by Constance D. Sherman, Charlotesville, 1976.

McAllister, Ward. *Society as I Have Found It*. New York, 1890.

McArthur, Benjamin. *Actors and American Culture 1880–1920*. Philadelphia, 1984.

McCarthy, Mary. *The Company She Keeps*. Harmondsworth, 1966 [1942].

McCarthy, Patrick. *Camus: a Critical Study of his life and his work*. London, 1982.

McCarthy, Patrick. *Céline*. London, 1975.

McCluny, Robert and Gale S. McCluny. 'Tammany's Remarkable Gardiner Baker. New York's First Museum Proprietor, Menagerie Keeper, and Promoter Extraordinary' in *The New York Historical Society Quarterly* vol. 42, 1958 (143–169).

McCormick, Charles H. 'Governor Sloughter's Delay and Leisler's Rebellion, 1689–1691' in *The New York Historical Society Quarterly* vol. 62, 1976, (238–252).

Melder, Keith. 'Ladies Bountiful. Organized Women's Benevolence in Early 19th-Century America' in *New York History* vol. 48, 1967, (231–254).

Meskil, Paul. "In the Eyes of the Storm" The Old Tongs Have Made Peace, but There Are Other New Invaders in Chinatown' in *Daily News Magazine*. New York, February 5 1989, (10–16).

Metropolitan Transportation Authority. *Report to the Governor*. New York, 1988.

Metropolitan Transit Authority. *The Capital Program of the MTA*. New York, February 1989.

Metropolitan Transit Authority. *1988 MTA Financial Statements*. New York, 1989.

Metropolitan Transit Authority. *1988 MTA Annual Report*. New York, 1989.

Meyer, Egon. *From Suburb to Shtetl. The Jews of Boro Park*. Philadelphia, 1979.

Miguéis, José Rodriguez. *Léah e Outras Obras*. Lisboa, 1983 [1958].

Mikhail, E.H. *Oscar Wilde: Interviews and Recollections, vol. I*. New York, 1979.

Miller, Agnes. 'Centenary of a New York Statue' in *New York History* vol. 38, 1957 (167–176).

Miller, Douglas T. 'Immigration and Social Stratification in Pre-Civil War New York' in *New York History* vol. 49, 1968 (157–168).

Miller, Samuel. 'A Discourse Designed to Commemorate the Discovery of New York by Henry Hudson.' New York, 4 September 1859.

Miller, Terry. *Greenwich Village and How It Got that Way*. New York, 1990.

Minsky, Morton and Milt Machlin. *Minsky's Burlesque*. New York, 1986.

Misceric, Dusanka and Peter Kwong. 'The Chinese Exodus' in *Village Voice*. 31 October 1989, (29–32).

Mitchell, William E. *Mishpokhe; A Study of New York City Jewish Family CLubs*. Morton, 1978.

Model, Suzanne Windholz. 'Ethnic Bonds in the Work Place: Blacks, Italians and Jews in New York City.' PhD dissertation, Department of Social Work and Sociology, University of Michigan, 1955.

Mohl, Richard. *Poverty in New York, 1783–1825*. New York, 1971.

Mohl, Raymond A. 'Poverty in Early America, a Reappraisal: The Case of Eighteenth-Century New York' in *New York History* vol. 50, 1960 (5–27).

Moore, Deborah D. *At Home in America*. New York, 1981.

Moorhouse, Geoffrey. *Imperial City. The Rise and Rise of New York*. London, 1988.

Morales, Julio. *Puerto Rican Poverty and Migration. We Just Had to Try Elsewhere*. New York, 1986.

Morand, Paul. *New York*. New York, 1930.

Morgan, Thomas B. 'So This Is How Ed Koch Ends? Not with a Bang but with a Kvetch' in *Manhattan Inc.* January 1989 (43–51).

Morris, Jan. *Manhattan '45*. Harmondsworth, 1987.

Morris, Jan. *The Great Port. A Passage Through New York*. New York, 1985 [1969].

Moscow, Warren. *The Last of the Big Time Bosses: The Life and Times of Carmine de Sapio and the Rise and Fall of Tammany Hall*. New York, 1971.

Murdock, James E. *The Stage or Recollections of Actors and Acting from Experience of Fifty Years*. Philadelphia, 1880.

Murphy, Henry C. *Henry Hudson in Holland*. New York, 1972 [1909].

Murphy, Henry C. *Anthology of New Netherland*. Amsterdam, 1966 [1865].

Mustain, Gene and Jerry Capeci. *Mob Star. The Story of John Gotti*. New York, 1988.

Myers, Bernard S. *Problems of the Younger American Artist*. New York, 1957.

Myers, John Bernard. *Tracking the Marvelous. A Life in the New York Art World*. New York, 1983.

Naifeh, Steven, and Gregory White Smith. *Jackson Pollock: An American Saga*. New York, 1989.

Narret, David E. 'Preparations for Death and Provisions for the Living: Notes on New York Wills (1665–1760)' in *New York History* vol. 57, 1976 (417–437).

Nash, Gary B. *The Urban Crucible: Social Change, Political Consciousness and the Origins of the American Revolution*. Cambridge, 1979.

Natural Resources Group, City of New York Parks and Recreation. 'Landscape Management and Restoration Program for the Woodlands of Central Park' (mimeo) New York, 1989.

Natural Resources Group, City of New York Parks and Recreation. 'Natural Areas Management Plan. Van Cortlandt Park, Bronx 1989' (mimeo) New York, 1989.

Nellis, Andrew J. *The Law of Street Surface Railroads*. Albany, 1902.

Nevis, Allan. *John D. Rockefeller: The Heroic Age of American Enterprise*. New York, 1969 [1940].

New York State Urban Development Corporation. '42nd Street Development Project. Final Environmental Impact Statement.' (mimeo) New York, 1984.

New York City Transit Authority. *1989 Goals*. New York, January 1989.

New York City Transit Authority. *Opening Budget Proposal 1989–1991*. New York, 1989.

New York City Transit Authority. 'Draft Strategic Business Plan 1990–1994' (mimeo). New York, June 1989.

New York City Transit Authority. *Proposed 1988 Capital Budget and 1987–1991 Capital Program Revision*. New York, 1987.

New York Colonial Manuscripts: Dutch. 'Principal Secretary, vol. I 1628–1641.' 'Principal Secretary, vol. II 1642–1647.' 'Principal Secretary, vol. III 1648.'

Newfield, Jack and Paul du Brul. *The Abuse of Power*. Harmondsworth, 1978.

Newfield, Jack, and Wayne Barrett. *City for Sale. Ed Koch and the Betrayal of New York City*. New York, 1977.

Nicols, Jack. *Welcome to Fire Island*. New York, 1976.

Nicosia, Gerald. *Memory Babe: A Critical Biography of Jack Kerouac*. New York, 1983.

Norse, Harold. *Memoirs of a Bastard Angel*. New York, 1981.

O'Connor, John E. 'The Rattle Watch of New Amsterdam' in *De Halve Maen* vol. 43, 1978 (65–66).

O'Connor, Richard and Dale L. Walter. *The Last Revolutionary: A Biography of John Reed*. New York, 1967.

Ogren, Kathy J. 'Controversial Sounds: Jazz Performance and Language in the Harlem Renaissance' in Amritjit Singh et al, eds. *The Harlem Renaissance: Revaluations*. New York, 1989.

Older, Mrs Fremot. *William Randolph Hearst, American*. New York, 1936.

Oliva, L. Jay. 'Maxim Gorky Discovers America' in *The New York Historical Society Quarterly* vol. 51, 1967 (45–60.)

Oppenheim, Samuel. *The Early History of the Jews in New York 1654–1664*. New York, 1909.

Ormsbee, Helen. *Backstage with Actors*. New York, 1938.

Osofsky, Gilbert. 'A Decade of Urban Tragedy: How Harlem Became a Slum' in *New York History* vol. 46, 1965 (331–355).

Page, Walter Hines. *A Publisher's Confessions*. New York, 1905.

Page, William F. 'The African Slave During the Early English Period, 1664–1700' in *The Journal of the Afro-American Historical and Genealogical Society* vol. 5, nos.3 and 4, 1984 (123–132).

Perry, Albert. *Garrets and Pretenders. A History of Bohemianism in America*. New York, 1960 [1933].

Pessen, Edward. 'The Marital Theory and Practice of the Antebellum Urban Elite' in *New York History*. vol. 53, 1972 (389–410).

Pessen, Edward. 'The Wealthiest New Yorkers of the Jacksonian Era: A New List' in *The New York Historical Society Quarterly* vol. 54, 1970 (145–172).

Pessen, Edward. 'The Social and Economic Portrait of Jacksonian Brooklyn. Inequality, Social Immobility, and Class Distinction in the Nation's Seventh City' in *The New York Historical Society Quarterly* vol. 54, 1970 (318–353).

Peterson, Virgil W. *The Mob, 200 Years of Organized Crime in New York*. Ottawa, Illinois, 1983.

Phelps Stokes, I.N. *The Iconography of Manhattan Island, 1498–1901*. New York, 1967 [New York, 1926].

Pitkin, Thomas. 'High Tide at Ellis Island' in *The New York Historical Society Quarterly* vol. 52, 1968 (311–353).

Piwonka, Ruth. 'Chronology of Dutch Settlements in New Netherland, 1614–1664' in *New World Dutch History* 1986 (xi-xii).

Pointer, Richard Wayne. 'Seedbed of American Pluralism: The Impact of Religious Diversity in New York, 1750–1800.' PhD dissertation, John Hopkins University, 1981.

Pomerantz, Sidney I. 'The Press of a Greater New York, 1898–1900.' in *New York History*, vol. 39, 1958 (50–68).

Pound Arthur. *The Golden Earth. The Story of Manhattan's Landed Wealth*. New York, 1935.

Pratt, John D. 'Boss Tweed's Public Welfare Program' in *The New York Historical Society Quarterly* vol. 45, 1961 (396–411).

President's Commission on Organized Crime. *Record of Hearing III*. New York, 23–25 October 1984.

Pulitzer, Ralph. *New York Society on Parade*. New York, 1910.

Purchas, Samuel. 'Henry Hudson's Voyages.' From *Purchas his Pilgrims*. Ann Arbor, 1966.

Ramsey, James B. 'Selling the Subways in New York: Wild Eyed Radicalism or Feasible Solution?' (mimeo) New York University, 1981.

Rand, Ayn. *The Fountainhead*. New York, 1961 [1943].

Ratzel, Friedrich. *Sketches of Urban and Cultural Life in North America*. Translated and edited by Stwart A. Stehlin, New Brunswick, 1988 [1876].

Read, Henry Hope and Sophia Duckworth. *Central Park. A History and a Guide*. New York, 1967.

Reich, Jerome R. *Leisler's Rebellion. A Study of Democracy in New York, 1664–1720*. Chicago, 1953.

Renzetti, Claire Marie. 'Purity vs Politics: The Legislation of Morality in Progressive New York, 1840–1920.' PhD dissertation, University of Delaware, 1982.

Resseguie, Harry E. 'A.T. Stewart's Marble Palace – The Cradle of the Department Store' in *The New York Historical Society Quarterly* vol. 48, 1964 (131–162).

Reynolds, Donald Martin. *The Architecture of New York. Histories and Views of Important Structures, Sites and Symbols*. London, 1984.

Reynolds, Quentin. *The Fiction Factory*. New York, 1985.

Rhodes, Benjamin. 'A Modern "Black Hole of Calcutta"? The Anglo American Controversy over Ellis Island, 1921–1924' in *New York History* vol. 66, 1985,(230–248).

Richard, Pamela Spence. *Scholars and Gentleman. The Library of the New York Historical Society, 1804–1982*. Howden, Conn., 1984.

Richardson, James F. 'Mayor Fernando Wood and the New York Police Force, 1855–1857' in *The New York Historical Society Quarterly* vol. 50, 1966 (5–40).

Richardson, James F. 'The Struggle to Establish a London Style Police Force for New York City' in *New York Historical Society Quarterly* vol. 49, 1965 (175–197).

Rink, Oliver H. 'Unraveling a Secret Colonialism: Part I' in *De Halve Maen* vol. 59, no. 4, 1987 (13–16). Part II in *De Halve Maen* vol. 60, no. 1, 1987 (8–11).

Rink, Oliver H. *Holland on the Hudson*. Ithaca, 1986.

Ritchie, Robert C. 'The Duke of York's Commission of Revenue.' in *The New York Historical Society Quarterly* vol. 58, 1974 (177–187).

Robbe-Grillet, Alain. *Project for a Revolution in New York*. Translated from French by Richard Howard New York, 1972.

Robeson, E.G. *Paul Robeson, Negro*. London, 1970.

Rock, Howard B., ed. 'A Woman's Place in Jeffersonian New York: The View From the Independent Mechanic' in *New York History* vol. 63, 1982 (435–458).

Rogers, W.E. and Mildred Weston. *Carnival Crossroads. The Story of Times Square*. New York, 1960.

Romig, Edgar Franklin. 'The English and Low-Dutch School-Master. New York: William Bradford, 1730' in *The New York Historical Society Quarterly* vol. 43, 1959 (149–159).

Rooney, Gerald F. 'Daniel Denton, Publicist of Colonial New York' in *The New York Historical Society Quarterly* vol. 55, 1971 (272–276).

Rosenberg, Bernard, and Ernest Goldstein. *Creator and Disturbers*. New York, 1982.

Ross, J.H. *What I Saw in New York*. New York, 1851.

Rowse, A.L. *The Poet Auden: A Personal Memoir*. London, 1987.

Rubin, Israel. *Satmar – An Island in the City*. New York, 1972.

Ruche, John F. 'The Uranian Society: Gentlemen and Scholars in Federal New York' *New York History*. vol. 52, 1971 (121–131).

Sagarin, Edward. *Structure and Ideology in an Association of Deviants*. New York, 1975.

Scanlon, James Edward. 'British Intrigue and the Governorship of Robert Hunter' in *The New York Historical Society Quarterly* vol. 57, 1973 (199–21).

Schama, Simon. *The Embarrassment of Riches*. London, 1987.

Scharnhorst, Gary and Jack Bales. *The Lost Life of Horatio Alger, Jr*. Bloomington, Indiana, 1985.

Scharnhorst, Gary. *Horatio Alger Jr. An Annotated Bibliography of Comment and Criticism*. London, 1981.

Scheiner, Seth M. 'The New York City Negro and the Tenement, 1880–1910' in *New York History* vol. 46, 1964 (304–315).

Schilivek, Louis B. *Man in Metropolis*. New York, 1965.

Schlesinger, Elizabeth Baneroff. 'The Nineteenth-Century Woman's Dilemma and Jennie June' in *New York History* vol. 42, 1961 (365–379).

Scott, Kenneth. 'The Slave Insurrection in New York in 1712' in *The New York Historical Society Quarterly* vol. 45, 1961 (43–74).

Secrest, Meryl. *Salvador Dali – The Surrealist Jester*. London, 1986.

Seraille, William. 'The Struggle to Raise Black Regiments in New York State, 1861–1864' in *The New York Historical Society Quarterly* vol. 58, 1974 (215–233).

Shanor, Rebecca Read. *The City that Never Was*. New York, 1988.

Sherard, R.H. *At the Closed Door*. London, 1902.

Sinclair, David. *Dynasty The Astors and Their Times*. London, 1983.

Singer, Isaac Bashevis. *Love and Exile; the Early Years – A Memoir*. Garden City, 1984.

Singer, Isaac Bashevis. *Enemies, a Love Story*. New York, 1988 [1972].

Singer, Mark. *Mr Personality*. London, 1989.

Sizer, Theodore, ed. 'The Recollections of John Ferguson Weir (1841–1926)' in *The New York Historical Society Quarterly* vol. 41, 1957 (351–175).

Skolnik, Richard. 'Civic Group Progressivism in New York City' in *New York History* vol. 51, 1970 (411–439).

Smith, George L. *Religion and Trade in New Netherland: Dutch Origins and American Development*. Ithaca, New York State, 1973.

Smith, Howden Arthur D. *John Jacob Astor: Landlord of New York*. Philadelphia, 1929.

Smith, J.C. *Witnessing for Jesus in the Houses of the Poor*. London, 1868.

Smith, Mary Ann. 'John Snook and the Design for A.T. Stewart's Stores' in *The New York Historical Society Quarterly* vol. 58, 1978 (18–33).

Snow, Dean R. and Kim M. Lamphear. 'European Contact and Indian Depopulation in the Northeast: The Timing of the First Epidemics' in *Ethnohistory* vol. 35, no.1, 1988, (15–33).

Solomon, Poll. *The Hasidic Community of Williamsburg*. New York, 1962.

Spalleto, Matteo. 'Divorce in Colonial New York' in *The New York Historical Society Quarterly* vol. 39, 1955 (422–440).

Spico, Robert H. Jr. 'John Loudin McAdam, Revolutionary in New York' in *The New York Historical Society Quarterly* vol. 40, 1956 (24–59).

Stansell, Christine. *City of Women. Sex and Class in New York, 1789–1869*. Chicago, New York, 1983, 1987.

Steen, Ivan D. 'Palaces for Travelers: New York City's Hotels in the 1850s As Viewed by British Visitors' in *New York History* vol. 51, 1970 (269–286).

Stehle, R.L. 'The Dusseldorf Gallery of New York' in *The New York Historical Society Quarterly* vol. 58, 1974 (305–317).

Sterling, David L. 'John Pintard (1794–1844). The First City Inspector of New York' in *The New York Historical Society Quarterly* vol. 43, 1959 (453–463).

Stern, Robert A.M. et al. *New York 1900: Metropolitan Architecture and Urbanism 1890–1915*. New York, 1983.

Stern, Steve J. 'Knickerbockers Who Asserted and Insisted. The Dutch Interest in New York Politics, 1664–1691' in *The New York Historical Society Quarterly* vol. 58, 1974, (113–138).

Sterngold, James. 'Too Far, Too Fast. Salomon Brothers' John Gutfreund' in *New York Times Magazine* 10 January 1988.

Stevens, Thomas Ward. *The Theatre from Athens to Brooklyn*. New York, 1932.

Stevenson, Robert Louis. *The Amateur Emigrant*. London, 1989.

Stewart, Ian R. 'Politics and the Park. The Fight for Central Park' in *The New York Historical Society* vol. 61, 1977 (124–155).

Still, Bayrd. *Mirror for Gotham. New York as Seen by Contemporaries from Dutch Days to the Present*. Westport, 1980 [1956].

Still, Bayrd. 'New York's Mayoralty: The Formative Years' in *The New York Historical Society Quarterly* vol. 47, 1963 (239–256).

Still, Bayrd. 'New York City in 1824: A Newly Discovered Description' in *The New York Historical Society Quarterly* vol. 62, 1962 (137–169).

Stott, Richard Briggs. 'The Worker in the Metropolis: New York City 1820–1860' PhD dissertation, Graduate School, Cornell University, 1983.

Sukenick, Donald. *Down and In: Life in the Underground*. New York, 1987.

Sutton, Peter C. *Masters of Seventeenth-Century Dutch Landscape Painting*. Boston, 1987.

Swanberg, W.A. *Citizen Hearst* New York, 1986 [1961].

Szasz, Ferenc M. 'The New York Revolt of 1741: A Re-examination' in *New York History* vol. 48, 1967 (215–230).

Taylor, George Roger. 'Gaslight Foster: A New York "Journeyman Journalist" at Mid-Century' in *New York History* vol. 58, 1977 (298–312).

Taylor, John. *Circus of Ambition. The Culture of Wealth and Power in the Eighties.* New York, 1989.

Taylor, John. 'Hard to be Rich. The Rise and Wobble of the Gutfreunds' in *New York* 11 January 1988 (22–33).

Tebbel, John. *Between Covers: The Rise and Transformation of Book Publishing in America.* New York, 1987.

Temminck Groll, C.L. 'Nieuw Amsterdam in Noord-Amerika Vergeleken met Andere Nederlandse 17de Eeuwse Stedestichtingen' in *Leids Kunsthistorisch Jaarboekje* 1984.

Thelen, David P. and Leslie H. Fishel Jr. 'Reconstruction in the North: The World Looks at New York's Negroes, March 16, 1867' in *New York History* vol. 49, 1978 (405–440).

Thomas, Piri. *Down These Mean Streets.* New York, 1967.

Tomkins, Calvin. *Merchants and Masterpieces. The Story of the Metropolitan Museum of Art.* New York, 1989.

Tomkins, Calvin. *The Bride and the Bachelors.* Harmondsworth, 1968 [1962].

Tompsett, Christine. 'Note on the Economic Status of the Widows in Colonial New York' in *New York History* vol. 55, 1974 (319–332).

Trager, James. *Park Avenue. Street of Dreams.* New York, 1990.

Trauttman, Frederick, trans. and intro. 'New York Through German Eyes: The Travels of Ludwig Gall 1819' in *New York History* vol. 62, 1981 (439–461).

Trollope, Anthony. *North America, vol. I.* London, 1986 [1862].

Trotsky, Leon. *My Life: The Rise and Fall of a Dictator.* London, 1930.

Trump, Donald (with Tony Schwartz). *Trump. The Art of the Deal.* New York, 1987.

Turner, Fredrerick. *Spirit of Place: The Making of an American Literary Landscape.* San Francisco, 1989.

Turner, W.J. *A Trip to New York and a Poem.* London, 1929.

United States Commission on Civil Rights. 'The Economic Status of Americans of Asian Descent: An Explanatory Investigation' (mimeo). October 1988.

Van Wyck, Frederick. *Recollections of an Old New Yorker.* New York, 1933.

Van der Zee, Henry and Barbara van der Zee. *A Sweet and Alien Land* London, 1978.

Van Gelder, Roelof. *The Birth of New York, Nieuw Amsterdam 1624–1664.* Trans. from the Dutch by Gary Schwartz, Amsterdam, 1982.

Van Laer, A.J.F. trans. and *Records of New Netherland. Council Minutes vol. I 1638–1649.* Albany, 1939.

Van Laer, A.J.F. trans and *Documents Relating to New Netherland 1624–1626.* San Marino, Cal., 1924.

Van Rensselaer, Mrs. John King (with Frederick van De Wate). *The Social Ladder.* New York, 1929.

Vanderbilt, Arthur T. II. *Fortune's Children. The Fall of the House of Vanderbilt.* New York, 1989.

Varga, Nicholas. 'Election Procedures and Practices in Colonial New York' in *New York History* vol. 41, 1960 (249–277).

Versteeg, Dingman. *Manhattan in 1628*. New York, 1904.

Vitz, Robert C. 'Struggle and Response: American Artists and the Great Depression' in *New York History* vol. 57, 1976 (81–98).

Vitz, Robert C. 'Clubs, Congresses, and Unions: American Artists Confront the Thirties' in *New York History* vol. 54, 1973 (425–447).

Von Karlstein, H.O. *Gotham and the Gothamites*. London, 1887.

Von Hoffman, Nicholas. *Citizen Cohn*. New York, 1988.

Voorhees, David. 'Leisler's Pre-1689 Biography and Family Background' in *De Halve Maen* vol. 57, no. 4, December 1989.

Wagman, Morton. 'Liberty in New Amsterdam: A Sailor's Life in Early New York' in *New York History* vol. 64, 1983 (101–119).

Wagman, Morton. 'The Rise of Dieter Claessen Wyckoff: Social Mobility in the Colonial Frontier' in *New York History* vol. 53, 1972 (5–24).

Waldinger, Rogers D. *Through the Eyes of the Needle: Immigrants and Enterprise in New York's Garment Trades*. New York, 1986.

Wallace, David M., ed. 'From the Windows of the Mail Coach. A Scotsman Looks at New York State in 1811' in *The New York Historical Society Quarterly* vol. 40, 1956 (269–296).

Wallock, Leonard, ed. *New York, Culture Capital of the World 1940–1965*. New York, 1988.

Walter, William. *The Life of David Belasco*. New York, 1975 [1925].

Ward, David. *Poverty, Ethnicity, and the American City, 1840–1925. Changing Conceptions of the Slum and the Ghetto*. New York, 1989.

Weatherspoon Bowden, Mary. "Cocklofts and Slang-whangers": The Historical Source of Washington Irving's *Salmagundi*' in *New York History* vol. 61, 1980 (133–160).

Wechster Ph.D., Robert, ed. 'New York Heritage. A Selected Bibliography of New York City Labor History' (mimeo) Tamiment Institute Library, 1981.

Weintenkampf, Frank. 'New York in the Illustrated Weeklies' in *The New York Historical Society Quarterly* vol. 51, 1970 (301–309).

Weisz, Howard. 'Irish-American Attitudes and the Americanization of the English Language Parochial School.' in *New York History* vol. 53, 1972 (157–176).

Weld, Jacqueline Bograd. *Peggy The Wayward Guggenheim*. New York, 1986.

Wells, H.G. *The Future in America*. London, 1987 [1906].

Wharton, Edith. *A Backward Glance*. New York, 1964 [1934].

Wharton, Edith. *Hudson River Bracketed*. London, 1986 [1929].

Wharton, Edith. *The Mothers Recompense*. London, 1986 [1925].

Wharton, Edith. *Old New York*. London, 1985 [1924].

Wharton, Edith. *The Age of Innocence*. New York, 1987 [1920].

Wharton, Edith. *The Custom of the Country*. New York, 1987 [1913].

Wharton, Edith. *The House of Mirth*. Harmondsworth, 1985 [1905].

White, Edmund. *States of Desire*. New York, 1980.

White, Norval. *New York, a Physical History*. New York, 1987.

Whitman, Walt. *The Complete Poems*. Harmondsworth, 1989 [1975].

Whyte, William H. *City: Rediscovering the Center*. New York, 1988.

Wickham, Glynne. *A History of the Theatre*. Cambridge, 1985.

Wilcoxen, Charlote. *Dutch Trade and Ceramics in America in the Seventeenth Century*. Albany, 1987.

Wilkenfeld, Bruce M. 'New York City and Neighborhoods, 1730' in *New York History* vol. 57, 1976 (165–200).

Wilkenfeld, Bruce M. 'The New York City Common Council, 1689–1800' in *New York History* vol. 52, 1971 (249–273).

Willensky, Elliot and Norval White. *AIA Guide to New York City*. San Diego, 1988.

William, J.L. *New York Sketches*. London, 1903.

Williams, Tennessee. *Memoirs*. New York, 1975.

Williams, Terry. *The Cocaine Kids*. New York, 1989.

Wilson, Garff B. *Three Hundred Years of American Drama and Theatre*.

Yee, Chiang. *The Silent Traveller in New York*. New York, undated.

Yin Chang, Yuen. 'Riding the Dragon' in *Village Voice*. New York, 31 October, 1989 (33–35).

Zamper, Jules, ed. *Captain Frederick Marryat. Diary in America*. Bloomington, Indiana, 1960.

Zion, Sidney. *The Autobiography of Roy Cohn*. New York, 1988.

Zlotnick, Joan. *Portrait of an American City: The Novelist and New York*. London, 1982.

INDEX

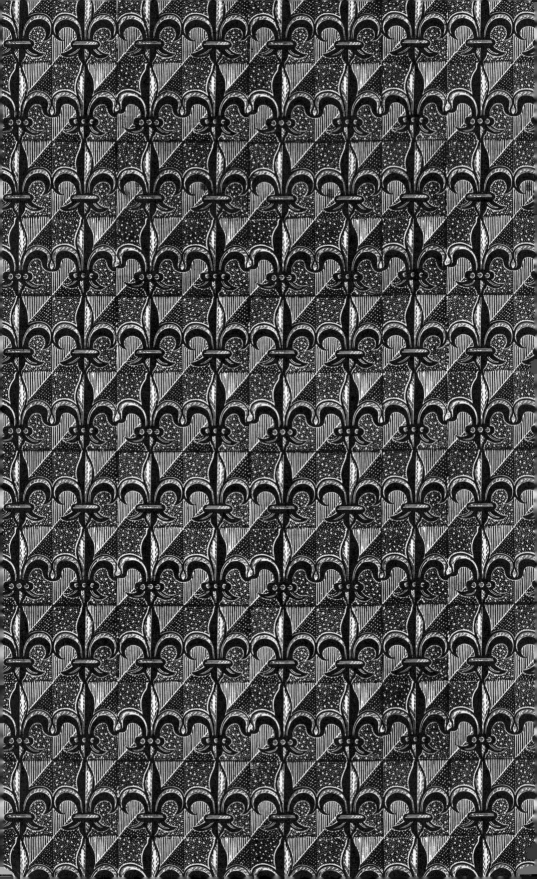